A BIBLIOGRAPHY OF NORFOLK HISTORY

Supplement, to December 1988

A BIBLIOGRAPHY

OF

NORFOLK HISTORY
II
1974–1988

Compiled and edited by

Barry Taylor

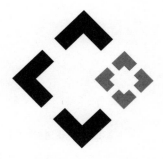

CENTRE OF EAST ANGLIAN STUDIES
UNIVERSITY OF EAST ANGLIA
1991

ISBN 0 906219 30 2

Printed in Great Britain at the
University Press, Cambridge

CONTENTS

Introduction   v

Abbreviations   vi

Notes and corrections to original edition   viii

DIRECTORIES   1

ALMANACS, ANNUALS, HANDBOOKS   1

NEWPAPERS AND MAGAZINES   1

GEOGRAPHY
  Landscape and climate   2
  Regions: the Coast; Breckland; Broadland; Fens   5
  Place-names   10
  Human geography: Population; Settlement patterns; Planning,
    resources, environmental issues   10

GUIDEBOOKS AND DESCRIPTIVE WORKS   15

HISTORY AND ARCHAEOLOGY
  Periodicals; bibliography and historical aids   18
  General history and archaeology   19
  Early man   20
  Roman period   22
  Anglo-Saxon and medieval   23
  Early modern   24
  Nineteenth and twentieth centuries   28
  General controversy   30
  Maritime and aviation history   31

POLITICS AND ADMINISTRATION
  General   32
  Finance and taxation   33
  Parliamentary representation   34
  Military affairs   34
  Law enforcement   34
  Social welfare   35
  Education   39

ECONOMIC HISTORY
  General   40
  Agriculture and fisheries   40
  Trade and industry   44
  Transport and communications   49

RELIGION   53

CULTURE AND RECREATION
  Folklore; dialect   57
  Arts and science   58
  Amusement and sport   60
  Clubs and societies   61

ART, ARCHITECTURE, MONUMENTS
  General and secular   63
  Church architecture and furnishings   65
  Painting; applied arts; gardens   68

BIOGRAPHY
  Collective biography; genealogy; heraldry; wills, etc.   70
  Individual and family biography, A-Z   73

INDIVIDUAL LOCALITIES
  ACLE-KIMBERLEY   100
  KING'S LYNN
    Directories; guidebooks; general history   130
    Municipal government   131
    Trade and industry   132
    Religion; culture and recreation   133
    Topography   133

  KIRSTEAD-NORTHWOLD   134

  NORWICH
    Directories; guides; general history   139
    Municipal government   145
    Trade and industry   152
    Religion; culture and recreation   155
    Topography   160

  ORMESBY-WYMONDHAM   165

  YARMOUTH, GREAT
    Directories; guides; general history   189
    Municipal government   191
    Trade and industry   193
    Religion; culture and recreation   193
    Topography   194

INDEX OF AUTHORS, INSTITUTIONS, ETC.   195

INTRODUCTION

It was my original hope that this would be the first in a series of decennial supplements to the *Bibliography of Norfolk History*, and would thus bear a 1985 imprint. For various reasons that target became impracticable, and I must apologise that slippage of time and accumulation of material have made this a somewhat bulkier publication than I would have wished.

In the main, the explanations set out in the introduction to the parent volume concerning arrangement and coverage apply also to the supplement. The same subject classification has been adopted, with only a few changes to accomodate new types of material (e.g. the greatly increased flow of local government planning documents) or to suppress subdivisions for which there were virtually no new entries. This is not to insist that the original classification is ideal – a good case could be made, I think, that it is over-elaborate, notably for anyone attempting a broad period approach to the county's history as a whole – but it seemed most sensible to link the volumes in this way for use in parallel. To make references unambiguous, numbering has been made consecutive to that of the original Bibliography.

Most entries relate to work written or published in the period 1974-88; but the opportunity has also been taken to add a certain amount of older material formerly overlooked or too summarily rejected as slight, derivative or otherwise inappropriate. Naturally it would have been possible to be considerably more inclusive still. Total consistency, however, let alone the concept of 'completeness', is a mirage constantly threatening to leave the bibliographer stranded in the wilderness...

An invaluable source in assembling the supplement has been the periodical *East Anglian Bibliography*, in which the county library services of Norfolk, Suffolk, and Cambridgeshire cooperate in recording their acquisition of a remarkably wide range of local publications, ephemera, and audio-visual materials. I am also indebted to its recent editor, Clive Wilkins-Jones, and to his colleague at the Local Studies Library in Norwich, Bill Beattie, for providing further information about a great many references on which I had only the most sketchy details. Ron Fiske, from the experience of a dedicated collector, drew my attention to numerous items which harboured unsuspected Norfolk material, particularly of a biographical nature. Robin Lucas and Bill Marsh of UEA Library provided valuable help on architectectural bibliography and local government documentation respectively. Finally let me pay tribute to Barbara Furze: undismayed by the recollection of typing several versions of the 1975 volume, she bravely took on this further exercise, mastered an unfamiliar word-processing system overnight, as it seemed, and again brought order out of chaos with a briskness that vastly speeded up our halting progress.

ABBREVIATIONS AND LOCATION SYMBOLS

Agric.	Agriculture, agricultural
Ann.	Annual
Antiq.	Antiquarian, antiquaries
App.	Appendix
Archaeol.	Archaeology, archaeological
Architect.	Architecture, architectural
Assoc.	Association
Bibliog.	Bibliography, bibliographical
Brit.	British
BL	British Library
B.N.H.	*Bibliography of Norfolk History* (1975)
Bull.	Bulletin
Chron.	Chronicle
Coll.	Collection
E.A.A.R.	*East Anglian Archaeology. Reports*
E.A.M.	*East Anglian Magazine*
Econ.	Economic
Ed.	Editor, edition
Eng.	English
FPL	Freemasons' Provincial Lodge library
Geneal.	Genealogy, genealogical
Geog.	Geography, geographical
GY	Great Yarmouth Public Library
H.C.	House of Commons papers
Hist.	History, historical
Inst.	Institute
J.	Journal
KL	King's Lynn Public Library
Mag.	Magazine
Ms.	Manuscript
N.& N.	Norfolk and Norwich
N.A.	*Norfolk Archaeology*
N.d.	No date of publication given
N.p.	No place of publication given
NPL	Norwich Public Library
N.R.S.	Norfolk Record Society
N.s.	New series
P	Pamphlet (32 pages or less)
Proc.	Proceedings
Publ.	Published, publisher
Quart.	Quarterly
RCF	Collection of R. C. Fiske Esq., North Walsham
Rept.	Report
Rev.	Review
Roy.	Royal

Ser.	Series
Soc.	Society
Trans.	Transactions
Univ.	University
UEA	University of East Anglia Library

NOTES AND CORRECTIONS TO ORIGINAL EDITION

Item no.

40 Delete. Merely a subset of no.33.

50 Should read *Aikin's Monthly...*

62 *Cromer and North Walsham Post*. From Dec. 1912 became *Cromer and North Norfolk Post*. Later incorporated in *Norfolk Chronicle*.

66 *Daylight*. BL dates last issue as 25 Dec. 1909.

76 *East Anglian*. Only 5 parts, Jan.– May 1814, seem to have been publ.

93 *Enigmatical Repository*. Mr. Fiske dates this Jan.– Dec. 1827.

132 *Norfolk Globe*. Should read 1858, not 1880.

140 *Norfolk News Ensign*. Extant 1952–63.

197 BL Newspaper Catalogue now records *South Norfolk News and Diss Mercury*, Oct. 1953 – Nov. 1955; then *South Norfolk News, Diss Mercury and Journal*.

202 *Temperance Monthly Visitor*. Mr. Fiske has run of this title covering 1859–62. Bodleian Lib. records set beginning 1891.

206 *Trawl Net*. B.L. Newspaper Catalogue now dates as July – Oct. 1884.

234 DUTT. Another ed. 1920.

247 Among following cross-references, 1536 should read 1356.

309 LONG. Published at Brundall.

313 CLARKE. 1937 ed. was revised by R. R. Clarke.

324 DAVIES. Variant titles of later eds. include: *The tourists' guide to the rivers...[etc.]*; and *Jarrold's illustrated guide to...[etc.]*

338 DUTT. 4th revised ed. 1930.

363 MARTINS. Duplicates entry no. 2229

368 HALL. Mr. Fiske's copy has parts dated 1814, 1816, and the last part undated.

511 1971 census. Should read 3 parts.

563 RYE. Other eds. noted: 1889, 1892.

565 WARD. 3rd ed. 1892.

573 DUTT. Illustrator's name: for Rennell, read Pennell. Another ed. 1932.

577 CLARKE. Add: Paintings by A. S. Cooper.

587 WALLACE. Other eds. 1943, 1948.

593 BLAKE. 3rd ed. 1975.

596 *Shell Guide*. Further eds. 1969, 1982.

599 SEYMOUR. 2nd ed. 1982; 3rd 1988.

656 ARMSTRONG. Author's name not carried on title page.

658 CHAMBERS. Ditto.

679 KETTON-CREMER. Date of publication should read 1948.

710–11 CLARKE, LEWIS. These items should be classed under Anglo-Saxon period.

712 CLARKE. Reprint ed. 1971.

758 SIEVEKING. Author's initials: for I read G. de G.

799 DASHWOOD. Misleading entry. Volume of 1881 was wholly edited by Rye. Dashwood had planned an edition of these documents, but only a specimen pamphlet of 16pp. appeared in 1863.

896 GEDDES. Appeared anonymously. Date should read 1792.

903 Author should read AMICUS VERITATIS.

976 TILLETT. Title should read *Progressive reform-true conservatism.*

995 MALSTER. 2nd ed. 1986.

996 SIMPER. 2nd ed. 1987.

1008 *Vicecomites...* Anonymous compiler was G. H. Dashwood.

1017 VIRGOE. Add: pp. 218–41.

1048 BRADFER-LAWRENCE. Misleading classification. Does not concern tax receipts, but administration of estate of Thomas Kervill or Carvell of Wiggenhall by his executors.

1049 HOOD. Deals almost exclusively with parish of Sidestrand.

1093 [BURGES]. Further edition appeared responding to item 1094.

1098 Appeared anonymously as 'By a Norfolk freeholder'.

1114 Date should read: 1896.

1121 UEA now has copy.

1184 Published at Swaffham.

1321 NPL and UEA now have copies.

1353 BALLS. Add to following cross-references: 2062.

1430 CRESSWELL. Appeared anonymously.

1461 *Farming World.* Till Oct. 1960 was titled *East Anglian farming world.*

1577 SPRINGHALL. Should read SPRINGALL.

1615 WILLIAMS. This thesis has been posthumously publ., with some updated references, by Oxford University Press in 1988.

1907 ANDERSON. Shortened and revised ed. 1981.

1977 ECTON. Various revised eds. appeared 1723–96.

2007 *Norwich Churchman.* Extant to 1978. Succeeded by *Norwich Diocesan Bulletin* (1983–86) and *Diocesan News Service* (1984–).

2029 HARMER. The *Remarks* were first publ. in 1777.

2044 *Defence of the people called Quakers....* BL attributes this to Richard Ashby and others.

2071 HALLIWELL. Author should read: HALLIWELL-PHILLIPPS.

2082–83 WILSON. These works should be in section on Dialect.

2086 HAGGARD. Inappropriate classification. See this supplement, under Biography.

2107 TRUDGILL. Line omitted. Publication details should read: Cambridge, 1974.

2119 THURLEY. 2nd ed., by N. Kelbrick, 1985.

2156 SAVORY. This work first publ. London, 1953.

2170 *Masonic Yearbook.* Complete run available at FPL.

2174 COZENS-HARDY. Vol. no. of *N.A.* should be 29.

2197 MINISTRY OF HOUSING. Listing became mandatory under Town and Country Planning Act, 1947. The Ministry and its successors (now Dept. of the Environment) have continued to issue revised and expanded lists following new local government boundaries.

2213 HAWKYARD. Add after this, as cross-reference for section on Halls and Manor-Houses: See also no. 4111.

2214 BIRKBECK. Author's initial: for R. read G.

2244 *Fen and Marshland churches.* Photographs attributed to Edward Johnson, date of publ. probably 1867–69.

2344 STARK. Engravings after Stark. Text by J. W. Robberds.

2385 RYE. There is also an *Index nominum* for this work, by C. Nowell, 1915.

2393 CARTHEN. Should read CARTHEW.

2427 RYE. Edition of work actually by Thomas Martin. Date of publ. should read [1892].

2439 ARCH. There are now alternative eds. of this work by J. G. O'Leary (1966); and A. Howkins (1986).

2513 RIX. BL catalogue records 2-part enlarged and illustrated copy of this work, dated Great Yarmouth 1863.

2518 WATKINS. For Alan Bloom see also no. 3614.

2524 NICHOLS. This comprises four etchings of scenery with Borrow associations.

2533 SHORTER. 2nd ed., with new documents, publ. as *Life of George Borrow* [c.1919].

2560 NORWICH CASTLE MUSEUM. Revised ed., by M. Allthorpe-Guyton, 1986.

2570 *Account of Robert Browne*. Page ref.: 867–72.

2600 JOHNSTON. Publ. at Carlisle.

2605–6 Item 2605 is incorporated in 2606, and authors should be identical (Hannah R., or Mrs. T., Geldart).

2692 REINAECKER. Should read RIENAECKER.

2757 EADE. Note also Eade's *Addresses and papers* (Norwich, 1908).

2803 LEWIS. Author publ. more substantial life of Elizabeth Fry in 1910.

2941 VALDAR. This work appeared in printed form, 1976.

2943 *Maid of the mill*. Attributed to Gwen M. Parry in NPL catalogue.

3134 FENN. Abridged ed., 2 vols., 1840.

3136 GAIRDNER. 6-vol. ed. should be dated 1904.

3139 KNOWLES. Author's initials: for M. V. read M. C. But author is better known as David Knowles, name adopted on entry to monastic order.

3181–5 For Humphrey read Humphry throughout.

3191 EVANS. Richards' year of death should read 1818, *not* 1810.

3201 ROBERTS. Author's initial S., not P.

3206 ROLFE. Though source of this narrative has been taken to be Frederick Rolfe, he is not identified in the text. Other eds., 1975, 1982.

3292 TROUBRIDGE. For Curneys read Gurneys in note.

3296 Dawson Turner sale. Add: catalogue of mss. for sale of 3–5 Apr. 1860.

3314 KETTON-CREMER. Add after this entry: George Walpole, *4th Earl of Orford*. See no. 367.

3440 *Aylsham illustrated almanack*. Eds. for 1929 and 1936 have since been noted.

3463 Delete this entry, which refers to honour of Bacton in Suffolk and Essex.

3471 H.,G. Publ. at Diss.

3547 BOND. Date should be 1948.

3614 BLOOM. Updated ed. 1986.

3700 HIGDON. Reprinted Scole, 1984.

3794 BELOE. A version of this article was separately publ. as *Castle Rising: the barony, the borough, the franchise* (Norwich, 1894). P.

3881 Insert after this item: COXFORD PRIORY. *See* TATTERSETT.

3915 DUTT. Somewhat misleading to pick out this version of 'Official guide', as similar work went through numerous editions from 1904 onwards.

3972 BOSTON. Mr. Fitch dates this guide to 1951. 2nd ed. 1955.

4034 DUNKIN. Date should be 1961.

4061 In subsequent cross-references 1491 refers to Ellingham near Bungay, and not to Great Ellingham.

4104 ROBERTSON. Garbled citation should of course read *Numismatic Chron.*

4123 *Church of St. Margaret.* This guide was written by R. W. Ketton-Cremer.

4129 SUTCLIFFE. Enlarged ed. 1974.

4130 HART. This item is in fact part of no.659.

4189 CUTTING. Date should read 1889.

4261 DAWSON. Should read DAVISON.

4293 ROYAL SOCIETY. This is an account by C. Blagden and E. Nairne in the *Philosophical Transactions* of the Society (vol.72).

4323 MARSHAM. Another ed. 1975. P.

4369 BRETTINGHAM. Another ed. 1773.

4442 JONES. Also publ. in her *Some Norfolk worthies* (1899), pp.153–214.

4451 WILSON. Several later eds., revised by G. Webster.

4587A Lynn poll books. Add: 1754 (NPL).

4267 K.L. CONSERVANCY BOARD. NPL has copy of this, and also briefer ed. of 1985.

4671 GLASIER. UEA now has copy of this.

4697 Guide to...Greenland Fishery Museum. Can be attributed to E. M. Beloe.

4936 COLE. 4th ed. 1950. This work better classed under Norwich 'Views' (p.333).

4940 LE GRICE. Date should read 1954.

4959 PARKIN. Virtually identical work was publ. in 1778 (also by Whittingham of Lynn), misleadingly titled *A new and complete history of Norfolk.* This does not specify Parkin's authorship.

4979 WAKE. 2nd ed. [1949].

5110 LE GRICE. Date of publication should read [1945].

5162 TILLETT. Date probably correct, but not specified. Substantially same work appears as essay in no. 5113 (*Book of Norwich Festival*).

5173 *Planning Handbook.* Another ed. 1981.

5179 *Case relating to election.* Should be dated [1702].

5204 *Municipal characters.* Seems that at least 18 nos. were publ., through to Oct. 1836. [Bookseller's catalogue].

5227 [*Workhouse Acts*]. Collected and issued as pamphlet, Norwich, 1827.

5260 *Charities Act.* See also Corporation's publ. scheme (Norwich, 1910).

5346B PERCIVAL. This should be followed by centred heading PUBLIC WORKS AND UTILITIES.

5308 JOHNSON. Add cross-reference to 5403 [*Edward VI charity*], which concerns Great Hospital as well as Grammar School.

5449 SPARKS. Publ. at Northampton.

5491 JARROLD AND SONS. This contains more on printing than on retail activities.

5533 RYE. For Chapel Road read Chapelfield Road.

5546 DAVIS. In following cross-references, add for Methodists nos. 5070–71.

5593 NORFOLK AND NORWICH LITERARY INSTITUTION. An inaugural catalogue seems to have been printed in 1823.

5617 SOUTHWELL. Abridged ed. 1913.

5725 WILLINS. Should be classed under Norwich 'Views' (facing page).

5726 KNIGHTS. Plates by P. E. Stimpson: these were also separately publ. as *Sketches from the highways [etc.]*.

5833 LE GRICE. For vols. read parts (pamphlet size).

5855 JAMES. This item should be credited to H. C. Beeching, whose article covers pp. 67–92, with addendum on p.174. James contributes an appendix on Norwich manuscripts now in other libraries, pp. 93–116.

5904 WHITTINGHAM. This item is a reprint from 19th annual report of Friends of Norwich Cathedral (1948).

5985 *Mousehold Heath Act*. See also Corporation bye-laws relating to Heath, 1885.

6040 TILLETT. Another ed. 1917.

6121 COZENS-HARDY. Joint author: GREEN, B.

6149 STONE. Published at Gloucester.

6175 Edited by J. H. Harrison.

6234 On Ringstead see also no. 728.

6236 Rockland St. Mary, in Broadland, should have been classified separately from the other Rockland parishes near Attleborough.

6294 LADY FARMER. Pseudonym for Mrs. G. Cresswell.

6298 GRANT. First publ. 1921 ? Many subsequent eds.

6359 STEPHEN. There appears to have been a guide of this title (not carrying Stephen's name) as early as 1909.

6388 HOARE. Add after this item: See also no. 1049.

6422 GOOD. Author's name should read HOOD.

6423 Southrepps Church. This work is by R. J. Simpson.

6440 On Sprowston see also nos. 1442, 1459.

6456 Following this item, add to cross-references for Stody: no. 4469.

6508 RIPPER. Another ed. 1979.

6510 RIX. Date should be 1950.

6557 *Thetford almanac*. This appears to have continued at least to 1929 (NPL has copy for this year).

6564 *Thetford: historical...sketch*. Author described as 'Wandering Will' (i.e. W. G. Clarke). 2nd ed. 1897.

6612 RABY. This version is 2nd ed. First publ. 1935 (by Raby alone). 3rd ed. 1979.

6702 FORDER. Revised ed. 1975.

6746 GILLETT. First ed. 1934.

6748 HOLE. First ed. 1939.

6786 LINGWOOD. UEA now has copy.

6834 On Wiggenhall St. Mary see also no. 1048.

6863 KETTON-CREMER. This version is 3rd ed. First publ. 1947. Other eds. 1951, 1957, 1973.

6887 TOYNBEE. Page nos. should read 20–27.

6941 PRESTON. Author's initial J., *not* I.

6978 CRISP. Later eds. extend coverage to 1877, 1879, and 1884.

6984 HEDGES. Revised ed. 1973.

7152 WICKSTEAD. Preliminary report of 1845 noted in bookseller's catalogue.

7190 AMICABLE SHIPPING ASSURANCE ASSOC. Earlier version of 1824 extant.

7210 EVANS. Author's initials G. E., *not* C. E.
7254 PALMER. NPL has typescript index compiled by P. E. Rumbelow (1943).
7259 *Town wall report*. Revised eds. 1973, 1977.
7291 *Guide to parish*. Author should read [LUPSON, G. *and others*].

Index
Insert Birkbeck, G., 2214
Birkbeck, R. Delete 2214
Add Blagden, C., 4293
Dashwood, G.H. Add 1008
Insert Davison, A.J., 4261
Delete Dawson, A.J.
Insert Dinmore, R., 938
Fussell, G.E. For 1417 read 1418
Geldart, H.R. Add 2606
Delete Geldart, T.
Green, B. Add 6121
Halliwell, J.O. should read Halliwell-Phillips, J.O.
Jones, W.H. For 5978 read 5980
Ketton-Cremer, R.W. Add 4123
King, P. Add 1974
Insert King, S.H., 239
Knowles, M.C. Add 3139
Delete Knowles, M.V.
McKisack, M. For 4586A read 4587B
Add Nairns, E., 4293
Add Parry, G.M., 2943
Patterson, A.H. Add 2134
Insert Pennell, J., 973
Preston, I. Delete 6941
Add Preston, J., 6941
For Reinaecker, V. read Rienaecker, V.
Delete Roberts, P.
Roberts, S. Add 3201
Rye, W. For 5977 read 5979
Sieveking, I. Initials should be G. de G.
Simpson, R.J. Add 6423
Snelling, J.H. Initials should be J.M.

DIRECTORIES

7305 King's Lynn and West Norfolk blue book. Hunstanton, 1967–70.
7306 East Anglian area trades directory. Vol.1: Norfolk. Harrow, [1974].
7307 Norwich, Great Yarmouth and Lowestoft Chambers of Commerce directory. Norwich, 1979/80–.
7308 LYNN NEWS AND ADVERTISER. Local directory for King's Lynn, Downham Market, Swaffham, Fakenham, Hunstanton and areas. King's Lynn, 1982–.
7309 MUSCROFT, S., *ed*. Alternative East Anglia: a directory. Haverhill, 1982.

ALMANACS, ANNUALS, HANDBOOKS

7310 The Eastern and Midland Counties annual. King's Lynn, [1865]. BL.
7311 The Norfolk handbook, containing a description of the county and history of the city... almanack for the year... [etc.]. 7th year. Norwich, 1866. UEA.
7312 FISHER'S Norwich almanac. Norwich, 1891–1918.
Title varies, at its most elaborate being *Norwich and Eastern Counties almanac and annual*.

NEWSPAPERS AND MAGAZINES

7313 Anglia Advertiser. Yarmouth ed., 1978–. Norwich ed., 1984–.
7314 Aylsham, Reepham and Foulsham Post. *Extant* Feb. 1919–Sept. 1933. *Incorporated* with Norfolk Chronicle. BL.
7315 City Herald: Norwich strike paper for the National Union of Journalists. Dec. 1978–Jan. 1979.
7316 Citywise Magazine. [Norwich]. 1985–.
7317 Democrat. [Norwich]. 1949–.
W.E.A. publication.
7318 Diss, Harleston, Bungay, Beccles and Eye Journal. *Extant* Jan. 1910–July 1922. *Incorporated with* Norwich Mercury. BL.
Diss Mercury and Advertiser. *See* South Norfolk News.
7319 Downham Market Gazette and Journal. 1987–.
7320 East Anglia Monthly. [Norwich]. Aug. 1976–.
7321 East Anglian Post. [Great Yarmouth]. 1985–.
7322 Eastern Counties Magazine and Suffolk Note-book. Aug. 1900–May 1902.
7323 Fakenham and District Advertiser. 1981–.
7324 Fakenham Post. May 1919–July 1932. *Incorporated with* Holt, Melton Constable and Wells Post. BL.
7325 Great Yarmouth Mid-Week Mercury. Apr.1986–.
7326 Harleston and Waveney Express. 1980–.
7327 Holt, Melton Constable and Wells Post [*from July 1932* Holt and Fakenham Post]. *Extant* Jan. 1919–Sept. 1933. *Incorporated with* Norfolk Chronicle. BL.
7328 King's Lynn Messenger. 1–12, 1875.
Religious magazine.

7329 King's Lynn Trader. 1980–.
7330 Lancaster Press and North and West Norfolk News. [Fakenham]. March–May 1905. BL.
7331 Mid-Norfolk Advertiser. [Dereham]. 1981–.
7332 NALGO Norfolk News. [Norwich]. *Extant* 1956–. BL.
See also Norwich Branch Bulletin, 1952–.
7333 Norfolk Advertiser: North Norfolk edition. [Sheringham]. 1981–.
7334 Norfolk Leader. [King's Lynn]. 1986–.
7335 North Walsham Post and East Norfolk Standard. *Extant* Jan. 1919–Sept. 1933. *Incorporated with* Norfolk Chronicle. BL.
7336 Norwich Co-operator. [*From 1889* Norwich Co-operative Monthly Herald; *from Apr. 1933*, Norwich Co-operative Herald and Wheatsheaf]. July 1876–July 1946. NPL. 1896–1926; BL. 1914–.
Corrects no. 155 of B.N.H.
7337 Norwich Mercury and Advertiser. 1983–.
7338 Norwich Scene. Oct. 1981–.
7339 South Norfolk News. [Diss; *from 1986*, Diss Mercury and Advertiser]. 1983–.
7340 Thetford and Brandon Advertiser. 1983–.
7341 Wymondham and Attleborough Express. 1975–.
7342 Yarmouth and Central Norfolk Citizen. Apr. 1961–Jan. 1962. BL.
7343 Yarmouth Standard [*from July 1923* Y.S. and Gorleston Standard]. N.s. July 1922–Apr. 1926. BL.
Revived issue of Yarmouth Weekly Standard [B.N.H 229].

See also nos. 7638–45, 7918–20, 7923, 7937, 8077, 8096, 8105, 8190, 8262, 8266–7, 8349, 8360.

GEOGRAPHY

LANDSCAPE AND CLIMATE

GENERAL FEATURES

7344 MURBY, T., *publisher*. Murby's county geographies: Norfolk. [c. 1875]. P.
7345 CLARKE, W. G. Norfolk lakes and meres. *Trans. N. & N. Naturalists' Soc.* 11, 1919/24, 269–94.
7346 FORESTRY COMMISSION. Forestry Commission areas in Norfolk and Suffolk. 1934. P.
7347 GODWIN, H. Age and origin of the 'Breckland' heaths of East Anglia. *Nature* 154, 1944, 6–7.
7348 DEBENHAM, F. A pictorial survey of England and Wales. Section 2: East Anglia. 1952. P.
7349 TURNER, J. Rivers of East Anglia. 1954.
7350 PRINCE, H. C. Pits and ponds in Norfolk. *Erdkunde* 16, 1962, 10–31.
7351 ROBINSON, A. H. W. *and* WALLWORK, K. L. Map studies. 1970. Chap.5: North-East Norfolk.
Study of Ordnance Survey sheet 126 (1″).

7352 CARTWRIGHT, A. R. An analysis of landscape types and a re-evaluation of traditional regional sub-divisions of Norfolk. M.Phil. thesis, Univ. of E. Anglia, 1972.

7353 SIMS, R. E. The anthropogenic factor in East Anglian vegetational history. *In* BIRKS, H. G. B. *and* WEST, R. G., *eds*. Quaternary plant ecology (1973), pp. 223–36.
See also author's M.Sc. thesis, 'The vegetational history of East Anglia related to agricultural practice' (Cambridge Univ., 1976).

7354 ARMSTRONG, P. The changing landscape. The history & ecology of man's impact on the face of East Anglia. Lavenham, 1975.

7355 BARRINGER, J. C. An introduction to Faden's map of Norfolk. *N.R.S.* 42, 1975.
Together with reproduction of the 1797 map by William Faden.

7356 JOBY, R. S., *ed*. Norfolk field studies. (Geographical Assoc., Norwich). 5 pts. Norwich, 1975.

7357 NORFOLK SOCIETY. Vanishing Norfolk. [Exhib. cat.]. 1975. P.

7358 HOSKINS, W. G. Landscapes of England, 3. North Norfolk. *Listener* 95, 1976, 136–7.

7359 WASHBOURN, R., *ed*. Nature in Norfolk: a heritage in trust. 1976.

7360 SOUTH NORFOLK DISTRICT COUNCIL. Walls, fences and hedges in South Norfolk. Long Stratton, 1976.

7361 TILLYARD, R. Hedge dating in north Norfolk: the Hooper method examined. *N.A.* 36, 1976, 272–9.

7362 NORFOLK COUNTY COUNCIL. Farmland tree survey of Norfolk. Norwich, [1977].

7363 YONEKAWA, S. I. Champion and woodland Norfolk: the development of regional differences. *J. European Econ. Hist.* 6, 1977, 163–76.

7364 SIMS, R. E. Man and vegetation in Norfolk. *In* LIMBREY, S. *and* EVANS, J. G., *eds*. The effect of man on the landscape: the Lowland Zone. (CBA research reports, 21, 1978), pp. 57–62.
Evidence from Hockham Mere.

7365 WRIGHT, D., *ed*. Interpreting Norfolk geography. Norwich, 1980.

7366 BRADSHAW, R. H. W. Quantitative reconstruction of local woodland vegetation using pollen analyses from a small basin in Norfolk. *J. Ecology* 69, 1981, 941–55.
Deductions about vegetational history and clearances of Oxborough Wood, near Stoke Ferry.

7367 JENYON, A. R., *ed*. Norfolk's changing wetlands. Norwich, [1981]. P.

7368 JOHNSON, W. E. The application of hedge-dating techniques in South Norfolk. *N.A.* 38, 1982, 182–91.

7369 FORESTRY COMMISSION. Census of woodlands and trees, 1979–82: county of Norfolk. Edinburgh, 1983.

7370 RAVENSDALE, J. *and* MUIR, R. East Anglian landscapes, past and present. 1984.

7371 DYMOND, D. The Norfolk landscape. 1985.

7372 WILLIAMSON, T. Parish boundaries and early fields: continuity and discontinuity. *J. Hist. Geog.* 12, 1986, 241–8.

7373 GILES, M. Rural landscape change in South Norfolk, 1964–80. [Unpubl. typescript]. 1987.

7374 WADE-MARTINS, P., *ed*. Norfolk from the air. Norwich, 1987.
Publ. by Norfolk Museums Service. Photographs credited principally to D. A. Edwards.

7375 FROSTICK, R. The Dutch connection: some Norfolk maps and their makers. Norwich, 1988. P.

7375A MANNING, M. Commons in Norfolk: historical and ecological studies of selected commons. Norwich, 1988.

See also nos. 7669, 10017.

GEOLOGY

7376 BENNETT, F. J. The geology of the country around Attleborough, Watton, and Wymondham. (Geological Survey). 1884. P.

7377 WOODWARD, H. B. The geology of the country around Fakenham, Wells and Holt. (Geological Survey). 1884.

7378 WHITAKER, W. *and* DALTON, W. H. The geology of the country around Halesworth and Harleston. (Geological Survey). 1887.

7379 BLAKE, J. H. The geology of the country around East Dereham. (Geological Survey). 1888.

7380 BLAKE, J. H. The geology of the country near Yarmouth and Lowestoft. (Geological Survey), 1890.

7381 WHITAKER, W. *and others*. The geology of south-western Norfolk and of northern Cambridgeshire (Geological Survey). 1893.

7382 WHITAKER, W. *and* JUKES-BROWN, A. J. The geology of the borders of the Wash, including Boston and Hunstanton. (Geological Survey). 1899.

7383 HUGHES, T. M. The gravels of East Anglia. Cambridge, 1916.

7384 MINISTRY OF HOUSING AND LOCAL GOVERNMENT. Report of the advisory committee on sand and gravel: parts 11–13 [Middle Anglia; East Anglia; Kent and E. Sussex]. 1954.

7385 SOIL SURVEY OF GREAT BRITAIN. Soils in Norfolk. 1: sheet TM 49 (Beccles North), 1970. 2: sheets TG 13/14 (Barningham, Sheringham), 1974. 3: sheet TG 31 (Horning), 1977. 4: sheet TM 28 (Harleston), 1979. 5: sheet TG11 (Attlebridge), 1980.

7386 GEOLOGICAL SURVEY. Records of wells. Area around Norwich (1973); Area around Fakenham (1974); North Norfolk (1974).

7387 INSTITUTE OF GEOLOGICAL SCIENCES. Sand and gravel resources. Country around Attlebridge (Rept. 73–15, by E. F. P. Nickless, 1973); Country around Diss (Mineral Assessment Rept. 137, by C. J. Wilcox and R. Stancsyszyn, 1983).

7388 INSTITUTE OF GEOLOGICAL SCIENCES. Geological and geophysical survey of the Wash. 1978. P.

7389 CLAYTON, K. M. *and* STRAW, A. Eastern and central England. (Geomorphology of the British Isles). 1979.

7390 WEST, R. G. *and others*. The pre-glacial Pleistocene of the Norfolk and Suffolk coasts. Cambridge, 1980.

7391 NORFOLK COUNTY COUNCIL. Sand and gravel in Norfolk. [1]: Sand and gravel workings in the Great Yarmouth area (1982). 2: Norwich area guidelines for... extraction (1987). P.

7392 MILLER, S. H., *ed*. Fenland meteorological circular and weather report. 1–24. Wisbech, 1874–75. UEA.

7393 METEOROLOGICAL OFFICE. Rainfall over the areas of East Suffolk and Norfolk and the Essex River Boards, 1916–1950. By H. Howsell. Bracknell, 1963. P.

7394 OLIVER, J. Norfolk weather 1778–1802 as recorded by Rev. James Woodforde. *Trans. N. & N. Naturalists' Soc*. 23, 1974, 120–39.

7395 HALLAM, H. E. The climate of eastern England, 1250–1350. *Agric. Hist. Rev*. 32, 1984, 124–32.

7396 GLENN, A. Weather patterns of East Anglia. Lavenham, 1987.

FLOODS AND STORMS

7397 Ordinance for reviving and continuing an Act of Parliament for recovery of many thousand acres of ground in Norfolk and Suffolk surrounded by the rage of the sea. [Thomason tracts E 1064 (43)]. 1654. P. BL.
Cf. *B.N.H* 275.

7398 COE, A. E. Photographs of the floods in Norwich and Norfolk, 1912. Norwich, 1912. P.

7399 JANSON, H. Britain's great flood disaster. 1953.

7400 STEERS, J. A. The East Coast floods, Jan.–Feb. 1953. *Geog. J*. 99, 1953, 280–98.

7401 INSTITUTION OF CIVIL ENGINEERS. Conference on the North Sea floods of 31 Jan.–1 Feb. 1953. 1954.

7402 POLLARD, M. North Sea surge: the story of the East Coast floods of 1953. Lavenham, 1978.

7403 SUMMERS, D. The East Coast floods. Newton Abbot, 1978.

7404 HARLAND, M. G. *and* HARLAND, H. J. The flooding of Eastern England. Deeping St. James (Peterborough), 1980.

See also nos. 9330–1.

REGIONS

THE COAST

7405 SCOTT, C. W. Poppy-land: papers descriptive of scenery on the East Coast. 1895.

7406 PARSONS-NORMAN, G. Poppyland illustrated in colour. Norwich, [c. 1900].

7407 PATTERSON, A. H. Man and nature on tidal waters. 1909.
Material on fishing industries, wildfowling, etc.

7408 KESTNER, F. J. T. The old coastline of the Wash. *Geog. J*. 128. 1962, 457–78.

7409 UNIVERSITY OF EAST ANGLIA. East Anglian coastal study. Reports 1–9 [by] S. J. Craig-Smith. Norwich, 1971–74. East Anglian coastal research programme. Reports, 1–7. Norwich, 1974–78.

7410 SOUTH, D. The recent sedimentology of the West Norfolk coast. Ph.D. thesis, London Univ., 1971.

7411 NORFOLK COUNTY COUNCIL. Heritage coast management plan: consultative draft. Norwich, 1978.

7412 CORNFORD, B. The Sea Breach Commission in East Norfolk, 1609–1743. *N.A.* 37, 1979, 137–45.

7413 STIBBONS, P. *and* CLEVELAND, D. Poppyland: strands of Norfolk history. Cromer, 1981. P. 2nd ed., 1985.
See also nos. 7553, 7594, 7609, 7627, 7629, 7632, 7863–85 *passim*, 8151–2, 8522.

BRECKLAND

7414 KENT, C. The land of the "babes in the wood"; or, the Breckland of Norfolk. [1910].

7415 COOK, O. Breckland. 1980.

7416 DAVISON, A. J. The Brecklands: a Norfolk field guide. Norwich, 1987.
See also nos. 7347, 7688.

BROADLAND

7417 DAVIES, G. C. The 'Swan' and her crew. The adventures of three young naturalists and sportsmen on the Broads and rivers of Norfolk. [1876]. Many later eds. Revised ed. by H. C. Davies, 1932.

7418 Broads and rivers of Norfolk; reprinted from the *Norwich Argus*. Norwich, 1882.
Presumably by H. Brittain who is credited with renamed 3rd ed., *Notes on Broads and rivers...* (1889). Cf. no. 7424.

7419 EMERSON, P. H. Idyls of the Norfolk Broads. Being 12 autogravure plates... with descriptive text. [1887].

7420 RYE, W. A month on the Norfolk Broads on board the wherry 'Zoe'. [1987].

7421 [DOUGHTY, H. M.] Summer in Broadland. Gipsying in East Anglian waters. 1889.

7422 EMERSON, P. H. English idyls. 1889. Another ed. 1924.
Lyrical work about Broads.

7423 ANNAN, T. *and* ANNAN, R. [Norfolk Broads and rivers]. N.p., n.d. [c. 1890]. UEA.
Photographic volume, no title-page.

7424 BRITTAIN, H. Rambles in East Anglia; or, holiday excursions among the rivers and Broads. [1891]. 3rd ed., 1899. BL.

7425 SUFFLING, E. R. How to organise a cruise on the Broads. [1891]. Another ed. 1899.

7426 EMERSON, P. H. Marsh leaves from the Norfolk Broadland. 1895. Another ed. 1898.

7427 DODD, A. B. On the Broads. 1896.

7428 PARSONS-NORMAN, G. Broadland illustrated in colour. Norwich, [c. 1900].

7429 SUFFLING, E. R. The innocents on the Broads. 1901.

7430 Pictures in colour of the Norfolk Broads, with descriptive notes... Norwich, [1909].

7431 LEEDS, H. Romance land. Norwich, [c. 1910].

7432 PATTERSON, A. H. The cruise of the 'Walrus' on the Broads. A Broadland voyage in a North Sea ketch boat. [1923].

7433 DALEY, P. V. Broadland in pictures. Norwich, 1949.

7434 HANNAFORD, C. A. The charm of the Norfolk Broads. Norwich. [c. 1950].
Brochure for Broads Tours Ltd., with paintings by author.

7435 DAY, J. W. Broadland adventure. 1951.
See also his *Marshland adventure. On Norfolk broads and rivers. Of wildfowlers... Essex isles and smugglers.* 1950.

7436 DAY, J. W. Portrait of the Broads. 1967.

7437 TULLETT, G. A. Broadland tour. St. Ives (Hunts), 1968.

7438 STEPHENSON, F. The story of the Broads. Holt, 1969. P.

7439 GEORGE, M. Land use and nature conservation in Broadland. *Geography* 61, 1976, 137–42.

7440 NATURE CONSERVANCY COUNCIL. A Broadland bibliography. Ed. by A. M. O'Riordan. Norwich, 1976.

7441 COUNTRYSIDE COMMISSION. The Broads: possible courses of action. Cheltenham, 1977. P.
See also earlier *The Broads: a consultative paper* (1976).

7442 MOSS, B. Conservation problems in the Norfolk Broads and rivers of East Anglia: phytoplankton, boats, and the causes of turbidity. *Biological Conservation* 12, 1977, 95–114.

7443 GOODEY, C. A century of Broadland cruising. Wroxham, 1978. P.

7444 MIDDLETON, C. S., *ed.* The Broadland photographers [J. P. Jennings, P. H. Emerson, G. C. Davies]. Norwich, 1978.

7445 MOSS, B. *and* O'RIORDAN, T. An ecosystem out of phase: signs of disaster and a policy for survival. *Geog. Mag.* 52, Oct. 1979, 47–59.

7446 MOSS, B. *and others*. Problems of the Norfolk Broads and their impact on freshwater fisheries. *In* Proc. First Brit. Freshwater Fisheries Conference (1979), pp. 67–85.

7447 O'RIORDAN, T. The Broads Authority. *Town and Country Planning* 48, 1979, 49–51.

7448 BROADS AUTHORITY. [Publications]. Norwich, 1980–.
A. [Strategy and Management Plans].
Strategy and management plan for Broadland (July 1981).
Reports of Ecology, Landscape, Recreation, Information and Interpretation Working Groups (SMP 5–8, 1981–82).
What future for Broadland? Strategy and management plan... draft consultation. (1982).
Broads plan (1987).

B. [Development proposals]. 3: Ranworth Staithe (1983). 4: Trinity Broads (1985). 5: Potter Heigham Bridge local plan (1985).

C. Research series:
1. Proposed Yare Basin flood control barrier: environmental impact assessment (1980).
2. Botanical survey of marsh dykes (C. Doarks, 1980).
3. Acid sulphate soils (D. Dent, 1981)
4. River management to reduce bank erosion (S. J. Payne and R. D. Hey, 1982).
5. Turf ponds (B. D. Wheeler, 1983).
6. Decline of reedswamp: causes, consequences, and solutions (C. E. Crook *and*

others, 1983).

7. Broadland research register (1984).

8. Economic approach to environmental management, incorporating a review of Anglian Water's Yare Basin flood control strategy (R. K. Turner, 1984).

9. Study of marsh dykes (C. Doarks, 1984)

10. Decline of reedswamp: the importance of rhizome structure (C. E. Crook *and others*, 1984).

11. Isolation of Broads as a technique for restoration (B. Moss *and others*, 1985).

D. Design guidance series. 1985–86.

7449 MANNING, S. A. Portrait of Broadland. 1980.

7450 CORNFORD, B. *and others*. Past water levels in Broadland. *Bull. Norfolk Research Committee* 27, 1982, 10–13; 28, 1982, 14–19; 33, 1985, 16–19.

7451 MOSS, B. *and others*. Study of the River Bure, Norfolk Broads: final report to the D.O.E. and Anglian Water. 2 vols. 1982.

7452 MOSS, B. The Norfolk Broadland: experiments in the restoration of a complex wetland. *Biological Rev.* 58, 1983, 521–61.

7453 STANDLEY, V. The drainage of Norfolk Broadland. *Bull. Norfolk Research Committee* 30, 1983, 7–11.

7454 COUNTRYSIDE COMMISSION. The Broads, a review: conclusions and recommendations. Cheltenham, 1984.

7455 DRISCOLL, R. J. Changes in land use in the Thurne catchment area, 1931/32 to 1973. *Trans. N. & N. Naturalists' Soc.* 26, 1984, 282–90.

7456 GRINT, B. S. The Halvergate chronicles. Acle, 1984.

7457 Looking after the Broads: the Broads Bill ... to set up a new authority for the Broads. [Issued by Norfolk County Council. Broadland District Council and other local authorities]. Norwich, 1985. P.
See also Norfolk County Council. *The Broads Bill: working for the future* (Norwich, n.d.).

7458 Norfolk and Suffolk Broads Act. Public General Acts, 1988: chap. 4.

7459 MOSS, B. The palaeolimnology of Hoveton Great Broad: clues to the spoiling and restoration of Broadland. *In* MURPHY, P. *and* FRENCH, C., *eds*. The exploitation of wetlands (Brit. Archaeol. Repts., 186, 1988), pp. 163–91.

   See also nos. 7530, 7589, 7591–2, 8074, 8151, 8155–6, 8184, 8293, 8354, 8359, 8369, 8521, 8678.

FENLAND AND MARSHLAND

7460 MILLER, S. H. *and* SKERTCHLY, S. B. J. The Fenland past and present. 1878.

7461 MILLER, S. H. The hand-book to the Fenland: being a brief account of all the towns, villages and parishes in the Fen district. [1889]. Another ed. 1890. BL.

7462 MARLOWE, C. The Fen country. 1925.

7463 BLOOM, A. The Fens. 1953.

7464 BEVIS, T. A. A guide to the Fens and Fenland churches. March, [1966].

7465 PARKER, A. *and* PYE, D. The Fenland. Newton Abbot, 1976.

7466 CORY, R. H. Fenland lighters and horse knockers. Ely, 1977. P.

7467 GODWIN, H. Fenland: its ancient past and uncertain future. Cambridge, 1978.

7468 COLES, J. M. *and* HALL, D. The Fenland project. *Antiquity* 57, 1983, 51–2.
Announcement of ambitious archaeological survey.

7469 DARBY, H. C. The changing Fenland. Cambridge, 1983.

7470 Fenland research. No. 1 (1983/84)–. Gressenhall, 1984–.

7471 HALL, D. *and others*. The fenlands of East Anglia: survey and excavation. *In* COLES, J. M. *and* LAWSON, A. J., *eds*. European wetlands in prehistory (Oxford, 1987), pp. 169–201.

7472 SILVESTER, R. J. The Norfolk fens. *Antiquity* 62, 1988, 326–30.
Part of special feature on Fenland archaeology.

See also nos. 7392, 7731, 7734, 7802, 8179, 8292, 8296, 8497, 8768, 8872–3, 8918, 9387–8.

FEN DRAINAGE

7473 ALBRIGHT, M. The entrepreneurs of Fen draining in England under James I and Charles I. *Explorations in Entrepreneurial Hist.* 1st ser. 8, 1955, 51–65.

7474 SUMMERS, D. The Great Level: a history of drainage and land reclamation in the Fens. Newton Abbot, 1976.

7475 POWELL, R. Fen dyke maintenance. *E.A.M.* Oct. 1980, 608–10.

7476 GROVE, R. Cressey Dymock and the draining of the Fens: an early agricultural model. *Geog. J.* 147, 1981, 27–37.

7477 BRATHWAITE, C. A. The changing politics of land drainage in rural East Anglia. M.Phil. thesis, Univ. of E. Anglia, 1984.

See also no. 8176.

EAU BRINK CUT

7478 Reasons attempting to shew the necessity of the proposed cut from Eau-Brink to Lynn...1793. P. BL.

7479 An abstract of the case and opinions that have appeared in print for and against the Eau Brink Cut... By a member of the Committee. 1794. P. BL.

7480 YORKE, P., *3rd Earl Hardwicke*. Observations upon the Eau Brink Cut, with a proposal offered to the consideration of the friends of drainage. 1794. P. BL.

7481 LENNY, J. G. Particulars referring to a plan of part of the Bedford Level and lands adjacent subject to Eau Brink tax. Halesworth, 1844. UEA.
Detailed list of proprietors subject to tax.

NORFOLK ESTUARY WORKS

7482 Norfolk estuary bill, 1876: the Ouse Outfall Board and the Lynn Corporation. 1876.
Also publ. in conjunction with this promotion: *Minute books of the original promoters...1837 to...1846; Argument and part of evidence...on the reference to Sir John Goode; Norfolk estuary bill, 1877.*

WAVENEY VALLEY

See nos. 7600, 7617, 7694, 8273, 9987.

PLACE-NAMES

7483 ANDERSON, O. S. The English hundred-names. Lund, 1934. Norfolk, pp. 63–83.

7484 COX, B. H. The significance of the distribution of English place-names in *-tun* in the Midlands and East Anglia. *J. Eng. Place-Name Soc.* 5, 1972/3, 15–73.

7485 ARNGART, O. The hundred-name Wayland. *J. Eng. Place-Name Soc.* 12, 1979/80, 54–8.

7486 PICKARD, I. *Ham* placenames in East Anglia. B.A. thesis, London Univ., 1979/80.

7487 SANDRED, K. I. Anglo-Saxon heritage in East Anglia. *Namn og Bygd* 61, 1973, 83–92.

7488 SANDRED, K. I. *and* LINDSTROM, B. Vad sager oss staden Norwichs ortnamn. *Ortnamnssallskapets i Uppsala Arsskrift* 1979, 5–26 [with Eng. summary].

7489 SANDRED, K. I. From the king's retainers to unfree peasants: some reflexes of Anglian social class groups in Norfolk place-names. *Nomina* 9, 1985, 21–30.

7490 SANDRED, K. I. Some reflexes of old Anglian and Viking settlement in Norfolk place-names. [Lecture summary]. *Bull. Norfolk Research Committee* 38, 1987, 10–12.

7491 SANDRED, K. I. The Vikings in Norfolk: some observations on the place-names in *-by*. *In* Proc. Tenth Viking Congress (Oslo, 1987), pp. 309–24.

See also nos. 8947A, 10116–17.

HUMAN GEOGRAPHY

POPULATION

7492 PATTEN, J. Population distribution in Norfolk and Suffolk during the 16th and 17th centuries. *Trans. Inst. Brit. Geog.* 65, 1975, 45–65. *Reprinted in his* Pre-industrial England: geographical essays (1979), pp. 71–91.

7493 PATTEN, J. Patterns of migration and movement of labour in 3 pre-industrial East Anglian towns. *J. Hist. Geog.* 2, 1976, 111–29. *Reprinted in his* Pre-industrial England: geographical essays (1979), pp. 143–61; *also in* CLARK, P. *and* SOUDEN, D., *eds*. Migration and society in early modern England (1987), pp. 77–106.
Deals with Norwich, Yarmouth and Ipswich.

7494 CLARK, P. Migration in England during the late 17th and early 18th centuries. *Past and Present* 83, 1979, 57–90.
Norwich is one of 6 diocesan courts furnishing evidence.

7495 DRUDY, P. J. *and* DRUDY, S. M. Population mobility and labour supply in rural regions: North Norfolk and the Galway Gaeltacht. *Regional Stud.* 13, 1979, 91–9.
See also no. 8065A.

7496 MCCLURE, P. Patterns of migration in the late Middle Ages: evidence of English place-name surnames. *Econ. Hist. Rev.* 2nd ser. 32, 1979, 167–82.
Norwich records form part of the evidence.

7497 CAMPBELL, B. M. S. The population of early Tudor England: a re-evaluation of the 1522 muster returns and 1524 and 1525 lay subsidies. *J. Hist. Geog.* 7, 1981, 145–54.
Uses evidence from hundreds of Tunstead and Happing.

7498 EDRICH, R. G. Population trends in Norfolk, 1600–1720. Ph.D. thesis, Reading Univ., 1984.

7499 EAST ANGLIA ECONOMIC PLANNING COUNCIL. Future population of East Anglia a report. Norwich, 1978.

7500 MOSELEY, M. J., *ed*. Planning for the future population of East Anglia [C.E.A.S. conference report]. Norwich, 1979. P.

7501 NORFOLK AREA HEALTH AUTHORITY. Population estimates, mid-1979. Norwich [1980]. P.

Census reports:

7502 1971: Report for the county... as constituted on 1 April 1974. 1976.
　　　　　Economic activity county leaflets: Norfolk. 1975. P
　　　　　Migration regional report: East Anglia. 3 parts. 1975–77.

7503 1981: County report. 2 parts. 1982–83.
　　　　　Regional migration, East Anglia. 2 parts. 1983–84.
　　　　　Parliamentary constituency monitors, 14: East Anglia. 1983. P.
　　　　　Economic activity [microfiche]. 1984.
　　　　　Ward and civil parish monitors, 29: Norfolk. 1984. P.

　　See also nos. 9381, 9488.

SETTLEMENT PATTERNS

7504 MOSELEY, M. J. The spatial impact of 'growth centres': case studies in Brittany and East Anglia. Ph.D. thesis, Reading Univ., 1971/72.

7505 LEMON, A. The small town: a study of changing functions, with special reference to the smallest urban settlements of Norfolk and Suffolk. D.Phil. thesis, Oxford Univ., 1972.

7506 WADE-MARTINS, P. The origins of rural settlement in East Anglia. *In* FOWLER, P. J., *ed*. Recent work in rural archaeology (Bradford-on-Avon, 1975), pp. 137–57.

7507 MCCUTCHEON, E. Recording deserted medieval villages. *Local Historian* 13, 1979, 471–4.
On work being done by a sub-group of the Norfolk Archaeology Rescue Group.

7508 CUSHION, B. *and others*. Some deserted village sites in Norfolk. *E.A.A.R.* 14, 1982, 40–101.

7509 ADDINGTON, S. Landscape and settlements in South Norfolk. *N.A.* 38, 1982, 97–139.
Surveys parishes of Fritton, Morningthorpe, Stratton St. Michael, Tasburgh and Hempnall.

7510 BECKETT, G. The Barwicks: one lost village or two? *N.A.* 39, 1984, 51–3.
See also *ib* 53–4 for note on deserted village of Caldecote, by A. Davison.

7511 DAVISON, A. Little Hockham. *N.A.* 40, 1987, 84–92.
Deserted village, adjoining Great Hockham.

　　See also nos. 7570, 7669, 7739, 7746, 9210, 9212, 9940, 9981, 10059.

PLANNING, RESOURCES, ENVIRONMENTAL ISSUES

7512 EAST ANGLIAN REGIONAL STUDIES GROUP. Regional planning and East Anglia: proceedings of the first annual conference. Cambridge, 1967.

7513 CONSERVATIVE AND UNIONIST PARTY (EASTERN AREA). East of England: a Tory study. Cambridge, 1968.

7514 DRUDY, P. J., *and* WALLACE, D. B. Towards a development programme for remote rural areas: a case study in North Norfolk. *Regional Stud.* 5, 1971, 281–8.

7515 East Anglia, where are we going? A conference held at the University of East Anglia to study the future social and economic objectives for the region. Norwich, 1971. P.
See also similar conference report. 1972.

7516 JAMIESON, MACKAY AND PARTNERS. Great Yarmouth-Lowestoft area: land use/transportation study. 2 vols. 1973.
Consultant engineers' report for joint D.O.E.-local authorities team.

7517 EAST ANGLIA REGIONAL STRATEGY TEAM. Strategic choice for East Anglia. 1974.

7518 AYTON, J. Rural settlement policy: problems and conflicts. In DRUDY, P. J., *ed.* Regional and rural development (Chalfont St. Giles, 1976). pp. 59–68.
See also in same collection essay on regional development in East Anglia by R. A. Bird, pp. 11–22.

7519 DEPT. OF THE ENVIRONMENT. East Anglia regional strategy. Government response to 'Strategic choice'. 1976. P.

7520 LABOUR PARTY. Look East: a prospect for the Eastern region. Report of a working party set up by the Eastern Regional Council. Ipswich, [1976].

7521 MOSELEY, M. J., *ed.* Social issues in rural Norfolk. Norwich, 1978.
11 papers dealing with problems of services to rural communities and questions arising from management of tourism and recreation.

7522 NEWBY, H. Urbanization and the rural class structure: reflections on a case study [E. Anglia]. *Brit. J. Sociol.* 30, 1979, 475–99.
Implications of urban population moving into countryside (commuters, pensioners, second-home owners, etc.).

7523 RAY, A. L. Second homes in North Norfolk. Swanton Novers, 1979.

7524 SMITH, S. Locational politics of local authority employment policies in Norfolk. M.Phil. thesis, London Univ., 1979.

7525 HILL, C. M. Leisure behaviour in Norfolk rural communities. Ph.D. thesis, Univ. of E. Anglia, 1980.

7526 WALMSLEY, M. Participation and non-participation in local and structure planning in small rural communities (Shipdham and Mundford). Ph.D. thesis, Univ. of E. Anglia, 1980.

7527 OWENS, S. E. Energy implications of alternative rural development patterns. Ph.D. thesis, Univ. of E. Anglia, 1981.
N.E. Norfolk (North Walsham area) taken as unit of study.

7528 MOSELEY, M. J., *ed.* Power, planning and people in rural East Anglia. Norwich, 1982.
Includes papers on Norfolk parish councils, second homes and retirement in N. Norfolk, newcomers and leisure in Norfolk villages, rural services in Norfolk and Suffolk, CoSIRA factories in employment provision, and survey of research on rural E. Anglia.

7529 O'RIORDAN, T. *and others.* Town and country: home and work. *J. Roy. Soc. of Arts* 131, 1983, 238–57.
Report of conference on rural environment, which includes paper by J. M. Shaw, Norfolk county planning officer (pp. 249–51).

7530 O'RIORDAN, T. Halvergate marshes: the story so far. *Ecos* 6 (i), 1985, 24–31.
On Halvergate issue see also Countryside Planning Yearbook 6, 1985, 101–6; and nos. 7456, 8074.

7531 PACKMAN, J. Rural deprivation and the loss of services: a case study of Norfolk. Ph.D. thesis, Univ. of E. Anglia, 1986.

See also nos. 7441, 7448, 7454, 7457–8, 7499–501, 7953–91 *passim*, 8013–21, 8091–107 *passim*, 8150–61, 8967, 9535–59, 10190–7.

EAST ANGLIA CONSULTATIVE COMMITTEE DOCUMENTS

7532 East Anglia: cause for concern. Ipswich, 1979. P.

7533 European Community policies and the region. Ipswich, 1982. P. Another ed., 1985.

7534 Regional development programme. Ipswich, 1982.

7535 Regional commentary [annual]. Ipswich, 1983–. P.

NORFOLK COUNTY COUNCIL PLANNING DOCUMENTS

7536 [Conservation area leaflets]. Norwich, 1971–.
Plans noted for Aylsham (1972); Bawburgh (1973); Castle Rising; Downham Market; Great Massingham (1973); Heydon (1971); New Buckenham; North Walsham (1973); Reepham (1973); Woodbastwick (1971).

7537 NORFOLK JOINT STRUCTURE PLAN STEERING COMMITTEE. Norfolk joint structure plan: issues and possibilities. Norwich, 1974.

7538 King's Lynn area land use/transportation study: summary report. Norwich, 1975.

7539 [Entry deleted]

7540 County structure plan: draft written statement for consultation. Norwich, 1976.
Also *Norfolk, the way ahead: a summary of the draft*, P.

7541 Norfolk structure plan. [1]: Written statement. [2]: Report of survey and studies. 2 vols. [3]: Statement on public participation and consultation. 4 vols. Norwich, 1977.
See also *Modifications for the written statement* (Dec. 1977); *Schedule of proposed amendments* (July 1978); *Written statements, as modified and approved by the Secretary of State... with approved alterations* (1983); *Draft explanatory memorandum* (1985).

7542 Norfolk structure plan: monitoring reports. Norwich, 1977–. 1st report, 1977; 2nd report (3 parts), 1978–9; 3rd report, 1980; 4th report, 1981; 5th report, 1982; 6th report, 1984; 7th report, 1986.

7543 Action plan for North Norfolk and proposed Central Norfolk special investment areas: submission to the Development Commission. [Norwich], 1978.
Submission jointly prepared with district councils of North Norfolk and Breckland. See also *Action plan for the proposed extensions...* (1983).

7544 NORFOLK COUNTY COUNCIL *and* SUFFOLK COUNTY COUNCIL. Action plan for the proposed Southern Norfolk/North Suffolk special investment area: submission to the Development Commission. 1979.
Issued in conjunction with appropriate district councils.

7545 Development control scheme: district councils. Norwich, 1979. Another ed. 1982. P.

7546 Nuclear power in the east of England: proceedings of a seminar...2 July 1979. Norwich, 1980.

7547 Services in rural Norfolk: survey of the changing pattern...over the last 30 years. Norwich, 1981.
Surveys decline in provision of public transport, garages, pubs, etc.

7548 Waste disposal plan. Norwich, 1981.
See also preliminary survey reports (1980); and *Draft consultative review*, 1988–97 (1987).

7549 Environmental resources directory. Norwich, 1982. P.

7550 The future of the River Yare valley at Colney, Bowthorpe and Bawburgh: a discussion document. Norwich, 1984. P.

7551 Norfolk rural development area: strategy and programme, 1986/87. Norwich, 1985. *Followed by* Rural development programme, 1988/89–90/91 (1987).

7552 Norfolk structure plan: technical reports. Norwich, 1985.
Comprise: *Job need; Financial resources; Development land requirement; Villages for estate development; Housing countrywide; Housing – Great Yarmouth policy area; Housing – Norwich policy area; Housing – King's Lynn policy area; Housing – Thetford and rural policy area; Norwich policy area boundary; Swaffham.*

7553 The North Norfolk heritage coast strategy and management plan: consultation draft. Norwich, 1987.
See also earlier *Heritage coast management plan: consultative draft* (1978).

7554 Norfolk countryside strategy. Topic paper series [consultative drafts]. 1: River valleys. 2: Woodlands. 5: Historic parklands. Norwich, 1988.
See also nos. 7362, 7391, 7411, 7985–6, 7989–90, 8100, 8103, 8157, 8159, 8161, 8409–10, 9158, 9318, 9542, 9547, 9557, 9790, 10076, 10141.

DISTRICT COUNCIL PLANNING DOCUMENTS
For local plans affecting individual towns and villages see under locality. Note also nos. 7360, 8016–17, 8101, 8106, 8172.

Breckland
7554A Design in Breckland: individual houses. 1975. P.

7555 Breckland 1: digest of information. [E. Dereham]. 1977.

7556 Norfolk structure plan: representations of the Breckland District Council. E. Dereham, 1977.

7557 Rural accessibility: a study of the Breckland district of Norfolk, prepared by R. P. Kilvington. Loughborough, 1982.

King's Lynn and West Norfolk
7558 Village development guidelines. [King's Lynn, 1981].

South Norfolk
7559 South Norfolk's heritage. By B. R. Joyce and H. M. Haslam. Loddon, 1975. P.

7560 [Conservation area leaflets]. Loddon, Long Stratton, 1976–.
Plans available for Bramerton (1982); Brockdish (1976); Brooke (1978); Cringleford (1980); Dickleburgh; Fritton (1978); Hingham (1979); Howe (1982); Loddon and Chedgrave; Long Stratton (1980); Mulbarton (1982); Old Costessey (1983); Saxlingham Nethergate and Saxlingham Green (1982); Shotesham (1982); Starston (1983); Stoke Holy Cross, Keswick, and Ellingham mills(1980); Tacolneston (1983); Trowse with Newton (1985); Wacton (1982).

7561 Planning in South Norfolk. Loddon, [1976]. P.

7562 West Costessey, Wensum and Yare valleys local plan. Loddon, 1980.
Preceded by *Draft local plan: a discussion document* (1978); and *Local plan: public participation and consultation* (1980).

7563 1981 census: journey to work in South Norfolk. Long Stratton, 1986. P.

7564 Rural policy area: potential for estate scale residential development. Long Stratton, 1986. P.

7565 HASLAM, M. *and* PARTRIDGE, B. Planning in South Norfolk. *Planning* 74, Feb. 1988, 87–91.

WATER RESOURCES PLANNING
7566 WATER RESOURCES BOARD. Water supplies in south-east England. 1966.
Includes E. Anglia. See also Board's *Combined use of surface and groundwater in the Ely, Ouse, and Nar catchments* (1974).
7567 EAST SUFFOLK AND NORFOLK RIVER AUTHORITY. First survey of water resources and demands. 2 vols. Norwich, 1971.
7568 ANGLIAN WATER AUTHORITY. Interim review of the long term water plan. 1975.
7569 DEPT. OF THE ENVIRONMENT. The Wash water storage scheme: report on the feasibility study. 1976.
7570 ALLERSTON, P. A. The coordination of rural settlement planning and water infrastructure planning in Norfolk. Ph.D. thesis, Univ. of E. Anglia, 1987.
Involves special attention to Swaffham, Horsford-Taverham-Drayton, and Downham Market areas.
See also nos. 9611–13, 10042.

YARE VALLEY PROPOSALS
7571 LAND USE CONSULTANTS. A landscape assessment of the Yare basin flood control study proposals. (Countryside Commission working paper, 13). Cambridge, 1978
7572 ANGLIAN WATER AUTHORITY. Yare basin flood control study: the options. [Norwich, 1978]. P.
7573 DENT, D. L. *and* HEY, R. D., *eds.* Environmental impact assessment of the proposed Yare Basin flood control scheme. (Broads Authority research ser. 1), Norwich, 1980.
7574 O'RIORDAN, T. The Yare barrier proposals. *Ecos* 1 (ii), 1980, 8–14.
7575 O'RIORDAN, T. The Yare barrier controversy. [UEA inaugural lecture]. Norwich, 1981.
7576 TURNER, R. K. A review of the Anglian Water's *Yare Basin flood control study*: draft report. (Broads Authority). 1983.
See also his subsequent paper (Broads Authority research ser. 8) in no. 7448.

GUIDE BOOKS AND DESCRIPTIVE WORKS

7577 Occasional reflections in a journey from London to Norwich and Cambridge. 1711. P. Yale Univ. Lib.
7578 SALMON, N. A new survey of England. Part 3: comprehending Norfolk, Cambridgeshire, and Huntingdonshire. 1728.
7579 SCARFE, N., *ed.* A Frenchman's year in Suffolk...1784...The *Mélanges sur l'Angleterre* of François de la Rochefoucauld, supplemented by the *journaux de voyage* of Alexandre de La Rochefoucauld and the *lettres à un ami* of their companion, Maximilien de Lazowski. *Suffolk Records Soc.* 30, 1988.
Includes two-week tour of Norfolk, pp.156–215. New translation of item 1387 in B.N.H.

7580 PRATT, S. J. Gleanings in England descriptive of the countenance, mind, and character of the country. 1794. BL.
Deals mainly with Norfolk. Forms vol. 4 of work entitled *Gleanings through Wales, Holland, and Westphalia* which went through several editions up to 1804, with the *Gleanings in England* eventually being itself expanded to 3 vols.

7581 JOHNSTON, L. Town and country in East Anglia 150 years ago. *Suffolk Rev.* 2, 1964, 249–59.
From a ms. *Tour to Cambridge, Norwich and Ipswich … 1815* in the Bodleian Library.

7582 TYMMS, S. A compendious account of the antient and present state of the Norfolk circuit. 1833.
Forms vol. 3 of his *The family topographer.*

7583 WHITE, W. Eastern England from the Thames to the Humber. 2 vols. 1865. BL.

7584 BARRETT, C. R. B. Barrett's illustrated [Eastern counties] guides. 9 parts. 1892–94. BL.

7585 HARBOUR, H. The way about Norfolk and Suffolk. 1893.

7586 ROPER, C. Where the birds sing. A selection of rustic sketches and idylls of common life. Manchester, 1894. BL.

7587 East Anglian health and holiday resorts illustrated. Norwich, [c. 1895]. RCF.

7588 DODWELL, R. Norfolk pocket county companion. 1896.

7589 HOMELAND ASSOCIATION. Handy guides. 1: King's Lynn [and Sandringham]. 13: Mundesley. 25: North Walsham and the Norfolk Broads. 1907–. BL.

7590 CARNIE, T. W. In quaint East Anglia. 1899. UEA.

7591 WARD, LOCK & CO. A new pictorial and descriptive guide to Cromer, Sheringham, Mundesley...with excursions to the Broads, Norwich, and Sandringham...1899.
Many other eds., also titled *Guide to North Norfolk...*

7592 WARD, LOCK & CO. A new pictorial and descriptive guide to Great Yarmouth and the land of the Broads, with excursions to Lowestoft, Norwich... 1900.
Many subseq. eds. with variant titles.

7593 LINDLEY, P. Holidays in Eastern counties. [1901].

7594 PEATON, A. Pictures of East Coast health resorts. 1901.

7595 BRITISH ASSOCIATION. Cambridge meeting, 1904. Excursion guides. RCF.
Consists of E. M. Beloe, *Lynn, Castle Rising and Sandringham*; L. G. Bolingbroke and T. Southwell, *Norwich*.

7596 ROBINSON, E. K. In the King's county. 1904.

7597 VINCENT, J. E. Through East Anglia in a motor car. 1907.

7598 JERROLD, W. Norwich and the Broads described... Pictured by E. W. Haslehurst. 1910.

7599 MORLEY, F. V. Travels in East Anglia. 1923.

7600 BAKER, B. G. Waveney. 1924.
Description of Waveney Valley towns and villages on both sides of Norfolk-Suffolk border.

7601 HOME, G. C. Through East Anglia. 1925. BL.

7602 MEREDITH, H. East Anglia from Colchester to Boston. [1929].

7603 DIXON-SCOTT, J. *and* JORDAN, J. A. The beauty of Norfolk. Camera pictures...1931. RCF.

7604 PRIEST, E. W. Hiking through Norfolk. Norwich, 1931.

7605 STIBBONS, F. In the King's country. 1931.

7606 FELCE, E. *and* BARRY, T. H. Picturesque Norfolk: a guide to some of the characteristic beauty spots... Norwich, 1939.

7607 COWLEY, J. [K.] East Anglia. [1949].

7608 COOPER. A. P. Camera cameos of Norwich and Norfolk. Norwich, [1950].

7609 COOPER, C. G. T. A fortnight on the East Coast. 1951.

7610 GRIGSON, G. E. H. East Anglia. (Festival of Britain Office: About Britain, 4). 1951.

7611 JONES, S. R. England east. [1954].

7612 COUNTRY LIFE. Picture book of East Anglia. 1958.

7613 FORREST, A. J. Under three crowns. Ipswich, 1961.

7614 HADFIELD, J. *and others*. East Anglian heritage. Ipswich, 1964.

7615 LAMB, C. Discovering Norfolk. Tring, 1968. Other eds. 1972, 1976.

7616 DORMAN, B. E. Norfolk. 1972.

7617 BUTCHER, D. R. Waveney Valley. Ipswich, 1975.

7618 HALES, J. Norfolk places. Ipswich, 1975. 2nd ed. Holt, 1987.

7619 CENTRAL OFFICE OF INFORMATION. East Anglia. (Reference pamphlets, 142). 1976.
General report on economy and amenities.

7620 HEPWORTH, P. The Batsford colour book of Norfolk. 1976.

7621 KUDO, N. A stranger in East Anglia. Ipswich, 1976.
See also sequel *East Anglia from abroad* (Ipswich, 1978).

7622 BROWN, R. The lowdown guide to North Norfolk. Melton Constable, 1976.

7623 WATKINS, M. A taste of East Anglia: a guide to 101 regional restaurants. Ipswich, 1977.

7624 YAXLEY, D. Portrait of Norfolk. 1977.

7625 BAX, A. *and* FAIRFIELD, S. Macmillan guide to the U.K., 1978/79. 1978. Norfolk: pp. 502–18.
Handy facts and figures on county government, economy etc.

7626 STEGGALL, P. East Anglia. 1979.

7627 DRACKETT. P. Inns and harbours of North Norfolk. N.p., 1980.

7628 ANCKORN, G. A West Norfolk camera. Sevenoaks, 1981.
Old photographs of Lynn, Wells, Sandringham etc.

7629 KENNETT, D. H. A guide to the Norfolk Way. 1983.
Guide to accompany Peddar's Way and coastal path.

7630 WATKINS, M. An East Anglian journey: landscape with figures. Ipswich, 1983.

7631 INNES, H. Hammond Innes' East Anglia. 1986.

7632 ROBINSON, B. The Peddars Way and Norfolk coast path. (Countryside Commission). 1986.

7633 AUTOMOBILE ASSOCIATION. East Anglia. 1987.

7634 HOPKINSON, B., *ed*. Norfolk in colour. Photography and text by Mark and Elizabeth Mitchels. Forncett St. Peter, 1987.

7635 BLOEMENDAL, F. A. H. East Anglia: heritage and landscape. Photographs. Text by F. Barran and A. Hollingsworth. 1988.

7636 HORDER, M., *ed*. In praise of Norfolk: an anthology for friends. Bury St. Edmunds, 1988.

7637 SIMMS, N. Orlando's guide to North Norfolk. Briston, 1988.
See also nos. 7669, 7673, 8400.

HISTORY AND ARCHAEOLOGY

PERIODICALS

7638 NORFOLK ARCHAEOLOGICAL RESCUE GROUP. NARG news. North Elmham, 1975–.
7639 East Anglian history workshop: a social history newsletter for East Anglia. Colchester, 1977–79.
7640 WEST NORFOLK LOCAL HISTORY SOCIETY. Journal. King's Lynn, 1978–.
7641 GREAT YARMOUTH AND DISTRICT ARCHAEOLOGICAL SOCIETY. Yarmouth Archaeology. Great Yarmouth, 1979–.
7642 HISTORICAL ASSOCIATION: NORFOLK AND NORWICH BRANCH. Newsletter. Norwich, 1979–.
7643 CENTRE OF EAST ANGLIAN STUDIES. Newsletter of the Friends of Earlham. Norwich, 1980–82.
7644 NORFOLK HERITAGE. Newsletter. Gressenhall, 1982–.
7645 CENTRE OF EAST ANGLIAN STUDIES. Newsletter. Norwich, 1984–.
Incorporates *East Anglian Film Archives Newletter.*

See also nos. 8539, 8556.

BIBLIOGRAPHY AND HISTORICAL AIDS

7646 EVERITT, A. T. *and* PERCEVAL, C. S. Documents relating to Suffolk and Norfolk. *Proc. Soc. of Antiq.* 2nd ser. 10, 1883–85, 97–105.
7647 RYE, W. A short calendar of the topographical and genealogical books and mss. in the Free Library at Norwich. *N.A.M.* 2nd ser. 2, 1908, 10–54.
Also publ. separately as *A catalogue of the topographical and antiquarian portions of the Free Library*
7648 BELOE, E. M. Report of lecture on seals: reprinted from the *Lynn Advertiser.* King's Lynn, 1911. P.
7649 HUMPHREYS, A. L. A handbook to county bibliography. 1917. Norfolk, pp. 173–81.
7650 NORFOLK COUNTY LIBRARY [WEST NORFOLK DIV.] Local history subject index to non-book materials. [1975].
7651 RUTLEDGE, P. Norfolk Record Office business and industrial records [for Norfolk Archaeological Society]. Norwich, 1977. P.
7652 CENTRE OF EAST ANGLIAN STUDIES. Catalogue of films in the East Anglian film archive. 3 vols. Colchester/Norwich, 1977–84.
See also nos. 7645, 7659.

7653 OPEN UNIVERSITY. Guide to libraries, record offices and other resource centres in the East Anglian region. Cambridge, [1978]. P. Another ed. 1982.

7654 THETFORD MUSEUM. Collection of late 18th and early 19th century broadsides, etc., mainly relating to Norfolk, in the Duleep Singh collection. Norwich, [c. 1978]. P.

7655 EVANS, N. Tithe books as a source for the local historian. *Local Historian* 14, 1980, 24–7.
Examines their survival in Norfolk and Suffolk.

7656 NORFOLK RECORD OFFICE. Parish registers deposited at the Norfolk Record Office. Norwich, 1980. P.

7657 CENTRE OF EAST ANGLIAN STUDIES. East Anglian studies: theses completed. Ed. by Janice Henney. Norwich, 1982.

7658 ANGLIA TELEVISION. A sense of the past. Norwich, 1984.
Guide to topographical research in East Anglia.

7659 CLEVELAND, D. East Anglia on film. North Walsham, 1987.

7660 NORWICH COMMUNITY WORKSHOP. Oral history archive [transcripts and cassettes]. Norwich, 1987.

See also nos. 8222, 8960, 9995, 10055, 10164.

GENERAL WORKS

7661 BAYNE, A. D. History of Norfolk and Suffolk, including a survey of the eastern counties. [c. 1870].

7662 KNIGHTS, M. Popular risings in Norfolk. [c. 1885]. P. BL.

7663 SYMES, E. S. The story of the East Country. 1904.

7664 NORWICH CASTLE MUSEUM. East Anglia and the Netherlands. Catalogue of a loan exhibition. Norwich, [1954]. P.

7665 BATES, M. Regional military histories: East Anglia. Reading, 1974.

7666 HALES, J. Norfolk patchwork. Wymondham, 1979.

7667 WATKINS, M. This other breed – East Anglians. Ipswich, 1979.

7668 FLETCHER, R. The East Anglians. (A popular regional history of the British people). Cambridge, 1980.

7669 KENNETT, D. H. Norfolk villages. 1980.

7670 LEWIS, C. Norfolk in Europe. Based on the text for the exhibition *Norfolk in Europe* written by K. Hudson and B. Green. Norwich, 1980.

7671 HALES, J. A family of no importance. Holt, 1984.
Collection of short essays and reprints on Norfolk history and tradition.

7672 WADE MARTINS, S. History of Norfolk. Chichester, 1984.

7673 WATKINS, M., *ed.* East Anglian golden book. Ipswich, 1984.
Anthology of pieces from *East Anglian Mag.* to commemorate its 50th anniversary.

ARCHAEOLOGY

7674 NORWICH CASTLE MUSEUM. Archaeological discovery in East Anglia. 1851–1951. [Exhib. cat.]. Norwich, 1951.

7675 CLARKE, H. Regional archaeology. East Anglia. 1971.

7676 NORFOLK ARCHAEOLOGICAL UNIT. The archaeological implications of the Norwich southern by-pass: a preliminary report. E. Dereham, 1974. P.

7677 WADE-MARTINS, P. The Norfolk Archaeological Unit. *Current Archaeol.* 4 (9), 1974, 281–4.

7678 East Anglian archaeology reports. Ipswich/Gressenhall/Norwich, 1975–.

7679 EDWARDS, D. The air photographs collection of the Norwich Archaeological Unit. *E.A.A.R.* 2, 1976, 261–9; 5, 1977, 225–37; 8, 1978, 87–105.

7680 AGRICULTURAL DEVELOPMENT AND ADVISORY SERVICE. Farming on ancient monuments in Norfolk. Norwich, [1978]. P.

7681 PRITCHARD, G. Farming on archaeological sites in Norfolk. *In* Historical landscapes: identification, recording and management. (Conference proc., Dept. of Geography. Polytechnic of North London, 1978), pp. 87–9.

7682 Some recent archaeological finds from Norfolk. *N.A.* 37, 1978–80. 129–36, 216–29, 329–57; 38, 1981–83, 88–95, 204–18, 363–83; 39, 1984–86, 65–99, 215–23, 315–30; 40, 1987–88, 122–30, 194–9.

7683 BECKLEY, R. Ancient walls of East Anglia. Lavenham, 1979.

7684 WILSON, D. R. Factors affecting the distribution of crop marks in the Anglian region. *Aerial Archaeol.* 4, 1979, 32–6.

7685 WILTON, J. W. Earthworks and fortifications of Norfolk. Lowestoft, 1979. P.

7686 Village sites in Launditch Hundred. *E.E.A.R.* 10, 1980.
Reports on Beetley, E. Bilney, Brisley, Horningtoft, Kempstone, Longham, Mileham, Stanfield, Tittleshall, Weasenham, Wellingham, Worthing; also Caldecote and Grenstein (deserted villages).

7687 MOATED SITES RESEARCH GROUP. Reports nos. 9–13. Liss (Hants.), 1982–86.
Several Norfolk sites dealt with.

7688 MURPHY, P. Iron age to late Saxon land use in the Breckland. *In* JONES, M., *ed.* Integrating the subsistence economy. (Brit. Archaeol. Repts., Internat. ser. 181, 1983), pp. 177–209.

7689 GREGORY, T. *and* ROGERSON, A. J. G. Metal detecting in archaeological excavation. *Antiquity* 58, 1984, 179–84.
Examples from Norfolk.

7690 MURPHY, P. Environmental archaeology in East Anglia. *In* KEELEY, H. C. M., ed. Environmental archaeology: a regional review (1984), pp. 13–42.

7691 GREGORY, T. *and* GURNEY, D. Excavations at Thornham, Warham, Wighton and Caistor St. Edmund. *E.A.A.* 30, 1986.
Reports excavations originally undertaken or encouraged by R. Rainbird Clarke.

7692 DOLLIN, B. W. Moated sites in north-east Norfolk. *N.A.* 39, 1986, 262–77.

7693 BEAGRIE, N. *and* GURNEY, D. The Norfolk excavations index. *N.A.* 40, 1988, 185–93.

See also nos. 7468, 7472, 7506, 8032, 8099, 8801, 8946, 9299, 9301, 9303–4, 9432–54, 9934, 10032, 10108, 10125, 10130, 10235.

HISTORY, BY PERIOD

EARLY MAN

7694 DUTT, W. A. The Waveney Valley in the Stone Age. Lowestoft, 1905.

7695 ROE, D. A., *ed.* A gazetteer of British lower and middle palaeolithic sites. (Council for Brit. Archaeol., research rept. 8). 1968. Norfolk, pp. 228–42.

7696 BURGESS, M. W. The standing stones of Norfolk and Suffolk. Lowestoft, 1978. P.

7697 LAWSON, A. J. Prehistoric earthworks in Norfolk: printed on the occasion of the Prehistoric Society's field excursion to Norwich. 12–14 May 1978. [Norwich], 1978. P.

7698 HEALY, F. M. A. The neolithic in Norfolk. Ph.D. thesis, London Univ., 1980.

7699 LAWSON, A. J. The evidence for later Bronze Age settlement and burial in

Norfolk. *In* BARRETT, J. *and* BRADLEY, R., *eds*. Settlement and society in the later British Bronze Age (Brit. Archaeol. Repts. 83, 1980), pp. 271–94.

7700 LAWSON, A. J. *and others*. The barrows of East Anglia. *E.A.A.R.* 12, 1981.

7701 ROBINSON, B. Hunters to first farmers. (Norfolk origins, 1). Fakenham, 1981.

7702 BAMFORD, H. M. Beaker domestic sites in the Fen edge and East Anglia. *E.A.A.R.* 16, 1982.
Relates largely to finds at Hockwold. Revised version of Ph.D. thesis, Edinburgh, 1970.

7703 BARRINGER, C., *ed*. Aspects of East Anglian pre-history (20 years after Rainbird Clarke): a collection of essays by Paul Ashbee [and others]. Norwich. 1984.

7704 WYMER, J. The palaeolithic sites of East Anglia. Norwich, 1985.

7705 LAWSON, A. J. *and others*. Barrow excavations in Norfolk 1950–82. *E.A.A.* 29, 1986.

7706 WILLIAMSON, T. Early co-axial field systems on the East Anglian boulder clays. *Proc. Prehistoric Soc.* 53, 1987, 419–31.

See also nos.7471, 8969, 8976, 8978, 9037, 9039, 9183, 9214, 9391, 9434, 9964, 10059.

ARTEFACTS

7707 STURGE, W. A. Implements of the later palaeolithic 'cave' periods in East Anglia. *P.P.S.* 1, 1910–12, 210–32.

7708 FOX, *Sir* C. The socketed bronze sickles of the British Isles, with special reference to an unpublished specimen from Norwich, *P.P.S.* n.s. 5, 1939, 222–48.

7709 NORWICH CASTLE MUSEUM. Bronze age metalwork in Norwich Castle Museum. Norwich, 1966. Rev. ed. 1977.

7710 KINNES, I. A beaker burial on Ringstead Downs, Old Hunstanton. *E.A.A.R.* 8, 1978, 19–22.

7711 HEALY, F. Recent finds of neolithic bowl pottery in Norfolk. *N.A.* 39, 1984, 65–82.

7712 LAWSON, A. J. Bronzes from Brettenham, Boxford, Barton Bendish, Boughton and Broadmoor Common. *N.A.* 39, 1985, 169–75.

See also nos. 9003, 9008, 9080, 9083, 9283, 9432, 9450, 10131.

GRIMES GRAVES

7713 GREENWELL, W. Grimes Graves. [Paper read to Wilts. Archaeol. and Natural History Soc.] Salisbury, 1870.

7714 GREENWELL, W. On the opening of Grimes Graves. *J. Ethnological Soc.* n.s.2, 1870, 419–39.

7715 STURGE, W. A. The polished axe found... at Grimes Graves. *Man* 8, 1908, 166–8.

7716 SMITH, R. A. A flint masterpiece [from Grimes Graves]. *Brit. Museum Quart.* 6, 1932, 103–104.

7717 GREEN, B. Young people's guide to Grimes Graves. 1964. P.

7718 MERCER, R. J. Grime's Graves... interim... conclusions drawn from the total excavation of a flint mine shaft and... surface area in 1971–2. *In* BURGESS, C. *and* MIKET, R., *eds*. Settlement and economy in the 3rd and 2nd millenia B.C. (Brit. Archaeol. Repts. 33, 1976), pp. 101–13.

7719 BURLEIGH, R. *and others*. A further consideration of neolithic dogs with special reference to a skeleton from Grimes Graves. *J. Archaeol. Sci.* 4, 1977, 353–66.

7720 SIEVEKING, G. de G. Grimes Graves and prehistoric European flint mining. *In* CRAWFORD, H., *ed*. Subterranean Britain: aspects of underground archaeology. (1979), pp. 1–43.

7721 BURTON, J. Making sense of waste flakes: new methods for investigating the technology and economics behind chipped stone assemblages. *J. Archaeol. Science* 7, 1980, 131–48.

7722 MERCER, R. J. *and others*. Grimes Graves, Norfolk: excavations, 1971–72. 2 vols. (D.O.E. archaeological rept. 11), 1981.

7723 Excavations at Grimes Graves, Norfolk, 1972–1976. Fasc. 1: Neolithic antler picks... By J. Clutton-Brock. Fasc. 2: The Neolithic, Bronze Age, and later pottery. By I. Longworth and others. 1984/88.

7724 HEALY, F. Recent work at Grimes Graves. *N.A* 39, 1975, 175–81.

ROMAN PERIOD

7725 SURTEES, S. F. Julius Caesar: showing beyond reasonable doubt that he never crossed the Channel but sailed from Zeeland and landed in Norfolk. 1868. P. BL. See also his *Julius Caesar. Did he cross the Channel?* (1866).

7726 TAYLOR, A. Papers in relation to the antient topography of the eastern counties of Britain, and on the right way of interpreting the Roman itinerary. 1869. BL.

7727 PLOUVIEZ, J. The Romano-British pottery kilns in East Anglia. Dissertation, London Univ. Institute of Archaeology, 1972.

7728 BAGSHAWE, R. A Roman road between Brisley and Terrington St. Clement. *E.A.A.R.* 5, 1977, 5–8.

7729 WADE-MARTINS, P. A Roman road between Billingford and Toftrees. *E.A.A.R.* 5, 1977, 1–3.

7730 SMALLWOOD, J. Roman settlement in north-west Norfolk. *NARG News* 25, 1981, 12–17.

7731 GREGORY, T. Romano-British settlement in West Norfolk and on the Norfolk fen edge. *In* MILES, D., *ed*. The Romano-British countryside (*Brit. Archaeol. Repts.* 103, 1982), part 2, pp. 351–75.

7732 JOHNS, C. *and* POTTER, T. The Thetford treasure: Roman jewellery and silver. 1983.

7733 TRETT, R. Roman bronzed 'grooved pendants' from East Anglia. *N.A.* 38, 1983, 219–34.

7734 GURNEY, D. *and others*. Settlement, religion and industry on the fen-edge: three Romano-British sites in Norfolk. *E.A.A.* 31, 1986. 'Backlog' reports on villa and bath-house at Feltwell (excavated 1962–64); Leylands Farm, Hockwold cum Witton (1957); salt-production site at Denver (1960).

7735 ROBINSON, B. *and* GREGORY, T. Celtic fire and Roman rule. (Norfolk origins, 3). North Walsham, 1987.

See also nos. 8943–4, 8947, 8981, 9006–7, 9009–11, 9014, 9021, 9032–5, 9038, 9246, 9434, 9909–10, 9912, 9916, 9932, 9969, 9976, 10031, 10033, 10102, 10107, 10125, 10139.

ANGLO-SAXON PERIOD

7736 CUMING, H. S. On the kings of East Anglia. *J. Brit. Archaeol. Assoc.* 21, 1865, 22–31.

7737 HURST, J. G. Saxo-Norman pottery in East Anglia: 2, Thetford ware. *Proc. Cambridge Antiq. Soc.* 50, 1957, 29–60.

7738 WADE-MARTINS, P. The linear earthworks of west Norfolk. *N.A.* 36, 1974, 23–38.

7739 THACKERAY, D. W. R. Defensive linear earthworks of East Anglia, with particular reference to Anglo-Saxon settlement. Ph.D. thesis, Cambridge Univ., 1980.

7740 INSLEY, J. Social structure and place-names in relation to the Danish settlement of East Anglia. Ph.D. thesis, Nottingham Univ., 1980.

7741 GREEN, B., MILLIGAN, W. F., *and* WEST, S. E. The Illington/Lackford workshop. *In* EVISON, V. E., *ed*. Angles, Saxons and Jutes: essays presented to J. N. L. Myres (Oxford, 1981), pp. 187–226.
Related pottery finds from sites in S. W. Norfolk, N. W. Suffolk and E. Cambridgeshire.

7742 HART, C. The East Anglian chronicle. *J. Mod. Hist.* 7, 1981, 248–82.
Reconsideration of source usually known as Annals of St. Neots.

7743 HILLS, C. Animal stamps on Anglo-Saxon pottery in East Anglia. *Studien zur Sachsenforschung* 4, 1983, 93–110.

7744 HINES, J. The Scandinavian character of Anglian England in the pre-Viking period. (Brit. Archaeol. Repts. 124). 1984.

7745 ATKIN, M. The Anglo-Saxon urban landscape in East Anglia. *Landscape Hist.* 7, 1985, 27–40.

7746 WILLIAMSON, T. Settlement chronology and regional landscapes: the evidence from the claylands of East Anglia and Essex. *In* HOOKE, D., *ed*. Anglo-Saxon settlements (Oxford, 1988), pp. 153–75.

See also nos. 7487–91, 8108–9, 8226, 8231, 8247, 8554, 8980, 8984, 9016, 9040, 9138–48, 9363, 9390, 9458–9, 10006, 10024, 10030.

MEDIEVAL PERIOD

DOMESDAY BOOK

7747 CARNELL, P. A study of the lay fiefs of Norfolk at the time of the Domesday Survey. M.A. thesis, Univ. of Wales, 1966.

7748 DARBY, H. C. *and* VERSEY. G. R. Domesday gazetteer. Cambridge, 1975. Norfolk section, pp. 262–96.

7749 BROWN, P., *ed*. Domesday book: vol. 33, Norfolk. (History from the Sources, general ed. J. Morris). 2 vols. Chichester, 1984.

OTHER SOURCES

7750 Rotuli hundredorum temp. Hen. III & Edw. I. (Publ. of the Record Commissioners). Norfolk: vol. 1 [1812], pp. 434–543.

7751 BEDELL, A. J. Unpublished muster-roll of the reign of Richard I: Norfolk and Suffolk. *East Anglian.* n.s. 4, 1891/92, 225–9.

7752 LIEBERMANN, F. Uber ostenglischen Geschichtsquellen des 12–14 Jahrhunderts. Neues Archiv 18, 1892, 225–67.

7753 PUBLIC RECORD OFFICE. Inquisitions and assessments relating to feudal aids, with other analogous documents, 1284–1431. Vol.3: Kent to Norfolk. 1904.

7754 HISTORICAL MSS. COMMISSION. Ancient deeds belonging to the Duke of Norfolk, and relating chiefly to manors in... Norfolk and Suffolk. *In* Report on Mss. in various collections, vol. 7. [Publications, ser. 55]. 1914.

7755 KILLINGSWORTH, V. An edition of the writs and charters of Henry II relating to Norfolk, Suffolk, Cambridgeshire and Huntingdonshire. B.Litt. thesis, Oxford Univ., 1975.

See also nos. 9300, 9305, 9805, 9808, 9455–6, 9460–1, 10171, 10174.

MISCELLANEOUS TOPICS, 12TH TO 15TH CENTURIES

7756 HOOD, C. M. Manorial history. Changes in the manor. *In her* Sequestered loyalists and Bartholomew sufferers (1922), pp. 150–204.
Sketch of manorial evolution largely drawing on Norfolk examples.

7757 BENNETT, H. S. Six medieval men and women. Cambridge, 1955.
Includes studies of Sir John Fastolf, Margaret Paston and Margery Kempe.

7758 FEENEY, B. J. East Anglian opposition to King John. Ph.D. thesis, Reading Univ., 1973.

7759 CLARK, E. G. Medieval debt litigation: Essex and Norfolk, 1270–1490. Ph.D. thesis, Univ. of Michigan, 1977.

7760 SAYER. M. Norfolk involvement in dynastic conflict, 1469–71 and 1483–87. N.A. 36, 1977, 305–26.

7761 MILNER, J. Sir Simon Felbrigg, K.G.: the Lancastrian revolution and personal fortune. N.A. 37, 1978, 84–91.

7762 SPENCER, B. Medieval pilgrim badges from Norfolk. Norwich, 1980. P

7763 VIRGOE, R. The Crown, magnates, and local government in 15th-century East Anglia. *In* HIGHFIELD, J. R. L. *and* JEFFS, R., *eds.* The Crown and local communications in England and France in the 15th century (Gloucester, 1981), pp. 72–87.

7764 FLETCHER, A. J. Chaucer's Norfolk reeve. *Medium Aevum* 52, 1983, 100–103.
Suggests medieval stereotype of Norfolk men as cunning and avaricious.

7764A CORNFORD, B., *ed.* Studies towards a history of the rising of 1381 in Norfolk. Norwich, 1984.

7765 CORNFORD, B. The Black Death in Flegg. *NARG News* 43, 1985, 7–15.

7766 MADDERN, P. C. Violence, crime, and public disorder in East Anglia, 1422–42. D.Phil. thesis, Oxford Univ., 1985.

7767 POST, J. B. Sir John Le Breton and the mutilation of Sir Godfrey Millers. N.A. 39, 1985, 189–92.
12th century episode involving revenge for seduction, somewhat reminiscent of Abelard and Heloise story.

See also nos. 7395, 7496, 7507–8, 7898–901, 7906, 7914, 7929–31, 7950, 8028–31, 8034–5, 8037–8, 8040, 8044–5, 8184, 8223–47 *passim*, 8553–4, 8590–1, 8697–9, 8823, 8827–8, 8855–65, 8877, 9073, 9226A, 9232, 9299–306, 9387, 9457, 9908, 9977, 10059, 10170–6.

LATER HISTORY

GENERAL EARLY MODERN

7767A Extracts from churchwardens' books. *East Anglian* 2, 1866, 356–8, 364–6; 4, 1869, 54–8, 126–8, 176–8; n.s. 3, 1889/90, 23–4.
Material from records of Forncett St. Peter, Redenhall, Bacton, Toft Monks.

7768 HARRIS, J. R. East Anglia and America. Ipswich, 1976.
For other material on emigration to America see nos. 7795–6, 8544, 8826, 9241–2.

7769 PATTEN, J. English towns, 1500–1700. Folkestone, 1978. Chap. 6: Towns in the national urban system – East Anglia.

7770 TILLY, C. Proletarianization and rural collective action in East Anglia and elsewhere, 1500–1900. *Peasant Stud.* 10, 1982, 5–34.

7771 CRESSY, D. Levels of illiteracy in England, 1530–1730. *Hist. J.* 20, 1977, 1–23.
Evidence based on depositions of Norwich consistory court. See also his 'Literacy in 17th century England: more evidence', *J. Interdisciplinary Hist.* 8, 1977, 141–50.

7772 PATTEN, J. Changing occupational structures in the East Anglian country-side, 1500–1700. *In* FOX, H. S. A. *and* BUTLIN, R. A., *eds*. Change in the countryside: essays on rural England, 1500–1900. (Inst. of Brit. Geographers, special publ. 10, 1979), pp. 103–122.

7773 MORGAN, V. Country, court and Cambridge University, 1558–1640: a study in the evolution of a political culture. Ph.D. thesis, Univ. of East Anglia, 1983.
Special emphasis on Norfolk connections with Cambridge. For preliminary study, see 'Cambridge University and the "country", 1560–1640' in L. Stone, ed. *The university in society* (Princeton, 1975), vol. 1, pp. 183–245.

7774 BEARMAN, P. S. Relations into rhetorics: elite transformation and the eclipse of localism in England, 1540–1640. Ph.D. thesis, Harvard Univ., 1985.
Case study of Norfolk.

7775 AMUSSEN, S. D. An ordered society: gender and class in early modern England. Oxford, 1988.
Reworks her Ph.D. thesis, 'Governors and governed: class and gender relations in English villages, 1590–1725'. (Brown Univ., 1982). Based largely on documents concerning Cawston, Winfarthing, Shelfanger, Stow Bardolph and Wimbotsham. See also related articles 'Gender, family, and the social order, 1560–1725' in A. Fletcher and J. Stevenson, eds., *Order and disorder in early modern England* (Cambridge, 1985), pp. 196–217; and 'Feminin/masculin: le genre dans l'Angleterre de l'epoque moderne', *Annales, E.S.C.* 40, 1985, 269–87.

See also nos. 7492–4, 7498, 7498A, 7951–2, 8002, 8028, 8033, 8036, 8039, 8041–3, 8047, 8149, 8174, 8254, 8541, 8544, 8548, 9265, 9466–77, 9482, 9487, 9590, 9593–5, 10146, 10180, 10217.

16th CENTURY

7776 VIRGOE, R. The recovery of the Howards in East Anglia, 1487–1529. *In* IVES, E.W., KNECHT, R. J. *and* SCARISBRICK, J. J., *eds*. Wealth and power in Tudor England (1978), pp. 1–20.

7777 STERN, E. Peckover and Gallyard, two 16th-century Norfolk tailors. *Costume* 15, 1981, 13–23.

7778 SMITH, A. H., *ed*. A case of piracy in the sixteenth century. (Creative history from East Anglian sources, 2). Norwich, 1983.

7779 TITTLER, R. *and* BATTLEY, S. L. The local community and the Crown in 1553: the accession of Mary Tudor revisited. *Bull. Inst. Hist. Res.* 57, 1984, 131–9.
Instances of Norfolk hostility to Mary in succession crisis of 1553.

7780 HOULBROOKE, R. The making of marriage in mid-Tudor England: evidence from the records of matrimonial contract litigation. *J. Family Hist.* 10, 1985, 339–52.
Based on records of Norwich consistory court.

See also nos. 7497, 8028, 8248, 8251–3, 8255, 8406, 8587, 8613, 8759–60, 8762, 8797, 8799, 8885, 9307, 9317, 9388, 10043.

KETT'S REBELLION

7781 WALKER, W. H. T. The Norfolk rising under Robert Kett, 1549. M.A. thesis. Univ. of Wales, 1921.

7782 NORWICH CASTLE MUSEUM. Catalogue of loan exhibition to commemorate the 4th centenary of Kett's rebellion, 1549–1949. Norwich, 1949. P.

7783 HOOD, C. M. The Norfolk rising. Robert Kett. *Eastern Daily Press* 8, 11, 15, 18, June 1949.

7784 BEER, B. L., *ed*. The commoyson in Norfolk, 1549: a narrative of popular rebellion in 16th-century England [by Nicholas Sotherton]. *J. Medieval & Renaissance Stud.* 6, 1976, 73–99.
Also edited as booklet by S. Yaxley. Stibbard, 1987.

7785 CORNWALL, J. Revolt of the peasantry, 1549. 1977.
Deals with both the Norfolk and the Western risings.

7786 LAND, S. K. Kett's rebellion. Ipswich, 1977,

7787 MACCULLOCH, D. Kett's Rebellion in context. *Past and Present* 84, 1979. 36–59; 93, 1981, 160–73 [debate with J. Cornwall]. Repr. in SLACK, P., *ed*. Rebellion, popular protest and the social order in early modern England (Cambridge, 1986), pp. 39–76.

7788 BEER, B. L. Rebellion and riot: popular disorder in England during the reign of Edward VI. Kent, Ohio, 1982.
Chaps. 4–5 deal with Norfolk rising.

7789 HOARE, A. In search of Robert Kett: guide to the places and people connected with Kett's Rebellion... Wymondham, [1982].
See also *On the trail of Robert Kett of Wymondham*. Wymondham, 1985. P.

7790 CARTER, A. The site of Dussindale. *N.A.* 39, 1984, 54–62.
Site of Kett's defeat near Mousehold.

ELIZABETHAN PERIOD

7791 PARRY, P. H. The Queen's progress to Norwich in 1578. M.A. thesis, Birmingham Univ., 1973.

7792 SMITH, A. H. *and* MACCULLOCH, D. The authorship of the chorographies of Norfolk and Suffolk. *N.A.* 36, 1977, 327–41.

7793 MOYNES, J. C. The reception of Elizabeth I at Norwich. Ph.D. thesis, Toronto Univ., 1978.

See also nos. 7902, 8001, 8250, 8270–1, 8560, 8576, 8578, 9067, 9463–4, 9597, 9989–91, 10084, 10181.

17th CENTURY

7794 LE STRANGE, *Sir* N. 'Merry passages and jeasts': a manuscript jestbook, 1603–1655. Ed. H. F. Lippincott. (Elizabethan & renaissance stud. 29). Salzburg, 1974.

7795 DEJOHN, V. A. To pass beyond the seas: the background to East Anglian emigration to New England, 1620–1660. M.A. thesis, Univ. of E. Anglia, 1978.
7796 TYACK, N. C. P. The humbler puritans of East Anglia and the New England movement: evidence from the court records of the 1630s. *New England Hist. & Geneal. Register* 138, 1984, 79–106.

    See also nos. 7473, 7944, 8042, 8249, 8311–12, 8414, 8576, 8578, 8798, 8966, 9111, 9241–2, 9309, 9462–3, 9465, 9810, 10178, 10182.

CIVIL WAR
7796A The foure petitions of Huntingtonshire, Norfolk, Suffolk and Essex, joyntly concerning the libertie of the subjects, to the...High Court of Parliament...1642. P. BL.
7797 An ordinance of Parliament for putting the associated counties and the cities of Lincoln and Norwich into a posture of defence. 1644. P. BL.
7798 COLLINGS, J. A cordial for a fainting soule... Being the sum of fourteen sermons, delivered in so many lectures in the chapell belonging to Chapel-field-house in Norwich. 1652. UEA.
7799 HOLMES, C. The Eastern Association in the English Civil War. Cambridge, 1974.
For a number of contemporary pamphlets relating to the Eastern Association in general, see A. V. Steward, *A Suffolk bibliography (Suffolk Records Soc.* 20, 1979), nos. 770, 771, 777, 782–6, 788, 789, 791–3, 797, 800, 802, 803, 807, 808, 813, 817.
7800 JAGGAR, G. Colonel Edward Whalley, his regimental officers, and crown land, with particular reference to the manors of Terrington and West Walton, 1650 to the Restoration. *N.A.* 36, 1975, 149–66.
7801 BUTTERFIELD, R. I. East Anglia, 1645–1660: provincial life and politics during the Great Interregnum. Ph.D. thesis, Michigan Univ., 1981.
7802 LINDLEY, K. Fenland riots and the English Revolution. 1982.
7803 IVE, J. G. A. The local dimensions of defence: the standing army and militia in Norfolk, Suffolk, and Essex, 1649–60. Ph.D. thesis, Cambridge Univ., 1987.

    See also nos. 9308, 9478, 9810.

LATER STUARTS
7804 NORWICH CITY COUNCIL. The restoration of Charles II. An exhibition at the Strangers' Hall... Norwich, 1960. P.
7805 MILNE, K. The political organization of dissent in Norfolk borough politics, 1660–1730. M.A. thesis, Univ. of E. Anglia, 1968.
7806 ROSENHEIM, J. M. An examination of oligarchy: the gentry of Restoration Norfolk, 1660–1720. Ph.D. thesis, Princeton Univ., 1981.

    See also nos. 7907–8, 7911, 7915–16, 7921, 7943, 8279–80, 8551, 9311, 10179.

18th CENTURY
7807 PATTERSON, A. H. In Norfolk bird haunts in A.D. 1755; reprinted from the *Norfolk Chronicle* series. Holt, 1930.
7808 KETTON-CREMER, R. W. Norfolk and the threat of invasion. *In* Norfolk portraits (1944), pp. 140–69.
Seven Years' War and Napoleonic Wars.

7809   The Norfolk list of 1721. *In* FRITZ, P. S. The English ministers and Jacobitism (Toronto, 1975), pp. 143–6.
Christopher Layer's estimate of Jacobite supporters in Norfolk.

7810   GOODWYN, E. A. *and* BAXTER, J. C., *eds*. East Anglian reminiscences. Ipswich, 1976.
Extracts from 18th and 19th century sources.

7811   MUSKETT, P. 'Riotous assemblies': popular disturbances in East Anglia, 1740–1822. Ely, 1984.

7812   MOORE, A. W. Norfolk and the Grand Tour. Norwich, 1985.
Incorporates catalogue of exhibition at Castle Museum.

   See also nos. 7909–10, 7917, 7948, 8259, 8261, 8281, 8348, 8551, 8627, 8806, 8889, 9312, 9323, 9383, 9385, 9479–87, 10081, 10219.

19th CENTURY

7813   A century ago. Extracts from the *Norwich Mercury*, 1802. Norwich, n.d.

7814   CLABBURN, P., *ed*. Working class costume from 'Sketches of characters' by William Johnstone White, 1818. (Costume Society). 1971.
White produced these sketches, 'illustrative of the counties of Norfolk, Cambridgeshire and Middlesex', as a specimen volume sent to Dawson Turner.

7815   EMERSON, P. H. Pictures from life in field and fen. Twenty plates in photogravure... with an introductory article. 1887

7816   EMERSON, P. H. Pictures of East Anglian life. 1888.

7817   PEACOCK, A. J. Village radicalism in East Anglia, 1800–1850. *In* DUNBABIN, J. P. D., *ed*. Rural discontent in nineteenth-century Britain (1974), pp. 27–61.

7818   JONES, D. Thomas Campbell Foster and the rural labourer: incendiarism in East Anglia in the 1840s. *Social Hist*. 1, 1976, 5–43.
See also 'Arson and the rural community: East Anglia in the mid-19th century' in his *Crime, protest, community, and police in 19th-century Britain* (1982), pp. 33–61.

7819   LIVINGSTONE, S. A penny a boy: Norfolk children at work in Victorian days. Ipswich, 1978.

7820   JAMES, H. V. The London-Yarmouth telegraph line, 1806–1814. *N.A*. 37, 1978, 126–9.

7821   CARTER, M. J. Peasants and poachers: a study in rural disorder in Norfolk. Woodbridge, 1980.

7822   ARCHER, J. E. Rural protest in Norfolk and Suffolk, 1830–1870. Ph.D. thesis, Univ. of East Anglia, 1981.
See also his paper of same title in A. Charlesworth, ed. *Rural social change and conflicts since 1500* (Hull, [1983]), pp. 83–95.

7823   FOWLER, E. Jonathan Mardle's Victorian Norfolk. Norwich, 1981.

7824   ARCHER, J. E. The Wells-Charlesworth debate: a personal comment on arson in Norfolk and Suffolk [1800–1830]. *J. Peasant Stud*. 9, 1982, 277–84.

7824A   BANKS, S. J. Open and close parishes in 19th-century England. Ph.D. thesis, Reading Univ., 1982.
Deals with landownership in large block of West Norfolk parishes. See also no. 7910.

7825   APFEL, W. H. Crisis in a rural society, 1790–1830: social change and class relationships in Norfolk. Ph.D. thesis, Brown Univ., 1984.

7826   CHARLESWORTH, A. A comparative study of the spread of the agricultural

disturbances of 1816, 1822, and 1830 in England. *Peasant Stud.* 11, 1984, 91–110.
Contrasts E. Anglian disturbances of 1816 and 1822 with more widespread Swing movement.

7827 MUSKETT, P. The East Anglian agrarian riots of 1822. *Agric. Hist. Rev.* 32, 1984, 1–13.

See also nos. 7945, 7947–8, 7963, 8048, 8059, 8067, 8072A, 8081, 8259–61, 8277, 8367, 8372, 8562, 8628, 8806, 9488–92, 10183–6, 10219.

20th CENTURY

7828 NORFOLK NEWS CO. Norfolk roll of honour, 1914–18. Norwich, 1920.

7829 HARRIS, C., *pseud.* Hennage – a social system in miniature. New York, 1974.
Sociological study of N. Norfolk village (place-name invented).

7830 EVANS, G. E. The days that we have seen. 1975.
Oral material on social conditions in E. Anglia c. 1880–1930.

7831 NORFOLK COUNTY COUNCIL. Visit to Norfolk by H.M. Queen Elizabeth II and H.R.H. Prince Philip... 11th July. Norwich, 1977. P.

7832 DIXON, G. M. *and others.* Life in Norfolk. Langtoft (Peterborough), 1979. 2nd ed. 1985.

7833 SHAW, M. All our yesterdays. Norwich, 1980.
Photographs illustrating social history of early 20th century Norfolk.

7834 JOHNSON, D. E. East Anglia and the Great War in old picture postcards. Zaltbommel (Netherlands), 1984.

7835 GLIDDON, G., *ed.* Norfolk and Suffolk in the Great War. Norwich, 1988.

See also nos. 8060, 8072A, 8075, 8078–9, 8081, 9493–510.

SECOND WORLD WAR

7836 JOHNSON, D. E. East Anglia at war, 1939–1945. Norwich, 1978.

7837 BOWYER, M. J. F. Wartime military airfields of East Anglia, 1939–1945. Cambridge, 1979.

7838 HASTINGS, M. Bomber Command. 1979. Chap. 2: 82 Squadron, Norfolk, 1940–41.

7839 BROWN, R. D. East Anglia, 1939. Lavenham, 1980.
See also sequel volumes *East Anglia, 1940* (1981); *East Anglia, 1941* (1986); and *East Anglia, 1942* (1988).

7840 ELLIOTT, C. R. The day Mr. Churchill dropped in. *E.A.M.* 40, Apr. 1981, 272–4.

7841 BOWYER, M. J. F. Air raid! The enemy offensive over East Anglia, 1939–45. Wellingborough, 1986.

See also nos. 8820, 9315, 9377, 9500–3, 9507.

U.S. FORCES

7842 FREEMAN, R. The mighty Eighth. 1970.
See also his *Airfields of the Eighth, then and now* (1978); and *Mighty Eighth war diary* (1981).

7843 LANCASTER-RENNIE, J. "... and over here!" Wymondham, 1976.

7844 BOWMAN, M. W. Fields of little America. An illustrated history of the 8th Air Force, 2nd Air Division, 1942–45. Norwich, 1977.

7845 VICKERS, R. E. The Liberators from Wendling: the combat story of the 392nd Bombardment Group (H) of the Eighth Air Force during World War Two. Ed. by J. V. Rogers. Alburquerque, New Mexico, 1977.

7846 [Entry deleted]

7847 HOSEASON, J. The thousand day battle. Oulton Broad, 1980.
Concentrates on operations of 448 Bomber Group stationed at Seething.

GENERAL CONTROVERSY: LOCAL REACTION TO NATIONAL ISSUES

7848 SCOT, T. The highwaies of God and the King...two sermons preached at Thetford in Norfolke...1620. 1623. UEA.

7849 SCOT, T. The projector: teaching a direct, sure, and ready way to restore the decays of the church and state in honour and revenue. Delivered in a sermon before the judges in Norwich. 1623. UEA.

7850 S[MYTHIES], W. The Norfolk feast: a sermon preached at St. Dunstan's in the East upon the 18th of July 1671, being the day of the anniversary feast for that county...By a minister of that county. 1671.

7851 CLEAVER, J. The subjects duty: a sermon preached at the Cathedral in Norwich... 1676. UEA.

7852 MERITON, H. A semon preacht at the Cathedral Church in Norwich upon the 11th of April, 1696, the day of His Majesties coronation. 1696. UEA.

7853 MARSTERS, T. A view of agricultural oppressions: and their effects upon society. Lynn Regis, 1798. BL.

7853A TWIDDY, J. Catholic claims considered, part 1. Popish miracles, part 2. Norwich, [c. 1826]. P.
Verses against Catholic empancipation. Provoked counter-squib, *Popish pinching irons, a poem dedicated without permission to James Twiddy, A.S.S., author, hairdresser and parish clerk of St. Peter's Mancroft. By Tweedle-dee.*

7854 TURNER, C. A sermon preached at the Cathedral Church at Norwich on... His Majesty's birthday. Norwich, 1835. P.

7855 W., C. Village musings on moral and religious subjects. By a villager. Norwich, 1837. Other eds. 1839, 1843.
Author from Pulham St. Mary. B.L. attributes to Cornelius Wher.

7856 OWEN, J. Riches and poverty. A sermon preached at the parish church of SS. Simon and Jude before a body of Chartists... Norwich, 1839.

7857 HALLATT, G. Infidel socialism calmly considered, and proved to be unphilosophical, irrational and absurd. Norwich, 1840.

7858 GREEN, J. The duty of Christians rightly to exercise the elective franchise... Norwich, [1841]. P.

7859 NORWICH COMPLETE SUFFRAGE UNION. Reconciliation between the middle and labouring classes. [Preface by Joseph Sturge]. Norwich, 1841.
Reprint of pro-Chartist article from *The Noncomformist*, which was also publ. in Manchester, and probably elsewhere.

7860 On petitioning in favour of the removal of Jewish disabilities: a few words on a Minister's letter to his parishioners. Yarmouth, 1847. P. RCF
See items 971–3 of *B.N.H.*

7861 TILLETT, J. H. Our dangers and our duty: an appeal to Christian people on the questions of the day. Norwich, [1873]. P.

7862 HENDERSON, F. Politics in the pulpit: an address delivered at the Norwich Labor Church. Norwich, n.d. P. UEA.
Author of *The case for socialism* [1911] and numerous other books and pamphlets, some locally printed.

MARITIME HISTORY

7863 BENHAM, H. Once upon a tide. 1955. Another ed. 1971.
Deals with East Coast shipping and fisheries, 1700–1830.

7864 MARSHALL, M. A. N. Norfolk ships. *Mariner's Mirror* 49, 1963, 62–8.

7865 MILLS, J. F. C. Prize taken by Captain Reynolds. An incident of the War of the English Succession [1689]. *N.A.* 33, 1965, 108–13.

7866 MALSTER, R. Maritime East Anglia. Great Yarmouth, 1969. P.

7867 STRUGNELL, K. W. Seagates to the Saxon Shore. Lavenham, 1973.

7868 HEDGES, A. A. C. East Coast shipping. Aylesbury, 1974.

7869 MALSTER, R. Saved from the sea: the story of life-saving services on the East Anglian coast. Lavenham, 1974.

7870 TEMPLE, C. R. East Coast shipwrecks. Norwich, 1974.
See also later version, *Shipwreck! Wrecks and rescues off the East Anglian coast* (Lowestoft, 1986).

7871 MILLER, C. D. The East Anglian beachmen. Diploma thesis, Ruskin College, Oxford, 1975.

7872 DAVIES, C. The passing of the wherrymen. *E.A.M.* 35, Sept. 1976, 428–30.

7873 WREN, W. J. Ports of the Eastern Counties: the development of harbours... from Boston... to Harwich. Lavenham, 1976.

7874 EAST ANGLIA ECONOMIC PLANNING COUNCIL. Seaports in East Anglia. N.p., [1977]. P.

7875 BRAY, D. The story of the Norfolk wherries. [Lingwood, 1978]. P.

7876 JOLLY, C. The loss of the *English Trader*: Henry Blogg's toughest mission. Fakenham, 1981.

7877 TONKIN, G. Sudden and violent storm. *E.A.M.*, Mar. 1981, 244–6.
Shipwrecks in storm of 1833.

7878 LEWIS, C. Pierhead paintings: ship portraits from East Anglia. [Exhib. cat.] Norwich, 1982.

7879 MASON, J. A Norfolk wreck [the smack *Mountaineer*, 1918]. *E.A.M.*, Feb. 1982, 186–7.

7880 YARHAM, E. R. Afloat with the ice skippers. *Ibid.*, Aug. 1982, 446–7.
Wherry trade in ice for refrigeration.

7881 LONG, N. Lights of East Anglia. Lavenham, 1983.
On lighthouses and their keepers.

7882 HAYES, D. R. His Majesty's late ship *Invincible*...the wreck off Happisburgh ... March 1801: a study based on contemporary documents. Ludham, 1985.

7883 FINCH, R. *and* BENHAM, H. Sailing craft of East Anglia. Lavenham, 1987.

7884 HIGGINS, D. The beachmen: the story of the salvagers of the East Anglian coast. Lavenham, 1987.

7885 GIBBS, A. W. Shipping intelligence of the Norfolk and Suffolk coast during the time of the war with France, 1793–1815, from weekly reports in the *Norwich Mercury*. 3 vols. [to date]. Norwich, 1987–88.
See also nos. 8082–90, 8813–14, 9041, 9046, 9094, 9096, 9281, 9301, 9303–4, 9938, 9952, 10166–7, 10214.

AVIATION

7886 CAMPAIGN AGAINST NORWICH AIRPORT EXPANSION. The case against...

expansion at St. Faith's. Norwich, 1974. P.

7887 DEPT. OF TRADE. Report on the accident near Norwich airport... 12 Dec. 1973. 1974. P.

7888 CIVIL AVIATION AUTHORITY. The developmemt of Norwich Airport: a report to the Norwich Airport Joint Committee by a research team. 1975.

7889 DEPT. OF TRADE. Report on the collision at Fordham Fen... 9 Aug. 1974. 1975. P.

7890 DEPT. OF TRADE. Cessna 310 G-APTK. Report on the accident at Norwich Airport, 25 Oct. 1974. 1976. P.

7891 KINSEY, G. Aviation: flight over the eastern counties since 1937. Lavenham, 1977.

7892 NORFOLK AND SUFFOLK AVIATION MUSEUM. Airfields of Norfolk and Suffolk. 4 parts. Lowestoft, 1977–83. [Revision in progress].

7893 NORWICH AIRPORT JOINT COMMITTEE. Norwich Airport: master plan for the development of new terminal facilities. [By] Sir Frederick Snow and Partners. Norwich, 1978.

7894 DEPT. OF TRANSPORT. Report on the mid-air collision between Cessna F 150M G-BFEL and a U.S. Air Force A-10A near Hardwick, 29 Feb. 1984. 1986.

7895 KINSEY, G. K. Pulham pigs. Lavenham, 1988.
History of airship station at Pulham St. Mary.

See also nos. 7837–8, 7841–7.

POLITICS AND ADMINISTRATION

GENERAL ADMINISTRATION

7896 JEWITT, L. *and* HOPE, W. H. St.J. Corporation plate and insignia of office of the cities and towns of England and Wales. 2 vols. 1895. Norfolk: vol 2, pp. 170–214.

7897 YOUNGS, F. A. Guide to the local administrative units of England. Vol. 1: Southern England. (Royal Hist. Soc. guide and handbooks, 10). 1979. Norfolk, pp. 351–87 (parishes); 652–61 (local govt. units); 751–4 (parl. constituencies); 781–2 (diocesan units).

MEDIEVAL PERIOD

7898 BARRINGER. J. C. Some remarks on the early administrative geography of Norfolk. *Bull. Norfolk Research Committee* 22, 1979, 2–5.

7899 FLOWER, C. T., *ed.* Public works in medieval law, vol. 2. *Selden Soc.* 40, 1923. Norfolk section, pp. 88–99.

7900 PUBLIC RECORD OFFICE. List of Escheators for England. Compiled by A. C. Wood. *List and Index Soc.* 72, 1971. Norfolk, pp. 85–93.

7901 ALSFORD, S. Office-holding in East Anglian boroughs, 1272–1460. M.Phil. thesis, Leicester Univ., 1982.

See also nos. 7763, 9316, 9519.

7902 GRIGG, A. J., *ed.* Selected letters of the Privy Council to Norfolk, c. 1580–1603. M.Phil. thesis, Univ. of E. Anglia, 1984.
See also nos. 7412, 7805, 8929–31, 9317, 9520–4.

7903 JAMES, D. E. H. The Norfolk County Council, 1889–1974. [Norwich, 1974].
7904 LOCAL GOVERNMENT OPERATIONAL RESEARCH UNIT. Review of transport in Norfolk County Council. 1977.
7904A HOLLIS, P. Ladies elect: women in English local government, 1865–1914. 1987.
Draws considerably on Norfolk and Norwich examples.
7905 SMITH, S. *and* SMITH, B. Shield and sword: a history of the Norfolk County branch of the National and Local Government Officers Association, 1920–1980. Lowestoft, 1987.
On Nalgo see also no. 7321.
See also nos. 7526, 7528, 7536–65, 9366, 9525–34, 10149, 10183–4, 10188–9.

FINANCE AND TAXATION

MEDIEVAL

7906 FEENEY, B. The effects of King John's scutages on East Anglian subjects. *In* BARBER, M. *and others, eds.* East Anglian and other studies presented to Barbara Dodwell (Reading, c. 1984), pp. 51–73.

7907 SEAMAN, P. J. A guide to the Norfolk hearth tax records in the Public Record Office. *Norfolk Ancestor* 2, 1980/82, 23–7; 30–34; 58–61; 73–7; 122–6.
7908 FRANKEL, M. S. *and* SEAMAN, P. J., *eds.* Norfolk hearth tax assessment, Michaelmas 1664. *Norfolk Geneal.* 15, 1983.
7909 WINSTANLEY, R. L. Parson Woodforde and the tax system. *Quart. J. Parson Woodforde Soc.* supplement 7, 1984.
7910 BANKS, S. Parish landownership and the land tax assessments in West Norfolk: a comparison with the tithe surveys. *In* TURNER, M. *and* MILLS, D., *eds.* Land and property: the English land tax, 1692–1832 (New York, 1986). pp. 40–52.
7911 SEAMAN, P., *ed.* Norfolk and Norwich hearth tax assessment, Lady Day 1666. *Norfolk Geneal.* 20, 1988.

7912 Returns of the amount levied for the purposes of the county rate... in... the last seven years. H.C. 1867, lviii. Norwich diocese. pp. 194–214.
7913 COLMAN, J. J. Local taxation. A paper read at the Social Science Congress at Norwich. Norwich, [1873]. P.

PARLIAMENTARY REPRESENTATION

PARTICULAR ELECTIONS; POLITICAL CONTROVERSY

7914 VIRGOE, R. An election dispute of 1483. *Bull. Inst. Hist. Res.* 60, 1987, 24–44.

7915 ROSENHEIM, J. M. Party organization at the local level: the Norfolk sheriff's subscription of 1676. *Hist. J.* 29, 1986, 713–22.

7916 HAYTON, D. Note on the Norfolk election of 1702. *N.A.* 37, 1980, 320–24.

7917 ALSOP, J. D. Contemporary remarks on the 1768 election in Norfolk and Suffolk. *N.A.* 38, 1981, 79–82.
From correspondence of Benjamin Gooch.

7918 Norwich Labour Elector. *Extant* May 1906. I.L.P. Archive.

7919 SOUTH NORFOLK LABOUR PARTY. South Norfolk Clarion. 4 issues. Wymondham, 1961–64.

7920 NATIONAL FRONT. Anglian news. Norwich, 1976–.

See also nos. 8682, 8931A, 9322–3, 9515–16, 9520, 9522–4, 9526–7, 9531–2, 10198.

MILITARY AFFAIRS

7921 DUNN, R. M. Norfolk lieutenancy journal, 1660–1676. *N.R.S.* 45, 1977.

7921A KENT, P. Fortifications of East Anglia. Lavenham, 1988.

See also nos. 7665, 7799, 7803, 7828, 7834–47, 9352, 9493, 9502–3, 9510, 9937, 10178, 10186.

PARTICULAR UNITS

7922 Records of the 54th West Norfolk Regiment. Roorkee (India), 1881.

7923 Norfolk Military Gazette: a service journal for Norwich and district. 12 issues. Norwich, 1896.

7924 A little chat about the 1st (City of Norwich) Battln., Norfolk Volunteers. N.p. [c. 1915].

7925 BRUMWELL, P. M. History of the 12th (Eastern Division) in the Great War, 1914–18. 1923.

7926 WILLIAMSON, T. The disappearance of the King's Company (Sandringham) in Gallipoli. Ilfracombe, 1979. P.
See also C. Crowther, 'Gallipoli and the missing "Norfolks".' *E.A.M.*, Apr. 1982, 251–3.

7927 BARTHORP, M. Crater to the Creggan. The history of the Royal Anglian Regiment, 1960–1974. 1976.

7928 BASTIN, J. The Norfolk Yeomanry in peace and war. Fakenham, 1986.
Mainly on Second World War campaigns.

LAW ENFORCEMENT; POLICE AND FIRE SERVICES; CRIME

MEDIEVAL PERIOD

7929 STENTON, D. M., *ed*. Pleas and assizes at Norwich, 1209. *Publ. Selden Soc.* 84, 1967, 168–282.

7930 WESTMAN, B. H. A study of crime in Norfolk, Yorkshire and Northamptonshire, 1300–1348. Ph.D. thesis, Univ. of Michigan, 1970.

7931 HANAWALT, B. A., *ed*. Crime in East Anglia in the 14th century: Norfolk gaol delivery rolls, 1307–1316. *N.R.S.* 44, 1976.
See also no. 7766.

LATER PERIODS

7932 HOWARD, J. Account of the prisons and houses of correction in the Norfolk circuit. 1789. Bodleian Lib.

7933 Report of the committee of magistrates for superintending and regulating the County Gaol of Norfork...and the report of the Hon. Edward Harbord on the state and condition of the House of Correction at Aylsham. Norwich, 1819. P.

7934 BRERETON, C. D. A refutation of the first report of the Constabulary Force Commissioners. 3 parts. Swaffham, [c. 1839].

7935 [LANE, R. M.] Recollections of a rural policeman, by an old member of the Norfolk constabulary. King's Lynn, 1882.

7936 KETTON-CREMER, R. W. Justices of the peace in Norfolk. Norwich, [1961]. P.

7937 NORFOLK FIRE SERVICE. Alarm: the annual journal. Norwich, 1983–.

7938 JARVIS, S. M. Smuggling in East Anglia, 1700–1846. Newbury, 1987.

7939 SLATTER, M. *and* MOSELEY, M. M'rural friend. *New Law J*. 136, 1986, 626–8, 641.
Provision of legal services in rural areas.

7940 CHURCH, R. Murder in East Anglia: a new look at some notorious cases. 1987.
See also nos. 7778, 7818, 7821–2, 7824, 8009, 9151, 9329, 9560, 9985.

SOCIAL WELFARE

POOR LAW

TO 1834

7941 ALEXANDER, W. A pastoral dialogue between two gentlemen... on the vacillancy of the Committees on the distresses of the poor. Yarmouth, 1818. P.

7942 RICHARDSON, J. A proposal for a change in the poor laws and the reduction of the poor's rate by the beneficial employment of the labourers, in a letter addressed to... Lord Suffield. Norwich, [1830]. P.
See also his *Letter to Lord Brougham on an alteration in the poor laws*...1831. (2 edns.)

7943 DITTBRENNER, C. H. The poor law and the treatment of poverty in Norwich and Norfolk, 1660–1760. Ph.D. thesis, Univ. of Wisconsin, 1973.

7944 WALES, T. Poverty, poor relief and the life-cycle: some evidence from 17th-century Norfolk. *In* SMITH, R. M., *ed*. Land, kinship and life-cycle (Cambridge, 1984). pp. 351–404.
See also nos. 8253, 9203, 9561, 9913, 10115.

AFTER 1834

7945 DIGBY, A. The labour market and the continuity of social policy after 1834: the case of the eastern counties. *Ec. Hist. Rev*. 2nd ser. 28, 1975, 69–83.

7946 McCUTCHEON, E. M. J. Aspects of the new Poor Law in St. Faith's Union, 1835–1939. Cert. in Local Hist., Cambridge Board of Extra-Mural Studies, 1977.
See on a specific case of 1836 her 'John Taylor's poor', *E.A.M*. Sept. 1979, 596–8.

7947 DIGBY, A. Pauper palaces. 1978.

7948 CROWLEY, J. *and* REID, A., *eds*. The poor law in Norfolk, 1700–1850: a collection of source material. Ely, 1983.

See also nos. 8853, 9217–18, 9562–5.

CHARITIES

7948A JORDAN, W. K. The charities of rural England, 1480–1660. 1961. Norfolk, pp. 89–213.

See also nos. 9562–3, 9599–600, 10200, 10210–11.

FRIENDLY SOCIETIES

7949 Rules of the Smithdon and Brothercross Friendly Society for the benefit of labourers, servants, and mechanics residing within ten miles of Docking, est. December 1837. Docking, 1838.

See also no. 10127.

PUBLIC HEALTH AND MEDICAL SERVICES

TO 1800

7950 GOTTFRIED, R. S. Epidemic disease in 15th century England: the medical response and the demographic consequences. New Brunswick, N.J., 1978.
Based on evidence from East Anglia, London and Hertfordshire wills. The evidence is extended into the 1480s in his 'Population, plague and the sweating sickness. *J. Brit. Stud.* 17, 1977, 12–37.

7951 PELLING, M. *and* WEBSTER, C. Medical practitioners. *In* WEBSTER, C., *ed*. Health, medicine, and mortality in the 16th century (1979), pp. 165–235.
Urban evidence drawn from London and Norwich, rural from Norfolk and Suffolk. See also Pelling's 'A survey of East Anglian medical practitioners, 1500–1640'. *Local Population Stud.* 25, 1980, 54–5.

7952 PELLING, M. Occupational diversity: barbersurgeons and the trades of Norwich, 1550–1640. *Bull. Hist. Medicine* 56, 1982, 484–511.

See also nos. 7765, 9592–5, 9597, 9977.

19th AND 20th CENTURIES

7953 Rules for establishing independent medical clubs in the parishes of Great Melton, Hethersett, East Carlton, Bracon Ash, Hethel and Wreningham. Norwich, 1835.

7954 WESBY. E. A few words of friendly advice composed by Mrs. E. Wesby, doctress. North Walsham, 1855. P.
Advertises her talents as cure-all herbalist.

7955 EADE, *Sir* P. Medical notes and essays. Fasciculus I. Notes on diptheria, and particularly on this disease as it has occured in Norfolk. 1883.

7956 NORFOLK COUNTY COUNCIL. Report upon the sanitary condition of... Norfolk for the year 1894. Compiled from the annual reports of the district Medical Officers of Health. Norwich, 1895. BL.

7957 THOMSON, D. G. The Norfolk County Asylum. 1903.

7958 MINISTRY OF HEALTH. Hospital survey: the hospital services of the Eastern Area. 1945.

7959 HALES, J. A tale of the Norfolk Red Cross. Watton, 1970. P.

7960 NORFOLK AREA JOINT LIAISON COMMITTEE. National Health Service reorganisation: proposals for a pattern of health districts. Great Yarmouth, 1973.
See also its *Area profile for Norfolk* [1973].

7961 BUSSEY, A. A century of service. A celebration of 100 years of the Norfolk and Suffolk Hospital Contributors Association. Norwich, 1974. P.

7962 NORFOLK AREA HEALTH AUTHORITY. [Strategic, operational, district plans. Health statistics. Reports, etc.]. Norwich, 1975–80. UEA.
Set includes some annual reports of associated Community Health Councils.

7963 MUNCASTER, M. J. Medical services and the medical profession in Norfolk, 1815–1911. Ph.D. thesis, Univ. of East Anglia, 1976.
Contains useful biographical directory of medical practitioners.

7964 EAST ANGLIAN REGIONAL HEALTH AUTHORITY. Strategic plan for health services, 1977–1982: draft. [With vol. of statistics]. [Cambridge], 1977. UEA

7965 CARO, A. J. A genetic problem in East Anglia: Huntington's chorea. Ph.D. thesis, Univ. of E. Anglia, 1977.

7966 HAYNES, R. M. *and* BENTHAM, C. G. Community hospitals and rural accessibility. Farnborough, 1979.
Case study of King's Lynn Health District.

7967 Norwich Health District hospitals: a brief history. Norwich, 1979. P.
Reissue of articles originally appearing in the NHD newsletter *Contract*.

7968 EAST ANGLIAN REGIONAL HEALTH AUTHORITY. Provisional proposals for the restructuring of health authorities in East Anglia: a consultative paper. N.p., [1980]. UEA.

7969 BATTY SHAW, A. Knapper's rot: silicosis in East Anglian flint-knappers. *Medical Hist.* 25, 1981, 151–68.

7970 NORWICH HEALTH AUTHORITY. Norwich Health Authority: a profile. Norwich, 1981.

7971 HAYNES, R. M. *and* BENTHAM, C. G. The effects of accessibility on general practitioner consultations, out-patient attendances, and in-patient admissions in Norfolk. *Social Sci. and Medicine* 16, 1982, 561–9.

7972 FEARN, R. M. G. The role of the branch surgery in accessibility to primary health care in rural Norfolk. Ph.D. thesis, Univ. of E. Anglia, 1983.

7973 NORWICH HEALTH AUTHORITY. Strategic plan, 1984–1994. [Norwich, 1984].
See also Authority's *Short term programme 1988/89 and 1989/90* [Norwich, 1987].

7974 BATTY SHAW, A. The Norfolk and Norwich Benevolent Medical Society, 1786–1986. Norwich, 1986.

7975 BOSANQUET, N. *and* MIDDLETON, J. Budgetary implications of cross boundary flows in East Anglia: a report to the Regional Health Authority. (Centre for Health Economics, Univ. of York). York, 1987.
See also nos. 9091, 9217, 9324–7, 9598–605, 10199, 10201.

SPECIAL MEDICAL AND OTHER WELFARE SERVICES

7976 NORWICH COUNCIL OF CHRISTIAN CONGREGATIONS. Occasional papers published by the Current Affairs Research Group. [Norwich, 1970–].
Includes papers on redundancy, homelessness, community care of mentally handicapped, etc.

7977 NORWICH INDUSTRIAL MISSION. From psychiatrist to employer: a report on the employment of mentally disabled persons. [Norwich, 1974].

7978 BRITISH ASSOCIATION OF SOCIAL WORKERS (NORFOLK SUB-BRANCH). On the street: [homelessness in Norfolk]. N.p., [c. 1975]. P.

7979 NORFOLK COUNTY COUNCIL *and* NORFOLK AREA HEALTH AUTHORITY. Report of the review body appointed to enquire into the case of Steven Meurs. 1975. P.

7980 EAST ANGLIAN REGIONAL HEALTH AUTHORITY. Care for the elderly: report of a regional nursing working party. N.p., 1979. UEA.

7981 NORFOLK AREA HEALTH AUTHORITY *and other bodies*. Report of the joint working group on services for the mentally handicapped. Norwich, 1979.

7982 COUNTY AUDIOLOGY SERVICE. Reports on services to hearing-impaired children in Norfolk. N.p., 1980. UEA.

7983 INTERNATIONAL HOSPITAL FEDERATION. Good practices in mental health. Norwich, 1980.
List of day centres, hostels etc. in Norfolk.

7984 FENNELL, G. *and others*. Day centres for the elderly in East Anglia. Norwich, 1981.

7985 NORFOLK COUNTY COUNCIL. Report of the Mental Handicap Study Group (Social Services Dept.). Norwich, 1981. P.

7986 NORFOLK COUNTY COUNCIL. A scheme of supervision facilities [for young offenders]. Norwich, 1983. P.

7987 NORWICH HEALTH AUTHORITY. A district mental handicap service. Discussion paper. Norwich, 1984.
Followed by *Services for people with mental handicap: a 10-year plan and NHS residential accomodation for people with mental handicap* (1984).

7988 NORWICH HEALTH AUTHORITY. A guide to services for physically disabled people in the Norwich district.

7989 NORFOLK COUNTY COUNCIL. Social Services Department: report of the study group on services to elderly people. Norwich, 1985.

7990 NORFOLK COUNTY COUNCIL. Social Services Department: report of the study group on mental health services. Norwich, 1985.
Note also in connection with above two reports Council's *Directory of day centres and luncheon clubs for the elderly and physically handicapped* (1985); *Directory of sheltered housing schemes in Norfolk* (1986); *Directory of registered private and voluntary residential care homes for the elderly and mentally disordered* (3rd ed., 1987).

7991 GIBBINS, R. W. The deprivation of the elderly in rural Norfolk. Ph.D. thesis, Univ. of E. Anglia, 1986.

See also nos. 9282, 9374, 9566–74, 9983, 10202.

HOUSING

7992 CROTCH, W. W. The cottage homes of England: the case against the housing system in rural districts. 2nd ed., 1901. 3rd ed., 1908. Chap. 7: The Norfolk experiment that failed.

See also nos. 7523, 7528, 7552, 7564, 7976, 7978, 9575–83.

EDUCATION

7993 ADKIN, L. The Sabbath. A sermon preached in... St. Stephen's... to promote the establishment of Sunday schools... [with] the rules adopted for this institution in that parish. Norwich, [1795].

7994 FARNELL, W. K. An address to the public... upon the subject of school recitations, exhibitions, etc., showing how the 'march of humbug' may be mistaken for the 'march of intellect'... Norwich, [c. 1830]. P.

7995 A congratulatory letter to the Rev. John Perowne, Rector of St. John's Maddermarket... occasioned by reading 'A Vindication' by Mr. John Alexander. By a member of the Church of England. Norwich, 1836. P.

7996 The visions of Somniator... a Congress Extraordinary convened by His Satanic Majesty for the purpose... of presenting the Rev. J. P-ro-ne with a vote of thanks for his late attempt to render Dissenterism contemptible... Norwich, [1836]. P.

See *B.N.H.* 1329–32 for the controversy on Church schools of which the above pamphlets are part.

7997 ALEXANDER, J. *and others.* A letter addressed to a Member of Parliament on the educational clauses in Sir James Graham's... Factory Bill. 1843. P.

7998 NEVILL, H. R. *and others.* Three papers on the management of Sunday schools. Norwich, 1862.

7999 JESSOPP, A. Some account of Norfolk endowed schools. N.p., n.d. P.

8000 NORFOLK COUNTY COUNCIL. Report on the supply of secondary education in the administrative county of Norfolk. Norwich, [c. 1903]. P.

8001 FEYERHAM, W. R. Education in Elizabethan East Anglia. Ph.D. thesis, Univ. of Wisconsin, 1972.

See also article derived fron this research, 'The status of the schoolmaster and the continuity of education in Elizabethan East Anglia', *Hist. of Education* 5, 1976, 103–15.

8002 CRESSY, D. A. Education and literacy in London and East Anglia, 1580–1700. Ph.D. thesis, Cambridge Univ., 1973.

8003 NORFOLK COUNTY COUNCIL. Norfolk development plan: high schools. Norwich, 1975.

8004 NATIONAL UNION OF TEACHERS. Norfolk school buildings. N.p., 1977.

8005 DIMMICK, R. Standards in danger: the future of secondary education in Central Norfolk. N. Walsham, 1978. P.

Publ. by N. Norfolk Constituency Labour Party.

8006 NATIONAL UNION OF TEACHERS. A report on special education facilities in Norfolk. [Gorleston], 1979. P.

8007 BULL, J., *ed.* 1839–1981: story of Keswick Hall Church of England College of Education. Norwich, 1981.

8008 AMISON, P. The Attleborough experiment: a handbook. Cambridge, 1982.

On adult education methods. Publ. by National Extension College Trust.

8009 THOMAS, D. H. The Home Office certified schools in Norfolk, 1855–1933. *N.A.* 38, 1983, 358–61.

Reformatories and industrial training schools at Buxton and Fakenham.

8010 DEPARTMENT OF EDUCATION AND SCIENCE. Report by H.M. inspectors on educational provision and response in some Norfolk schools. 1984. P.

8011 NORFOLK COUNTY COUNCIL. HMI report... the authority's response: draft for consideration. Norwich, 1985, P.

8012 NORFOLK EDUCATION INDUSTRY AND COMMERCE GROUP. Norfolk schools: industry/commerce links. Norwich, 1986.

See also nos. 7317, 7773, 8765, 8955, 9029–30, 9076, 9082, 9095, 9141, 9261–2, 9282, 9287, 9363A, 9614–42, 9875, 9931, 9967, 10011, 10014–15, 10022, 10074, 10077–8, 10080, 10111–12, 10143.

ECONOMIC HISTORY

GENERAL WORKS

8013 EAST ANGLIA ECONOMIC PLANNING COUNCIL. Regional economic review. [Annual]. 1973–78.

8014 EAST ANGLIA ECONOMIC PLANNING COUNCIL. Earnings, other incomes, and household expenditure in East Anglia. 1977. P.

8015 MOSELEY, M. J. *and* DARBY, J. The determinants of female activity rates in rural areas: an analysis of Norfolk parishes. *Regional Stud.* 12, 1978, 297–309.

8016 SOUTH NORFOLK DISTRICT COUNCIL. Report of the Chief Officers' management team on employment. Loddon, 1978.

8017 KING'S LYNN AND WEST NORFOLK BOROUGH COUNCIL.Employment survey of West Norfolk. By K. E. Harrington. King's Lynn, 1982.

8018 GUIVER, J. *and others*. Employment and unemployment in the Norwich diocese: discussion paper commissioned by the Norwich Diocesan Synod. 1985.

8019 SAPSFORD, D. A study of aspects of local economic development initiatives. (UEA Economics Research Centre, working paper no. 2). Norwich, 1985.

8020 UNIVERSITY OF EAST ANGLIA. East Anglian economic newsletter. April 1985–.

8021 [Entry deleted]

See also nos. 9646, 10202.

AGRICULTURE

GENERAL WORKS

8022 EVERITT, W. S. Practical notes on grasses and grass growing in East Anglia. Ed. by N. Everitt. 1897. BL.

8023 SAYER, F. D. Early horticulture and the Norwich market. [Unpubl. typescript]. 1966.

8024 HASLAM, S. M. The reed... in relation to its cultivation and harvesting in East Anglia for the thatching industry. Norwich, 1969. 2nd ed. 1972.

8025 WILLS, N. T. Woad in the Fens. Long Sutton, 1975. Another ed. 1979. P.

8026 EBBAGE, S. Barns and granaries in Norfolk. Ipswich, 1976.

8027 HARRIS, S. Farm wagons of East Anglia. Woodbridge, 1979.

See also nos. 7353, 7474, 8420, 8429, 9232.

8028 LADE, R. Agricultural and social developments in manors in North Norfolk in the 15th and 16th centuries. M.Sc. thesis, Bristol Univ., 1972.

8029 CAMPBELL, B. M. S. Field systems in eastern Norfolk during the Middle Ages... with particular reference to the... fourteenth century. Ph.D. thesis, Cambridge Univ., 1974.

8030 WILLIAMSON, J. G. Norfolk: thirteenth century. *In* HARVEY, P. D. A., *ed.* The peasant land market in medieval England (Oxford, 1984), pp.30–105.
Examines manors of Gressenhall, Martham and Sedgeford. See also her Reading Univ. Ph.D. thesis, 'Peasant holdings in medieval Norfolk' (1976).

8031 MORIMOTO, N. The sheep farming of Norwich Cathedral Priory in the 13th and 14th centuries. *Nagoya Gakuin Univ. Rev.* (Japan), March 1977, 1–37.

8032 EDWARDS, D. A. Air photography and early fields in Norfolk. *In* BOWEN, H. C., *and* FOWLER, P. J., *eds.* Early land allotment in the British Isles (Brit. Archaeol. Rept. 48, 1978), pp. 99–102.

8033 OVERTON, M. Estimating crop yields from probate inventories: an example from East Anglia, 1585–1735. *J. Econ. Hist.* 39, 1979, 363–76.

8034 CAMPBELL, B. M. S. The extent and layout of commonfields in eastern Norfolk. *N.A.* 38, 1981, 5–32.

8035 CAMPBELL, B. M. S. Regional uniqueness of English field systems? Some evidence from eastern Norfolk. *Agric. Hist.* 29, 1981, 176–28.

8036 OVERTON, M. Agricultural change in Norfolk and Suffolk, 1580–1740. Ph.D. thesis, Cambridge Univ., 1981.

8036A HALLAM, H. E. Rural England, 1066–1348. 1981. Eastern England, pp. 32–74.
Hallam has also edited *Agrarian history of England and Wales, 2: 1042–1350* (1988), to which he contributed sections on region.

8037 CAMPBELL, B. M. S. Agricultural progress in medieval England: some evidences from eastern Norfolk. *Econ. Hist. Rev.* 2nd ser. 36, 1983, 26–46.

8038 CAMPBELL, B. M. S. Arable productivity in medieval England: some evidence from Norfolk. *J. Econ. Hist.* 43, 1983, 379–404.

8039 HOLDERNESS, B. A. East Anglia and the Fens. *In* THIRSK, J. *ed.* Agrarian history of England and Wales, vol. 5 (i): Regional farming systems, 1640–1750. (Cambridge, 1875), pp. 197–238.

8040 GRIFFITHS, G. R. Three Norfolk estates: a study of their development and economic performance. M.Phil. thesis, Nottingham Univ., 1985.
Deals with N. Elmham, Sedgeford, and Saxthorpe in pre-Reformation period.

8041 OVERTON, M. The diffusion of agricultural innovations in early modern England: turnips and clover in Norfolk and Suffolk, 1580–1740. *Trans. Inst. Brit. Geographers* 10, 1985, 205–21.

8042 GRIFFITHS, E. The management of two East Norfolk estates in the 17th century: Blickling and Felbrigg. Ph.D. thesis, Univ. of E. Anglia, 1987.

8043 STRIDE, K. B. Engrossing in sheep-corn-chalk areas: evidence in Wiltshire and Norfolk, 1530–1641. Cambridge diploma thesis, 1987.
Evidence comes from W. Raynham.

8044 BAILEY, M. The rabbit and the medieval East Anglian economy. *Agric. Hist. Rev.* 36, 1988, 1–20.

8045 CAMPBELL, B. M. S. The diffusion of vetches in medieval England. *Ec. Hist. Rev.* 41, 1988, 193–208.
Evidence mainly from Norfolk grange accounts.
    See also nos. 7473, 7476, 8862, 9073, 9381, 10084.

1750–1850

8046 MUNNINGS, T. C. An account of some experiments for drilling and protecting turnips, with some miscellaneous observations on agricultural subjects. Norwich, [1802]. BL.

8047 EDEN, P. Land surveyors in Norfolk. 1550–1850. 2: The surveyors of inclosure. *N.A.* 36, 1975, 119–48.

8048 ROE, P. J. The development of Norfolk agriculture in the 19th century, 1815–1914. M.Phil. thesis, Univ. of East Anglia, 1975.

8049 WADE-MARTINS, S. The farm buildings of the agricultural revolution. *Local Historian* 12, 1977, 407–15.

8050 WADE-MARTINS, S. A great estate at work: the Holkham estate and its inhabitants in the 19th century. Cambridge, 1978.
See also her Ph.D. thesis, 'The Holkham estate in the 19th century, with special reference to farm building and agricultural improvement'. (Univ. of E. Anglia, 1975).

8051 STANDLEY, V. H. Some effects of parliamentary inclosure on northern Broadland and upon selected parishes. [Unpubl. typescript, 1982].
Deals mainly with Potter Heigham and E. Ruston.
    See also nos. 7853, 8945.

AFTER 1850

8052 NORFOLK AGRICULTURAL ASSOCIATION. Lord Leicester's prize essays on agriculture. No. 1 by A. J. Smith... no. 2 by J. Darby. Norwich, 1875.

8053 MOSCROP, W. J. Report on the farm prize competition in Norfolk and Suffolk in 1886. *J. Roy. Agric. Soc.* 2nd ser. 22, 1886, 566–664.

8054 BRUCE, R. Typical farms in East Anglia. *Ibid.* 3rd ser. 5, 1894, 497–530.

8055 BIRD, M. C. H. The cost of winter grazing in East Norfolk. *Ibid.* 70, 1909, 82–98.

8056 ORWIN, C. S. *and* ORR, J. The cultivation of sugarbeet in Norfolk and Suffolk. *J. Board of Agriculture* 21, 1915, 969–87.

8057 Royal Commission on agriculture. Minutes of evidence. H.C. 1919, viii–ix. Norfolk evidence: vol. 1 (Cmd 345), pp. 178–89; vol. 2 (Cmd 365), pp. 91–114; vol. 3 (Cmd 391), pp. 18–30.

8058 [REEVE, L. M.] The earth no longer bare. By a Norfolk woman. Wymondham, [c. 1945].
Tottington connection. By same author and roughly contemporary are *Farming on a battleground* and *The pheasants had no tails and other tales.*

8059 FUSSELL, G. E. 'High farming' in the East Midlands and East Anglia, 1840–80. *Econ. Geog.* 27, 1951, 72–89.

8060 DAY, J. W. The new yeomen of England, 1952
On post-war farming situation in E. Anglia. Chap. 10 deals with Wretham.

8061 The Sprowston Farm. A report for members of the Norfolk Agricultural Station. 1953–.

8062 KEITH, J. Fifty years of farming. 1954.
Reminiscences of large-scale farmer in Aberdeenshire and Norfolk.

8063 SHOTTON, F. E. Norfolk farming – an outline of certain trends and problems. *J. Brit. Grasslands Soc.* June 1955, 87–95.

8064 NATIONAL AGRICULTURAL ADVISORY SERVICE (EASTERN DIVISION). Agriculture in the Eastern region. 1968.
Several subsequent editions (some as Agricultural Development and Advisory Service reports).

8065 HENDERSON, H. J. R. *and* COOPER, R. R. The livestock markets of Norfolk, 1928–64. *Tijdschrift voor Econ. en Sociale Geografie* 61, 1970, 358–65.

8065A DRUDY, P. J. A study of selected aspects of agricultural adjustment and rural depopulation in North Norfolk. Ph.D. thesis, Cambridge Univ., 1973.

8066 NUNN, H. L. Managerial and economic aspects of hardy nursery stock production: a study involving 40 nurseries in Hampshire, Norfolk and Surrey. Ashford, 1974.

8067 DODD, J. P. Norfolk agriculture in 1853–54. *N.A.* 36, 1976, 253–64.

8068 OWERS, A. C. The role of the independent experimental station and its impact on local farming. (Lord Hastings Memorial lecture). Norwich, 1978. P.

8069 HUTCHINSON, *Sir* J. *and* OWERS, A. C. Changes and innovation in Norfolk farming: 70 years... at the Norfolk Agricultural Station, 1908–78. Chichester, 1980.

8070 TOOKE, C., *ed*. Harvest [at Repps-cum-Bastwick, Sept. 1879. Farmer's diary]. *J. Norfolk Industrial Archaeol. Soc.* 2 (5), 1980, 52–6.

8071 BURGESS, B. 19th century tile drainage and the specialist tools of South Norfolk. Norwich. [1981]. P.

8072 MURRAY, G. C. Co-operation, capital and control: a study of member and management behaviour in agricultural co-operation in the East Anglian region. Ph.D. thesis, Univ. of East Anglia, 1981.

8072A BARNES, P. B. The economic history of landed estates in Norfolk since 1880. Ph.D. thesis, Univ. of E. Anglia, 1984.

8073 POTTER, C. Countryside change in lowland England: a survey of farmer investment behaviour. Ph.D. thesis, Univ. of E. Anglia, 1985.
Survey centred on Norfolk, Suffolk, and Shropshire.

8074 LOWE, P. *and others*. Countryside conflicts: the politics of farming, forestry, and conservation. 1986. Pp.265–300: 'Ploughing into the Halvergate marshes'.

8075 DOUET, A. Norfolk agriculture 1914–39 [lecture summary]. *Bull. Norfolk Research Committee* 37, 1987, 4–6.

8076 SAYER, M. A pattern of contraction: the changing face of Norfolk estates. *Country Life* 19 Mar. 1987, 104–5.

See also nos. 7477, 7680–1, 7824A, 8805, 8873A, 8876, 9053, 9055, 9408, 9926.

AGRICULTURAL LABOUR

8077 The Labourer. Organ of the National Agricultural Labourers' and Rural Workers' Union [Norwich]. 1–13, Feb. 1915 – Jan. 1918. BL.

8078 HOWKINS, A. The Norfolk farm labourer, 1900–1923. *Bull. Soc. for Study of Labour Hist.* 33, 1976, 7–9.

8079 HOWKINS, A. Structural conflict and the farmworker: Norfolk, 1900–20. *J.*

Peasant Stud. 4, 1977, 217–29.

8080 NEWBY, H. The deferential worker: a study of farm workers in East Anglia. 1977.
Some Norfolk references, but mainly based on survey of Suffolk workers.

8081 HOWKINS, A.J. Poor labouring men: rural radicalism in Norfolk, 1870–1912. 1985.
Based on similarly titled Ph.D. thesis, Essex Univ., 1982.

See also nos. 7813–27 passim, 8260, 8277, 8915, 9055, 9989, 10113.

FISHERIES

8082 WALTON, P. C. Geography of the East Anglian herring industry. M.A. thesis, Univ. of London, 1948.

8083 LEATHER, J. The sailing shrimpers of Great Yarmouth. *Mariner's Mirror 56*, 1970, 429–37.

8084 CLARK, R. The longshoremen. 1974
Contains autobiographical material from Norfolk fishermen.

8085 FESTING, S. Fishermen. Newton Abbot, 1977.
Much material on North Norfolk longshoremen.

8086 LUMMIS, T. The occupational community of East Anglian fishermen: an historical dimension through oral evidence. *Brit. J. Sociology* 28, 1977, 51–74.

8087 LEWIS, C. Whaling from Great Yarmouth, 1627–1797. *Yarmouth Archaeol.* 1 (v), 1983, [unpaginated].

8088 LUMMIS, T. Close-up: East Anglia. *In* THOMPSON, P. *and others*. Living the fishing (1983), pp. 182–202.

8089 STIBBONS, P. *and others*. Crabs and shannocks: the longshore fishermen of North Norfolk. Cromer, 1983.
See also pamphlet of same title by Stibbons, 1975.

8090 LUMMIS, T. Occupation and society: the East Anglian fishermen, 1880–1914. Cambridge, 1985.
Based on Ph.D. thesis, 'The fishermen in 19th and 20th century East Anglia' (Univ. of Essex, 1981).

See also nos. 7446, 9297, 10214, 10216, 10220–1, 10223.

TRADE AND INDUSTRY

GENERAL WORKS

8091 DICKINSON, R. E. Markets and market areas of East Anglia. *Econ. Geog.* 10, 1934, 172–82.

8092 CENTRAL OFFICE OF INFORMATION. Industrial trends in the Eastern region: looking ahead... 1958.

8093 STRATTON, D. G. The ports of Yarmouth and Norwich, 1800–1957. [Unpubl. typescript], 1958.

8094 LYNN, R. The entrepreneur: 8 case studies. 1974.
Studies incl. Colin Chapman (Lotus Cars) and Bernard Matthews (poultry-rearing).

8095 LEMON, A. Postwar industrial growth in East Anglian small towns: a study of migrant firms, 1945–1970. (School of Geography research papers, 12). Oxford, 1975.

8096 NORWICH TRADES COUNCIL. The Link. Sept. 1976–.

8097 SANT. M. E. C. *and* MOSELEY, M. J. The industrial development of East Anglia. Norwich, 1977.

8098 NORWICH INDUSTRIAL MISSION. Man at work: a collection of articles from the *Norwich Churchman*. Norwich, 1979.

8099 ALDERTON, D. *and* BOOKER, J. Batsford guide to the industrial archaeology of East Anglia. 1980.
See also Alderton's *Industrial archaeology in and around Norfolk* [Directory of sites; n.p., c. 1981]; and 'The industrial archaeology of regions of the British Isles, 1: East Anglia' *Industrial Archaeol. Rev.* 8, 1984, 7–23.

8100 NORFOLK COUNTY COUNCIL. Survey of activity on industrial estates in rural Norfolk, 1980. By John Packman. [Norwich], 1980.

8101 BRECKLAND DISTRICT COUNCIL. Industrial development handbook. E. Dereham, 1982. Other eds., 1983, 1985.
Similar handbooks publ. by Broadland D.C. (1983) and North Norfolk D.C. (1987).

8102 GOULD, A. *and* KEEBLE, D. New firms and rural industrialization in East Anglia. *Regional Stud.* 18, 1984, 189–201.
See also same authors' 'Entrepreneurship and manufacturing firm formation in rural regions: the East Anglian case' in M. J. Healey and B. W. Ilbery, eds., *The industrialization of the countryside* (Norwich, 1985), pp. 197–219.

8103 NORFOLK COUNTY COUNCIL. Norfolk industrial land register. Norwich, 1984.
See also Council's *Industrial premises register* (1985); and *Norfolk industrial directory* (1986, 1988).

8104 KIVELL, M. S. Industrial development initiatives in Norfolk: a review of the role of local authorities and public sector agencies. [Research report]. Wellington (New Zealand), 1985.
See also associated report by D. Sapsford (Univ. of E. Anglia, School of Economics and Social Studies), *Norfolk new industrial premises survey...1979–85* (Norwich, 1985).

8105 Business. The journal of the Norwich and Norfolk Chamber of Commerce and Industry. May, 1987–.

8106 SOUTH NORFOLK DISTRICT COUNCIL. Possible industrial and commercial development in the countryside. Long Stratton, [1985].
See also Council's *Longwater employment area development brief* (1986).

8107 UNIVERSITY OF EAST ANGLIA. SCHOOL OF DEVELOPMENT STUDIES. Norfolk economy and information project. Company files. Norwich. [c. 1985–].
Press cuttings files. Companies incl. Rowntree Mackintosh; Reckitt & Colman; Laurence, Scott & Electromotors; Boulton & Paul; Footwear sector; May and Baker; Norwich Brewery; Heatrae Sadia.

See also nos. 7651, 8012, 9332–4, 9373, 9463, 9466, 9643–7, 10180, 10217, 10219, 10222

COINS AND TOKENS

8108 CLOUGH, T. H. M. Sylloge of coins of the British Isles, 26. Museums of East Anglia. Part 1: the Morley St. Peter hoard. Part 2: Anglo-Saxon, Norman and Angevin coins, and later coins of the Norwich Mint. Oxford, 1980.

8109 PAGAN, H. E. The coinage of the East Anglian kingdom from 825 to 870. *Brit. Numismatic J.* 52, 1982, 41–83.

8110 WHITTET, T. D. Norfolk apothecaries' tokens and their issuers. N.A. 40, 1987, 100–9.

See also nos. 9107, 9211, 9213, 9909, 9912.

PARTICULAR TRADES, FIRMS, ETC.

BANKING AND INSURANCE

8111 LLOYD-PRICHARD, M. F. Savings banks in Norfolk. *Notes & Queries* 98, 1953, 441–5.

8112 VALLANCE, A. Very private enterprise: an anatomy of fraud and high finance. [1955]. Pp. 101–9: failure of Farrow's Bank, Norwich.

8113 WHITES, RENARD AND CO. [agents for M. S. Emerson, Norwich, solicitor]. High Court of Justice, Chancery Division. Boswell and Baxter v. Coaks and others. Copy correspondence *and* Copy supplemental correspondence. Norwich, [c.1886].
Relates to failure of Harveys and Hudsons, 1870, and subsequent litigation.

8114 The Norfolk and Norwich Savings Bank, 1816–1901. Norwich, [1901].

8115 Proceedings of the meetings of members of the Norwich Union... Associations held at the York Hotel... and at the City of London Tavern... 1818.

8116 FELCE, E. Norwich Union Fire Insurance Society. An historical sketch... 1797–1897. [1897].

8117 NORWICH UNION. A souvenir of the inauguration of the new head offices... Norwich, 1906. P.

8118 NORWICH UNION. Peeps into the past. A souvenir of the bi-centenary of the old Amicable Society and the centenary of the Norwich Union Life Office. Norwich, 1908.

8119 NORWICH UNION. Official opening of the new head offices. Norwich, 1962. P.

8120 NORWICH UNION. Review of building development schemes. Norwich, 1962. P.

8121 RYAN, R. J. History of the Norwich Union Fire Life Insurance societies from 1797 to 1914. Ph.D. thesis, Univ. of E. Anglia, 1983.

8122 RYAN, R. The Norwich Union and the British fire insurance market in the early 19th century. *In* WESTALL, O. M., *ed.* The historian and the business of insurance (Manchester, 1984), pp. 39–73.

8123 RYAN, R. The early expansion of the Norwich Union Life Insurance Society, 1808–37. *Business Hist.* 27, 1985, 166–96.

8124 Overend, Gurney and Co. Ltd: a plain statement of the case. By a barrister. 1867. P.

8125 XENOS, S. Depredations; or, Overend, Gurney and Co. and the Greek and Oriental Steam Navigation Co. Ltd. 1869.

See also nos. 8752, 9854.

BRUSHMAKING

8126 JONES, M. G. The story of brushmaking: a Norfolk craft. [Wymondham], 1974. P.
On presentation of Briton & Chadwick collection to Norfolk Museums. See also no. 10150.

BRICK AND TILE-MAKING
See nos. 8401–2, 8406, 8999, 9248, 9885, 9899, 9962, 9965.

BUILDING
See no. 10218

CHEMICALS
8127 [Entry deleted]
See nos. 8107, 9338, 9652, 10039.

CLAY PIPES
8128 ATKIN, S. The clay pipe-making industry in Norfolk. *N.A.* 39, 1875, 118–49.
See also nos. 9671–2.

CRAFTS
8129 SMEDLEY, N. East Anglian crafts. 1977.
8130 STANNARD, J. Norfolk craftsmen. Woodbridge, 1979.
8131 COUNCIL FOR SMALL INDUSTRIES IN RURAL AREAS. Norfolk county crafts directory. Norwich, 1983. P.
See also nos. 8766, 8770, 8882, 9027, 9653.

ELECTRICITY AND GAS
8132 MELLING, C. T. Light in the east: first decade of the Eastern Electricity Board. [Ipswich], 1987.
See also 8143, 9153, 9609–10.

ENGINEERING
8133 HARVEY, C. Lotus: the complete story. 1982.
See also nos. 8094, 8107, 8637, 8940, 9112, 9335–7, 9339, 9379, 9655–6, 10008, 10037–8.

FOOD AND DRINK
8134 BRIGDEN, R. Norfolk maltings. *J. Norfolk Industrial Archaeol. Soc.* 1 (8), 1975, 6–13, 20.
8135 OWEN, A. E. B. Medieval salting and the coastline in Cambridgeshire and N-W. Norfolk. *In* DE BRISAY, K. W. *and* EVANS, K. A., *eds.* Salt: the study of ancient industry (Colchester, 1975), pp. 42–4.
8136 MALSTER, R. Drink and be merry: a history of the drinks industry in East Anglia. Hadleigh, 1980. P.
8137 WATSON, J. Bernard Matthews labour dispute, Feb. – March 1982. [Unpubl. typescript, 1983].
8138 CHAPMAN, K. R. Breweries of Norwich and Norfolk. Taverham, 1984. 2nd ed., 1986.
8139 GOURVISH, T. Norfolk beers from English barley: a history of Steward and Patteson, 1793–1963. Norwich, 1987.
See also nos. 8094, 8107, 8525, 9657–62, 10212–13.

GLASS-MAKING
See nos. 9340, 9663, 10215.

GRAIN TRADE

8140 [NORGATE, T. S.] Letters to corn merchants who frequent the Norwich market. By Incognitus. Norwich, [1810].

On mills and milling see nos. 8433–40 and cross references given there.

IRON AND STEEL

8141 FEWSTER, M. Thomas Smithdale and Sons: a study of a Victorian ironfounder. *J. Norfolk Industrial Archaeol. Soc* 3 (1), 1981, 23–33.

Works at Norwich, Panxworth and Acle.

See also nos. 8952, 9342, 10008, 10225.

LEATHERWORK AND SHOE-MAKING

See nos. 9664–9, 10120, 10138.

LIMEBURNING

8142 JONES, J. *and* JONES, J. Limeburning in Norfolk. *J. Norfollk Industrial Archaeol. Soc.* 2 (2), 1977, 21–31.

See also no. 10114.

MOULDED PRODUCTS

See nos. 10040–1.

OIL AND NATURAL GAS

8143 HINDE, P. Fortune in the North Sea. The story of oil and gas off the East Coast of Britain. 1966.

See also no. 8967.

PAPER

8144 STOKER, D. The early history of paper-making in Norfolk. *N.A.* 36, 1976, 241–52.

POTTERY MANUFACTURE

See nos. 7727, 7737, 7741, 9006, 9033, 9363, 9389, 9441, 9446, 10048.

PRINTING

See nos. 9155, 9712, 9715–16.

RADIO AND TELEVISION

8145 ANGLIA TELEVISION. Anglia Television, the first 21 years. Norwich, 1980.

8146 [Great Yarmouth and Norwich independent local radio contract: applications to the IBA]. 1983.

Applications from GYN Radio; Nelson Radio; Norfolk on the Air Ltd.; Radio Broadland; Suffolk Group Radio PLC. Lowestoft PL.

ROAD HAULAGE

See no. 8174.

TEXTILES

8147 WARNER, Sir F. The silk industry of the United Kingdom: its origin and development. [1921]. Norfolk, pp. 265–96.

8148 BISHOP, J. S. The historical geography of the Norfolk and Suffolk woollen industry. M.A. thesis, London Univ., 1929.

8149 EVANS, N. The East Anglian linen industry: rural industry and local economy, 1500–1850. Aldershot, 1985.

See also nos. 9208, 9367, 9676–81, 10224.

TIMBER

See nos. 9135, 9197.

TOURISM AND RECREATION

8150 RICHARDS, A. B. Recreation in Thetford Chase: a study of recreation provision within the structure of a commercial national forest. M.Phil. thesis, Univ. of E. Anglia, 1974.

8151 JOBY, R. S. The Norfolk seaside. *East Anglian Mag.* June 1975, 361–3.
On beginnings of holiday industry 1860s to 80s. See also similar article on Broads area, *ibid.* Nov. 1976, 38–40.

8152 ARCHER, B. H. *and others.* Tourism in the coastal strip of East Anglia: a report prepared for the East Anglia Economic Planning Council. 1977.

8153 EAST ANGLIA TOURIST BOARD. A tourism policy for East Anglia: a draft discussion document. Ipswich, 1977.

8154 HEELEY, J. Tourism and local government, with special references to the county of Norfolk. Ph.D. thesis, Univ. of E. Anglia, 1980.
Chaps. 5–9 deal with historical development of tourist resorts and areas in the county.

8155 WALKER, S. E. Recreational behaviour among boat users on the Norfolk Broads. Ph.D. thesis, Univ. of E. Anglia, 1981.

8156 ASHWORTH, G. J. *and* BERGSMA, J. R. Impacts of the boat-hire industry in the Broads. Groningen (Netherlands), 1982.

8157 NORFOLK COUNTY COUNCIL. Report on the Norfolk holiday industry. Norwich, 1984. P.

See also nos. 8539, 9101, 9558, 10197.

TRANSPORT AND COMMUNICATIONS
GENERAL WORKS

8158 CLOUT, H. D. *and others.* A study of public transport in North Norfolk. (University College, London: Dept. of Geography, occasional paper, 18). 1973. UEA.

8159 NORFOLK COUNTY COUNCIL. A transportation strategy for 1986. Norwich, 1974.
Revised study, 1975, entitled *A transportation strategy for 1990.*

8160 MOSELEY, M. J. *and others.* Rural transport and accessibility. 2 vols. Norwich, 1978.
Research carried out at Centre of E. Anglian Studies, Univ. of E. Anglia, under contract to Dept. of Environment. See also Moseley's *Accessibility: the rural challenge* (1979).

8161 NORFOLK COUNTY COUNCIL. Transport policies and programme, 1980/81. 2 vols. Norwich, 1979.

See also nos. 7516, 7538, 7547, 7563.

POSTAL SERVICE

8162 CHAMPNESS, M. V. D. East Anglian helicopter mails. (E. Anglia Postal Hist. Study Circle. Monographs, 3). Bishop's Stortford, 1973.

8163 PEGG, R. E. F. Norfolk penny posts. (E. Anglia Postal Hist. Study Circle. Monographs, 5). Bishops Stortford, 1976.

8164 SUSSEX, V. J. *and* SHELTON, S. S. Continental mail service, 1793–1815: especially by Yarmouth packet boat. (E. Anglia Postal Hist. Study Circle. Monographs, 6). Bishop's Stortford, [1978].

8165 SUSSEX, V. J. The Norwich Post Office, 1568–1980: its postmasters, services and postal markings. (Postal history of E. Anglia, 7). Coggeshall, 1980.

See also no. 9117.

TRACKS

8166 ROGERS, D. The Peddar's Way. Wymondham (Leics.), 1974.

8167 TOULSON, S. East Anglia: walking the ley lines and ancient tracks. 1979.

See also nos. 7629, 7632.

ROADS

8168 KENNETT, D. H. The pattern of coaching in early 19th century Norfolk. *N.A.* 36, 1977, 355–72.

8169 BRITISH ROAD FEDERATION. County road needs in Norfolk and Suffolk. [1978]. P.

8170 FONE, J. F. The Stoke Ferry turnpike. *N.A.* 38, 1982, 195–203.

8171 ROBINSON, B. *and* ROSE, E. J. Roads and tracks. Cromer, 1984.

8172 KING'S LYNN AND WEST NORFOLK BOROUGH COUNCIL. Trunk roads: problems for West Norfolk. King's Lynn, 1985. P. *Followed by* Trunk roads: the need for action (1986).

8173 HAINES, C. W. Norfolk milestones. *J. Norfolk Industrial Archaeol. Soc.* 4, 1986/87, 27–30, 46–52.

8174 BRANFORD, C. W. Carriers and carrying in early modern Norfolk, c.1540–1750. M.A. thesis, Univ. of East Anglia, 1988.

See also nos. 7728–9, 9014.

BRIDGES

8175 JERVOISE, E. Ancient bridges of mid- and Eastern England. 1932.

INLAND WATERWAYS

8176 Navigation prejudiced by the Fenn drainers. As appears by the petition... of the town of Lynn concerning... navigation. N.p., n.d. [c. 1700?]. P. R.C.F.

8177 DISNEY, H. B. The voice of truth, in reply to a pamphlet entitled 'A warning voice... on the plan for making Norwich a port.' Norwich, [1823]. P. Cf.*B.N.H.* no. 1764.

8178 MANBY, G. W. Hints and observations on the improvement of the Yarmouth navigation. Yarmouth. 1830. P.

8179 ROULSTON, M. Fenland waterways: a pictorial anthology. St. Ives, 1974.

8180 BOYES, J. *and* RUSSELL, R. The canals of Eastern England. Newton Abbot, 1977.

8181 JOBY, R. S. North Walsham and Dilham Canal. Norwich, 1977. P.

8182 PIERSSENE, A. Water transport in Norfolk. Gressenhall, 1977. [Booklet and cards, portfolio].

8183 GRISTON, J. The North-Walsham-Dilham Canal. Mundesley, 1981. P.

8184 CORNFORD, B. Water transport on the Broads in the 13th and 14th centuries. *NARG News* 29, 1982, 4–8; 31, 1982, 11–14.

See also nos. 7478–81, 9648–50.

RAILWAYS AND TRAMWAYS

8185 YARMOUTH AND NORWICH RAILWAY. Stephenson's or Valley Line: prospectus. 1842. P.

8186 EASTERN COUNTIES RAILWAY CO. Report of the committee of investigation to the shareholders. 1849. BL.

8187 EASTERN COUNTIES RAILWAY CO. Report of the committee of investigation and minutes of evidence taken before the committee. 1855. BL.
See also D. Waddington, *The Chairman's answer to the report...* ; *Observations of the investigation committee on Mr. Waddington's answer...* ; and *The Chairman's final answer...* [1856]. Inst. of Civil Engineers Lib.

8188 Petition of the Corporation of Norwich and merchants etc. of Norwich...against...[a bill to constitute certain railways...a separate undertaking...]. Norwich, 1867. P.
Also similar petition, same date, against bill to close Victoria Station, Norwich.

8189 TAYLOR, G. H.Tramways of East Anglia. 1950.

8190 GREAT EASTERN RAILWAY SOCIETY. Great Eastern news. *Continued as* Great Eastern journal. Ingatestone, 1973–.
See also their *Information sheets* (1977–) providing reproductions of old timetables etc.

8191 MARRIOTT, W. Forty years of a Norfolk railway. Ed. by C. Beckett. (Publ. Midland and Great Northern Joint Railway Soc. 1). Sheringham, 1974.

8192 JOBY, R. S. [Klofron railway albums and histories]. Norwich, 1975–82.
Albums: Great Eastern Railway, 1913; The Great Eastern in Norfolk from the 1860s until the present.
Histories: Norfolk and Suffolk Joint Railways; Rails across Breckland; East Norfolk Railway; Railways of North-Western Norfolk; Waveney Valley Railway.

8193 MANN, J. D., *ed*. Great Eastern Railways, a pictorial collection. Frinton, 1975. P.

8194 JOBY, R. S. East Anglia (Forgotten railways). 1977. 2nd ed. 1985.

8195 WRIGHT, A. C. Development at Great Yarmouth. *Railway Mag.* 123, 1977, 530–5, 584–8.

8196 CLARK, R. H. Scenes from the Midland and Great Northern Joint Railway. Ashbourne, 1978.

8197 FISHER, C. The narrow gauge tramways of Norfolk. *J. Norfolk Industrial Archaeol. Soc.* 2 (3), 1978, 36–41
Additional note on chalk tramway at Whitlingham, *ibid.* 3 (2), 1982, 89–91.

8198 PERRY, G. North Norfolk Railway. Sheringham, [1978]. P,

8199 MIDLAND AND GREAT NORTHERN CIRCLE. Booklets. 1980–.
Includes *Running a Norfolk railway*, ed. A. C. Whittaker (no. 12), photograph catalogues, track surveys, etc.

8200 TOOKE, C. S. The Valley Line [Norwich to Yarmouth railway]. *Yarmouth Archaeol.* 1 (ii), 1980, 11–17.

8201 ALLEN, G. F. The Eastern since 1948. 1981.

8202 BECKETT, M. D. *and* HEMNELL, P. R. M. & G.N. in action. Norwich, 1981.

8203 ALLEN, I. C. 55 years of East Anglian steam. Oxford, 1982.

8204 JOBY, R. S. F. The development of railways in N-E. Norfolk, 1872–1914. M.Phil. thesis, Leicester Univ., 1982.

8205 RAILWAY DEVELOPMENT SOCIETY. Ten years on, 1972–1982: the story of railway development in East Anglia. [Lowestoft, 1982].

8206 RHODES, J. The Midland and Great Northern Joint Railway. 1982.

8207 NEVE, E. East Coast from King's Cross. 1983.

8208 SWINGER, P. W. Railway history in pictures: East Anglia. Newton Abbot, 1983.

8209 DARSLEY, R. The Wissington Railway: a fenland enterprise. Sheffield, 1984.

8210 ROTHERY, C. The Poppyland flier: the story of the railway line from Cromer to North Walsham, 1906–1953. Trimingham, 1984.

8211 POPPLEWELL, L. A gazetteer of the railway contractors and engineers of East Anglia. Southbourne, [c. 1985].

8212 COWLEY, I. Anglia East: the transformation of a railway. 1987.

8213 JENKINS, S. C. The Lynn and Hunstanton Railway and the West Norfolk Branch. Headington, 1987.

8214 JOBY, R. S. East Anglia (Regional railway handbooks, 2). Newton Abbot, 1987.

8215 MOFFAT, H. East Anglia's first railways: Peter Bruff and the Eastern Union Railway. Lavenham, 1987.

See also nos. 8391, 10060, 10133, 10207–8.

MOTOR BUSES

8216 COLLINS, R. N. and others. British bus fleets. No. 4: East Anglia. 4th ed., 1967.

8217 EVERETT, C. G. G. From Tilling to National Bus Company: the story of Eastern Counties Omnibus Co. Ltd. Thesis, Keswick Hall College, 1970.

8218 CLARK, P. Bus operation in East Anglia, the private sector: a list of independent bus operators and their services in the Eastern Traffic Area. (Omnibus Society). Cambridge, 1971. P.

8219 BREWSTER, D. E. Motor buses in East Anglia, 1901–31. Lingfield, 1974.

8220 DOGGETT, M. Eastern Counties: the first 50 years. Norwich, [1981].

See also no. 10207.

RELIGION

CHURCH HISTORY

GENERAL WORKS

8221 PUDDY, E. I. A short history of the Order of the Hospital of St. John of Jerusalem in Norfolk. From Knights Hospitallers to Ambulance Brigade, 1163–1961. Dereham, 1961.

8222 SMITH, D. M. Guide to bishops' registers of England and Wales. 1981. Norwich diocese, pp. 150–62.

See also no. 9380.

THE PRE-REFORMATION CHURCH

8223 HOWLETT, R. Early parochial clergy in Norfolk not mentioned by Blomefield. *N.A.M.* 2, 1883, 427–33.

8224 FIRTH, C. B. Some aspects of the religious history of Norfolk in the 15th century. M.A. thesis, London Univ., 1910.

8225 BRADLEY, E. The story of the English abbeys, told in counties. Vol. 2: the eastern counties. 1939. BL.

8226 WHITELOCK, D. The conversion of the Eastern Danelaw. *Saga-book of Viking Soc.* 12, 1941, 159–76.

8227 FINES, J. D. Studies in the Lollard heresy... evidence from the dioceses of Norwich, Lincoln, Coventry and Lichfield, and Ely: 1430–1530. Ph.D. thesis, Sheffield Univ., 1964.

8228 NICHOLS, J. A. The history and cartulary of the Cistercian nuns of Marham Abbey. Ph.D. thesis, Kent State Univ. Graduate College, 1974.

8229 BURNHAM, B. The episcopal administration of the diocese of Norwich in the later middle ages. B.Litt. thesis, Oxford Univ., 1971.

8230 CARSON, T. E. A socio-economic study of East Anglian clergy in the time of Henry Despencer, 1370–1406. Ph.D. thesis, Michigan Univ., 1972.

8231 SCARFF, E. P. The Fenland abbeys in the 10th and 11th centuries. Ph.D. thesis, Leeds Univ., 1974.

8232 HARPER-BILL, C. A late medieval visitation: the diocese of Norwich in 1499. *Proc. Suffolk Inst. Archaeol.* 34, 1977, 35–47.

8233 TANNER, N. P., *ed.* Heresy trials in the diocese of Norwich, 1423–31. *Camden Soc.* 4th ser. 20, 1977.

8234 COTTON, S. Domesday revisited – where were the 11th-century churches? *NARG News* 21, 1980, 11–17.

8235 WILTON, J. W. Monastic life in Norfolk and Suffolk. Fakenham, 1980.

8236 SEAL-COON, F. W. The history of the Templar province of East Anglia. Great Yarmouth, 1982.

8237 SHINNERS, J. R. Religion in 14th-century England: clerical standards and popular practice in the diocese of Norwich. Ph.D. thesis, Univ. of Toronto, 1982.

8238 MARZAC-HOLLAND, N. Three Norfolk mystics. Burnham Market, 1983. Richelde de Faverches, Julian of Norwich, Margery Kempe.

8239 FARMER, D. H. Some saints of East Anglia. *In* BARBER, M. *and others, eds.* East Anglian and other studies presented to Barbara Dodwell (Reading, c.1984), pp. 31–49.

8240 GLASSCOE, M., *ed.* The medieval mystical tradition in England. Woodbridge, 1984.
Contains S. Dickman, 'Margery Kempe and the continental tradition of the pious woman', pp. 150–68; and D. Wallace, 'Mystics and followers in Siena and East Anglia: a study in taxonomy, class, and cultural tradition', pp. 169–91.

8241 HARPER-BILL, C. Bishop William Turbe and the diocese of Norwich, 1146–1174. *In* BROWN, R. A., *ed.* Anglo-Norman studies, 7: proceedings of the Battle Conference, 1984. (Woodbridge, 1985), pp. 142–60.

8242 CARSON, T. E. The problem of clerical irregularities in the late medieval church: an example from Norwich. *Catholic Hist. Rev.* 72, 1986, 185–200.

8243 COTTON, S. In search of some Norfolk churches and their dedications. *NARG News* 47, 1986, 12–18.

8244 NICHOLS, A. E. The etiquette of pre-Reformation confession in East Anglia. *Sixteenth-Century J.* 17, 1986, 145–63.
Concerns depiction of penance ritual on seven-sacrament fonts of Norfolk and Suffolk.

8245 WARNER, P. Shared churchyards, freemen church builders, and the development of parishes in 11th-century East Anglia. *Landscape Hist.* 8, 1986, 39–52.

8246 COTTON, S. Indulgences for building Norfolk churches. *NARG News* 51, 1987, 11–16.

8247 RIDYARD, S. J. The royal saints of Anglo-Saxon England: a study of West Saxon and East Anglian cults. Cambridge, 1988.

See also nos. 8444–95 passim, 8778–86, 8788–93, 9185, 9369–72, 9686–92, 10043–5, 10156.

TUDOR AND EARLY STUART PERIOD

8248 Valor ecclesiasticus temp. Henrici VIII (Publ. of the Record Commissioners). Norfolk: vol. 3 (1817), pp. 281–402.

8249 JUKES, H. A. L. Bishop Matthew Wren and the non-conforming ministers of the diocese of Norwich. *Hist. Stud.* 1 (ii), 1968, 13–20.

8250 HOULBROOKE, R. A., *ed.* The letter book of John Parkhurst, Bishop of Norwich... 1571–75. *N.R.S.* 43, 1974/75.

8251 HOULBROOKE, R. A. Church courts and the people during the English Reformation, 1520–1570. Oxford, 1979.
Based on Norwich and Winchester diocesan records.

8252 PEET, D. J. The mid-16th century parish clergy, with particular consideration of the dioceses of Norwich and York. Ph.D. thesis, Cambridge Univ., 1980.

8253 POUND, J. Clerical poverty in early 16th-century England: some East Anglian evidence. *J. Eccles Hist.* 37, 1986, 389–96.

8254 CORNFORD, B. The Reformation in Flegg, 1500–1650. *Bull. Norfolk Research Committee* 37, 1987, 10–15.

8255 LYONS, S. M. The resignation [1549] of William Rugg: a reconsideration. *Catholic Hist. Rev.* 73, 1987, 23–40.

See also nos. 8738–41, 8937, 9310, 9693–4, 9905, 10018, 10177.

8255A The case of the Rev. C. Le Grice. [Norwich, 1788?]. P. BL.
Charged with non-residence in his cures of Wickhampton and Thwaite.

8256 A letter to the Rev. Robert Forby, M.A., Rector of Fincham. 1815.
See *B.N.H.* no. 1989.

8257 [STANLEY, E.] Speech of the Lord Bishop of Norwich in the House of Lords, on subscription. 1840.

8258 Scheme for redistribution of the East Anglian dioceses. Norwich, [1880]. P. RCF.

8259 WHITFIELD, P. W. Change and continuity in the rural church: Norfolk, 1760–1840. Ph.D. thesis, Univ. of St. Andrew's, 1977.

8260 SCOTLAND, N. Rural war in later Victorian Norfolk. *N.A.* 38, 1981, 82–7.
On hostility of agricultural labourers' unions to Anglican clergy.

8261 JACOB, W. M. Clergy and society in Norfolk, 1707–1906. Ph.D. thesis, Exeter Univ., 1982.

See also nos. 8572, 8640, 8769, 8787, 8807, 9106, 9310, 9695–6, 9979, 10179, 10226–7.

8262 North-east Norfolk country churchman [journal]. North Walsham, 1963–76.

8263 TYLER, M. The rural clergy of the Anglican Church: an introductory study of south and south-west Norfolk incumbents. M.A. thesis, Univ. of E. Anglia, 1969.

8264 RUSSELL, A., *ed.* Groups and teams in the countryside. 1975.
The 'group parish' system in Norfolk.

8265 NORFOLK CHURCHES TRUST. Annual reports. Holt, 1977–.

8266 Norwich diocesan news service. Norwich, 1979–.
Successor to *Norwich Churchman*.

8267 Church Post: the publication of the diocese of Norwich. Norwich, 1986–.
Replaces *Diocesan Bulletin*

See also nos. 8705, 9005, 9128–9, 9219, 9697.

8268 Directions... George [Horne]. 1791. UEA.

ROMAN CATHOLICISM

8269 NATIONAL CATHOLIC CONGRESS. The Catholic faith in East Anglia: three papers read at the...Congress at Norwich. 1912.

8270 CALTHROP, M. M. C. *and others, eds.* Recusant rolls, nos. 1–4, 1592–1596. [Norfolk sections]. *Catholic Record Soc.* 18, 1916, 218–34; 57, 1965, 99–113; 61, 1970, 55–64, 187–96.

8271 RYAN, *Rev.* P., *ed.* Diocesan returns of recusants for England and Wales, 1577. (Norfolk section]. *Catholic Record Soc.* 22, 1921, 54–63.

8272 The installation of the first Bishop of Anglia, the Rt. Rev. Alan C. Clark. 1976.

See also nos. 8974, 9310, 9698.

NONCONFORMITY

8273 JORDAN, R. A study of nonconformism in the Waveney Valley during the 19th century. B.A. thesis (Historical geography), Cambridge Univ., 1976.

8274 NORFOLK AND SUFFOLK ASSOCIATION OF BAPTIST CHURCHES [*later* SUFFOLK AND NORFOLK NEW ASSOCIATION]. Circular letters. 1771–c. 1880. NPL (incomplete); BL (incomplete).

8275 PALGRAVE-MOORE, P. Norfolk Baptists and their records. *Norfolk Ancestor* 3 (3), 1983, 39–41.

8276 KEY, R. The gospel among the masses; or, a selection of remarkable scenes, incidents and facts connected with the missionary work and experience of the Rev. Robert Key, now a superannuated minister of the Primitive Methodist Connexion. 1866. 2nd ed. 1872.
See also C. Jolly, 'The apostle to the Norfolk villagers', *E.A.M.* Sept. 1976, 438–9.

8277 SCOTLAND, N. A. The role of Methodism in the growth and development of the 'Revolt of the Field' in Lincolnshire, Norfolk and Suffolk, 1872–95. Ph.D. thesis, Aberdeen Univ., 1975.
See also his 'Methodism and the "Revolt of the Field" in East Anglia, 1872–96'. *Proc. Wesley Hist. Soc.* 41, 1977, 2–11, 39–42.

8278 HUGHES, H. T. A progress of pilgrims, 1980.
Portraits of 7 Methodist ministers with E. Anglian links, incl. Sidney Dye, M.P. for S.W. Norfolk.

8279 BECKHAM, E. *and others*. A brief discovery of some of the blasphemous and seditious principles and practices of the people called Quakers... By Edward Beckham... rector of Gayton-Thorpe; Hen. Meriton, rector of Oxborrow; Lancaster Topcliffe... 1699. P. BL.
See also their *Principles of the Quakers further shown to be blasphemous... In a reply to Geo. Whitehead's answer...* (1700); and Whitehead's pamphlets *Truth and innocency vindicated* (1699) and *Truth prevalent...* (1701).

8280 [FIELD, J.] Apology for the people called Quakers, and an appeal to the inhabitants of Norfolk and Suffolk. 1699. BL.

8281 ASHBY, R. A relation of a visit to three malefactors [Quakers] condemn'd at the assizes at Thetford... anno 1721–2. 1724. P. BL.

8282 GRAY, M. G., *ed*. The records of the Society of Friends in Norfolk: a catalogue. Diploma in Archive Admin., Univ. of London, 1965.

8283 JONES, G. R. Notes on the history of the Eastern Union of Unitarian and other Free Christian churches. *Trans. Unitarian Hist. Soc.* 4, 1929, 45–57.

> On Baptists see also nos. 9052, 9699, 10136; Congregationalists, nos. 9106, 9700–1, 9777, 10072, 10099; Methodists, nos. 8683, 8921, 8965, 9047, 9084, 9194, 9245, 9702–6, 10065; Quakers, nos. 8950, 9707–8, 10148.

JUDAISM

8284 MARGOLIOUTH, M. Vestiges of the historic Anglo-Hebrews in East Anglia. 1870.

> See also nos. 9455–6.

CULTURE AND RECREATION

FOLKLORE

8285 KNIGHTS, M. Norfolk stories. The phantom horseman, The lost village, Our bells. Norwich, [c. 1880]. RCF.

8286 JAMES, M. H. Bogie tales of East Anglia. Ipswich, 1891.

8287 HOOPER, J. Horkeys, or harvest frolics. *In* ANDREWS. W., *ed*. Bygone Norfolk (1898), pp. 196–209.

8288 GILLETT, H. E. H. Some saws and proverbs of Norfolk. *Ibid.*, pp. 210–28.

8289 GILLETT, H. E. H. Sports and pastimes of old Norfolk. *Ibid.*, pp. 240–270.

8290 SMITH, A. H. East Anglian songs and lays. 1903.

8291 ELWES, H. Fairy tales from Norfolk. [1916].

8292 MARLOWE, C. Legends of the Fenland people. 1926.

8293 SAMPSON, C. Ghosts of the Broads. 1931. Another ed. 1973.

8294 LONGE, A. The old nightwatchman. The ghost of Spixworth Hall. A Norfolk ghost story and other anecdotes. Ipswich, 1950. BL.

8295 COLEMAN, S. J. Traditional lore of East Anglia. Douglas (Isle of Man), [1961]. P.

8296 BARRETT, W. H. Tales from the Fens. Ed. E. Porter. 1963.
Followed by *More tales from the Fens*. 1964.

8297 [Entry deleted].

8298 FORMAN, J. Haunted East Anglia. 1974.

8299 BARRETT, W. H. *and* GARROD, R. P. East Anglian folklore and other tales. 1976.

8300 DIXON, G. M. Folktales and legends of Norfolk. Peterborough. 1980.

8301 SIMPER, R. Traditions of East Anglia. Woodbridge, 1980.

8302 RABUZZI, D. A. In pursuit of Norfolk hyter sprites. *Folklore*, 95, 1984, 74–89.

8303 WEST, H. M. Ghosts of East Anglia. Woodbridge, 1984.

8304 WESTWOOD, J. Albion: a guide to legendary Britain, 1985. East Anglia, pp. 141–74.

8305 CROWE, G. At great-grandmama's knee: 14 rare rhymes of long ago remembered by Gladys Crowe. Ed. K. Bartlett. Highfield (Pretoria), 1986.
Early 19th-century rhymes from Norwich.

8306 GIFFORD, A. Ghosts and legends of Lynn. King's Lynn, 1986.

See also nos. 9423, 9900, 9970.

See also nos. 9423, 9900, 9970.

RECIPES

8307 POULSON, J. Old Anglian recipes. Nelson, 1976.

8308 NORWAK, M. East Anglian recipes: 300 years of housewife's choice. Ipswich, 1978.

8309 NORFOLK RECORD OFFICE. Recipes on record from Norfolk cookery books of the 18th and 19th centuries. Ed. D. Clewes and S. Maddock. Norwich. 1979.

8310 DIXON, G. M. Traditional Norfolk recipes. Peterborough, 1982.

WITCHCRAFT

8310A NEWMAN, L. F. Notes on the history and practice of witchcraft in the Eastern Counties. *Folk-Lore* 57, 1946, 12–23.

8311 DEACON, R. Matthew Hopkins: Witch-Finder General. 1976.

8312 GARDINER, T. Broomstick over Essex and East Anglia: introduction to witchcraft in the eastern counties during the 17th century. Hornchurch, 1981.

GYPSIES

8313 THOMPSON, T. W. Youngs, Gibsons, and their associates. *J. Gypsy Lore Soc.* 3rd ser. 24, 1945, 144–56; 25, 1946, 39–45.

8314 WINSTEDT, E. O. Records of gypsies in the Eastern counties. *Ibid.* 40, 1961, 26–35.

DIALECT

8314A STONE, R. K. Middle English prose style: Margery Kempe and Julian of Norwich. Ph.D. thesis, Univ. of Illinois, 1963.

8315 ECCLES, M. *Ludus Coventriae*: Lincoln or Norfolk? *Medium Aevum* 40, 1971, 135–41.
Argues that the English of this play cycle indicates a Norfolk origin.

8316 BENNETT, J. The language and the home of the *Ludus Coventriae*. *Orbis* 22, 1973, 43–63.

8317 BENNETT, J. The *Mary Magdalene* of Bishop's Lynn. *Stud. in Philology* 75, 1978, 1–10.
Analysis of Norfolk idiom of this 15th century play.

8318 HILL, L. A. A detailed analysis of the word-order of 102 letters dictated by Margaret Paston to members of her family... Ph.D. thesis, London Univ., 1978.

8319 DAVIS, N. Language in letters from Sir John Falstolf's household. *In* HEYWORTH, P. L. Medieval studies for J. A. W. Bennett (Oxford, 1981), pp. 329–46.
See also no. 8330.

ARTS AND SCIENCE

8320 WRIGHT, L. The arts in Norfolk: a survey and plan for their development. Commissioned by Norfolk Arts Forum. Norwich, 1986.
See also nos. 9092, 9154, 9239, 9274, 9485, 9717–32, 10214, 10229.

BOOKS AND LIBRARIES

8321 DUTT, W. A. Some literary associations of East Anglia. 1907.

8322 DRAPER, W. H. A course of twelve lectures on some notable writers of Norfolk. [Compilation of press reports, 1922].

8323 STOKER, D. An eighteenth-century map piracy. *N.A.* 37, 1978, 123–6.
Concerns pirated edition of James Corbridge's Norfolk map of 1730.

8324 SMITH, J. Book use in East Anglia. [British Library Research and Development Dept. report]. 1979.

8325 GOODWYN, E. A. East Anglian literature: a survey from Crabbe to Adrian Bell. [Beccles, c. 1982].

8326 KELBRICK, N., *ed*. Library resources in East Anglia. 2nd ed. 1985. Supplement: medieval libraries, 1986.
First ed. by C. A. Thurley noted in *B.N.H.* 2119.

    See also nos. 8571, 8595–7, 8605–11, 8619–23, 8649, 8662–3, 8677, 8732–5, 8748, 8759–60, 8794–5, 8799, 8817, 8819, 8824–5, 8896, 8898, 8902, 8904, 8924, 8926, 8991, 8997, 9251–2, 9258, 9344, 9471, 9711–16, 10012.

THEATRE

8327 NORFOLK DRAMA COMMITTEE. East Anglian theatre: an exhibition devoted to the history of the players and playhouses of Norfolk and Suffolk [at the] Castle Museum. [Norwich, 1952].

8328 WRIGHT, R. R. Medieval theatre in East Anglia... with special reference to game, interlude and play in the late 15th and early 16th century. M.Litt. thesis, Bristol Univ., 1971.

8329 GRICE, E. Rogues and vagabonds; or, the actors' road to respectability. Lavenham, 1977.
Deals with 'Norfolk Circuit' of East Anglian theatres.

8330 BEADLE, H. R. L. The medieval drama of East Anglia: studies in dialect, documentary records and stagecraft. D.Phil. thesis, York Univ., 1978.

8331 BEADLE, R. Plays and playing at Thetford and nearby, 1498–1540. *Theatre Notebook* 32, 1978, 4–11.

8332 GALLOWAY, D. *and* WASSON, J. Records of plays and players in Norfolk and Suffolk, 1330–1642. *Malone Soc. Collections* 11, Oxford, 1980.

    See also nos. 8315–17, 9733–40, 10043, 10228. On cinemas see nos. 9741, 10230.

MUSIC

8333 NORFOLK RURAL MUSIC SCHOOL. Annual reports. Norwich, 1941–58. RCF.
See also programmes of the County Music Festival, assoc. with the Rural Music Schools Association, 1968–72. RCF.

8334 PAGET, G. An account of the organs in the diocese of Norwich. 2 vols. [Unpubl. typescript]. Bury St. Edmunds, 1976.
Note also Paget's numerous contributions to journal *Organ*, notably 'Some Norfolk village church organs' (no. 44, 1932, 245–8); 'Some organs in Norwich' (no. 35, 1930, 172–80); 'John Rayson organs in Norfolk' (vol. 63, 1984, 7–14); and on instruments at Cromer (no. 114, 1949, 67–76), Sandringham (no. 102, 1946, 62–7), Wymondham Abbey (no. 138, 1955, 66–76), Norwich Cathedral (no. 84, 1942, 137–48), and St. Peter Mancroft (vol. 57, 1978, 5–12).

8335 BOOTMAN, R. Organ 'migrations' in the county of Norfolk and the diocese of Norwich. Stoke Holy Cross, 1977. P.

8336 HUGHES, A. 15th-century English polyphony discovered in Norwich and Arundel. *Music and Letters* 58, 1978, 148–58.

8337 FAWCETT, T. C. Music in 18th century Norwich and Norfolk. Norwich, 1979.

8338 [Entry deleted]

    See also nos. 8627, 8672–3, 9237, 9358, 9742, 10019, 10154.

SCIENCE

8339 SMITH, *Sir* J. E. Biographical memoirs of several Norwich botanists. *Trans. Linnean Soc.* 1804, section B, 1–7.

    See also nos. 8390, 8579, 8592, 8691, 8866.

AMUSEMENT AND SPORT

GENERAL

8340 SPORTS COUNCIL (EASTERN REGION). Regional strategy for sport and recreation. March, 1980.

8341 JOHNSON, D. E. East Anglian sporting days. Ipswich, 1981.

8342 EASTERN COUNCIL FOR SPORT AND RECREATION. A regional strategy for sport and recreation: seminar reports, 1–2. Bedford, 1987.

ATHLETICS

8343 POTTER, H. E., *ed.* Norfolk athletes and athletics. Norwich, [1904].

CHESS

8344 NORFOLK COUNTY CHESS ASSOCIATION. Bulletin. 1979–.

CRICKET

8345 COLMAN, J. Cricket records [1845–46; 1870–87]. Privately printed, 1887.

8346 Norfolk cricket annual, season 1891; ed. R. H. Legge and F. W. Watson. Norwich, 1891.

8347 Norfolk county cricket club, 1905: souvenir of a record season. Norwich, 1905.

8348 PENNY, J. S. Cricketing references in Norwich newspapers, 1701–1800. Norwich, 1979.

See also no. 8690.

CYCLING

8349 East Anglian Cyclist. [Diss]. Aug. 1948 – Jan. 1949. BL.

8350 MORRISS, A. H. Cycling in the 1880s. *E.A.M.* 41, Nov. 1981, 34–5.

FISHING

8351 FISHER, E. C. Trout in Norfolk. 1936. BL.

8352 SAVORY, A. Lazy rivers. 1956.

8353 COOPER, B. Angling in Norfolk and Suffolk waters, Norwich, [1958].

8354 COLLINS, P. Fishing the Norfolk Broads. 1967. 3rd ed. 1977.

8355 GILLESPIE, I. Sea fishing: the Wash to the Thames Estuary. 1969.

8356 WILSON, J. Fresh and saltwater fishing in Norfolk and Suffolk. Norwich, 1974.

8357 ANGLIAN WATER AUTHORITY. A guide to angling in the Norfolk and Suffolk River Division. Gloucester, 1975.

8358 WILSON, J. A specimen fishing year: John Wilson's fishing diary. 1977.

8359 OWENS, L. Recreational conflict and the behaviour of coarse anglers and boat users in the Norfolk Broads. Ph.D. thesis, Univ. of E. Anglia, 1983.

See also no. 8630.

FOOTBALL

8360 Eastern Football News. [Norwich]. Aug. 1919–Sept. 1939; Aug. 1946–. BL.

8361 BELL, T., *ed*. Canary crusade. Norwich, 1959. Another ed., 1972. P.

8362 BELL, T., *ed*. Norwich City: The Division One story. Norwich, 1978.

8363 SPURDENS, D. Norwich City, our way. Ed. and designed by M. Shaw. Norwich, 1980.

8364 EASTWOOD, J. *and* DAVAGE, M. Canary citizens: the official history of Norwich City F.C. Sudbury, 1986.

GOLF

8365 DARWIN, B. The Royal West Norfolk Golf Club. (Golf Club Assoc.). 1921/22. P.

8366 DARWIN, B. A round of golf on the London and N. Eastern Railway. York, [1924]. BL.
Cf. similar work. *A round of golf* (1937).
See also nos. 9102, 9745.

HUNTING AND SHOOTING

8367 JONES, H. Norfolk game duty certificates, 1800, extracted from the *Norwich Mercury. Norfolk Ancestor* 2 (12), 1983, 163–7.
Also 'Norfolk game duty: gamekeepers (registered), 1801', *ibid.* 4, 1987, 109–12, 153–5.

8368 A list of Lord Hastings' hounds. 1862. P. RCF.

8369 EVERITT, N. Broadland sport. 1902.

8370 MCLEAN, C. At dawn and dusk: being my record of nearly 60 years' wildfowling. 1954.

8371 GREAVES, R., *ed*. Short histories of hunts, 32 pts. 1952–3.
Includes Norwich Staghounds, North Norfolk Harriers and West Norfolk Hunt.

8372 JOHNSON, D. E. Victorian shooting days: East Anglia, 1810–1910. Ipswich, 1981.
Includes list of E. Anglian gunsmiths.

8373 GIBBS, A. W. Norfolk gunmakers, 1700–1900. [N.p., 1987].

8374 BRIGHAM, R. Guns and goshawks: country life and country sports. 1988.
See also nos. 8675, 8802, 10007.

RACING

8375 FAIRFAX-BLAKEBOROUGH, J. F. A short history of Great Yarmouth Racecourse [Yarmouth, 1951]. P.

WATER SPORTS

8376 CLARKSON, A. T. A short history of the Royal Norfolk and Suffolk Yacht Club. Lowestoft, [1930].

8377 NORFOLK CANOEING ASSOCIATION. Newsletter. 1979–.

8378 BARNES, P. The Norfolk Broads Yacht Club: a short history. Norwich, [1983].

CLUBS AND SOCIETIES

FREEMASONS

8378A NORFOLK PROVINCIAL GRAND LODGE. Transactions. Norwich, 1876–1939. FPL.

8378B [LOFTUS, G. W. F.] Reminiscences of 26 years of freemasonry; by a past Provincial Grand Officer of Norfolk. 1890. FPL.

8379 DAYNES, G. W. 200 years of freemasonry in Norfolk. [1924]. P.

8380 EATON, F. R. Some Masonic events relating to the province of Norfolk, 1724–1944. Norwich, 1945.

8380A The Ashlar, a journal for Norfolk freemasons. 1–24; n.s.1–. Norwich, 1946–59; 1975–.

8381 BROWN, A. S. The Gregorians in Norfolk. *Ars Quatuor Coronatorum* 69, 1957, 127–32.

See also nos. 9109A, 9152A, 9205A, 9345, 9345A, 9745A, 9745B, 10042A, 10072A, 10141A, 10227A.

OTHER SOCIETIES

8382 CAMPAIGN FOR REAL ALE. Norfolk nips: newsletter of the Norfolk and Norwich branch. Norwich, 1982–.

8383 A full report of the proceedings at the annual meeting of the Norfolk and Norwich Archaeological Society held at Lynn, Sept.18 and 19, 1850. Norwich, 1850. P.

8384 CRESSWELL, I. Summary of the activities of the [Norfolk and Norwich Archaeological] Society, 1941–76. *N.A.* 36, 1977, 399–407.

8385 NORFOLK AND NORWICH HORTICULTURAL SOCIETY. Newsletter. Norwich, 1980–.

8386 NORFOLK AND NORWICH NATURALISTS' SOCIETY. Norfolk Natterjack: quarterly bulletin. Norwich, 1983–.

8387 NORFOLK ARCHITECTS ASSOCIATION. Broadsheets. Lyng, 1971–.

8388 NORFOLK CLUB. Trustees, President and committee, with a list of members. Norwich, 1947. P.

8389 NORFOLK CONSERVATION CORPS. Newsletter. 1980–.

8390 BASSETT, P., *ed.* A list of the historical records of the Norfolk Naturalists' Trust (Centre for Urban and Regional Studies, Univ. of Birmingham, and Institute of Agricultural History, Univ. of Reading: Lists of historical records). 1980. P. UEA.

See also Society's *Newsletter* (1974–78), continued as *Tern* (1978–).

8391 ADDERSON, R. S. *and others.* The Norfolk Railway Society, 1955–1980. Costessey, 1981. P.

See also Society's *Newsletter* (1962–).

8392 WAKE, T. Coordinating regional research: the Norfolk Research Committee. *East Anglian Mag.* Jan. 1939, 124–8.

8393 NORFOLK SOCIETY. Newsletter. Norwich, 1973–.

8394 SCOUT ASSOCIATION. Norfolk Scouting [periodical]. Norwich, 1968–.

See also nos. 8265, 8344, 8376–8, 9744–57, 10231.

ART, ARCHITECTURE, MONUMENTS

ARCHITECTURE

GENERAL WORKS

8395 PRIEST, E. W. Piety and pride. Castles, convents and crosses of the county. Norwich, 1932.

8396 OFFICE OF WORKS. Ancient monuments and historic buildings. Illustrated regional guides, 3: East Anglia and the Midlands. 1936. 2nd ed. 1955. 3rd ed. 1967.

8397 CUDWORTH, C. L. The Dutch gables of East Anglia. *Architect. Rev.* March 1939, 113 ff.

8398 [Entry deleted].

8399 ROYAL ARCHAEOLOGICAL INSTITUTE. Report of the summer meeting at Norwich, 1979. *Archaeol. J.* 137, 1980, 280–368.
Notes on local buildings and antiquities.

8400 McKEAN, C. Architectural guide to Cambridge and East Anglia since 1920. 1982.

8401 MOORE, N. J. Brick building in medieval England: a study of its later development with special reference to East Anglia. M.Phil. thesis, Univ. of E. Anglia, 1969.

8402 HARLEY, L. S. Bricks of eastern England, to the end of the Middle Ages. *Essex J.* 10, 1975/76, 134–41.

8403 NORTON, T. W. Traditional Norfolk building materials. R.I.B.A. thesis, 1979.

8404 ELLIS, R. Shaped gables in Norfolk and Suffolk. *Trans. Assoc. Study & Conservation Hist. Buildings* 8, 1983, 3–20.

8405 KING, D. J. C. Castellarium Anglicanum: an index and bibliography of the castles in England, Wales, and the Islands. 2 vols., 1983. Norfolk: vol. 2, pp. 305–13.

8406 KENNETT, D. H. Taxes and bricks: wealthy men and their buildings in early Tudor Norfolk. *Brit. Brick Soc. Information* 32, Feb. 1984, 5–12.

8407 ORNA, B. *and* ORNA, E. Flint in Norfolk buildings. Norwich, 1984. P.

8408 NORWICH, J. J. The architecture of southern England. 1985. Norfolk. pp. 410–43.

8409 NORFOLK COUNTY COUNCIL. Historic buildings in Norfolk: problems and opportunities. A monitoring report, consultative draft. *Followed by* Result of public consultation: a summary report. Norwich, 1987.

8410 NORFOLK COUNTY COUNCIL. Historic buildings at risk in Norfolk. 1988. P.
Grade 2 buildings not listed except for Breckland District.

See also nos. 7554A, 7559, 8387, 8684, 8871, 8925, 9583A, 9922.

HALLS AND MANOR HOUSES

8411 COUNTRY LIFE. English country houses [series]:
Caroline, 1625–1685 (*by* O. Hill and J. Cornforth, 1966): Raynham Hall, pp. 57–60.
Early Georgian, 1715–1760 (*by* C. Hussey, 1956, rev.ed. 1965): Houghton Hall,

pp. 72–66; Holkham Hall, pp. 134–49; Langley Park, pp. 182–4.
Late Georgian, 1800–1840 (*by* C. Hussey, 1958): Sheringham Hall, pp. 103–114.

8412 WAKELING, C. Change or decay: an exhibition of photographs looking at the ways in which various Norfolk houses have been adapted to new uses. [Held at Centre of East Anglian Studies, Earlham Hall]. Norwich, 1976. P.

8413 YAXLEY, D. *and* VIRGOE, N. The manor house in Norfolk. Ipswich, 1978,

8414 AIRS, M. The designing of five East Anglian country houses, 1595–1637. *Architect. Hist.* 21, 1978, 58–67.
Incl. Raynham and Stiffkey Halls.

8415 PEART, S. Picture houses of East Anglia. Lavenham, 1980.

8416 KENWORTHY-BROWNE, J. *and others*. Burke's and Savill's guide to country houses. Vol. 3: East Anglia. [Norfolk section by M. Sayer]. 1982.

8417 WINKLEY, G. The country houses of Norfolk. Lowestoft, 1986.

VERNACULAR ARCHITECTURE

8418 BARNETT, P. W. Clay-lump building in Norfolk. *In* Building in cob and pisé de terre. (Building Research Board special reports, 5, 1922), pp. 14–18.

8419 GRIMSLEY, G. E. The country cottage in Norfolk. B.A. thesis, Manchester Univ., 1953.

8420 Norfolk farmhouses. [Series in *Eastern Daily Press* March–June, 1966].

8421 BILLETT, M. Thatching and thatched buildings. 1978. East Anglia, pp. 129–147.

8422 PENOYRE, John *and* PENOYRE, Jane. House in the landscape: a regional study of vernacular building styles in England and Wales. 1978. E. Anglia, pp. 62–79.

8423 PROCTOR, J. M. East Anglian cottages. Ely, 1979.

8424 CARTER, A. Variations in small houses plan-forms in Norfolk. N.p., 1980 [conference paper]. P.

8425 TOLHURST, P. D. The vernacular architecture of Norfolk: a sample survey. M.A. thesis, Manchester Univ., 1982.

8426 DARLEY, G. Built in Britain. 1983. North Norfolk, pp. 66–81.
Based on Channel 4 series on vernacular architecture of 8 regions.

8427 Three parsonage houses. *Bull. Norfolk Research Committee* 29, 1983, 12–18.
Descriptions of Besthorpe Vicarage (C. Barringer); Rollesby Rectory (B. Cornford); S. Elmham, Suffolk (L. McMurdo).

8428 RUTLEDGE, P. Vernacular buildings in Norfolk before 1580: some documents. *NARG News* 38, 1984, 1–4.

8429 CARTER, A. *and* WADE-MARTINS, S. A year in the field: the Norfolk historic farm buildings project. Norwich, 1987.
See also S. Wade-Martins 'Farm buildings – some basic questions', *J. Hist. Farm Buildings Group* 1, 1987, 37–41.

8430 COTTON, B. D. Cottage and farmhouse furniture in East Anglia: regional styles in the 18th and 19th centuries. Norwich, 1987.

8431 McCANN, J. Is clay lump a traditional building material? *Vernacular Architecture* 18, 1987, 1–16.
Suggests this technique was introduced in East Anglia only in early 19th century.

8432 BOUWENS, D. Clay lump in south Norfolk: observations and recollections. *Ibid.* 19, 1988, 10–18.

See also nos. 8026, 8049–50, 8593, 9883, 9892, 9936.

MILLS

8433 FLINT, B. Windmills of East Anglia. Ipswich, 1972. P.

8434 RYE, C. G. The end of the corn mills in the Fleggs. *N.A.* 36, 1975, 185–90.

8435 BROWN, R. J. Windmills of England. 1976. Norfolk. pp. 144–59.

8436 SCOTT, M. The restoration of windmills and windpumps in Norfolk. Drawings by M. Harris. Norwich, 1977.

8437 SMITH, A. C. Drainage windmills of the Norfolk marshes: a contemporary survey. Stevenage, 1978.

8438 NORFOLK WINDMILLS TRUST. Windmills to visit: a guide to prominent Norfolk windmills and windpumps. Norwich, 1979. P.

8439 SMITH, A. C. Corn windmills in Norfolk: a contemporary survey. Stevenage, 1982.

8440 APLING, H. Norfolk corn and other windmills. Vol.1. Norwich, 1984.

See also nos. 8982, 8986, 9109, 9189, 9222, 9286, 9401, 9848, 9894, 10112–3, 10119.

SPECIAL FEATURES

8441 PROCTOR, F. *and* MILLER, P. The story of village and town signs in Norfolk. 3 vols. Norwich, 1973–83.

8442 HEDGES, A. A. C. Inns and inn signs of Norfolk and Suffolk. Fenstanton, 1976.

8443 BOURNE, U. East Anglian town and village signs. Princes Risborough, 1986.

CHURCH ARCHITECTURE

GENERAL WORKS

8444 FREEMAN, E. A. The perpendicular of Somerset compared with that of East Anglia. *Trans. Somerset Archaeol. and Natural Hist. Soc.* 5, 1855, 1–28.

8445 BRANDON, R. *and* BRANDON, J. A. The open timber roofs of the Middle Ages. 1860.
Plates deal in large part with Norfolk examples.

8446 FAIRWEATHER, F. H. Additions to the plans of Norman priory churches in Norfolk. *In* INGLEBY, C., *ed.* Supplement to Blomefield's Norfolk (1929), pp. 317–40.

8447 PAGE, G. G. East Anglian niches during the perpendicular period. R.I.B.A. thesis, 1938.

8448 WILKS, J. C. A study of the Norman church doorways of Norfolk parish churches. R.I.B.A. thesis, 1938.

8449 MAW, P. G. The evolution of medieval church architecture in Norfolk. R.I.B.A. thesis, 1947.

8450 BREWSTER, K. A. Timber features of Norfolk parish churches. R.I.B.A. thesis, 1948.

8450A MESSENT, C. J. W. The round towers to English parish churches. Norwich, 1958. Norfolk, pp. 2–249, 364–6.

8451 BRISLEY AND ELMHAM RURAL DEANERY. Church tours. [Mileham, 1969–72].
Collection of brochures giving brief histories of parish churches of deanery.

8452 FAWCETT, R. The architecture and furnishings of Norfolk churches (Norfolk Soc.). Norwich, 1974. P.

8453 FAWCETT, R. Late Gothic architecture in Norfolk: an examination of the work of some individual architects in the 14th and 15th centuries. Ph.D. thesis, Univ. of E. Anglia, 1975.

8454 ROAST, T. R. Sound-holes: a feature of Norfolk church towers. B.A. thesis, N.E. Essex Technical College, 1975.

8455 Some Broadland churches. Norwich, 1975. P.

8456 MANSFIELD, H. O. Norfolk churches: their foundations, architecture furnishings. Lavenham, 1976.

8457 CHERRY, B. Romanesque architecture in eastern England. *J. Brit. Archaeol. Assoc.* 131, 1978, 79–109.

8458 COTTON, S., TRICKER, R. *and others.* [Norfolk Churches Trust: brief guides]. Holt, 1978–.

Churches for which guides have been issued incl. Barney, Barnham Broom, Barton Bendish, Blo' Norton, Brandiston, Bressingham, Brettenham, Bridgham, Burgh-next-Aylsham, Burlingham, North Creake, Deopham, Dunton, Eccles, Edgefield, Flordon, Forncett (S. Edmund; S. Mary; S. Peter), Framingham Earl, Garboldisham, Griston, Guestwick, Hackford, Hargham, Hillington, Great Hockham, Horsey, Ickburgh, Illington, Larling, Merton, Northwold, Reymerston, Riddlesworth, Rockland (All Saints; S. Peter), Rushford, Scottow, Stow Bedon, Swanton Abbot, Thompson, Thorpe Market, Thursford, Walpole (St. Andrew), Westwick. Wiggenhall (S. Mary Magdalen; S. Mary the Virgin), Wilby, Wood Dalling, East Wretham.

8459 COTTON, S. Building the late medieval church. *NARG News* 16, 1979, 10–16.

See also his article on medieval brickwork, *ibid.* 20, 1980, 7–9.

8460 DEAN, M. A. The beginnings of decorated architecture in the Southeast Midlands and East Anglia. Ph.D. thesis, Univ. of California, 1979.

8461 MARR, L. From my point of view: a personal record of some Norfolk churches. Sculthorpe, 1979.

8462 FAWCETT, R. A group of churches by the architect of Great Walsingham. *N.A.* 37, 1980, 277–94.

Identifies features of churches of G. Walsingham, Beeston St. Mary, Tunstead, Beetley, Little Fransham, Rougham, Narborough, Mileham and Houghton-Le-Dale (Slipper Chapel) as work of same architect. c. 1350.

8463 COTTON, S. Tradition and authority in church building. *NARG News* 26, 1981, 8–13.

Compares some statements in Blomefield relative to medieval church building with other evidence.

8464 MORTLOCK, D. P. *and* ROBERTS, C. V. Popular guide to Norfolk churches. 1: North-East Norfolk. 2: Central and South Norfolk [with Norwich]. 3: West and South-West Norfolk. Fakenham, 1981 [vol.1]; Cambridge, 1985 [vols.2–3].

8465 COTTON, S. *and* FAWCETT, R. Further aspects of medieval church building. *NARG News* 28, 1982, 5–14; 31, 1982, 1–7; 33, 1983, 20–21.

8466 GOODE, W. J. East Anglian round towers and their churches. Lowestoft, 1982.

8467 CATTERMOLE, P. *and* COTTON, S. Medieval parish church building in Norfolk. *N.A.* 38, 1983, 235–79.

Gazeteer, compiled from references in wills etc.

8468 COTTON, S. On the coexistence of curvilinear and perpendicular. *NARG News* 32, 1983, 1–8.

8469 SAVE BRITAIN'S HERITAGE. The fate of a thousand churches. Part 1: East Anglia. Introd. by Celia de la Hey. 1984.
Photographs of redundant churches.

8470 COTTON, S. Some Norfolk medieval architects. *NARG News* 40, 1985, 11–18.

8471 COTTON, S. The medieval church's development. *Ibid.* 44, 1986, 1–11.

8472 THOROLD, H. Collins guide to cathedrals, abbeys and priories. 1985. Norfolk, pp. 173–9.
Brief description of Norwich Cathedral, Binham, Ingham, Weybourne, and Wymondham abbeys.

8473 BATY, E. Victorian church building and restoration in the diocese of Norwich, Ph.D. thesis, Univ. of E. Anglia, 1987.

8474 COTTON, S. Nice things in small packages. *NARG News* 49, 1987, 8–14.
On small village churches.

8475 LINDLEY, P. G. The 'Arminghall Arch' and contemporary sculpture in Norwich. *N.A.* 40, 1987, 19–43.
Fourteenth-century sculptured archways, prob. from Carmelite convent at Norwich (later incorporated into Arminghall Old Hall, and now into Norwich Magistrates' Court).

8476 BATCOCK, N. The parish church in Norfolk in the 11th and 12th centuries. *In* BLAIR, J., *ed.* Minsters and parish churches: the local church in transition (Oxford Univ. Committee for Archaeology, monograph 17, 1988), pp. 179–90.

8477 HEYWOOD, S. The round towers of East Anglia. *Ibid.*, pp. 169–77.

8478 JACKMAN, B. England's god-forsaken churches. *Sunday Times Mag.* 16 Oct. 1988, 40–48.

See also nos. 7464, 8972, 10132.

STAINED GLASS

8479 DRAKE, M. The Costessey collection of stained glass, formerly in the possession of... [the] 8th Baron Stafford. Exeter, 1920.

8480 KING, D. J. Stained glass tours around Norfolk churches. (Norfolk Society). Norwich, 1974.

See also nos. 9108, 9134, 9375.

SCREENS AND MURALS

8481 HENFREY, H. W. *and* WATLING, H. East Anglian rood screens. *J. Brit. Archaeol. Soc.* 37, 1881, 135–40.

8482 BRINDLEY, H. H. Saint Christopher. *In* INGLEBY, C., *ed.* Supplement to Blomefield's Norfolk (1929), pp. 299–314.
Murals representing Christopher in Norfolk churches.

8483 CAMM, B. Some Norfolk rood-screens. *Ibid.*, pp. 239–95.

8484 TALBOT, H. J. The Gothic rood-screen in Norfolk. R.I.B.A. thesis, 1958.

8485 PLUNKETT, G. A. F. Norfolk church screens – 1865 survey. *N.A.* 37, 1979, 178–89.

8486 COTTON, S. Medieval roodscreens in Norfolk – their construction and painting dates. *N.A.* 40, 1987, 44–54.

See also nos. 9015, 9065, 9068, 9891, 10121.

FONTS

8487 TOMLINSON, H. Some Norfolk fonts. *In* INGLEBY, C., *ed*. Supplement to Blomefield's Norfolk (1929), pp. 207–36.

See also no. 8244.

BRASSES

8488 HAINES, H. A manual of monumental brasses. 1861. Norfolk, pp. 133–54.
RCF copy enlarged by E. M. Beloe.

8489 BELOE, E. M. Some lost brasses of Norfolk. *In* INGLEBY, C., *ed*. Supplement to Blomefield's Norfolk (1929), pp. 99–121.

8490 LINNELL, C. L. S. East Anglian chalice brasses. *Trans. Monumental Brass Soc.* 8, 1950, 356–65; 9, 1952/54, 76–9, 168–9.

8491 LE STRANGE, R. A complete descriptive guide to British monumental brasses, 1972. Norfolk. pp. 89–96.

8492 The complete brass-rubbing guide to the figure brasses in ... Norfolk. Norwich, [c. 1973].

8493 GREENWOOD, R. *and* NORRIS, M. The brasses of Norfolk churches. [Norwich], 1976.

8494 SPINKS, W. A memento from old England. Bardwell, 1977.
Describes notable brasses. mostly E. Anglian.

8495 BLATCHLY, J. M. The lost cross brasses of Norfolk, 1300–1400. *Trans. Monumental Brass Soc.* 13, 1981, 87–107.

See also nos. 8614, 8959, 9022, 9149, 9176, 9359, 9784, 9863, 9944, 9978.

MONUMENTS

8496 SPENCER, N. Sculptured monuments in Norfolk churches. Norwich, 1977.
See also no. 8758, 10124.

BELLS

8497 BEVIS, T. A. Church bells of the Fens: Isle of Ely and Lynn Marshland, [March, 1957].

See also no. 9811.

PAINTING

8498 EAST OF ENGLAND ART UNION. First exhibition. Norwich, 1842. P. RCF.

8499 STEPHEN, G. A. Norfolk artists. Norwich, 1915. P.

8500 NORWICH CASTLE MUSEUM. Catalogue of the Norwich school pictures. Norwich, 1937.
Cf. *B.N.H.* 2330, 2333.

8501 BARNARD, G. V. Paintings of the Norwich School, Norwich, [1950]. BL.

8502 WILLIAMS, I. A. Early English watercolours. 1952. Reprint ed., 1970. Chap. 8: the East Anglians.

8503 NEWBY, D., *ed*. East Anglian arts, crafts. and antiques. Halesworth, 1967–
Annual guide to galleries, workshops, etc.

8504 ROYAL INSTITUTE GALLERY. East Anglian art today. An exhibition... sponsored by the East Anglian Daily Times. 1969.

8505 BORSA, J. Printmaking and the Norwich School in the early 19th century. M.A. thesis, Univ. of E. Anglia, 1974.

8506 MALLALIEU, H. The Norwich School. Crome, Cotman and their followers. 1974.

8506A OSCAR AND PETER JOHNSON LTD. East Anglian art. [Exhibition cat.]. 1975.

8507 RAJNAI, M. *and* STEVENS, M. The Norwich Society of Artists, 1805–1833: a dictionary of contributors and their work. Norwich, 1976.

8508 FAWCETT, T. C. Eighteenth century art in Norfolk. *Walpole Soc.* 46, 1976/78, 71–90.

8509 RAJNAI, M. The Norwich schools of painters. (Jarrold Colour publications). Norwich, 1978. P.

8510 HEMINGWAY, A. The Norwich School of painters, 1803–33, Oxford, 1979.

8511 JACOBS, M. *and* WARNER, M. Art in East Anglia. Norwich, 1980.

8512 TILLYARD, V. Painters in 16th and 17th century Norwich. *N.A.* 37, 1980, 315–9.

8513 MOORE, A. The Norwich School of artists. Norwich, 1985.

8514 NORFOLK AND NORWICH ART CIRCLE. Norfolk and Norwich Art Circle, 1885–1985: a history of the Circle and the centenary exhibition. Norwich, 1985.

8515 RAJNAI, M. The Norwich School of etching. *In* HARTLEY, C. *and* RIDYARD, S., *eds*. The print in England, 1790–1830 (Cambridge, 1985), pp. 70–95.

8516 MOORE, A. W. Dutch and Flemish painting in Norfolk: a history of taste and influence, fashion, and collecting. 1988.

See also nos. 8567–9, 8582, 8635, 8650–60, 8665, 8668–71, 8678–9, 8830–5, 8846, 8886, 8890–5, 8901, 8905, 9489, 9629, 9866.

NORFOLK 'VIEWS'

8517 DIXON, R. Sketches illustrative of the picturesque scenery of Norfolk. Norwich, 1811.

8518 HODGSON, D. Antiquarian remains, principally confined to Norwich and Norfolk. N.p., [1842].

8519 SIMPSON, R. J. Leaves from my sketchbook. 8 parts. N.p., [c. 1890]–1896. A few parts have titles: 1. *From Bacton to Weybourne*. 6. *The churches of Tunstead and Worstead*. 7. *Brasses in Blickling Church*. 8. *North Creake Church and Abbey*.

8520 COOPER. A. H. Norfolk: water colours. 1926. RCF.

8521 POOLE, D. Broadland sketches. Horning, 1979.

8522 POOLE, D. Norfolk coast sketches. Norwich, 1980.

8523 BARLOW, J. North Norfolk landscapes. [Text] by M. Pedrick. Field Dalling, 1985.

8524 TOOKEY, J. East Anglia. Watercolours by John Tookey. Words by Paul Jennings, 1986.

See also nos. 7406, 7434, 9348, 9778–83, 10232.

APPLIED ARTS

8525 DAVY, T. *and* CLAIRFIELD, D. Norfolk ginger beer bottles. E. Dereham, 1977.

8526 COLMAN FOODS. The Colman collection of silver mustard pots. Norwich, 1979.

8527 HENIG, M. *and* HESLOP, T. A. Three thirteenth-century seal matrices with intaglio stones in the Castle Museum, Norwich. *N.A.* 39, 1986, 305–9.

8528 WEEDON, G. Painted fairground panels by the Whiting family of Norwich from Hatwells' Galloping Horse Roundabout. *National Art-Collections Fund Rev.* 1987, 123–5.

See also no. 9743.

GARDENS AND PARKS

8529 BARDSWELL, F. A. Sea coast gardens and gardening. 1908.

8530 HOLME, C., *ed.* The gardens of England, in the Midland and Eastern Counties. 1908.

8531 THACKER, C. Register of parks and gardens of special historic interest: part 29, Norfolk. [English Heritage dossier]. 1988.

See also nos. 8569, 8874–5, 9019, 9172, 9365, 9877, 9943.

BIOGRAPHY

COLLECTIVE BIOGRAPHY

GENERAL WORKS

8532 FULLER, T. History of the worthies of England endeavoured by Thomas Fuller. 1662. Other eds. 1811, 1840.

Contains Norfolk section (vol. 2, pp. 444–95, of 1840 ed.)

8533 [LANGHAM, G. H.] Eminent East Anglians. (London Society of E. Anglians). 1804.

8534 JONES, *Mrs.* H. The worthies of Norwich. Norwich, 1892.

First sketched in *Edinburgh Rev.* July 1879, 41–76; and later incorporated in her *Some Norfolk worthies* (See *B.N.H.* 2363, 2366).

8535 STEPHEN, G. A. Earlham roads: notes on local celebrities after whom the roads on the Earlham Housing Estate are named. Norwich, 1930. P.

8536 HENDRY, H. D. The city of Norwich, West Earlham estate: derivation of road names. Norwich, 1981. P.

8537 MARSDEN, W. Resting places in East Anglia. Romford, 1987.

Guide to burial places of some E. Anglian notables.

See also nos. 7951, 7963, 8047, 8339, 8373, 8499, 8507.

GENEALOGY

8538 NORFOLK RECORD OFFICE. Notes for the assistance of genealogists. Norwich, 1966. Revised eds., 1970, 1978. P.

8539 NORFOLK AND NORWICH GENEALOGICAL SOCIETY. Journal, 1972–77. *Continued as* The Norfolk Ancestor.

8540 PALGRAVE-MOORE, P. *and* SAYER, M. J. A selection of revised and unpublished Norfolk pedigrees. 4 pts. *Norfolk Geneal.* 6, 1974; 8, 1976; 13, 1981; 17, 1985.

8541 SAYER, M. J. Norfolk visitation families: a short social structure. *N.A.* 36, 1975, 176–82.

Families recorded by heralds' visitations, 1563–1664. See also postscript on disclaimers, *ibid* 37, 1980, 319–20.

8542 NORFOLK AND NORWICH GENEALOGICAL SOCIETY. Norfolk families: a list of Norfolk and Norwich Genealogical Society members and the family names they are researching. Norwich, 1979. 2nd ed. 1982. 3rd ed. 1986. Supplements, 1987, 1988. P.

8543 FONE, J. F., *ed*. Index to Norwich marriages, 1813–1837. *Norfolk Gen* 1l. 14, 1982.

8544 COLDHAM, P. W. Bonded passengers to America. 9 vols. in 3. Baltimore, 1983. Vol. 7: Norfolk circuit, 1663–1775.

8545 SOCIETY OF GENEALOGISTS. National index to parish registers. Vol. 7: Norfolk, Suffolk, and Cambridgeshire. [Ed. P. T. R. Palgrave-Moore]. 1983. Norfolk, pp. 46–177.

8546 NORFOLK AND NORWICH GENEALOGICAL SOCIETY. Norfolk nonconformist registers. Norwich, 1983–. 1: Mattishall and Dereham Congregational, 1772–1837; Mattishall and Watton Primitive Methodist, 1832–37. 2: Framingham Pigot Particular Baptist, 1808–36. 3: Downham Market Weslyan Methodist, 1814–37. 4: Shelfanger Particular Baptist, 1795–1837. 5: Diss Particular Baptist, 1806–36.

8547 BELLINGER, R. The Amicable Society for a Perpetual Assurance office. *Norfolk Ancestor* 3 (4), 1984, 47–51.
Lists Norfolk names in first policy register (1706–07) of this early insurance society

8548 HAMLIN, P. E. *and others*. Norfolk Peculiar jurisdictions: index to probate records, 1416–1857; index of marriage licence bonds, 1624–1860. *Norfolk Geneal*. 16, 1984.

8549 NORFOLK AND NORWICH GENEALOGICAL SOCIETY. The parish registers of Norfolk. Monograph series. Norwich, 1984–. 1: Rackheath. 2: Bodney. 3: Dunston. 4: Threxton. 5: Shingham. 6: Frenze. 7: Ryston cum Roxham. 8: Taverham. 9: Didlington with Colveston. 10: Cranwich. 11: Fordham. 12: Boughton. 13: Cockley Cley. 14: Barton Bendish, All Saints. 15: Barton Bendish, St. Andrew. 16: Santon. 17: Bexwell. 18: Langford. 19: Ickburgh. 20:Little Cressingham. 21: West Tofts. 22: Stanford with Sturston. 23: Gooderstone. 24: Colney. 25: Shelfanger. 26: Royden.

8550 NORFOLK AND NORWICH GENEALOGICAL SOCIETY. Norfolk strays. Ed . Perkins. 1: Yorkshire and Chesterfield. 2: Miscellaneous. Norwich, 1985/8 .

8551 NORFOLK AND NORWICH GENEALOGICAL SOCIETY. Index to bishops' transcripts from the diocese of Norwich. Ed. S. Bell. 3 parts: 1685–91; 1705; 1715. Norwich, 1986.

8552 CHURCH OF JESUS CHRIST OF LATTER DAY SAINTS. The parish and vital records lists of England for the *International Genealogical Index*, 3: Norfolk, Suffolk, Essex. Salt Lake City (Utah), 1987.
NPL holds current fiches of Index for British Isles as a whole.

See also nos. 7647, 8275, 8951, 8963, 9124, 9312, 9488, 9830, 9858, 9986, 9988, 10023, 10056.

PERSONAL NAMES

8553 McKINLEY, R. Norfolk and Suffolk surnames in the Middle Ages. (English Surnames Ser. 2). 1975.

8554 SELTEN, B. The Anglo-Saxon heritage in Middle English personal names: East Anglia, 1100–1399. 2 parts. Lund (Sweden), 1972/79.
See also his *Early English nicknames* (Lund, 1975).

HERALDRY

8555 DULEEP SINGH, *Prince* F. V. Some arms in Norwich houses. *N.A.M.* 2nd ser. 1, 1906, 100–113.

8556 NORFOLK HERALDRY SOCIETY. The Norfolk Standard [periodical], Norwich, 1976–.

8557 SUMMERS, P., *ed.* Hatchments in Britain, Vol. 2: Norfolk and Suffolk. 1976.

8558 NORFOLK HERALDRY SOCIETY. A display of heraldry held at the Tourist Information Office, Tombland, on the occasion of the Norwich-Rouen twinning weekend. Norwich, 1978. P.

8559 FISKE, R. C. Norfolk heraldic artists. *Norfolk Standard* 2, 1980/81, 78–6 (Charles Catton, sr.); 99–103 (W. R. Weyer); 115–7 (C. N. Elvin).

See also nos. 9291, 9878.

WILLS

8560 PALGRAVE-MOORE, P., *ed.* Index of wills proved in the Norfolk Archdeaconry court, 1560–1603/04. *Norfolk Geneal.* 10, 1978.

8561 LEVINE, G. J. More Norwich goldsmiths' wills. *N.A.* 37, 1979, 208–12.

8562 FROSTICK, C., *ed.* Index of wills proved in the Consistory Court of Norwich, 1819–1857. *N.R.S.* 47, 1980.

INSCRIPTIONS

8563 RYE, W. Copies of the inscriptions in the churches of Swafield and Edingthorpe., and the churches of Edingthorpe, Acle, Stokesby, and Hoveton St. John. *N.A.M.* 2, 1883, 509–23.

8564 CRISP, F. A. Fragmenta Genealogica. 14 vols. 1889–1910.
Various Norfolk references, but note esp. vol. 3, pp. 1–28: 'Norwich church notes'; and vol. 9 'Suffolk and Norfolk church notes'.

8565 LAMONT-BROWN, R. East Anglian epitaphs. Fakenham, 1980.

8566 HAMLIN, P. E., *ed.* Rosary Cemetery: monumental inscriptions, 1819–1986; and burials, 1821–37. *Norfolk Geneal.* 18, 1986,

See also nos. 9170, 9192, 9992, 10079.

PORTRAITS

8567 [Portraits of distinguished characters connected with the county of Norfolk. Etched by W. C. Edwards.] UEA.
Series of prints done in 1840s, and bound by a collector.

8568 FARRER, E. Catalogue of collection of Norfolk and Suffolk portraits, the gift of... Prince F. V. Duleep Singh, exhibited at the Guildhall, Thetford. [Thetford], 1927.

8569 NORWICH CASTLE MUSEUM. Loan exhibition of portraits in the landscape park, from Norfolk and Suffolk houses. Norwich, 1948. P.

INDIVIDUAL AND FAMILY BIOGRAPHY A – Z

ARTERTON
8570 JONES, A. The Felthorpe Artertons, 1811–1933. *Norfolk Ancestor* 4 (6), 1987, 88–90.

ASHFORD
8571 MALCOLMSON, R. Daisy Ashford: her life. 1984.

ASTLEY
8572 MILLER, A. C. Herbert Astley, Dean of Norwich: 'a man of good comfortable spirit'. *N.A.* 38, 1982, 149–67.
Prebendary 1663, Dean 1670–81.

ATKYNS
8573 TISDALL, E. E. P. Mrs. 'Pimpernel' Atkyns. 1965.
Charlotte Atkyns, of Ketteringham Hall.

AUSTIN
8574 HAMBURGER, L. Troubled lives: John and Sarah Austin. Toronto, 1985.
Sarah Austin, daughter of John Taylor of Norwich.

BACON
8575 MAHL, M. R. Giles Fletcher and the Bacons. *N.A.* 36, 1976, 280–82.
8576 PREST, W. An Australian holding of Norfolk mss: the Bacon-Townshend papers at the University of Adelaide. *N.A.* 37, 1978, 121–3.
Small collection, with docs. ranging from 1542 to 1629.
8576A KEY, J. The letters and will of Lady Dorothy Bacon, 1597-1629. M.A. thesis, Univ. of E. Anglia, 1986.
8577 LINDSAY, D. Sir Edmund Bacon: a Norfolk life. Maldon, 1988.
8578 SMITH, A. H., BAKER, G. M. *and* KENNY, R.W., *eds.* The papers of Nathaniel Bacon of Stiffkey. 2 vols. [to date]. *N.R.S.* 46, 1978/79; 49, 1982/83.
See also nos. 8932, 9989–91.

BAGNALL-OAKLEY
8579 LOCKHART, B. L. Dick Bagnall-Oakley: a tribute to a Norfolk naturalist. Norwich, 1987.

BAGSHAW
8580 BAGSHAW, R. Poppies to Paston. Wymondham, 1986.

BAINES
8581 LUCKETT, H. Thomas Baines, 1820–1875. [Exhib. cat.] [Norwich], 1975. P.
See also associated *Handlist [of exhibits]*, publ. by King's Lynn Museum, where exhibition was staged.

BARBER
8582 FRYER, F. A. A sculptor of Felbrigg [Judy Barber]. *E.A.M.* Nov. 1981, 30–31.

BARR
8583 BARR, D. A family way. Norwich, [1976].

BARRITT
8584 BARRITT, R. A. Barrits of the Fenlands. Upminster, [c. 1968]. P.

BATES
8585 BATES, F. Reminiscences and autobiography of a musician in retirement. Norwich, 1930.
Dr. Frank Bates, Cathedral organist, 1885–1928.

BEAUMONT
8586 WALKLETT, H. The swift witness: George Beaumont, a radical reformer, 1763–1841. Oxford, 1985.
Minister at Ebenezer Chapel, Ber St.

BEDINGFELD
8587 WEIKEL, A. The rise and fall of a Marian privy councillor: Sir Henry Bedingfeld, 1509/11–1585. N.A. 40, 1987, 73–83.

BENTINCK
8588 SCHAZMANN, P-E. The Bentincks: the history of a European family. 1976.

BENTON
8589 BENTON, E. O. Man and boy in a Norfolk village. Weston Longville, 1981.

BIGOD
8590 MILLER, R. G. The Bigod brothers in 13th century England, 1212–1270. Ph.D. thesis, Mississippi State Univ., 1973.
8591 ATKIN, S. J. The Bigod family and its estates, 1066–1306. Ph.D. thesis, Reading Univ., 1980.

BISHOP
8592 BISHOP, B. Cley Marsh and its birds: 50 years as warden. Woodbridge, 1983.

BLACKBURN
8593 BLACKBURN, S. The life of a Norfolk thatcher. Ed. R. Precy. N.p., [1982].

BLOFELD
8594 [BLOFELD, G.] An account of the Blofeld family of Hoveton House. N.p., [c. 1978].

BLOGG See no. 7896.

BLOMEFIELD
8595 NORWICH PUBLIC LIBRARY. Francis Blomefield, 1705–1752, historian and topographer. [Exhib. cat.]. Norwich, 1952. P.

8596 HAWES, T. L. M. Genealogy of the Rev. Francis Blomefield, *N.A.* 33, 1981, 59–66.

8597 STOKER, D. The compilation and production of a classic county history: Francis Blomefield's *History of Norfolk*. M.Phil. thesis, Reading Univ., 1982.

8598 BLOMEFIELD, M. The bulleymung pit: the story of a Norfolk farmer's child. 1946.
Presented as children's literature. See also sequels *Nuts in the rookery* (1946) and *Bow-net and water lilies* (1948).

BLOOM
8599 BLOOM, A. Prelude to Bressingham. Lavenham, 1975.
Cf. *B.N.H.* 3614.

8600 BLOOM, U. The rose of Norfolk [Frances Graver Bloom, b. 1809]. 1964.

8601 BLOOM U. Price above rubies. [Mary Gardner Bloom, b. 1860]. 1965.

BLYTH
8602 BLYTH, M. M. The family of Blyth of Norfolk. N.p., 1937. P.
Updates item 2520 in *B.N.H.*

BODHAM
8603 JOHNSON, M. B. Mrs. Bodham. *Quart. J. Parson Woodforde Soc.* 19 (2), 1986, 7–26.
Nee Anne Donne (1748–1846), daughter of Rev. Roger Donne, rector of Catfield.

BOOTY
8604 BOOTY, H. Some Bootys and their forebears: a family history... Privately publ., 1976.
Further elaborated in *The Bootys of Norfolk, Suffolk, Kent and Devonshire.* (N.p., 1983).

BORROW
8605 DEARDEN, S. The gypsy gentleman: a study of George Borrow. 1939.

8606 FITZGERALD, B. S. V. Gypsy Borrow. 1953.

8607 NORFOLK COUNTY LIBRARY. George Borrow, 1803–1881. [Exhibition cat.]. Norwich, 1981. P.

8608 COLLIE, M. George Borrow: eccentric. Cambridge, 1982.

8609 RIDLER, A. M. Norwich libraries and George Borrow. *Library Hist.* 6, 1983, 61–71.
Details libraries accessible to Borrow.

8610 COLLLIE, M. *and* FRASER, A. George Borrow: a bibliographical study. 1984.

8611 FENWICK, G., *ed.* Proceedings of the 1987 George Borrow conference. Toronto, 1988.

BRADFIELD
8612 Ted Bradfield of Heacham. King's Lynn, 1980. P.

BRANDON
8613 GUNN, S. J. Charles Brandon, Duke of Suffolk, c. 1484–1545. Oxford, 1988.
Influential in Norfolk as well as Suffolk.

BRASYER

8614 BADHAM, S. Brasses to the Brasyer family in St. Stephen's Church, Norwich. *Trans. Monumental Brass Soc.* 12, 1978, 295–9.

BREWER

8615 JEWSON, C. B. The Brewer family [of Norwich]. *Baptist Quart.* n.s. 13, 1950, 213–20.

BROOM

8616 BROOM, A. S. Bob's boy: the life story of a Norfolk countryman. Illustr. and ed. David Poole. Sprowston, 1984.

BROWNE

8617 Browne of Elsing, co. Norfolk. [Repr. from *Miscellanea Geneal. et Herald.*] 1937. P.

8618 MILEHAM, J. Dame Dorothy Browne and the family of Mileham of Burlingham. *Norfolk Ancestor* 2 (8), 1982, 104–9.
Wife of Sir. T. Browne.

8619 BATTY SHAW, A. Sir Thomas Browne: the man and the physician. *J. Royal College of Surgeons* 60, 1978, 336–44.

8620 PATRIDES, C. A., *ed.* Approaches to Sir Thomas Browne: Ann Arbor tercentenary lectures and essays. Columbia, Miss., 1982.

8621 ROYAL COLLEGE OF PHYSICIANS. Sir Thomas Browne and the baroque. [Exhib. cat.]. 1982.

8622 BATTY SHAW, A. Sir Thomas Browne of Norfolk. (Browne 300 Committee). Norwich, 1982. P.

8623 FINCH, J. S., *ed.* A catalogue of the libraries of Sir Thomas Browne and Dr. Edward Browne, his son: a facsimile reproduction, with an introduction, notes, and index. Leiden, 1986.
Reprints auction catalogue of 1710/11.

On Sir Thomas Browne see also no. 8848.

BUCK

8624 MALING, J. J. Comment on a Norfolk parson. [Rev. E. J. Buck of Wicklewood]. *E.A.M.* Dec. 1981, 72–4.

8625 GEDGE, D. Zechariah [Buck] and his choir. *Musical Opinion* 109, 1986, 82–5, 124–7, 167–70, 209–12, 248–50.

BURN

8626 BURN, M. P. [Memoir of William Pelham Burn, 1859–1901, Vicar of St. Peter Mancroft]. [Duplicated], N.d.

BURNEY

8627 RIBEIRO, A. F. V. An edition of the letters of Dr. Charles Burney, from 1751–1784. D.Phil. thesis, Oxford Univ., 1980.

8628 WOOD, F. A. A great-niece's journals: being extracts from the journals of Fanny Anne Burney (Mrs. Wood), from 1830–1842. Ed. M. S. Rolt, 1926.

BURTON
8629 BURTON, J. Transport of delight. 1977.
Year's diary of Methodist minister-cum-bus driver.

BUSH See no. 9406.

BUTTES See no. 8932.

BUXTON
8630 BUXTON, A. Fisherman naturalist. 1946.
See also *Happy year: the days of a fisherman naturalist* (1950).
8631 BUXTON, E. E. Family sketchbook: a hundred years ago. Arranged by her granddaughter Ellen R. C. Creighton. 1964. Rev. ed. 1969.
Extends item 2598 of *B.N.H.*
8631A ANDERSON, M. Noel Buxton, a life. 1952.
M.P. for N. Norfolk, 1910–30, and first Baron Noel-Buxton.
8632 STUART, F. C. A critical edition of the correspondence of Sir Thomas Fowell Buxton, with an account of his career to 1823. M.A. thesis, London Univ., 1957.
8633 PUGH, P. M. Calendar of the papers of Sir Thomas Fowell Buxton (List and Index Soc., special ser. 13). 1980.

CAMPBELL
8634 CAMPBELL, C. The peewit's cry: a Norfolk childhood. Ipswich, 1980.
West Runton connections.

CARR
8635 ROBERTSON, B. *and* ALLEY, R. David Carr: the discovery of an artist. 1987.
1915–68. Lived at Starston. Among founders of Norfolk Contemporary Art Society.

CATTON See no. 8559.

CASTELL
8635A JACOB, D. E. Castells of Norfolk and Suffolk. N.p., 1983.

CAVELL
8636 RYDER, R. Edith Cavell. 1975.

CHAPMAN
8637 CROMBAC, G. Colin Chapman: the man and his cars. Wellingborough, 1986.
See also no. 8094.

CHESNEY
8638 CHESNEY, R. W. L. The Chesney family of Norfolk: medieval history and arms. *Norfolk Ancestor* 1 (7), 1979, 87–94.

CLARKE
8639 COLLINS, R. P. A journey in ancestry. Gloucester, 1984.
8640 FERGUSON, J. P. An 18th century heretic: Dr. Samuel Clarke. Kineton, 1976.

CLERE
8641 CORNFORD, B. The Cleres of Ormesby. *Yarmouth Archaeol.* 1 (iv), 1982, [unpaginated].

COKE
8642 COKE, *Hon.* H. J. Tracks of a rolling stone. 1905.
3rd son of T. W. Coke.
8643 SCHMIDT, L. Thomas Coke, 1st Earl of Leicester: an 18th century amateur architect. Exhibition at Holkham Hall, 1980. Freiburg, 1980. P.
8644 BARBER, J. A. A review of Mr. Gibbs' letter to Mr. Tuttell Moore... Holt, 1822. P. RCF.
See *B.N.H.* 2646–7; and also E. H. Gibbs, *A letter to T. W. Coke Esq., pointing out his connection with Mr. Barber's review* (Holt, 1822). RCF.
8645 PARKER, R. A. C. Coke of Norfolk: a financial and agricultural study, 1707–1842. Oxford, 1975.
8646 [HASSALL, W. O.] Coke of Norfolk: published on the 200th anniversary of the first Holkham Sheep Shearings. Holkham, [1978]. P.

COLMAN
8647 TILLETT, J. H. The land where sorrow is unknown. An address . . . to the working men of Stoke Holy Cross... occasioned by the lamented death of Mr. James Colman. Norwich, 1854. P.
8648 FOWLER, E. Russell James Colman (1861–1946). Some sketches for a family portrait... Norwich, 1954.

COOPER See no. 9019.

CORBET
8649 CORBET, R. Poems. 4th ed., to which is prefixed biographical notes and a life of the author by O. Gilchrist. 1807.

COTMAN
8650 HOLME, C., *ed.* Masters of English landscape painting: J. S. Cotman, David Cox, Peter de Wint. 1903.
8651 OPPÉ, A. P. The water-colour drawings of John Sell Cotman, with commentary. 1923. P.
8652 Art of John Sell Cotman. *Burlington Mag.* 81, 1942, 159 ff.
8653 PIDGLEY, M. R. John Sell Cotman's patrons, and the romantic subject picture in the 1820s and 1830s. Ph.D. thesis, Univ. of E. Anglia, 1975.
8654 RAJNAI, M. *and* ALLTHORPE-GUYTON, M. John Sell Cotman: drawings of Normandy in Norwich Castle Museum. Beccles, 1975.
8655 HOLCOMB, A. M. John Sell Cotman. (British Museum Publications). 1978.
8656 RAJNAI, M. *and* ALLTHORPE-GUYTON, M. John Sell Cotman: early drawings (1798–1812) in Norwich Castle Museum. Norwich. 1979.
8657 NORTH YORKSHIRE COUNTY RECORD OFFICE. John Sell Cotman in the Cholmeley archive: ed. A. M. Holcomb and M. Y. Ashcroft. Northallerton, 1980.
8658 MOORE, A. W. John Sell Cotman, 1782–1842 [with cat. of bicentenary exhib.]. Norwich, 1982.

8659 RAJNAI, M., *ed.* John Sell Cotman, 1782–1842. 1982.

8660 HEMINGWAY, A. Meaning in Cotman's Norfolk subjects. *Art Hist.* 7, 1984, 57–77.

COTTON

8661 HENDERSON, H. And she who gives. The story of Dorothy Cotton, S.R.N. Wymondham, 1985.

COWPER

8662 COWPER, W. Letters and prose writings. Ed. J. King and C. Ryskamp. 5 vols. Oxford, 1979–86.

8663 KING, J. William Cowper, a biography. Durham (N. Carolina), 1986.

COZENS-HARDY

8664 COZENS-HARDY, H. T. The glorious years. Random recollections of prominent persons...1897–1952. 1953.

CRASKE

8665 FESTING, S. East Anglia's artists: 5 – John Craske, *E.A.M.* Oct. 1974, 625–7.

CREMER

8666 KETTON-CREMER, R. W. Acton Cremer. *In* Norfolk Assembly (1957), pp. 92–6.

CRESSWELL

8667 DUFF, D. Whisper Louise. Edward VII and Mrs. Cresswell. 1974.

CROME

8668 GOLDBERG, N. L. John Crome and the Norwich cathedral: an enigma. *Connoiseur Year Book*, 1962, 118–25.

8669 OSCAR AND PETER JOHNSON LTD. The influence of Crome in East Anglia. [Exhib. cat.]. 1968.

8670 GOLDBERG, N. L. John Crome the elder. 2 vols. Oxford, 1978.

8671 FAWCETT, T. John Crome and the idea of Mousehold. *N.A* 38, 1982, 168–81.
On social and aesthetic implications of Crome's painting of the heath.

CROTCH

8672 RENNERT, J. William Crotch, 1775–1847: composer, artist, teacher. Lavenham, 1975.

8673 CLARK, C. L. The lectures of Dr. William Crotch. M.A. thesis, McGill Univ. (Montreal), 1981.

CUBITT

8674 UNWIN, P. A. Norfolk millwright. *E.A.M.* Apr. 1975, 278–80.
On early career of Sir William Cubitt, engineer.

See also no. 9968.

CULLUM

8675 CULLUM, F. Both sides of the fence: the autobiography of a poacher turned gamekeeper. Lowestoft, 1987.
Keeper at Great Witchingham and Raynham.

CUSTANCE

8676 CUSTANCE, T. Custance family portraits. *Quart. J. Parson Woodforde Soc.* 21 (1), 1988, 19–35.
8677 SEWELL, B. Olive Custance: her life and work. 1975.
Weston Longville family; poet and wife of Lord Alfred Douglas.

DANE

8678 PASTON, E. The Broadsman: David Dane – artist and Broadsman. Norwich, 1986.

DANIELL

8679 THISTLETHWAITE, J. The etchings of Edward Thomas Daniell (1804–42), *N.A.* 36, 1974, 1–22.

DAVIES See no. 7444.

DAWSON

8680 In memoriam. John Withers Dawson, Feb. 1800–July 1879. [Norwich, 1879]. P.

DAYNES

8681 The late Samuel Daynes P.H.M. A short biographical sketch. Norwich, [c. 1892].

DE CHAIR

8682 DE CHAIR, S. A mind on the march. 1945.
Somerset De Chair, M.P. for S.W. Norfolk, 1935–45.

DENNIS

8683 JOLLY, C. Norfolk's Peter Mackenzie. Abel Dennis of Swaffham. *E.A.M.* Feb. 1979, 226–7.

DONNE See no. 8603.

DONTHORN

8684 O'DONNELL. R. W. J. Donthorne (1799–1859): architecture with great hardness and decision in the edges. *Architect. Hist.* 21, 1978, 83–92.

DOUGHTY

8685 ROSENHEIM, J. M. Robert Doughty of Hanworth, a Restoration magistrate. *N.A.* 38, 1983, 296–312.

D'OYRY

8686 MAJOR, K. The D'Oyrys of South Lincolnshire, Norfolk and Holderness, 1130–1275. Lincoln, 1984.

DUFF

8687 PIGOTT, B. A. F. Lillian Duff. Recollections and letters...[Privately printed, 1911]. RCF.

8688 HOPE, N. Mildred Duff. A surrendered life. [1933].
Salvationists. Westwick and N. Walsham connections.

DULEEP SINGH

8689 ALEXANDER, M. *and* ALNAND, S. Queen Victoria's Maharajah. 1980.

DYE See no. 8278.

EDRICH

8690 BARKER, R. The cricketing family Edrich. 1976.

ELLIS

8691 STONE, E. Ted Ellis, the people's naturalist. Norwich, 1988.

ELWIN

8692 ELWIN, *Rev.* W. Some 18th century men of letters... with a memoir [of Elwin] by his son. 2 vols. 1902.

EMERSON

8693 TURNER, P. *and* WOOD, R. P. H. Emerson, photographer of Norfolk. 1974.

8694 NEWHALL, N. P. H. Emerson: the fight for photography as a fine art. New York, 1975.

8695 McWILLIAM, N. *and* SEKULES, V., *eds.* Life and landscape: P. H. Emerson: art and photography in East Anglia, 1885–1900. [Exhib. cat.] Norwich, 1986.

On P. H. Emerson see also no. 7444.

EYRE

8696 HOLT, T. G. A Note on Bury's Hall in Norfolk. *Recusant Hist.* 18, 1987, 440–3.
Concerns Eyre family of Holme Hale and their chaplains in early 18th century. Further material in R. Meredith, 'The Eyres of Hassop', *ibid.* 9, 1967/68, 5–38, 267–87.

FASTOLF

8697 ARMSTRONG, C. A. J. Sir John Fastolf and the law of arms. *In* ALLMAND, C. T., *ed.* War, literature and politics in the late Middle Ages (Liverpool, 1976), pp. 46–56.

8698 SMITH, A. R. Aspects of the career of Sir John Fastolf, 1380–1459. D.Phil. thesis, Oxford Univ., 1982.

8699 SMITH, A. Litigation and politics: Sir John Fastolf's defence of his English property *In* POLLARD, A. J., *ed.* Property and politics: essays in later medieval English history (Gloucester, 1984), pp. 59–75.

See also nos. 7757, 8319.

FAVERCHES See no. 8238.

FELBRIGG See no. 7761.

FENN
8700 FENN, I. Tales of Norfolk. Wymondham, 1976.
Childhood reminiscences.
8701 SERPELL, M. F. Sir John Fenn, his friends, and the Paston letters. *Antiq. J.* 63, 1983, 95–121.

FILBY
8702 BOWYER, B. Filby roots: a record of the Filby family for over 250 years. N.p., [c. 1984].

FISHER
8703 [FISHER, F. O.] De stemmate Piscatoris: a tale of sea toilers. [1909].
Deals with family Fisher of Great Yarmouth. An additional chapter, described as vol. iv. was publ. in 1932 (Norwich).
8704 FISHER, *Lady* R. My jungle babies. 1979.
Deals with her work at Kilverstone Wild Life Park.

FLEMING
8705 LINDSAY, D. Friends for life: a portrait of Launcelot Fleming. Seaford, 1981.
Bishop of Norwich, 1959–71.

FOUNTAINE
8706 FORD, B. Sir Andrew Fountaine, one of the keenest virtuosi of his age, *Apollo* 122, Nov. 1985, 353–63.
8707 FOUNTAINE, M. Love among the butterflies; travels and adventures of a Victorian lady. Ed. W. F. Cater. 1980.
Later diaries publ. as *Butterflies and late loves* (1986).

FRY
8708 JONES, *Mrs.* H. Elizabeth Fry. *In* Some Norfolk worthies (1899), pp. 113–50.
8709 PRINGLE, P. The prisoners' friend: the story of Elizabeth Fry. 1953.
8710 ROSE, J. Elizabeth Fry. 1980
8711 VANSITTART, J., *ed.* Katharine Fry's Book. 1966.
Daughter of Eliz. Fry (1801–66).

FYSH
8712 FYSH, J. P. G. *and* FYSH, A. V. G. A. Fysh: the varying fortunes of a 19th-century family. *Norfolk Ancestor* 1 (8), 1979, 106–10.
Mainly King's Lynn connection. See also their 'Some notes on the Fysh family of Ringstead', *ibid.* 4 (9), 1987, 146–8.

GAWDY
8713 TRETT, R. Thomas Gawdy of Shotesham and a 16th century gold finger ring from East Rudham. *N.A.* 38, 1981, 94–5.

GILBERT

8714 FARROW, C. The arms of Gilbert of Norfolk. *Norfolk Standard* 3 (2), 1982, 18–21.

GILMAN

8715 AMES, C. L. The story of the Gilmans and a Gilman genealogy of the descendents of Edward Gilman of Hingham... 1550–1950. Yakima (Washington), 1950.

GIRLING

8716 WINSTANLEY, R. L. The Girlings: chronicles of a farming family [at Lyng]. *Quart. J. Parson Woodforde Soc.* 8 (2), 1975, 4–43.

GLOVER

8717 GLOVER, J. The hidden and happy life of a Christian... exemplified in an extract from the diary of Mr. John Glover, late of Norwich. Publ. by John Carter. [1780?]

8718 COWLIN, D. An ingenious lady of Norwich [Sarah Ann Glover]. *E.A.M.* Oct. 1979, 670–71.

GOGGS

8719 FONE, J. F. The Goggs family: Norfolk farmers from the 16th to 19th century. Norwich, 1983.

GOOCH

8720 [GOOCH, R.] Memoirs, remarkable vicissitudes, military career, and wanderings in Ireland...of Cassiel, the Norfolk astrologer. Norwich, 1844.

8721 FISKE, R. C. Richard Gooch. *Norfolk Fair*, May 1975.

GOODWINS

8722 GOODWINS, B. M. Obiter dicta: end pages of a priest's pocket book. [Norwich, 1976].
Assistant priest at St. Alban's Church, Lakenham.

GOULBURN

8723 JACKSON, J. C. K. Dean Edward Meyrick Goulburn, 1818–1897: a study of his devotional writings. Ph.D. thesis, Edinburgh Univ., 1955.

GREEN

8724 GREEN, G. C. Panorama of adventure in the realm of art and education. 5 parts. Halesowen, 1961–67. BL.
Collected work of writer and artist born Norwich, 1877.

GREEVES

8725 GREEVES, J. Maria's legacy, or, the experience of a suffering Christian delineated in a memoir of the late Mrs. Greeves of Lynn... compiled from her diary and... correspondence. 1823.

GURNEY

8726 SMITH, W. D. Changing attitudes to physical recreation in the early 19th century as evinced by a Norfolk Quaker family. *In* Proc. 9th International HISPA Congress (Lisbon, 1982), pp. 345–51.
Attitudes of Gurney family.

8727 ANDERSON, V. Friends and relations: 3 centuries of Quaker families. 1980.
On the Gurneys of Northrepps.

8728 AUSTIN, *Mrs.* S. Notice of Miss Anna Gurney... from the obituary of the *Gentleman's Magazine*, Sept. 1857. Norwich, [1857]. P.

8729 MOTT, R. F. Memoir and correspondence of Eliza P. Gurney. Philadelphia, 1884.
Nee Kirkbride. Wife of J. J. Gurney of Earlham.

8730 Record of the death of J. J. Gurney Esq. of Earlham... extracted from the Norfolk Chronicle of January 9th and 16th, 1847. Norwich, [1847]. P.

8731 SWIFT, D. E. Joseph John Gurney and the economic life of Norwich. *J. Friends' Hist. Soc.* 49, 1959/61, 96–110.

HAGGARD

8732 NORWICH CASTLE MUSEUM. Catalogue of the holograph manuscripts of novels, romances and works on agriculture and sociology by Sir. H. Rider Haggard. Norwich, 1920. P.
Mss. bequeathed to Norwich Corporation in 1917.

8733 ELLIS, P. B. H. Rider Haggard: a voice from the infinitive. 1978

8734 HAGGARD, *Sir* H. R. Private diaries, 1914–25. Ed. D. S. Higgins. 1980.

8735 WHATMORE, D. E. H. Rider Haggard: a bibliography. 1987.

8736 HAGGARD, L. R. Norfolk life. Ed. H. Williamson. 1943. *Followed by* A Norfolk notebook (1946); *and* A country scrap-book (1950).

HALES

8737 HALES, J. One thing and another. Wisbech, 1982.

HALL

8738 WHITEFOOTE, J. Deaths alarum, or the presage of approaching death... a funeral sermon preached at St. Peters in Norwich... For... Joseph Hall late Bishop of Norwich. 1656. UEA.

8739 HUNTLEY, F. L. Bishop Joseph Hall, 1574–1656. Cambridge, 1979.

8740 McCABE, R. A. Joseph Hall: a study in satire and meditation. Oxford, 1982.

8741 LACASSAGNE, C. Les avatars du pouvoir episcopal a Norwich, 1642–1656. *In* LIVET, G. *and* VOGLER, B., *eds*. Pouvoir, ville et société en Europe, 1650–1750 (Paris, 1983), pp. 461–70.
On experiences of Joseph Hall during Civil War and Commonwealth.

HARBORD

8742 HARBORD, R. P. A history of the family of Harbord. [Draft]. 1977.

8743 *Sale catalogue*. Gunton Park library... historical note on family. Ireland's, Norwich, 12 Sept. 1980.

8744 KETTON-CREMER, R. W. Charles Harbord. *In* Norfolk Assembly (1957), pp. 41–62.
Cf. *B.N.H.* item 2882.

HARLAND
8745 HARLAND, E. M. Wheelbarrow Farm. 1954.

HASTINGS
8746 HOOPER, B. *and others*. The grave of Sir Hugh de Hastyngs, Elsing. *N.A.* 39, 1984, 88–89.

HAYMON
8747 HAYMON, S. Opposite the Cross Keys: an East Anglian childhood. 1988.

HEADLEY
8748 Select beauties of ancient English poetry, with remarks by the late Henry Headley... and a biographical sketch [of Headley] by the Rev. Henry Kett. 1810.
Poet and critic, 1765–88, with Norwich and N. Walsham connections.

HENDERSON
8749 Alderman Fred Henderson, J.P., Lord Mayor of Norwich, 1939–40. [Norwich, 1940]. P. BL.

HENLEY See no. 9918.

HERVEY
8750 Dictionary of Herveys of all classes, callings, counties and spellings from 1040–1500. (Suffolk Green Books, 20). 5 vols. Ipswich, 1924–29. Vol.2: Norfolk.

HOARE
8751 HOARE, L. Six generations. Fakenham, 1960.
Memories of Cromer.
8752 PRYOR, F. P., *ed*. Memoirs of Samuel Hoare by his daughter Sarah and his widow, Hannah... 1911. BL.
18th century banker: married into Gurney of Keswick family.

HOME
8753 HOME, M. *pseud*. Autumn fields. 1945. *Followed by* Spring sowing (1946).
Predecessors of item 2908 in *B.N.H.*

HOPKINS See no. 8311.

HORTH
8754 HORTH, J. R. The Horths of Norwich, 10 parts. Goodmayes, Essex, 1981–83.
See also *An early Horth family of Norwich worsted weavers, 1455–1633* (1980); and no. 9858.

HOSTE

8755 HOSTE, *Sir* W. Memoirs and letters. 2 vols. 1833.
Shorter version with some supplementary information publ. as *Service afloat* (1887). Prominent naval captain, 1780–1828, son of Norfolk rector.

8756 POCOCK, T. Remember Nelson: the life of Captain Sir William Hoste. 1977.
See also his 'In search of Captain Hoste', *E.A.M.* Nov. 1977, 31–3.

HOWARD

8757 ROBINSON, J. M. The Dukes of Norfolk: a quincentennial history. Oxford, 1982.

8758 MARKS, R. The Howard tombs at Thetford and Framingham: new discoveries. *Archaeol. J.* 141, 1984, 252–68.

8759 CHAPMAN, H. W. Two Tudor portaits: Henry Howard, Earl of Surrey, and Lady Katherine Grey. 1960.

8760 SESSIONS, W. A. Henry Howard, Earl of Surrey. Boston (Mass.), 1986.

8761 ROSS, A. The career of John Howard, Duke of Norfolk, 1420–85. M.Phil. thesis, London Univ., 1975.

8762 HARRIS, B. J. Marriage 16th-century style: Elizabeth Stafford and the 3rd Duke of Norfolk. *J. Social Hist.* 15, 1982, 371–82.

See also nos. 7754, 7776.

HOWMAN

8763 HOWMAN, R. History of the Howman family. Salisbury (Rhodesia), 1974.

8764 HOWMAN, P. J. L. The Howman heritage. Part 1. [Norfolk]. Hataitai (New Zealand), 1983.

HOWSON

8765 SIMPSON, J. H. Howson of Holt. A study in school life. 1925.
G. W. S. Howson, headmaster of Gresham's School, Holt, c. 1900–1918.

HUGGIN

8766 JAY, D. John Huggin – clockmaker [of Ashwellthorpe]. *E.A.M.* May 1975, 316–17.

ILKETSHALE See no. 9288.

IVORY

8767 EVANS, M. C. The descendants of Thomas Ivory. *N.A.* 39, 1985, 206–14.

JAMES

8768 JAMES, A. Memoirs of a fen tiger: the story of Ernie James of Welney. Newton Abbot, 1986.

JEFFERY

8769 JEFFERY, J. A complete collection of the sermons and tracts [with memoirs of the author by S. Jones]. 2 vols. 1751.
Archdeacon of Norwich, 1694–1720.

JENKINS
8770 HARLEY, B. Toyshop steam. Watford, 1978.
Deals with work of Geoffrey Beaumont Jenkins of E. Dereham

JENNINGS See no. 7444

JERMY
8771 VALDAR, S. A brief history of the Jermy family of Norfolk and Suffolk. 1976. P.
8772 MILLMAN, J. The Norfolk roots of Capt. Seth and Capt. John Jermy. *Norfolk Ancestor* 4(8), 1987, 125–8.

JERNINGHAM
8773 UNIVERSITY OF BIRMINGHAM LIBRARY. Report on correspondence and diaries of Charlotte Georgiana, Lady Bedingfield (formerly Jerningham). [Reproduced by Hist. Mss. Commission]. 1982.
8774 DIXON, E. S. "Abstulit qui dedit." A sermon preached on occasion of the lamented death of ... Francis Xaveria Stafford Jerninghamn, Baroness Stafford... Norwich, 1832. P.

JEWSON
8775 [JEWSON, C. B.] P. W. Jewson. Verses and a biographical note. Norwich, 1964. P.

JONES
8776 JONES, B. A. Memoirs, 1888–1974. Colchester, 1974.
Bertha Jones: deals mainly with youth spent at King's Lynn.
8777 JONES, *Sir* L. E. A Victorian boyhood. 1955.
Early childhood at Cranmer Hall, near Fakenham. See also chap. on 'Return to Norfolk' in his *Georgian afternoon* (1958).

JULIANA
8778 MOLINARI, P. Julian of Norwich: the teaching of a 14th century English mystic. 1958.
8779 COLLEDGE, E. *and* WALSH, J., *eds.* A book of showings to the anchoress Julian of Norwich. 2 vols. Toronto, 1978.
New standard text with valuable introduction.
8780 SAWYER, M. E. A bibliographical index of 5 English mystics. Pittsburgh, 1978.
Incl. Julian of Norwich and Margery Kempe.
8781 GLASSCOE, M., *ed.* The medieval mystical tradition in England: papers read at the Exeter Symposium, July 1980. Exeter, 1980.
Papers on Julian by A. M. Allchin, R. Maisonneuve and B. A. Windeatt; and on Margery Kempe by S. Dickman.
8782 LAGORIO, V. M. *and* BRADLEY, R. The 14th-century English mystics: a comprehensive annotated bibliography. New York, 1981. Julian, pp. 105–25; Margery Kempe, pp. 127–32.
8783 PELPHREY, B. Love was his meaning: the theology and mysticism of Julian of Norwich. Salzburg, 1982.
Based on Ph.D thesis, Univ. of Edinburgh, 1976.

8784 McILWAIN, J. T. The "bodelye syeknes" of Julian of Norwich. *J. Medieval Hist.* 10, 1984, 167–80.

8785 LLEWELYN, R., *ed.* Julian: woman of our day. 1985.

8786 JANTZEN, G. M. Julian of Norwich: mystic and theologian. 1987.

See also nos. 8238, 8314A.

JULIUS

8787 ELWORTHY, G. *and* ELWORTHY, A. A power in the land: Churchill Julius, 1847–1938. Christchurch (New Zealand), 1971.

Curate in Norwich. Later Archbishop of New Zealand.

KEMPE

8788 COLLIS, L. The apprentice saint [Margery Kempe]. 1964.

8789 GOODMAN, A. E. The piety of John Brunham's daughter of Lynn. *In* BAKER, D., *ed.* Medieval women (Studies in Church Hist. subsidia, 1. Oxford, 1978), pp. 347–58.

8790 SIEGMUND-SCHULTZE, D. Some remarks on the *Book of Margery Kempe.* *15th-Century Stud.* 7, 1983, 329–44.

8791 ATKINSON, C. W. Mystic and pilgrim: the book and the world of Margery Kempe. Ithaca, N.Y., 1984.

8792 LOCHRIE, K. The *Book of Margery Kempe*: the marginal woman's quest for literary authority. *J. Medieval & Renaissance Stud.* 16, 1986, 33–55.

8793 MUELLER, J. M. Autobiography of a new 'creatur': female spirituality, selfhood, and authorship in *The book of Margery Kempe.* *In* ROSE, M. B., *ed.* Women in the Middle Ages and the Renaissance: literary and historical perspectives (Syracuse, N.Y., 1986).

See also nos. 7757, 8238, 8240, 8314A.

KETTON-CREMER

8794 GRETTON, J. R. A bibliography of the printed works of R. W. Ketton-Cremer (1906–1969). *N.A.* 36, 1974, 85–96.

8795 GRETTON, J. R. R. W. Ketton-Cremer. *In his* Essays in book-collecting (East Dereham, 1985), pp. 41–7.

See also no. 9161.

KEY See no. 8276.

KING

8796 KING, J., *ed.* A family remembers. N.p., [1981].

Family of Herbert Alfred King, Rector of Hales.

KNYVETT

8797 MACKENZIE, M. L. Dame Christian Colet: her life and family. Cambridge, 1923.

Daughter of Sir John Knyvett of Ashwellthorpe, and mother of John Colet, Dean of St. Paul's.

8798 OWENS, G. L., *ed.* Two unpublished letters of Thomas Knyvett of Ashwellthorpe, 1641–1642. *N.A.* 35, 1972, 428–32.

8799 CAMBRIDGE UNIVERSITY LIBRARY. The library of Sir Thomas Knyvett of Ashwellthorpe, c. 1539–1618. Ed. D. J. McKitterick. Cambridge, 1978.

LAMBERT
8800 LAMBERT, D. Don't quote me, but... 1979.
Cub reporter for Eastern Daily Press, 1950s.

LANKESTER
8801 MOIR, J. R. Prehistoric archaeology and Sir Ray Lankester. Ipswich, 1935.

LAWS
8802 CROWN, J. The wildfowling man [Jim Laws of Dersingham]. *E.A.M.* Jan. 1981, 132–4.

LE GRICE
8803 LE GRICE, J. Charles Le Grice of Attleborough, 1832–1914. *Norfolk Ancestor* 4(8), 1987, 128–31.

LIND
8804 BISHOP, S. M., *and others*. Jenny Lind in Norwich: a centenary celebration (1820–1887). Norwich, 1987.

LING
8805 LING, W. E. More time to mardle. Ed. R. P. Garrod. Ipswich, 1981.
Farming autobiography.

LITTLEWOOD
8806 NORMAN, J. C., *ed.* The diary of John Littlewood of Hempstead with Eccles, 1789–1818. *Norfolk Ancestor* 2 (10), 1982, 135–40.

LLOYD
8807 MILLER, A. C. William Lloyd, Bishop of Norwich, 'a very able and worthy pastor'. *N.A.* 39, 1985, 150–68.
Bishop 1685–91.

LOFTUS
8808 LOFTUS, C. [Autobiography]. 1. My youth, by sea and land, from 1809 to 1816. 2. My life from 1815 to 1849. 4 vols. 1876–77. BL.
Grandson of 1st Marquess Townshend.

LONG
8809 LONG, U. The heraldry of Long of Dunston and family connections. *Norfolk Standard* 2, 1981, 120–23, 137–9.

LUPSON
8810 LUPSON, E. J. Cupid's pupils from courtship to honeymoon, being the recollections of a parish clerk... 1899.
Yarmouth associations.

MACK
8811 MACK, M. The educated pin. 1944.
Marjorie Mack's recollections of Paston Hall. See also her *Hannaboys Farm* (1942).

McKAY
8812 SHAW, M. N. The history of the McKay family of Wymondham. Waikanae (New Zealand), 1986.

MANBY
8813 MANBY, G. W. Commemorative address to the founder, managers and friends of the National School at Gorleston. Yarmouth, 1844. P.
Cf. also similar brief resumés by Manby of his services to sea-rescue: *Memorial to the Rt. Hon. Richard Cardwell, M.P.* (Yarmouth, 1853); *Statement of endeavours and exertions* (Yarmouth, 1852); *A brief and faithful historic sketch of the life and public services... addressed to the Rt. Hon. Gen. Lord Raglan* (Yarmouth, 1852).
8814 MANBY, G. W. Anastatic drawings of gold and silver medals presented by sovereigns and public bodies to Capt. Manby for services rendered. Yarmouth, 1851. BL.
8815 MILLER, C. Captain Manby and the Joy brothers. B.A. dissertation, Cambridge, 1975.
8816 WALTHEW, K. Captain Manby and the conflagration of the Palace of Westminster. *Hist. Today* 32, Apr. 1982, 21–5.

MANN
8817 GOODWYN, E. A. Norfolk's finest short story writer [Mary Mann]. *E.A.M.* Aug. 1976, 389–91.

MARSHAM
8818 KETTON-CREMER, R. W. Robert Marsham. *In* A Norfolk gallery (1948), pp. 149–61.

MASSEY
8819 JEWSON, C. B. Lucy Massey, a forgotten poet. *Baptist Quart.* 28, 1980, 280–83.

MATTHEWS See no. 8094.

MAYHEW
8820 MAYHEW, P., *ed.* One family's war. 1985.
Mayhews of Felthorpe Hall.

METHWOLD
8821 Pedigree of the Methwold family, now called Methold, from 1180–1870. By some members of the family. 1870. BL.

MILLATT
8822 MILLATT, T. B. Jonathan Millatt, schoolmaster of Ringland. N.p., [c. 1976]. P.

MONCK   See 9736.

MORLEY
8823 RICHMOND, C. Thomas Lord Morley (d. 1416) and the Morleys of Hingham. *N.A.* 39, 1984, 1–12.

MOTTRAM
8824 MOTTRAM, R. H. The window seat; or, life observed. 1954. *Followed by* Another window seat: vol.2, 1919–1953 (1957).
8825 MOTTRAM, R. H. Vanities and verities. 1958.

MOULTON
8826 JONES, W. H. The English background of some early settlers of Hampton, New Hampshire, from Ormesby St. Margaret. *New England Hist. & Geneal. Register* 141, 1987, 313–29.

MOWBRAY
8827 ARCHER, R. E. The Mowbrays, Earls of Nottingham and Dukes of Norfolk to 1432. D.Phil. thesis, Oxford Univ., 1984.
8828 MOYE, L. E. The estates and finances of the Mowbray family, Earls Marshal and Dukes of Norfolk, 1401–76. Ph.D. thesis, Duke Univ., 1984.

MUIR
8829 MUIR, D. E. Lift the curtain. 1955.
Daughter of John Sheepshanks, Bishop of Norwich 1893–1912.

MULLER
8830 THOMAS, D. William James Muller and the Norwich connection. *Connoisseur* 197, 1978, 78–82.

MUNNINGS
8831 NORWICH CASTLE MUSEUM. A. J. Munnings: loan collection of pictures exhibited... Aug. 16 – Sept. 30. Norwich, 1928.
8832 MUNNINGS, *Sir* A. [Autobiography]. An artists's life; The second burst; The finish. 3 vols. 1950–52. 1 vol. ed. 1961.
8833 POUND, R. The Englishman. A biography of Sir Alfred Munnings. 1962.
8834 BOOTH, S. Sir Alfred Munnings, 1878–1959: an appreciation of the artist and a selection of his paintings. 1978.
8835 GOODMAN, J. What a go! The life of Alfred Munnings. 1988.

NELSON
8836 FOLEY, T., *pseud.* The Nelson centenary. Norwich, 1905.
8837 NAISH, G. P. B., *ed.* Nelson's letters to his wife, and other documents, 1785–1831. *Navy Records Soc.* 100, 1958.
8838 NATIONAL MARITIME MUSEUM. Catalogue of the library. Vol. 2, pt.1 (1969), pp. 292–347: Nelson bibliography.

8839 WINTER, L. Hero's country: Nelson and the Norfolk he knew. Burnham Thorpe, [1975].
8840 HARRIS, N. The Nelsons. 1977.
8841 BRADFORD, E. Nelson: the essential hero. 1977.
8842 WINTER, L. Heritage and Nelson: a salute to both. Burnham Thorpe, 1980.
8843 FISKE, R. C. Nelson and associated heraldry. (Nelson Society). North Walsham, 1983.
See also no. 9026.

NEVILL
8844 NEVILL, *Lady* D. Reminiscences... Ed. by... R.H. Nevill. [1906].
Nee Walpole. A few Norfolk memories. See also *Leaves from the notebooks of...* (1907); *Under five reigns* (1911); *My own times* (1912); and R. Nevill, *Life and letters of Lady Dorothy Nevill* (1919); G. Nevill, *Exotic groves: a portrait of Lady Dorothy Nevill* (1984).

NORTON
8845 NORTON, W. E. The Nortons of South Creake. [Forncett St. Peter, 1980].

OFFORD
8846 FRYER, F. Two Norwich art sisters [Georgina and Gertrude Offord]. *E.A.M.* March 1980, 228–9.

OPIE
8847 NORWICH PUBLIC LIBRARIES. Amelia Opie, 1769–1853. Norwich, 1953. P.

OSLER
8848 BATTY-SHAW, A. Sir William Osler, Sir Thomas Browne and Norfolk. Norwich, 1985.
Eminent medical writer and historian (1849–1919). Chronicles his visits to Norfolk and interest in Browne.

PAGE
8849 DUFF, D. Man of God. The story of a Norfolk parson. Privately publ., 1956.
Rev. R. C. Page of Trimingham.

PALGRAVE
8850 PALGRAVE, D. A. The history and lineage of the Palgraves. Doncaster, 1978.
See also his *The Palgraves of Rollesby: a brief history, 1773–1973* [1973]; *Archives of Flegg relating to the Palgraves* [1975]; and no. 8971. Also P.T. R. Palgrave-Moore, *The Palgraves of Ludham* (Doncaster, 1977).

PARISH
8851 PARISH, E. J. Reminiscences. Dereham, 1985. P.

PARKHURST See no. 8250.

PARRY

8852 HAMMOND, *Mrs.* P. Catherine Edwards Parry. A record of her life told chiefly in letters. Norwich, [1898].
Nee Hankinson. Born Lynn, 1808.

8853 PARRY, A. Parry of the Arctic: the life story of Admiral Sir Edward Parry, 1790–1855. 1963.
Pp. 176–88 deal with Parry's months as Assistant Poor Law Commissioner in Norfolk 1835–6.

PASQUA

8854 GOFFIN, M. Maria Pasqua. 1979.
Italian child model later married to Norfolk landowner Philip Shepheard.

PASTON

8855 DAVIS, N. A scribal problem in the Paston letters. *Eng. & Germanic Stud.* 4, 1951/52, 31–64.

8856 DAVIS, N. A Paston hand. *Rev. Eng. Stud.* 3, 1952, 209–21.

8857 HASKELL, A. S. The Paston women on marriage in 15th-century England. *Viator* 4, 1973, 459–71.

8858 WYNDHAM, K. S. H. An Elizabethan search: the Norfolk Pastons and the Tower archives. *Archives* 14, 1980, 211–16.

8859 BARBER, R., *ed.* The Pastons: a family in the wars of the Roses. 1981.
Folio Soc. selection from letters.

8860 HEARN, S. Law and order in 15th century England, with particular reference to the Paston family. M.Phil. thesis, St. Andrews Univ. 1982.

8861 RICHMOND, C. The Pastons revisited: marriage and the family in 15th-century England. *Bull. Inst. Hist. Res.* 58, 1985, 25–36.

8862 BRITNELL, R. H. The Pastons and their Norfolk. *Agric. Hist. Rev.* 36, 1988, 132–44.

8863 LESTER, G. A. Sir John Paston's 'grete boke'. Cambridge, 1984.
Introduction to and descriptive index of compilation on chivalry made for Sir John c. 1470.

8864 DAVIS, N. The text of Margaret Paston's letters. *Medium Aevum* 18, 1949, pp. 12–28.

8865 DAVIS, N. The letters of William Paston. *Neophilologus* 37, 1953, 36–41.
See also nos. 7757, 8318, 8701, 9048, 9880.

PATTERSON

8866 TOOLEY, B. John Knowlittle: the life of the Yarmouth naturalist Arthur Henry Patterson. Sprowston, 1985.

PAUL

8867 PAUL, L. Heron lake. A Norfolk year. 1948.

PEEL

8868 NAPIER, P. A memoir of Lady Delia Peel, born Spencer, 1889–1981. 1984.
Barton Turf connection.

PENRICE
8869 *Sale catalogue*. Catalogue of the furniture, plate, wine, library...of the late John Penrice Esq. throughout the spacious mansion at [St. George's Plain] Great Yarmouth. Yarmouth, 1845.

PERCIVAL See no. 9583A

PIGOTT
8870 PIGOTT, B. A. F., *ed*. Recollections of our mother, Emma Pigott [of Sheringham]. 1890. BL.

RAMSEY
8871 WHITTINGHAM, A. B. The Ramsey family of Norwich. *Archaeol. J.* 137, 1980, 285–9.
Medieval masons.

RANDELL
8872 RANDELL, A. R. Fenland molecatcher. Ed. E. Porter. 1970.
8873 Arthur Randell, fenman. (Bygones series, ed. R. Joice). Ipswich, 1976.

READ
8873A FISHER, J. R. Clare Sewell Read, 1826–1905: a farmer's spokesman of the late 19th century. Hull, 1975.

REEVE See no. 8058

REPTON
8874 SANECKI, K. N. An illustrated life of Humphry Repton, 1752–1818. Aylesbury, 1974.
8875 SAINSBURY CENTRE FOR VISUAL ARTS. Humphry Repton, landscape gardener, 1752–1818. [Exhibition cat.]. Norwich, 1982.

RICHARDS
8875A ODDY, J. A. The Rev. William Richards (1749–1818) and his friends: a study of ideas and relationships. M.Phil. thesis, Nottingham Univ., 1973.
Baptist minister and historian of Lynn.

RICHARDSON
8876 RICHARDSON, R. C. Some fell on stony ground. Wymondham, 1979.
Farmer's autobiography. Hethersett & Little Melton connections.

RIDOUT See no. 9363A.

RISLEY
8877 VIRGOE, R. Sir John Risley (1443–1512), courtier and councillor. *N.A.* 38, 1982, 140–8.

RITCHIE
8878 RITCHIE, J. E. Christopher Crayon's recollections: life and times of the late J. E. Ritchie, as told by himself. 1898.

RIX
8879 RIX FAMILY ALLIANCE. Rix register [family history newsletter]. Vol.3, 1984–. UEA.

ROLFE
8880 BERRY, V. The Rolfe family, 1559–1908. Colney, 1980.

ROXBY
8881 Father Roxby of Timberhill: a memoir. Norwich, 1939.

RUGG See no. 8255.

RUMBELOW
8882 BERRY, G. *and* TRETT, P. Philip Rumbelow, plumber extraordinary. *Yarmouth Archaeol.* 2 (i), 1984, 3–8.
Noted marine modeller.

RYE
8883 RYE, W. Rubbish and nonsense. Norwich, 1887.
Whimsical miscellany which includes some autobiographical detail.

SADGROVE
8884 SADGROVE, M. How I became a healer: an autobiography. King's Lynn, 1976.

SALTER
8885 GREENWOOD, J. R. The will of Thomas Salter of London, 1558. *N.A.* 38, 1983, 280–95.
B. 1478, Norwich. Many legacies to Norfolk relatives.

SANDYS
8886 WOOD, E. A consideration of the art of Frederick Sandys. *The Artist*, special winter no., 1896.

SCOTT
8887 WRIGHT. S. Memoir of the Rev. Thomas Scott. 1862. RCF.
Baptist minister in Norwich, 1831–61.

SCOTTOWE
8888 BACKHOUSE, J., *ed.* John Scottowe's alphabet books. (Roxburghe Club). 1974.
Elizabethan writing-master at Norwich.

SCURLL

8889 BUNTING, G. Notes towards a life of Brettingham Scurll, manservant. *Quart. J. Parson Woodforde Soc.* 15(1), 1982. *Followed by* More about the Scurll family. *Ibid.* 19(4), 1986, 5–17.

SEAGO

8890 SEAGO, E. A canvas to cover. 1947.

8891 Edward Seago: painter in the English tradition. Introductory text by Horace Shipp. 1952.

8892 Edward Seago. A review of the years 1953–1964. Introd. by F. W. Hawcroft. 1965. P.

8893 GOODMAN, J. Edward Seago. 1978.

8894 GREEN, R. Edward Seago, 1910–74. 1981.

8895 RANSON, R. Edward Seago. Newton Abbot, 1987.

SEWELL

8896 SEWELL, M. Mrs. [Mary] Sewell's poems and ballads, with a memoir by E. Boyd-Bayley. [1886]. Another ed. [1899]. BL.

On theatrical Sewell family see no. 9740.

SHEEPSHANKS See no. 8829.

SIMPSON

8897 SIMPSON, W. Statement of the facts which occurred in the late affair between Mr. Bulkeley of the 40th Regiment and Mr. William Simpson. Norwich, 1826. P.
See also L. Bulkeley, *A reply to Mr. Simpson's statement.*

SKELTON

8898 KINSMAN, R. S. John Skelton, early Tudor laureate: an annotated bibliography, c. 1488–1977. Boston, Mass., 1979.

SMITH

8899 Lady Margaret Barry and Mrs. Gertrude Smith. (Bygones series, ed. R. Joice). Ipswich, 1976.
Contrasting lives of landed gentlewoman and Norwich brewery worker's daughter.

On Arthur Smith of Langham see no. 9363A.

STANLEY

8900 VINCENT, J., *ed.* Disraeli, Derby and the Conservative Party: journals and memoirs of Edward Henry, Lord Stanley, 1849–1866. Hassocks, 1978.
M.P. for King's Lynn, 1848–69.

STANNARD See no. 9489.

STARK

8901 OSCAR AND PETER JOHNSON LTD. James Stark and the Norwich school. [Exhibition cat.]. 1983.

STIBBONS
8902 STIBBONS, F. Norfolk's 'caddie' poet. His autobiography, impressions, and some of his verses. Holt, 1923.

STYLEMAN See no. 9974.

SUTHERLAND
8903 An authentic and irrefutable statement of Mrs. Sinclair Sutherland's unfortunate intimacy with Mr. Whichcote Turner...To be had...of Mrs. Sutherland...at her cottage, New Buckenham. [1810].

TAYLOR
8904 BOENING, J. William Taylor of Norwich, 1765–1836, and the reputation of German literature in England. Ph.D. thesis, Indiana Univ., 1971.

THIRTLE
8905 ALLTHORPE-GUYTON, M. John Thirtle, 1777–1839: drawings in Norwich Castle Museum. Norwich, 1977.

THOMPSON
8906 MELLOR, I. Poet and peasant [Thomas Thompson of Little Dunham]. *E.A.M.* July 1976, 360–2.

THORESBY See no. 9388.

TILLETT
8907 The life and political career of Solomon White, Esq., our coming M.P. Norwich, [1875].
Attack on J. H. Tillett, Liberal M.P.

TOWNSHEND
8908 ATHERTON, H. M. George Townshend [1st Marquess Townshend] caricaturist. *18th Century Stud.* 4, 1971, 437–46.
See also short articles by C. R. Grundy, *Connoisseur* 94, 1934, 94–7; and R. W. Ketton-Cremer, *Country Life* Jan. 1964, 214–16.
8909 TOWNSHEND, G. E. G. E., *Marchioness.* It was – and it wasn't. 1937.
Wife of 6th Marquess.
8910 The trial between William Fawkener... plaintiff, and the Hon. John Townshend... defendant, for criminal conversation with the plaintiff's wife... with some particulars relative to the duel between the plaintiff and defendant. 1786. P. BL.
8910A CATTERMOLE, R. H. A study of the servants of Sir Roger Townshend. M.A. thesis, Univ. of E. Anglia, 1985.
8911 EDWARDS, E. H. The Raynham superhorses, bred by the Marchioness and Marquis Townshend. *Connoisseur* 212, 1982, 114–20.
See also nos. 8576, 8808.

TREWIN
8912   TREWIN, I. Norfolk cottage. 1977.
On renovating cottage at Wiggenhall St. Germans.

TURNER See no. 8903.

UPCHER See no. 9956.

VANCOUVER
8913   GIFFORD, A. George Vancouver: a portrait of his life. King's Lynn, 1986.

VENNING
8914   HENDERSON, T. S. Memorials of John Venning Esq., 1862.
Penal reformer, 1776–1858. Settled in Norfolk, 1830.

WALKER
8915   SCOTLAND, N. Zacharias Walker (1843–1900), Norfolk radical and agricultural trade unionist. *N.A.* 37, 1979, 212–15.

WALPOLE
8916   WALPOLE, *Lady* N. The Walpoles of Wolterton. Lewes, 1986.
8917   DAY, J. W. Sporting exploits of a mad earl [George Walpole, 3rd Earl of Orford]. *Country Life Annual*, 1963, 69–71.
8918   DAY, J. W. Lord Orford's voyage through the Fens. *E.A.M.* 37, Aug. – Sept. 1978, 508–11, 552–5.
Cf. *B.N.H.* 367.
   See also nos. 8844, 9060, 9323.

WEYER See no. 8859.

WHALL
8919   WHALL, W. B. Whall of the county of Norfolk. Taunton, 1905.

WHALLEY See no. 7800.

WHEATLEY
8920   KEYMER, T. The wolf in sheep's clothing, being a faithful and true narrative of the affair between Mr. James Wheatley, Mrs. Mary Mason and T. Keymer... Norwich, 1754.
8921   O'SULLIVAN, D. S. The case of James Wheatley, Methodist. *N.A.* 36, 1975, 167–75.

WHITING
8922   WHITING, A. Gal Audrey: a Norfolk childhood. 1986.
   On Whiting family of Norwich see no. 8528.

WIGBY

8923 WIGBY, F. C. Just a country boy. Wymondham, 1976.
Reminiscences of youth at Wicklewood. Further autobiography in *Travels of a country boy* (1981) and *A shilling, a shutknife and a piece of string* (1984).

WILKIN

8924 JEWSON, C. B. Simon Wilkin of Norwich. Norwich, 1979.

WILKINS

8925 LISCOMBE, R. W. William Wilkins, 1778–1839. Cambridge, 1980.
Architect, born in Norwich, whose commissions in county incl. Nelson memorial at Yarmouth and Bylaugh House. See also no. 9031.

WILLIAMSON

8926 FARSON, D. Henry: an appreciation of Henry Williamson. 1982.

WILSON

8927 WILSON, A. M. Friends of yesterday. 1903.
Details on Forncett area.

8928 YOUNG, *Sir* C. G. Statement of the claim of Robert Wilson Esq. of Didlington and of Ashwellthorpe... in relation to the Barony of Berners. 1822. P. BL.

WINDHAM

8929 WINDHAM, W. The diary of the Rt. Hon. William Windham, 1784–1810. Ed. Mrs. H. Baring. 1866.

8930 RUDDY, I. M. William Windham: a political biography, 1760–1801. Ph.D. thesis, Univ. of St. Louis, 1975.

8931 GADDIS, E. R. William Windham and the conservative reaction in England, 1790–1796: the making of a Conservative Whig and the Norwich electoral response. Ph.D. thesis, Pennsylvania Univ., 1979.

WINFREY

8931A WINFREY, *Sir* R. Leaves from my life. King's Lynn, [1936].
M.P. for S.W. Norfolk, 1906–23. See also his *Great men and others I have met* (Kettering, 1943).

WODEHOUSE

8932 HISTORICAL MANUSCRIPTS COMMISSION. Report on muniments in the possession of Edmond R. Wodehouse, Esq., M.P. 13th rept., app. 4, pp. 405–94. [Publ., ser. 31]. 1892.
Contains also material on the Bacon and Buttes family.

8933 CLARK, A. M. Pompeo Batoni's portrait of John Wodehouse [1st Baron]. *American Memorial Art Museum Bull.* 30, 1972, 3–11.

WOODFORDE

8934 WOODFORDE, J. Diary. (The first six Norfolk years 1776–1781). Ed. R. L. Winstanley. 3 vols. N.p., 1981–84.
See also nos. 7394, 7909.

WOODWARD
8935 RIBBANS, F. B. A brief memoir of Bernard Bolingbroke Woodward. Windsor, 1873.
See also his *Reasons for publishing the brief memoir* (Windsor, 1873).

WREN See no. 8249.

YALLOP
8936 HOLLEYMAN, G. A. A history of the Yallop family, 1767–1986: an account of the descendants of James Yallop born in Great Yarmouth... Henfield, 1987.

YATES
8937 SPRUNGER, K. L. John Yates of Norfolk: the radical puritan preacher as Ramist philosopher. *J. Hist. Ideas* 37, 1976, 697–706.

YOUELL
8938 YOUELL, G. Lower class. Washington, D.C., 1938.
Reminiscences of seaman, including early days at Toft Monks.

INDIVIDUAL LOCALITIES

ACLE

8939 ACLE SOCIETY. A guide to Acle. Acle, 1974. New ed. 1986. P.
8940 BEAUMONT, C. *and* JORDAN, C. Thomas Smithdale and Sons, Acle: millwrights and engineeers. *J. Norfolk Industrial Archaeol. Soc.* 1 (6), 1974, 25–8.
See also 8141, 8563.

ALBY

8941 VYSE, J. W. M. The parish church of St. Ethelbert, Alby. N.p., 1974. P.

ARMINGHALL

See no. 8475.

ASHBY

8942 KIRK, T. St. Mary's Church, Ashby, [c. 1975]. P.

ASHILL

8943 GREGORY, A. Some fragments of decorated daub from Ashill. *Britannia* 4, 1973, 268–9.
8944 GREGORY, T. The enclosure at Ashill. *E.A.A.R.* 5, 1977, 9–30.
Roman period. See also note by R. C. Fiske, *NARG News* 29, 1982, 13–17.
8945 REID, A. W. The process of parliamentary enclosure in Ashill. *N.A.* 37, 1979, 169–77.

8946 REID, A. *and* WADE-MARTINS, P. Re-examination of the Panworth Ditch, Ashill. *N.A.* 37, 1980, 307–12.

8947 LAWSON, A. K. A fragment of lifesize bronze equine statuary from Ashill. *Britannia* 17, 1986, 333–9.

8947A REID, A. Some medieval road and place-names in Ashill. *Bull. Norfolk Research Committee* 32, 1984, 18–21.

ASHWELLTHORPE

See nos. 8766, 8799.

ASLACTON

8948 LAW, J. R., *and others.* Aslacton St. Michael, Moulton. Holt, [c. 1978]. P.
See also no. 10054.

ATTLEBOROUGH

8949 BARRINGER, J. C. College House, Attleborough. *Bull. Norfolk Research Committee* 11, 1973, 4–5.

8950 PARTRIDGE, E. G. Quakerism in Attleborough and district, 1650–1900. Cert. in Local Hist., Cambridge Board of Extra-Mural Studies, 1977.

8951 PALGRAVE-MOORE, P., *ed.* Attleborough parish registers, 1552–1840. Transcribed by E. W. Sanderson. *Norfolk Geneal.* 12, 1980.

8952 The Hill Foundry, Attleborough. *J. Norfolk Industrial Archaeol. Soc.* 3 (4), 1984, 145–6.

8953 ATTLEBOROUGH CHAMBER OF TRADE AND COMMERCE. Attleborough town guide and directory. Attleborough, 1985.

8954 PARTRIDGE, E. Point Cottage, Attleborough. *NARG News* 42, 1985, 6–12.

8955 PARTRIDGE, E. View of Attleborough from pages of the school log, 1872–1946. N.p., 1985.

8956 BRECKLAND DISTRICT COUNCIL. Attleborough local plan. E. Dereham, 1987. Preceded by *Consultation draft* (1986).

8957 BUJAK, P. E. Bunn's Bank. *NARG News* 49, 1987, 21–5.

8958 BUJAK, P. E. Attleborough in the Great War. *In* GLIDDON, G., *ed.* Norfolk and Suffolk in the Great War (Norwich, 1988), pp.47–60.

See also no. 8008.

ATTLEBRIDGE

8959 GREENWOOD, J. R. Lost brasses from Attlebridge. *Trans. Monumental Brass Soc.* 13, 1983, 347–9.

AYLSHAM

8960 SAPWELL, J. Catalogue of the contents of the muniment room, Town Hall, Aylsham. [Aylsham, c. 1974]. P.

8961 ROWLANDS, S. The Three Black Boyes Inn and the manor of Aylshamwood. Aylsham, [1979]. P.

8962 VYSE, J. W. M. The parish church of St. Michael, Aylsham, 1380–1980. Aylsham, 1980. P.

8963 LODEY, M. J. Introduction of civil registration. A case history from Norfolk. *Genealogists' Mag.* 20, 1981, 223–31.

8964 PHILLIPS, B. Methodist Church, Aylsham: a short history of the buildings. Vol.1: 1784–1884. Aylsham, 1984. P.

8965 [Entry deleted].

8966 AYLSHAM LOCAL HISTORY SOCIETY. Aylsham in the 17th century: documents from the manor of Aylsham Lancaster. Aylsham, 1988.
A rental of 1624.
See also no. 7536.

BACTON

8967 GREGORY, R. The price of amenity: 5 studies in conservation and government. Chap. 5: Bacton and North Sea Gas, pp. 203–44.
See also no. 7767A.

BALE

8968 BLATCHLY, J. The church of All Saints, Bale, alias Bathley. [N.p., c. 1978]. P.

BANHAM

8969 LAWSON, A. J. The investigation of a mesolithic and later site at Banham. *E.A.A.R.* 8, 1978, 9–18.

BARMER

8970 LONGSDON, E. H. The Barmer estate. 1957. [And addenda, 1959, 1966].

BARNEY

See no. 8458.

BARNHAM (near Thetford)

See no. 9105.

BARNHAM BROOM

See no. 8458.

BARNINGHAM

8971 PALGRAVE, D. A. North Barningham: the church, the Hall, and the Palgrave family. Doncaster, [1974]. P.
See also *Heraldry at North Barningham Church* (Doncaster, 1976). P. Also article in *Norfolk Ancestor* 1(8), 1979, 103–5.

BARTON BENDISH

8972 ROGERSON, A. *and* ASHLEY, S. J. The parish churches of Barton Bendish: the excavation of All Saints' and the architecture of St. Andrew's and St. Mary's. *In* Three Norman churches in Norfolk (*E.A.A.R.* 32, 1987), pp. 1–66.
See also nos. 7712, 8458, 8549.

BARTON TURF

Sale catalogue
8973 Barton Hall estate. 5 Oct. 1935.
See also no. 8868.

BARWICK

See no. 7510.

BAWBURGH

8974 FARROW, C. Lodge Farm, Bawburgh – a recusant hideout? *Norfolk Standard* 3(13), 1987, 167–8, 175.
See also nos. 7536, 7550

BAWDESWELL

8975 WATSON, J. F. Bawdeswell Church. *The Builder* 190, Jan. 6 1956, 10–15.

BAWSEY

8976 WYMER, J. Excavation of the Bawsey barrow, 1984: summary report. *NARG News* 38, 1984, 1–6.
See also *Current Archaeol.* 9, 1985, 42–5.

BEESTON-NEXT-MILEHAM

8977 BRECKLAND DISTRICT COUNCIL. Beeston village plan. Dereham. 1982.
See also no. 8462.

BEESTON REGIS

8978 LAWSON, A. J. A late Bronze Age hoard from Beeston Regis. *Antiquity* 54, 1980, 217–19.
See also *NARG News* 22, 1980, 6–11.

BEESTON ST. LAURENCE

8979 HASLAM, R. Beeston Hall. *Country Life* 173, 1983, 270–4.

BEETLEY

See nos. 7686, 8462.

BERGH APTON

8980 GREEN, B. *and* ROGERSON, A. The Anglo-Saxon cemetery at Bergh Apton: catalogue. *E.A.A.R.* 7, 1978.

BESTHORPE

See no. 8427.

BEXWELL

See no. 8549.

BILLINGFORD

8981 GALE, C. H. Evidence of a Roman fort at Billingford. *Proc. Suffolk Inst. Archaeol.* 23, 1939, 173–4.
8982 NORFOLK WINDMILLS TRUST. Billingford windmill. Norwich, 1980. P.

BILNEY, EAST

See no. 7686.

BINHAM

8983 WORKERS' EDUCATIONAL ASSOCIATION. Binham: a social survey by the Binham W. E. A. student group, session 1942–43. Cambridge, [1943]. P. UEA.
See also no. 8472.

BIRCHAM

8984 ROGERSON, A. *and* ADAMS, N. Saxo-Norman pottery kiln at Bircham. *E.A.A.R.* 8, 1978, 33–44.
8985 YAXLEY, D. The Old Rectory, Great Bircham. *N.A.* 37, 1979, 146–52.
8986 CROWN, J. I. The Bircham windmill. *E.A.M.* 41, Jan. 1982, 142–4.

BLACKBOROUGH END

8987 SAMPSON, A. Blackborough End and its changing character. North Walsham, 1981. P.

BLAKENEY

8988 Proposed restoration of the parish church of St. Nicholas, Blakeney. Norwich, [c. 1885]. P. UEA.

8989 B., J. Blakeney, Norfolk. Saffron Walden, 1929. P.

8990 LINNELL, C. L. S. The Blakeney Book... printed for members of the [Linnell] family. Norwich, n.d. P.

8991 MUIR, P. Minding my own business. 1956.
Deals with firm of Elkin Mathews, booksellers. See also B. Kaye, *The company we kept* (Blakeney, 1986).

8992 HAYWARD, W. G. R. Thirty years of Blakeney. Blakeney, [1978]. P.

8993 SAYERS, G. R. Old Blakeney: a brief history of Blakeney and its haven... by the Blakeney Preservation Society. [Blakeney, c. 1979]. P.

8994 BROOKS, P. Have you heard about Blakeney? Cromer, 1981. P.

8995 CATLING, M. History of Blakeney and its havens. [Unpubl.] 1986.

BLICKLING

8996 GRAVES, C. L. Blickling. *In* INGLEBY, C., *ed.* Supplement to Blomefield's Norfolk (1929), pp. 3–12.

8997 NATIONAL TRUST. Blickling Library: books from Blickling Hall... at the National Book League exhibition 'Fine books from famous houses'. 1958. P.

8998 UNIVERSITY OF EAST ANGLIA LIBRARY. Books and pamphlets of the Civil War period in the library of Blickling Hall. Norwich, 1974.

8999 DURST, D. W. Blickling bricks. *J. Norfolk Industrial Archaeol. Soc.* 2 (2), 1977, 4–8.
Estate brickworks.

9000 STANLEY-MILLSON, C. The architecture and decoration of Blickling Hall up to 1629. M.Phil. thesis, Univ. of E. Anglia, 1981.
See also her articles 'Blickling Hall: the building of a Jacobean mansion', *Architect. Hist.* 29, 1986, 1–42; and (with J. Newman) 'Blickling Hall: the building of a great house', *J. Roy. Soc. of Arts* 135, Dec. 1986, 58–74.

9001 NATIONAL TRUST. Blickling Hall. 1987.
Revised, enlarged guide.

9002 MADDISON, J., CORNFORTH, J. Blickling Hall. *Country Life* March 1988, 104–9, 128–31, 136–9.
Notes on restoration of Peter the Great Room. Separate articles.

See also nos. 8042, 8519.

BLO' NORTON

See no. 8458.

BODNEY

9003 GLENDENNING, [S. E.] A handled beaker from Bodney. *P.P.S.* 7, 1932/34, 107–10.
See also no. 8549.

BOUGHTON

9004 COATES, D. E. The story of Boughton. Henley-on-Thames, 1982. P.
See also nos. 7712, 8549.

BRACON ASH

See no. 7953.

BRAMERTON

9005 BRAMERTON GROUP COUNCIL. Eleven churches: a guide to the Bramerton group. Ashby, 1978.
See also no. 7560.

BRAMPTON

9006 GREEN, C. J. S. Excavations in the Roman kiln field at Brampton, 1973–74. *E.A.A.R.* 5, 1977, 31–96.
9007 KNOWLES, A. K. The Roman settlement at Brampton, Norfolk: interim report. *Britannia* 8, 1977, 209–21.
9008 HEALY, F. Neolithic and later material from a shaft at Brampton. *N.A.* 38, 1983, 363–74.

BRANCASTER

9009 EDWARDS, D. A. *and* GREEN, C. J. S. The British evidence – the Saxon Shore fort and settlement at Brancaster. *In* JOHNSTON, D. E., *ed.* The Saxon Shore (C. B. A. research report, 18; 1977), pp. 21–9.
9010 HINCHLIFFE, J. *and others.* Excavations at Brancaster, 1974 and 1977. *E.A.A.R.* 23, 1985.
9011 FLACK, S. *and* GREGORY, T. Excavations at Brancaster, 1985. *N.A.* 40, 1988, 164–71.

BRANDISTON

See no. 8458.

BRESSINGHAM

9012 BRESSINGHAM AND FERSFIELD PARISH COUNCIL. Village appraisal. [Bressingham, 1981].
See also 8458, 8599.

BRETTENHAM

See nos. 7712, 8458.

BRIDGHAM

See no. 8458.

BRINTON

9013 FRIENDS OF BRINTON. Village history papers. 1: Brinton's former trades (J. A. Walton, 1981). 2: Brinton from the 1838 tithe map (J. A. Walton, 1982). 3: Brinton's parish chest (*Rev.* J. F. Lord, 1983).

BRISLEY

9014 WADE-MARTINS, P. Exacavation of a Roman road at Brisley. *E.A.A.R.* 8, 1978, 29–32.
See also no. 7686.

BRISLEY AND ELMHAM (Rural deanery)

See no. 8451.

BROCKDISH

See no. 7560.

BROOKE

9015 JAMES, M. R. The wall paintings in Brooke Church. *In* INGLEBY, C., *ed.* Supplement to Blomefield's Norfolk (1929), pp. 17–25.
9016 KENNETT, D. H. Anglo-Saxon finds from Brooke, Norfolk, 1867–1869. *Proc. Cambridge Antiq. Soc.* 66, 1975/76, 93–118.
See also no. 7560.

BRUNDALL

9017 LEVINE, G. J. A concise history of Brundall and Braydeston. Brundall, 1977. P.
9018 BROADLAND DISTRICT COUNCIL. Brundall local plan. Norwich, 1980.
9019 PEART, S. F. H. Cooper and a slice of woodland borrowed from Eden [Brundall Gardens]. *E.A.M.* Aug. 1981, 456–8.

BUCKENHAM, NEW

See no. 7536.

BUNWELL

9020 DAY, P. History of Bunwell: research notes. 2 vols. [Unpubl. typescript]. 1981/82.

9021 GREGORY, A. The Bunwell horse. *Britannia* 17, 1986, 330–2.

BURGH-NEXT-AYLSHAM

See no. 8458

BURLINGHAM PARISHES

9022 WILLIAMS, J. F. North Burlingham, Norfolk. *Trans. Monumental Brass Soc.* 7, 1939, 266–70.
See also nos. 8458, 8618.

BURNHAM PARISHES

9023 WALFORD, E. A pilgrimage to the birthplace of Nelson. *Gentleman's Mag.* Oct. 1879, 471–7.

9024 EARLE, A. St. Clement's Church, Burnham Overy. 1963. RCF.

9025 BARWOOD, N. E. The Burnhams' handbook. Burnham Market, [1981].

9026 LOCKWOOD, J. Norfolk's liveliest museum [The Lord Nelson at Burnham Thorpe]. *E.A.M.* Sept. 1981, 514–16.

9027 POWELL, R. A Norfolk saddler's ledger. *Ibid.* Aug. 1982, 442–3
Concerns George Hudson of Burnham Market.

9028 EVERITT, G. Industrious Burnham: a conducted tour of the businesses of Burnham Market over the last 150 years. Burnham Market, 1987.
See also nos. 8836–43.

BURSTON

9029 ZAMOYSKA, B. The Burston Rebellion. 1985.

BUXTON

9030 MELLOR, D. A history of the Red House Farm School, Buxton. Kelling, 1976.
See also no. 8009.

BYLAUGH

9031 LISCOMBE, R. W. Designs by William Wilkins for Bylaugh Hall. *Burlington Mag*, 116, 1974, 396–8.

CAISTOR ST. EDMUND

9032 WACHER, J. Caistor-by-Norwich. *In* The towns of Roman Britain (1975), pp. 227–38.

9033 SWAN, V. G. Caistor-by-Norwich reconsidered and the dating of Romano-British pottery in East Anglia. *In* ANDERSON, A. C. *and* ANDERSON, A. S., *eds*. Roman pottery research in Britain and north-west Europe (Brit. Archaeol. Repts., Internat. ser. 123, 1981), pp. 123–55.

9034 RICKWOOD, D. Caistor St. Edmunds: a study of the historical and present-day geography. [Unpubl., c. 1984].

9035 DARLING, M. J. The Caistor-by-Norwich 'massacre' reconsidered. *Britannia* 18, 1987, 263–72.

See also no. 7691.

CAISTER-NEXT-YARMOUTH

9036 PESTELL, R. E. Caister-on-Sea. Norwich, n.d.

9037 HAWKES, C. F. C. *and* CLARKE, R. R. Gahlstorf and Caister-on-Sea. Two finds of late Bronze Age Irish gold. *In* FOSTER, I. L. *and* ALCOCK, L., *eds*. Culture and environment: essays in hon. of Sir Cyril Fox (1963), pp. 193–250.

9038 ARTHUR, P. *and* WILLIAMS, D. An unusual late Roman mortarium from Caister-by-Yarmouth. *Britannia* 9, 1978, 394–5.

9039 LAWSON, A. J. A late Bronze Age hoard from West Caister. *In* BURGESS, C. *and* COOMBS, D., *eds*. Bronze Age hoards (Brit. Archaeol. Repts. 67, 1979), pp. 173–9.

9040 McEWEN, A. Anglo-Saxon cemetery at Caister by Yarmouth [excavated Aug. 1979]. *Yarmouth Archaeol.* 1 (iii), 1981, [unpaginated].

9041 [TOOKE, C. S.] The Beach Company. Caister, 1981. P.
See also his article in *J. Norfolk Industrial Archaeol. Soc.* 3 (2), 1982, 63–82.

9042 [TOOKE, C. S.] Caister churches: a short history and guide. Caister-on-Sea, 1981. P.

9043 CALVERT, D. K. Like little Topsy, it just growed. Colchester, 1983.

9044 GREAT YARMOUTH BOROUGH COUNCIL. Caister-on-Sea local plan: draft policies and proposals. Great Yarmouth, 1985.
See also *Written statement* (1985); and *Statement on public participation* (1986). P.

9045 TOOKE, C. Caister: 2000 years a village. North Walsham, 1985.

9046 TOOKE, C. Caister beach, boats, and beachmen. North Walsham, 1986.

9047 TOOKE, C. Caister-on-Sea Methodist Church: centenary, 1886–1986. Caister, 1986.

9048 BURTON, W. P. Margaret Paston and her castle at Caister. (Burton's Yarmouth Tractates, 11). [Yarmouth, n.d.]. P. RCF.

9049 Caister Castle. Illustr. by E. C. Allerton. Lowestoft, 1922. P.

CALDECOTE

See nos. 7510, 7686.

CANTLEY

9050 WEBSTER, S. This farewell address to the inhabitants of the parish of Cantley... Norwich, 1795. P. UEA.

CARBROOKE

9051 SAUNDERS, D. *and* SAUNDERS, S. Carbrooke in the past. Watton, 1986.

CARLETON, EAST

See no. 7953.

CARLETON RODE

9052 Carleton Rode Baptist Church ter-jubilee, 1812–1962: souvenir booklet. [Carleton Rode, 1962].

CASTLE ACRE

9053 Farm reports: the Lodge Farm, Castle Acre. *J. Roy. Agric. Soc.* 2nd ser. 5, 1869, 460–74,

9054 SIMPSON, R. J. Illustrations of Castle Acre. N.p., 1894. BL.

9055 MORRIS, S. E. The gang system as practised at Castle Acre in the 19th century. Unpubl. typescript. [1980].

9056 WILCOX, R. Castle Acre Priory excavations, 1972–76. *N.A.* 37, 1980, 231–76,

9057 FARLEY, V. Pictures from a village, Ipswich, 1981,
1920s photographs of Castle Acre.

9058 COAD, J. G. *and* STREETEN, A. D. F. Excavations at Castle Acre Castle, 1972–77. *Archaeol. J.* 139, 1982, 138–301.
See also interim reports by Coad, *Chateau Gaillard* 7, 1975, 173–82; 11, 1982, 55–67..

9059 COAD, J. G. *and others.* Excavations at Castle Acre Castle, Norfolk, 1975–1982: the bridges, lime kilns and eastern gatehouse. *Archaeol. J.* 144, 1987, 256–307.
See also Coad's guidebook to castle publ. by English Heritage (1984). P.

CASTLE RISING

9060 BRADFER-LAWRENCE, H. L. Castle Rising and the Walpoles. *In* INGLEBY, C., *ed.* Supplement to Blomefield's Norfolk (1929), pp. 29–46.

9061 BROWN, R. A. Castle Rising. (Dept. of the Environment: official handbook). 1978.
Updates previous Ministry of Works guide (1965).

9062 DENCE, C. S. Portrait of a village: Castle Rising. Castle Rising, 1980.
See also nos. 7536, 7595.

CASTON

9063 BARNES, J. S. A history of Caston. 3 parts. Orpington, 1974–77.

CATTON

9064 MANNING, I. M. A history of Old Catton. Catton, [1982]. P.

CAWSTON

9065 Cawston Church. An account of the rood screen and of works of restoration undertaken during 1952. 1952. P.
9066 KETT, J. Yesterday's children: tales of Cawston's past. Cawston, [1980].
9067 AMUSSEN, S. D. A Norfolk village: Cawston, 1595–1605. *Hist. Today* 36, Apr. 1986, 15–20.
See also no. 7775.

CHEDGRAVE

See no. 7560.

CLEY

9068 ROSE, E. *and* POOLEY, G. A medieval wall painting from Cley-next-the-Sea. *N.A.* 37, 1978, 115–16.
9069 STARR, F. A village shop. Woodbridge, 1979.
Memories of Cley.
9070 BROOKS, P. Cley: living with memories of greatness. North Walsham, 1984. P.
9071 St. Margaret's Church, Cley-next-the-Sea. N.p., 1984. P.
See also no. 8592.

COCKLEY CLEY

9072 ROBERTS, *Sir* P. A diversion at Cockley Cley. Swaffham, 1970. P.
Description of forge cottages (now private museum) and church.
See also no. 8549.

COLNEY

See nos. 7550, 8549

COLTISHALL

9073 CAMPBELL, B. M. S. Population pressure, inheritance and the land market in a 14th-century peasant community. *In* SMITH, R. M., *ed.* Land, kinship, and life-cycle (Cambridge, 1984), pp. 87–134.
9074 BOND, R. Coltishall: heyday of a Broadland village. North Walsham, 1986.
9075 SINCLAIR, O. When wherries sailed by: recollections of a Broadland village. North Walsham, 1987.
See also no. 10140.

CORPUSTY

9076 WILSON, J. *and* HOUSTON, W. Corpusty village school. Corpusty, 1974. P.

COSTESSEY

9077 JOLLY, W. T. F. St. Walstan's, Costessey. Rougham, [1976]. P.
See also nos. 7560, 7562, 8479.

COSTON

9078 BUTCHER, D. R. Faces of a village. *E.A.M.* March 1977, 188–90.

CRANWICH

9079 STONE, M. C. Cranwich camp. [Unpubl. study]. 1975.
9080 JACOBI, R. M.. *and* MARTINGELL, H. E. A later-glacial shouldered point from Cranwich. *N.A.* 37, 1980, 312–14.
See also no. 8549.

CREAKE PARISHES

9081 POOLEY, G. Eleven hundred years: South Creake. Fakenham, 1985.
See also nos. 8458, 8519, 8845.

CRESSINGHAM PARISHES

9082 GARROD, R. R. Little Cressingham Free School. *E.A.M.* May 1976, 274–5.
9083 LAWSON, A. J. A hand-axe from Little Cressingham. *E.A.A.R.* 8, 1978, 1–8.
9084 CHAPMAN, C. F. Cressingham and its chapels: Great Cressingham New Methodist Chapel 50th anniversary, 1932–82. Watton, 1982. P.
See also no. 8549.

CRINGLEFORD

9085 FENNER, A. *and* FENNER, G. Pond Farm, Cringleford. *NARG News* 17, 1979, 1–4.
With note on documentary evidence by T. L. M. Hawes, *ibid.* 18, 1979, 7–9.
9086 CRINGLEFORD HISTORICAL SOC. The history of St. Peter's Church, Cringleford. Cringleford, 1986.
See also no. 7560.

CROMER

9087 JARROLD's illustrated guide to Cromer and neighbourhood. [c. 1880]. Revised eds. by J. Hooper, M. Knights, G. Stephen, 1880–1930.
9087A SIMPSON, R. J. The Cromer scrap book. N.p., 1884.

9088 Opening of the new promenade pier of the Cromer Protection Commissioners. 1901. P. RCF.

9088A MACE, H. Some comments on the financial policy of the Cromer District Council. With Messrs. Hansell and Hales' rejoinder. [Cromer, c.1907]. P. RCF.

9089 HOARE, W. P. Guide to Cromer. Season 1912. Cromer, 1912. RCF.

9090 LOADS AND SONS. All about Cromer and district. 1913. P. RCF.

9091 Illustrated souvenir programme to commemorate the official opening of the Cromer and District Hospital. 1932. P. RCF.

9092 CROMER AND NORTH NORFOLK FESTIVAL OF MUSIC AND DRAMA. Programme catalogues. 1950–72. RCF.

9093 CLARKE, S. K. Some notes concerning Cromer churches. [Unpubl. typescript, 1974].

9094 HOLDEN, C. C. A history of Cromer lifeboats. [Unpubl. typescript]. 1975.

9095 BARRETT, K. D. L. A history of Cromer Girls' School, 1872–1949. Revised ed. Cromer, 1977. P.

9096 MALSTER, R. W. *and* STIBBONS, P. J. R. The Cromer lifeboats, 1804–1979. Cromer, 1979. 2nd ed. 1981. P.

9097 GOODWYN, E. A. Cromer past. Beccles, 1980. P.

9098 Cromer residents' directory. Wisbech, [c. 1981].

9099 STIBBONS, B. *and* STIBBONS, P. A Cromer album. North Walsham, 1985.

9100 GROSE, J. Those seaside days: memories of East Anglian family seaside holidays in the 1940s. North Walsham, 1986.
Concentrates on Cromer.

9101 REID, A., *ed.* Cromer and Sheringham: the growth of the holiday trade, 1877–1914. Norwich, 1986.

9102 EATON, R., *ed.* A hundred years of Royal Cromer Golf Club. [Cromer, 1987].

Sale catalogue
9103 Cromer Hall Estate. 1918.
See also nos. 7591, 8334, 8751.

CROSTWICK

9104 ROSE, E. J. *and* KING, D. J. Recent discoveries at Crostwick St. Peter. *N.A.* 39, 1985, 192–202.

CROXTON

9105 CLOVER, R. D. Tale of an area: a village study and history of Croxton, Kilverstone and Barnham, and the infancy of Thetford. Thetford, 1975. P.

DENTON

9106 SURMAN, C. E. Church briefs [Denton, 1724–1804]. *Trans. Congregational Hist. Soc.* 16, 1949, 137–42.

9107 CLOUGH, T. H. M. A small hoard of English hammered coins from Denton. *N.A.* 36, 1977, 391–2.
6 coins dated 1578–1606.

9108 INGLEBY, C. Denton and its glass. *In* Supplement to Blomefield's Norfolk (1929), pp. 49–69.

DENVER

9109 NORFOLK WINDMILLS TRUST. Denver windmill. Norwich, 1981. P.
See also no. 7734.

DEOPHAM

See no. 8458.

DEREHAM, EAST

9109A MACK, A. H. Centenary of Sondes Lodge no. 996 [Freemasons], 1863–1963. N.p., 1963. FPL.

9110 BRECKLAND DISTRICT COUNCIL. Dereham town centre plan: 1976 review: discussion document. Dereham, 1976. P.

9111 HOLLIS, D. W. A mid-17th century view of East Dereham manor. *N.A.* 36, 1977, 342–54.

9112 MONOPOLIES AND MERGERS COMMISSION. The Fruehauf Corporation and Crane Fruehauf Ltd: a report on the proposed merger. 1977.

9113 BRECKLAND DISTRICT COUNCIL. Dereham policy map review. 1978 review. Dereham, 1978. P.
Followed by *Responses to the discussion document*; and *Revised plan*.

9114 COOK, M. *and* DAVY, T. Memories of Dereham. Dereham, 1984. *Followed by* Looking back at Dereham (1984); More memories of Dereham (1986). P.

9115 DAVY, T. Dereham past and present. Dereham, 1987.
See also no. 8546.

DERSINGHAM

See no. 8802.

DICKLEBURGH

See no. 7560.

DIDLINGTON

See no. 8549.

DISS

9116 WHYTEHEAD, R. L. An account of the church of S. Mary the Virgin, Diss. 1922. P. RCF.

9117 SUSSEX, V. J. Diss, Norfolk: a postal history. (East Angla Postal Hist. Study Circle: monographs, 4). Bishops Stortford, 1974.

9118 Diss town guide. [Biennial]. Diss, 1976–.

9119 Diss walkabout [survey of industrial sites]. *J. Norfolk Industrial Archaeol. Soc.* 1 (7), 1974, 15–22.

9120 GRAYSTON, C. Some Diss industries. *J. Norfolk Industrial Archaeol. Soc.* 1 (9), 1975, 17–22.

9121 MALING, J. J. [Diss memories]. *E.A.M.* Dec. 1978, 106–8; Nov. 1979, 32–3; Jan. 1980, 138–9.
On shops, Guy Fawkes Day, and amateur music-making in 1930s.

9122 PIPER, C. Diss: the pictorial past, 1860–1905. Diss, 1982.

9123 SOUTH NORFOLK DISTRICT COUNCIL. Diss local plan. 2 pts. [Long Stratton], 1982.

9124 FARROW, C. W., *ed.* The parish registers of Diss, 1551–1837. *Norfolk Geneal.* 19, 1987.

Sale catalogue.

9125 Wingfield Castle, Diss. Christie, London, 30 May, 1980.
See also no. 8546.

DITCHINGHAM

9126 FAIRHEAD, A. E. The Ditchingham that I knew. Norwich, [1975].

9127 CHEYNE, N. The Bathhouse and Vineyard Hills in Ditchingham. [Type-script]. 1975.

9128 The community of All Hallows, Ditchingham. Centenary. 1855–1955. Norwich, 1955. P.

9129 All Hallows: an Anglican religious community. Ditchingham, [1979]. P.
Another ed. [by *Sister* Violet]. Oxford, 1983.

DOCKING

9130 HAGAN, G. Dry Docking: being some account of the history and records of a Norfolk village. King's Lynn, 1975. 2nd ed. 1983.
See also no. 7949.

DOWNHAM MARKET

9131 St. Dominic's. Downham Market, 1980. P.

9132 WEST NORFOLK DISTRICT COUNCIL. Downham Market draft district plan: consultative draft. King's Lynn, [1980].
Followed by: *Statement of public participation and consultation* [1981].
See also nos. 7536, 8546.

DRAYTON

9133 DRAYTON ASSOCIATION. Drayton directory... of associations and activities, festival edition, 1975–76. Drayton, 1975. P.

DUNHAM, LITTLE

See no. 8906.

DUNSTON

See nos. 8549, 8809.

DUNTON

See no. 8458.

EARSHAM

9134 ACOMB, H. W. The Flemish glass at Earsham. *In* INGLEBY, C., *ed*. Supplement to Blomefield's Norfolk (1929), pp. 73–80.
9135 FLEMING, M. Earsham timberyard. *J. Norfolk Industrial Archaeol. Soc.* 2 (5), 1980, 27–32.

EASTON

9136 BURT, R. M. A brief history of Easton. Easton, 1984. P.

ECCLES

See no. 8548.

EDGEFIELD

See no. 8458.

EDINGTHORPE

See no. 8563.

ELLINGHAM (near Bungay)

See no. 7560.

ELLINGHAM, GREAT

9137 ELTON, D. H. Great Ellingham – St. James' Church. N.p., 1979. P.

ELMHAM, NORTH

9138 HILLS, C. A runic pot from Spong Hill, North Elmham. *Antiq. J.* 54, 1974, 87–91.
9139 WADE-MARTINS, P. *and* WADE-MARTINS, S. The Anglo-Saxon cathedral, North Elmham. N. Elmham, 1976. P.

9140 WADE-MARTINS, P. *and* WADE-MARTINS, S. St. Mary's Church, North Elmham. N. Elmham, 1976. P.

9141 DODDS, M. *and* VIRGOE, N. The village school, North Elmham. Ed. P. Wade-Martins. N. Elmham, [1977]. P.

9142 HILLS, C. M. *and others*. The Anglo-Saxon cemetery at Spong Hill, North Elmham. *E.A.A.R.* 6, 1977; 11, 1981; 21, 1984; 34, 1987; 39, 1988.
See also Hills' Ph.D. thesis of this title, London Univ., 1976.

9143 HILLS, C. Chamber grave from Spong Hill, North Elmham. *Medieval Archaeol*, 21, 1977, 167–76.

9144 HILLS, C. Anglo-Saxon chairperson. *Antiquity* 54, 1980, 52–4.
Figured lid, probably of pagan funeral urn, found at Spong Hill.

9145 HILLS, C. Anglo-Saxon cremation cemeteries, with particular reference to Spong Hill. *In* RAHTZ, P. *and others, eds.* Anglo-Saxon cemeteries (Brit. Archaeol. Repts. 82, 1980), pp.197–207.
See also in same collection, G. Putnam 'Spong Hill cremations', pp.217–19.

9146 WADE-MARTINS, P. *and* YAXLEY, D. Excavations in North Elmham Park, 1967–72. *E.A.A.R.* 9, 1980. 2 vols.

9147 HEYWOOD, S. The ruined church at North Elmham. *J. Brit. Archaeol. Assoc.* 135, 1982, 1–10.
Excavated cathedral.

9148 RICHARDS, J. D. Anglo-Saxon pot shapes: cognitive investigations. *Science & Archaeol.* 24, 1982, 33–46.
Based mainly on evidence from Spong Hill cremation urns. See also his 'Funerary symbolism in Anglo-Saxon England', *Scottish Archaeol. Rev.* 3, 1984, 42–55.

See also no. 8040.

ELSING

9149 BINSKI, P. The coronation of the Virgin on the Hastings brass at Elsing. *Church Monuments* 1, 1985, 1–9.

9150 MUMBY, J. Elsing: a village history. Elsing, 1987.

See also nos. 8617, 8746.

ELVEDON

See no. 8689.

FAKENHAM

9151 FAKENHAM ASSOCIATION AGAINST HORSE STEALERS. Rules and orders...[1783]. P.

9152 HUMPHREYS, A. E. Borough guide to Fakenham. Fakenham, 1910.

9152A KERRISON, A. E. Centenary of Jappa Lodge no. 114 [Freemasons], 1866–1966. N.p., 1966. FPL.

9153 EASTERN GAS. Fakenham Gasworks. Potter's Bar, 1974. P. UEA.

9154 FAKENHAM FESTIVAL OF MUSIC AND THE ARTS. Programmes, 1975–.

9155 MORAN, J. Cox and Wyman Ltd., a company history. 1977.

9156 FAKENHAM LOCAL HISTORY SOCIETY. The town sign of Fakenham. Fakenham, 1979. P.

9157 BALDWIN, J. Fakenham: town on the Wensum. Cromer, 1982. P.

9158 NORFOLK COUNTY COUNCIL. Fakenham area shopping studies. [Norwich, 1984].

9159 PARTRIDGE, E. Fakenham Friends' Meeting House. *NARG News* 52, 1988, 5–9.

See also no. 8009.

FELBRIGG

9160 SIMPSON, R. J. Illustrations of St. Margaret's Church, Felbrigg. N.p., [1875?]. BL.
See also his *Brasses in St. Margaret's Church* (N.p., n.d.)

9161 FORD, B. Staying at Felbrigg as the guest of Wyndham Ketton-Cremer. *National Trust Yearbook*, 1977/78, 52–62.

9162 BACK, D. H. L. Firearms at Felbrigg. *National Trust Stud.*, 1979, 51–9.

9163 COOK, B. The 'headless lady' of Felbrigg Hall. *Ibid.*, 1980, 133–9.
Sculpture identified as part of Athenian grave monument.

9164 WATERSON, M. Marine pictures at Felbrigg Hall. *Country Life* 180, 1986, 438–40, 904–6.

See also nos. 8042, 8582.

FELMINGHAM

9165 GILBERT, H. The Felmingham Hall hoard. *Bull. Board Celtic Stud.* 28, 1978, 159–87.

FELTHORPE

See nos. 8570, 8820.

FELTWELL

9166 D[AUBENEY], A. R. V. A Feltwell family. The borough, registers [etc.]... King's Lynn, 1949. P. RCF.

9167 Feltwell coronation souvenir: the aerodrome, the churches, the school, the parish. King's Lynn, 1953. P.

9168 DAUBENEY, A. R. V. Feltwell: some further notes and tales. King's Lynn, 1954. *Followed by* Feltwell: some oddments (1956). P.

9169 Feltwell St. Nicholas and St. Mary. Some notes and remarks. Coventry, n.d. P. RCF.

See also no. 7734.

FERSFIELD

9170 GREENWOOD, J. R. Extracts from wills on gravestones at Fersfield and Stratton St. Michael. *Trans. Monumental Brass Soc.* 13, 1984, 381–6.

FILBY

9171 SKELTON, P. N. Historical notes on the manors of Filby. King's Lynn, [c. 1975].

FINCHAM

9172 HELLYER, A. The gardens of a great collector: Talbot Manor and Larchwood, Norfolk. *Country Life* 171, Mar. 1982, 550–52.
Gardens of Mr. M. Mason at Fincham.

FLEGG HUNDREDS

See nos. 8254, 8434, 8850.

FLORDON

9173 JOHNSON, C. J. The industrial archaeology of Flordon [and Hopton]. *J. Norfolk Industrial Archaeol. Soc.* 2 (3), 1978, 29–35.
See also no. 8458.

FORDHAM

See nos. 7889, 8549.

FORNCETT PARISHES

See nos. 7767A, 8458, 8927.

FRAMINGHAM PARISHES

9174 HARRIS, A. P. The twelfth century church of St. Andrew, Framingham Earl. *In* Three Norman churches in Norfolk (*E.A.A.R.* 32, 1987), pp. 81–9.
Excavation report.
See also nos. 8458, 8546.

FRANSHAM PARISHES

9175 FARRAR, J. M. Manor of Mills on the Moor together with Great Fransham, Norfolk: complete translation of the leet roll of 1670. *Geneal. Quart.* 23, 1956, 89–91.
See also no. 8462.

FRENZE

9176 GOODALL, J. A. Death and the Impenitent Avaricious King: a unique brass discovered at Frenze. *Apollo* 126, 1987, 264–6.
See also no. 8549.

FRITTON

See nos. 7509, 7560.

FULMODESTONE

9177 WADE-MARTINS, P. Two post-medieval earthenware pottery groups from Fulmodeston. *E.A.A.R.* 19, 1983.

GARBOLDISHAM

See no. 8458.

GAYTON

9178 PIRIE, J. Setting the parameters for a village study project [Gayton area]. *NARG News* 20, 1980, 2–5; 21, 1980, 20–24.

GIMINGHAM

9179 ABIGAIL, R. Notes on the churches of Gimingham and Trimingham. N.p., n.d. RCF.

GOODERSTONE

9180 RING, G. St. George's Church, Gooderstone: brief guide and history. [Gooderstone, 1981].
     See also no. 8549

GORLESTON AND SOUTHTOWN

9181 PHILLIPS, F. A. Gorleston and its parish church. Norwich, 1894.
9182 GREAT YARMOUTH BOROUGH COUNCIL. Gorleston town centre: draft district plan. Yarmouth, 1977. P.
9183 CLOUGH, T. H. M. *and* GREEN, C. The first late Bronze Age founder's hoard from Gorleston. *N.A.* 37, 1978, 1–18.
9184 St. Mary's, Southtown, through the years. [Great Yarmouth, 1978]. P.
9185 McEWAN, A. History and archaeology of Gorleston Priory. *Yarmouth Archaeol.* 1 (i), 1979, 3–16.
9186 ECCLESTONE, A. W. Gorleston. Gorleston, [1980].
9187 READ, J. Gorleston's Shelter Hall [Pavilion] and J. W. Cockrill. *Yarmouth Archaeol.* 1 (iv), 1982, [unpaginated].
See also note on subsequent use by E. W. Goate, *ibid.* 1 (v), 1983.
9188 BULLOCK, D. A. The Augustinian priory excavation: Wheelwrights Arms – Beccles Road site, Gorleston. *Yarmouth Archaeol.* 2 (3), 1986, 60–66.

GRENSTEIN

See no.7686.

GRESSENHALL

9189 PUDDY, E. The watermill of the Chapell of St. Nicholas of Rougholm in Gressenhall. Ipswich, 1966. P.

9190 GOREHAM, G. The Norfolk Rural Life Museum, Gressenhall: a short history of the house. [Norwich, 1978]. P.

9191 Gressenhall News and Views. Gressenhall, 1978–84.

9192 CARRINGTON, A. C. *and others*. Record of the monumental inscriptions in the church and churchyard of St. Mary, Gressenhall. [Gressenhall], 1981.

9193 Directory of Gressenhall. Gressenhall, 1983. P.

9194 JOLLY, C. The story of Gressenhall Methodist Church, or God's cottage. Gressenhall, 1985. P.

See also. no. 8030.

GRISTON

See no. 8458.

GUESTWICK

9195 ROGERSON, A. *and* WILLIAMS P. The late eleventh century church of St. Peter, Guestwick. *In* Three Norman churches in Norfolk (*E.A.A.R.* 32, 1987), pp. 67–80.
Excavation report.

See also no. 8458.

GUNTHORPE

9196 STEFFENS, R. J. *and others*. The church of St. Mary Gunthorpe: a brief guide. N.p., 1977. P.

GUNTON

9197 MAJOR, J. K. Gunton Park sawmill. *Industrial Archaeol.* 13, 1978, 3–8.

9198 BINNEY, M. *and* MARTIN, K. The country house: to be or not to be? (Save Britain's Heritage). 1982. Gunton Park, pp. 75–85.

9199 BINNEY, M. The fight for Gunton Park. *Country Life* 179, 1986, 1296–9.

HACKFORD

See no. 8458.

HADDISCOE

9200 GRIMMER, H. S. Notes and records of Haddiscoe. Yarmouth, 1866. P.

9201 LAWSON, N. G. St. Mary's Church, Haddiscoe. Beccles, n.d. P.

HAINFORD

9202 STANLEY, E. A sermon preached at the consecration of Haynford Church...[by the Bishop of Norwich]. Norwich, 1840. P. UEA.

9203 McCUTCHEON, E. M. J. John Taylor's poor. *E.A.M.* Sept. 1979, 596–8.

HALES WITH HECKINGHAM

See nos. 8796, 9217–18.

HALVERGATE

See nos. 7456, 7530.

HANWORTH

9204 HASLAM, R. Hanworth Hall, Norfolk. *Country Life* 15 Jan. 1987, 52–5.
See also no. 8685.

HAPPISBURGH

9205 PESTELL, R. E. Happisburgh, the story of a coastal parish. [Reprinted from *Norfolk Fair*]. Norwich, 1975. P.

HARDWICK

See no. 7894.

HARGHAM

See no. 8458.

HARLESTON

9205A SMITH, W. R. List of members of Lodge Faithful 85 [Freemasons]. Harleston, 1929. FPL.

9206 SOUTH NORFOLK DISTRICT COUNCIL. Harleston town centre draft plan: a discussion document. Norwich, 1977. P.

9207 RICHES, R. Harleston: a guide to present-day Harleston and some aspects of the history of the district. Ed. B. Jakes. Harleston, 1980.

9208 THOMAS, C. Harleston hosiery factory. *J. Norfolk Industrial Archaeol. Soc.* 2 (5), 1980, 33–6.

9209 SOUTH NORFOLK DISTRICT COUNCIL. Harleston local plan: consultation draft. Long Stratton, 1987.

HARLING, WEST

9210 DAVISON, A. J. West Harling: a village and its disappearance. *N.A.* 37, 1980, 295–306.
9211 ARCHIBALD, M. M. A ship-type of Athelstan I of East Anglia [from W. Harling]. *Brit. Numismatic J.* 52, 1982, 34–40.
9212 DAVISON, A. J. The distribution of medieval settlements in West Harling. *N.A.* 38, 1983, 329–36.
9213 ARCHIBALD, M. M. *and others*. The coinage of Beonna in the light of the Middle Harling hoard. *Brit. Numismatic J.* 55, 1985, 10–54.

HARPLEY

9214 LAWSON, A. The excavations of a round barrow at Harpley. *E.A.A.R.* 2, 1976, 45–64.

HEACHAM

9215 NEVILLE-ROLFE, C. W. Heacham in the [18]50s. *In* INGLEBY, C., *ed.* Supplement to Blomefield's Norfolk (1929), pp. 83–96.
9216 KING'S LYNN AND WEST NORFOLK BOROUGH COUNCIL. Heacham: plan for the future. King's Lynn, 1987.
Preceded by *Consultative draft* (1986).

See also no. 8612.

HECKINGHAM

9217 BILYARD, J. Hales Hospital, a history: workhouse to hospital. Norwich, 1987.
Former Heckingham workhouse.
9218 REID, A. Fire at the workhouse: a study in cause and motive. Yarmouth, 1988. P.
Workhouse fire of 1836. See also accompanying teacher's guide.

HEMPNALL

9219 LATHE, A., *ed.* The group: 21 years of the Hempnall group of parishes...Hempnall, 1986.
9220 CUBITT, M. The churches of Hempnall. *NARG News* 49, 1987, 1–8.
See also no. 7509.

HEMPSTEAD

9221 ROGERSON, A. *and* ADAMS, N. A moated site at Hempstead near Holt. *E.A.A.R.* 8, 1978, 55–72.
See also their preliminary article in *NARG News* 7, 1976, 10–14.
9222 LEWIS, P. *and* LEWIS, A. Hempstead water mill. *J. Norfolk Industrial Archaeol. Soc.* 3 (2), 1982, 92–4.

HEMPTON

9223 NICHOLSON, N. Hamatuna-Hempton: a village community, 1066–1977. [Hempton], 1977.

HEMSBY

9224 GREAT YARMOUTH BOROUGH COUNCIL. Hemsby district plan. Yarmouth, 1979. P.

9225 BEECH, G. A history of Hemsby. Hemsby, 1980. P.

9226 CHRISTIE, P. [Village portraits]. *E.A.M.* Sept. 1980, 546–7; Oct. 1981, 552–3.
On George Beech and Ada Fakes (centenarian).

9226A CORNFORD, B. Hemsby in the later middle ages. *Bull. Norfolk Research Committee* 32, 1984, 22–7.

Sale catalogue
9227 Hemsby Hall estate. 29 June 1918.

HETHERSETT

9228 HETHERSETT [AMENITY] SOCIETY. Hethersett handbook. 3rd ed. 1979. 5th ed. 1988.

9229 HUGHES, G., *ed*. Hethersett: 200 years of change. Hethersett, 1983. P.

9230 SOUTH NORFOLK DISTRICT COUNCIL. Hethersett local plan: report of survey and written statement. Long Stratton, 1984.
Preceded by *Draft local plan, a discussion document* (1982); and see also *Local plan: public participation and consultation* (1984).

9231 SOUTH NORFOLK DISTRICT COUNCIL. Hethersett: Back Lane/Shop Lane residential development brief. Long Stratton, 1984. P.
See also nos. 7953, 8876.

HEVINGHAM

9232 CAMPBELL, B. M. S. The complexity of manorial structure in medieval Norfolk: a case study [Hevingham]. *N.A.* 39, 1986, 225–61.

HEYDON

9233 CORNFORTH, J. Heydon Hall, Norfolk, and its village. *Country Life* 172, 1982, 246–9.
See also no. 7536.

HILBOROUGH

9234 A guide to the churches and villages of the Hilborough group of parishes. [1974]. P.

Sale catalogue
9235 Hilborough Hall. Furniture etc. Christie's, 21–23 Oct. 1985.

HILGAY

9236 ARNELL, L. *and* ARNELL, B. A brief history of Hilgay. Hilgay, 1983. P.

HILLINGTON

See no. 8458.

HINDRINGHAM

9237 HULME, A.-M. *and* CLIFTON, P. Social dancing in a Norfolk village, 1900–1945. *Folk Music J.* 3, 1978, 359–77.
9238 WYER. S. Requiem for a village: Hindringham. Fakenham, 1983.

HINGHAM

9239 HINGHAM FESTIVAL OF MUSIC. Programmes, 1963–. RCF.
9240 HINGHAM SOCIETY. The future development of Hingham. Hingham, [c.1975]. P.
9241 ALLEN, D. G. A tale of two towns: persistent English localism in seventeenth-century Massachusetts. *In* ALLEN, H. C. *and* THOMPSON, R., *eds*. Contrast and connection: bicentennial essays in Anglo-American history (1976), pp. 1–35.
Deals with emigration from the English to the American Hingham. See also chap. 5 of his Ph.D. thesis, 'In English ways: the movement of societies and the transferal of English local law and custom to Massachusetts Bay, 1600–1690' (Univ. of Wisconsin, 1974).
9242 LONSDALE, M. E. The heyday of their strength: the story of the emigrants from Hinghan, Norfolk, to the New World in the 17th century. Wymondham, 1979.
9243 NORRIS, R. Hingham, a short guide. Hingham, 1988. P.
See also nos. 7560, 8715, 8823.

HOCKERING

9244 JOLLY, C. Hockering Methodist Church. *E.A.M.* Feb. 1976, 162–3.

HOCKHAM

9245 MOSBY, J. E. G. Hockham Mere. *Trans. N. & N. Naturalists' Soc.* 14, 1935, 61–7.
See also nos. 7364, 7511, 8458.

HOCKWOLD

9246 JOHNS, C. The Roman silver cups from Hockwold. *Archaeologia* 108, 1986, 1–13.
See also nos. 7702, 7734.

HOLKHAM

9247 ROBINSON, J. M. Estate buildings at Holkham. *Country Life* 156, 1974, 1554–7, 1642–5.

9248 IVES, R. The Peterstone brickyard. *J. Norfolk Industrial Archaeol. Soc.* 2 (5), 1980, 12–16.

9249 MANNING, K. *and others*. Longlands Farm, Holkham Estate. *Ibid.* 17–26.
See also nos. 8050, 8642, 8644–6.

HOLKHAM HALL

9250 NORWICH CASTLE MUSEUM. Exhibition of old master drawings... from the Holkham Hall collection. Norwich, 1949.

9251 SKEAT, T. C. *and others*. Manuscripts and printed books from the Holkham Hall Library. *Brit. Museum Quart.* 17, 1952, 23–40.

9252 ROGERS, D. The Holkham collection [of printed books]. *Bodleian Lib. Record.* 4, 1953, 255–67.

9253 HASSALL, W. O. View from the Holkham windows. *In* EMMISON, F. G. *and* STEPHENS, R., *eds*. Tribute to an antiquary: essays presented to Marc Fitch (1976), pp. 305–19.

9254 AGNEW AND SONS LTD. Old master drawings from Holkham, collected by the first Earl of Leicester (1697–1759). Catalogue by C. Whitfield and G. Naughton. 1977.

9255 HARTCUP, A. Below stairs in the great country houses. 1980.
Chap. 4 deals with Holkham Hall.

9256 SCHMIDT, L. *and* CORNFORTH, J. Holkham Hall. *Country Life* 167, 1980, 214–17, 298–301, 359–62, 427–31.

9257 SCHMIDT, L. Holkham Hall: Studien zur Architektur und Ausstattung. Inaugural-Dissertation, Albert-Ludwigs-Univ., Freiburg-im-Breisgau, [1980]. UEA.

9258 DE LA MARE, A. C. Further manuscripts from Holkham Hall. *Bodleian Lib. Record* 10, 1982, 327–38.

9259 CORNFORTH, J. Augustan vision restored. *Country Life* 4 Aug. 1988, 90–92.
On restoration of 2 pictures commissioned for Holkham by first Earl of Leicester.
See also nos. 8050, 8643.

HOLME HALE

9260 HUNT, A. The Holme Hale story. Ed. C. Dawes. Holme Hale, 1985. P.
See also no. 8696.

HOLT

9261 The dunces of Norfolk, a satire; or, Patroclus and his clan lately assembled at H... truly delineated. 2nd ed. 1740.
Squib against Gresham's School masters.

9262 The history of Woodlands, Gresham's School, Holt. Holt, 1955.

9263 MACKEOWN, M. Holt and its environs. Salthouse, 1981. P.

9264 BROOKS, P. Holt: historical market town. Cromer, 1982. P.
See also no. 8765.

HOPTON

See no. 9173.

HORNING

9265 EDWARDS, W. F. A study of Horning parish registers under Elizabeth I and the early Stuarts. *Bull. Norfolk Research Committee* 22, 1979, 10–14.
9266 ROSE, E. A linear earthwork at Horning. *E.A.A.R.* 14, 1982, 35–9.
May have been defences of early monastic site.

HORNINGTOFT

See no. 7686.

HORSEY

See no. 8458.

HORSHAM ST. FAITH

9267 BARRETT-LENNARD, T. A Norman door from Horsham St. Faith's Priory. *N.A.M.* 2nd ser. 1, 1906, 52–5.
9268 BURTON, J. R. An English village: Horsham St. Faiths. [Unpubl. typescript, 1973]. P.
9269 SHERLOCK, D. Discoveries at Horsham St. Faith Priory, 1970–1973. *N.A.* 36, 1976/77, 202–23, 386–7.
9269A ST. FAITH'S SOCIETY. St. Faiths directory. [Horsham St. Faith], 1976. P.

HOUGHTON HALL

9270 A set of prints, engraved after the most capital paintings in the collection of... the Empress of Russia, lately... at Houghton in Norfolk: with plans, elevations, sections, chimney pieces and ceilings. 2 vols. 1788. BL.
9271 MADDEN, D. C. The building of Houghton Hall. M.A. thesis, London Univ., 1970.
9271A YAXLEY, D., *ed.* Survey of the Houghton Hall estate by Joseph Hill, 1800. *N.R.S.* 50, 1984 [publ. 1986].
9272 BOWDEN-SMITH, R. The water house, Houghton Hall. Illustr. W. A. Thompson. Woodbridge, 1987.
9273 CORNFORTH, J. Houghton Hall, Norfolk. *Country Life* 30 Apr. 1987, 124–9; 7 May, 104–8; 14 May, 162–8.
Concentrates on inventories of 1745 and 1792 and contemporary descriptions.

See also no. 8411.

HOUGHTON ST. GILES.

See no. 8462.

HOVETON

See nos. 7459, 8563, 8594, 10141.

HOWE

See no. 7560.

HUNSTANTON

9274 HUNSTANTON AND DISTRICT FESTIVAL OF ARTS. Programmes. 1958–. RCF.

9275 MARTIN, R. G. These hundred years: a picture of Union Church, Hunstanton. [Hunstanton, c. 1970]. P.

9276 WEST NORFOLK DISTRICT COUNCIL. Hunstanton: coast and country. King's Lynn, 1978. P.

9277 LAWSON, A. J. A late middle Bronze Age hoard from Hunstanton. *In* BURGESS, C. *and* COOMBS, D., *eds*. Bronze Age hoards (Brit. Archaeol. Repts. 67, 1979), pp. 42–92.

9278 GORE, L. L. The history of Hunstanton. Bognor Regis, 1983.

9279 KING'S LYNN AND WEST NORFOLK BOROUGH COUNCIL. Hunstanton draft district plan. King's Lynn, [1983].

9280 PAWLEY, M. Hunstanton School. *Architects' J.* 23 May 1984, 39–42.

9281 STIBBONS, T. The Hunstanton lifeboats. North Walsham, 1984. P.

9282 UNIVERSITY OF EAST ANGLIA: ECONOMICS RESEARCH CENTRE. The particular problems of educational provision for seasonally unemployed people in rural coastal areas. Hunstanton, a case study. Norwich, 1986.

9283 WYMER, J. J. Early Iron Age pottery and a triangular loom weight from Redgate Hill, Hunstanton. *N.A.* 39, 1986, 286–96.

See also no. 7712.

ICKBURGH

See nos. 8458, 8549.

ILLINGTON

See nos. 7741, 8458.

INGHAM

9284 PARK, D. A lost 14th-century altar-piece from Ingham. *Burlington Mag.* 130, 1988, 132–6.

See also no. 8472.

INGWORTH

9285 SCOTT, W. *and* WELCH, C. A brief history of St. Lawrence Church, Ingworth. Illus. J. Partner. 1971. P.

ITTERINGHAM

9286 SMITH, E. G. Transformation of a Norfolk watermill [Itteringham]. *E.A.M.* Aug. 1939. 501–504.

KELLING

9287 COLEMAN, J. Kelling School, 1877–1977: a look back. N.p., 1977. P.
9288 DOLLIN, B. W. Discovery and recovery at Kelling. *NARG News* 46, 1986, 1–6.
Discusses site of original manor house of Ilketshale family.

KEMPSTONE

See no. 7686.

KENNINGHALL

9289 SERPELL, M. F. Kenninghall history and St. Mary's Church. Kenninghall, [1982].

KESWICK

See nos. 7560, 8007.

KETTERINGHAM

See no. 8573.

KILVERSTONE

9290 WATSON, J. N. P. Latin America in East Anglia. The Kilverstone Wild Life Park. *Country Life* 164, 1978, 14–16.
See also nos. 8704, 9105.

KIMBERLEY

9291 WELLS, W. Heraldic relics from Kimberley. *Scottish Art Rev.* 8, 1962, 17–21, 31.

KING'S LYNN

DIRECTORIES

9292 TURNER's directory of King's Lynn. King's Lynn, 1901.

GUIDE-BOOKS

9293 KING'S LYNN SOCIETY OF ARTS AND SCIENCES. King's Lynn. Ed. C. N. Veal. Wisbech, 1981. Other eds. 1983, 1985.

9294 KING'S LYNN ROTARY CLUB. King's Lynn through Rotarian eyes. King's Lynn, 1984.

See also nos. 7589, 7595, 9346–52.

HISTORY

GENERAL WORKS

9295 LYNN NEWS AND ADVERTISER. King's Lynn charter story, celebrating 750 years, 1204–1954. King's Lynn, 1954. P.

9296 DAY, J. W. King's Lynn and Sandringham through the ages. Ipswich, 1977.

9297 MIDGLEY, P. W. The Northenders, a disappeared community. An account of the fisher folk of King's Lynn, 1185–1940. [King's Lynn], 1987.
See also L. Rix, *Community and segregation: a study of the North End fishing community of King's Lynn* (1987).

9298 WILSON, R. Bygone Lynn. King's Lynn, 1987.

See also no. 8306.

MEDIEVAL PERIOD

9299 CLARKE, H. *and* CARTER, A. Excavations in King's Lynn, 1963–1970. (Soc. for Medieval Archaeol. monograph ser. 7). 1977.

9300 RUTLEDGE, E. *and* RUTLEDGE, P. King's Lynn and Great Yarmouth: 2 thirteenth century surveys. *N.A.* 37, 1978, 92–114.
King's Lynn survey (c. 1279), pp.92–110.

9301 CLARKE, H. Archaeology, history and architecture of the medieval ports of the east coast of England, with special reference to King's Lynn. *In* McGRAIL, S., *ed.* The archaeology of medieval ships and harbours in Northern Europe (Brit. Archaeol. Repts., internat. ser. 66, 1979), pp. 155–65.

9302 OWEN, D. M. Bishop's Lynn: the first century of a new town? *Anglo-Norman Stud.* 2, 1980, 141–53.

9303 CLARKE, H. The medieval waterfront of King's Lynn. *In* MILNE, G. *and* HOBLEY, B., *eds.* Waterfront archaeology in Britain and Northern Europe (C.B.A. research rept., 41, 1981), pp. 132–5.

9304 CLARKE, H. English East Coast ports in the Middle Ages: an historical and archaeological survey. In Seehandelszentren des nordlichen Europa: der Strukturwandel vom 12. zum 13. Jahrhundert (Bonn, 1983), pp.69–75.
Emphasis on Lynn.

9305 OWEN, D. M., *ed.* The making of King's Lynn: a documentary survey. 1984.
9306 BEAUROY, J. Family patterns and relations of Bishop's Lynn will-makers in the 14th century. *In* BONFIELD, L. *and others, eds.* The world we have gained: essays presented to Peter Laslett... (Oxford, 1986), pp. 23–42.

See also nos. 9316, 9332, 9359.

TUDOR AND STUART

9307 Ms. Western 30745: a chronicle of Lynn [1477–1542]. *In* FLENLEY, R. *ed.* Six town chronicles of England (Oxford, 1911), pp. 84–95, 184–201.
9308 DYKE, G. W. The siege of King's Lynn. *NARG News* 25, 1981, 4–11.
9309 METTERS, G. A. The rulers and merchants of King's Lynn in the early 17th century. Ph.D. thesis, Univ. of E. Anglia, 1982.
9310 MILLER, A. C. A man of "unquiet spirit". *Recusant Hist.* 17, 1984, 1–16.
Concerns Mordaunt Webster, Restoration cleric at King's Lynn and alleged convert to Catholicism.
9311 COOPER, S. M. Family, household and occupation in pre-industrial England; social structure in King's Lynn, 1689–1702. Ph.D. thesis, Indiana Univ., 1985.

See also nos. 8176, 9317.

18TH TO 20TH CENTURIES

9311A ARMES, W. Memories of Lynn. King's Lynn, 1872.
9312 BRADFER-LAWRENCE, H. L. The merchants of Lynn. *In* INGLEBY, C., *ed.* Supplement to Blomefield's Norfolk (1929), pp. 145–203.
Genealogical study of prominent 18th century families.
9313 RABY, J. W. The alloted span in King's Lynn. King's Lynn, 1950.
Deals with politics and personalities, c. 1920–1950.
9314 Installation of H.R.H. the Duke of Kent as 19th High Steward of King's Lynn. Programme and narrative. King's Lynn, 1975. P.
9315 WILSON, R. Red alert: the bombing of King's Lynn, 1939–1942. King's Lynn, 1985.

See also nos. 8712, 8725, 8776, 8875A, 9347–8, 9351.

MUNICIPAL GOVERNMENT

THE CORPORATION

9316 GREEN, *Mrs.* J. R. The Common Council of Lynn. *In* Town life in the 15th century (1894), vol. 2, pp. 402–426.
9317 BATTLEY, S. M. Elite and community: the mayors of 16th century King's Lynn. Ph.D. thesis, State Univ. of New York, Stony Brook, 1981.

PLANNING

9318 NORFOLK COUNTY COUNCIL. King's Lynn town map. Gaywood Clock C.D.A. Report of survey and written analysis. Norwich, 1965. P.
9319 WEST NORFOLK DISTRICT COUNCIL. The Friars draft action plan, incorporating

the general improvement area. [King's Lynn, 1978].

9320 WEST NORFOLK DISTRICT COUNCIL. Gaywood clock. Draft district plan. King's Lynn, 1979. KL.
See also the *Consultative draft* (1977); and the *Statement of public participation and con-sultation* [1979].

9321 KING'S LYNN AND WEST NORFOLK BOROUGH COUNCIL. King's Lynn town centre local plan: consultative draft. 1984.
See also nos. 7538, 7552.

PARLIAMENTARY REPRESENTATION

9322 LYNN ADVERTISER. A full report of the King's Lynn election petition, March 1911. King's Lynn, 1911.

9323 WOOD, S. Walpole's constituency: King's Lynn. *History Today* 30 April, 1980, 40–44.
See also no. 8900.

PUBLIC HEALTH

9324 LYNN DISPENSARY. Report of the committee of directors for the year 1817. King's Lynn, 1818. P.

9325 WEST NORFOLK AND LYNN HOSPITAL. Rules and orders. King's Lynn, 1834. P.

9326 WEST NORFOLK AND LYNN HOSPITAL. Centenary souvenir, 1835–1935: pro-gramme...opening the new outpatients, medical, and ophthalmic block by H.M. Queen Mary...Feb. 9th. King's Lynn, 1935.

9327 LEWIN, J. A history of the West Norfolk and King's Lynn Hospital. King's Lynn, [1978].

9328 PEACOCK, A. C. Reaction in the borough of King's Lynn to the Public Health Reform acts of the mid-19th century. [Unpubl. typescript, 1980].

PUBLIC WORKS, UTILITIES, ETC.

9329 Rules for the Lynn Fire Brigade... King's Lynn, 1861. RCF.

9330 KING'S LYNN CIVIC SOCIETY. A study of options for King's Lynn flood defences. King's Lynn, 1980. P.

9331 Anglian Water Authority (King's Lynn tidal defences) Act. 1984.

TRADE AND INDUSTRY

TO 1750

9332 CLARKE, H. King's Lynn and East Coast trade in the Middle Ages. *In* BLACKMAN, D. J., *ed.* Marine archaeology: proceedings of the 23rd symposium of the Colston Research Soc. (1973), pp. 277–90.

9333 ASHTON, R. A note on trade between King's Lynn and Livorno in the first decade of the 17th century. *In* Atti del Convegno 'Gli Inglesi a Livorno e all'Isola d'Elba' (Livorno, 1980), pp. 178–80.
See also no. 9359.

MODERN

9334 KING'S LYNN BOROUGH COUNCIL. King's Lynn: industrial and commercial development at King's Lynn. [Lynn], 1948.

9335 CLARK, R. H. 100 not out. To commemorate the centenary of Savages Ltd., Engineers (1850–1950). King's Lynn, [1950].
Continued in 2nd ed. titled *Savages Ltd., Engineers... a short history, 1850–1964* (1964).

9336 SPARKES, W. Mr. Frederick Savage, King's Lynn. *J. Norfolk Industrial Archaeol. Soc.* 1 (6), 1974, 3–10.
From a 19th century ms.

9337 BRAITHWAITE, D. Savage of King's Lynn: inventor of machines and merry-go-rounds. Cambridge, 1975.
For account of one notable Savage fairground ride see S. R. White, 'The Sea in Land', *E.A.M.* Feb. 1979, 218–19.

9338 DEPT. OF EMPLOYMENT. The explosion at the Dow chemical factory, Kings Lynn, 27 June 1976. A report by HM Factory Inspectorate. 1977. P.

9339 TRETT, R. *and* TUCK, D. W. Alfred Dodman and Co. of King's Lynn. *N.A.* 36, 1977, 373–82.

9340 JAMES, E. M. King's Lynn and the glass-making industry. Norwich, 1979. P.

9341 HOLMAN, R. A. F. Holman and Son. *J. Norfolk Industrial Archaeol. Soc.* 2 (4), 1979, 62–9.
Stone masons, Railway Rd.

9342 AICKMAN, D. J. John Aickman's foundery MDCCCXXVII [1827], King's Lynn: a fragment of Lynn history. King's Lynn, 1980.

9343 CUNLIFFE, R. Factory extension for Bespak Industries, King's Lynn. *Architects' J.* 172, July 1980, 17–32.

RELIGION

See nos. 7328, 8788–93, 9360.

CULTURE AND RECREATION

BOOKS AND LIBRARIES

9344 WILSON, R. King's Lynn Library, 1905–1974. King's Lynn, 1980. P.

SOCIETIES AND CLUBS

9345 OSWELL, G. R. History of Freemasonry in King's Lynn. Lynn, 1956. FPL.
See also his *King's Lynn and the Holy Royal Arch* (1958).

9345A WEBB, D. H. Philanthropic Royal Arch Chapter no. 107. King's Lynn, 1968. FPL.

TOPOGRAPHY

GENERAL ARCHITECTURAL FEATURES

9346 KING'S LYNN MUSEUM. The town scene. Selected topographical material from the King's Lynn Borough collections exhibited in King's Lynn Museum. [Lynn, 1973].

9347 WINTON, M. Vintage King's Lynn. Nelson, 1976.
Photographic history of late Victorian and early 20th century Lynn.

9348 AUKER, R. H. Ancient Lynn, 1766–1848 [from drawings by Edward Edwards]. King's Lynn, [1977]. P.

9349 KING'S LYNN PRESERVATION TRUST. Heritage in danger. King's Lynn, 1977.

9350 SENIOR, C. Inns and taverns of Lynn. [Typescript and press cuttings]. 8 vols. 1978.

9351 WILSON, R. King's Lynn in old picture postcards. Zaltbommel (Netherlands), 1983.

9352 KENT, P. King's Lynn [fortifications]. *Fort* 13, 1985, 49–60.
See also no. 7628.

DISTRICTS, STREETS, BUILDINGS, A–Z

9353 BARTON, C. Bowker's Warehouse and the Hovel, King's Lynn. *NARG News* 9, 1977, 7–14.

9354 RICHMOND, H. *and* TAYLOR, R. 28, 30 and 32 King Street, King's Lynn: interim report. *E.A.A.R.* 2, 1976, 247–9.
See also illustrated article by Teresa Snowdon. *E.A.M.* Oct. 1975, 554–6.

9355 WADE-MARTINS, P. No. 22 King Street, King's Lynn. *E.A.A.R.* 14, 1982, 125–8.

9355A KELLY, G. I. Lattice House, King's Lynn: a full documentary account. [Unpubl. 1982].

9356 RICHMOND, H. *and others*. Nos. 28–34 Queen Street, King's Lynn. *E.A.A.R.* 14, 1982, 108–24.

9357 The priory and parish church of S. Margaret... King's Lynn, [1975].

9358 HESFORD, B. The organs and masters of the music in St. Margaret's, King's Lynn. *Organ* 55, 1977, 120–36.

9359 CAMERON, H. K. 14th-century Flemish brasses at King's Lynn, commemorating merchants in St. Margaret's Church. *Archaeol. J.* 136, 1979, 151–72.

9360 WODEHOUSE, *Canon* C. N. A sermon preached in St. Nicholas' Chapel... with appendix... on the pew rights in St. Margaret's parish. King's Lynn, [1853]. P. RCF.

9361 SMITH, T. P. The date of the King's Lynn South Gate. *N.A.* 36, 1976, 224–32.

9362 JAMES, E. A fresh study of the South Gate at King's Lynn, in the light of recent restoration work. *N.A.* 40, 1987, 55–72.

KIRSTEAD

9363 WADE, K. Excavations at Langhale, Kirstead. *E.A.A.R.* 2, 1976, 101–30.
Unearthing of Saxon/Norman kiln.

LANGFORD

See no. 8549.

LANGHAM

9363A HONER, D. E. A village schoolmaster: an account of the careers of Arthur Smith and his wife Amy Ridout, and of the village school at Langham ... where they taught. Goring (Sussex), 1986. P.
9364 VAN DAMME, E. *and* HONER, D. E. Aspects of Langham, a Norfolk village. Fakenham, 1987.

LANGLEY

9365 PEARSON, R. Farm into garden [Langley Grange]. *Country Life* 170, 1981, 758–60.

See also no. 8411.

LARLING

See no. 8458.

LODDON R. D. C.

9366 LODDON RURAL DISTRICT COUNCIL. 80 years of Loddon R.D.C., 1894–1974. [Loddon, 1974]. P.

LODDON (Parish)

See no. 7560.

LONGHAM

See no. 7686.

LOPHAM PARISHES

9367 A Norfolk linen centre: 'The Limes', North Lopham. *J. Norfolk Industrial Archaeol. Soc.* 1 (9), 1975, 3–9.
9368 SERPELL, M. F. A history of the Lophams. Chichester, 1980.

LUDHAM

9369 BATELY, J. An archaeological paper on the mitred abbey of St. Benet's. 1891. P.
9369A NEVILL, C. The ruined abbey in the marshes. Norwich, 1909. P.
9370 GRANSDEN, A. The 'Cronica Buriensis' and the abbey of St. Benet of Hulme. *Bull. Inst. Hist. Research* 36, 1963, 77–82.
9371 SNELLING, J. M. St. Benet's Abbey, Norfolk. Norwich, 1971. P. Another ed. 1974.
9372 EDWARDS, W. F. Studies towards a history of the Benedictine Abbey of St. Benet at Holme. Horning, 1981. P.

9373 A survey of Ludham. *J. Norfolk Industrial Archaeol. Soc.* 3 (1), 1981, 34–51.
9374 HOLMES, D. The How Hill story. Ludham, 1988. P.
See also no. 8850.

LYNG

See no. 8716.

LYNN, WEST

9375 CLARK, W. B. A William Jay Bolton window discovered: 'The Angel at the Tomb' at West Lynn. *J. Stained Glass* 18, 1983/84, 52–7.

MARHAM

9376 TRETT, R. Marham Pumping Station. *J. Norfolk Industrial Archaeol. Soc.* 2 (3), 1978, 18–21.
9377 ELLIOTT, C. R. A letter from Marham. *E.A.M.* 41, Nov. 1981, 24–6.
Written from R.A.F. station during Second World War.
See also no. 8228.

MARLINGFORD

9378 BURT, R. A brief history of Marlingford. Easton, 1986. P.

MARSHAM

9379 FISHER, C. Soame of Marsham. *J. Norfolk Industrial Archaeol. Soc.* 3 (1), 1981, 8–17.
Engineering works.

MARTHAM

9380 BRIDGES, A. The changing role of the Anglican Church from 1534 to 1976 as illustrated by the life of the village of Martham. Cert. in Local Hist., Cambridge Board of Extra-Mural Studies, 1977.
9381 CAMPBELL, B. M. S. Population change and the genesis of commonfields on a Norfolk manor: Martham. *Ec. Hist. Rev.* 33, 1980, 174–92.
9382 ORTON, C. Martham in times past. Chorley, 1984.
See also no. 8030.

MASSINGHAM, GREAT

See no. 7536.

MATTISHALL

9383 FUSSELL, G. E. Mattishall in the 1780s. *Suffolk Rev.* 3, 1966, 83–5.
9384 BARRINGER, J. C., *ed*. Towards a history of Mattishall; from research by the village history group of the Mattishall Society. Mattishall, 1977.
9385 JOHNSON, M. B. Mattishall. *Quart. J. Parson Woodforde Soc.* 10, 1977, 6–20.
See also no. 8546.

MELTON PARISHES

9386 ROBINS, P. A. The Great Melton mesolithic site. *NARG News* 51, 1987, 6–11.
See also nos. 7953, 8876.

MERTON

See no. 8458.

METHWOLD

9387 YATES, E. M. Land and life at the fen edge, as depicted in the medieval muniments of Methwold. (King's College, London, Dept. of Geography occasional paper, 17). 1984.

MIDDLETON

9388 YATES, E. M. The dispute of the salt fen. *N.A.* 38, 1981, 73–8.
Dispute over enclosure of Middleton fen by Thomas Thoresby of Lynn in 1540s.
9389 ROGERSON, A. *and* ASHLEY, S. J. A medieval pottery production site at Blackborough End, Middleton. *N.A.* 39, 1985, 181–9.

MILEHAM

See nos. 7686, 8462.

MORLEY

9389A HOARE, A. A history of Morley School, 1742–1978. [Unpubl. typescript, 1978].
See also no. 8108.

MORNINGTHORPE

9390 GREEN, B. *and others*. The Anglo-Saxon cemetery at Morning Thorpe, Norfolk. 2 vols. *E.A.A.R.* 36, 1987.
See also no. 7509.

MORSTON

9391 SOLOMON, J. D. Palaeolithic and Mesolithic sites at Morston. *Man* 31, 1931, 275–8.
9392 LINNELL, C. L. S. Morston Church, Norfolk. 1957. P. RCF.

MULBARTON

See no. 7560

MUNDESLEY

9393 Mundesley, Norfolk. Official guide. [c. 1936]. Several later eds.
9394 FISHER, B. Mundesley past and present. [Unpubl. typescript, 1976]. P.
9395 GOODWYN, E. A. Mundesley past. Beccles, 1979.
9396 READING, E. A Mundesley album. North Walsham, 1985.
See also nos. 7589, 7591.

MUNDFORD

9397 BRECKLAND DISTRICT COUNCIL. Mundford village plan. Discussion report. Dereham, 1977.
9398 YAXLEY, D. A decorated ceiling at Mundford. *NARG News* 20, 1980, 14–17.
9399 WALMSLEY, M. Non-participation in planning: the case of Mundford in Norfolk. *In* MOSELEY, M. J., *ed.* Power, planning and people in rural East Anglia (Norwich, 1982), pp. 43–74.
See also no. 7526.

NARBOROUGH

9400 TURNER, D. E. History of Narborough. 3 parts. Narborough, [1981–86].
9401 Narborough Mill. *J. Norfolk Industrial Archaeol. Soc.* 2 (2), 1977, 32–6.
See also no. 8462.

NARFORD

9402 PARISSIEN, S. *and others.* Narford Hall. *Georgian Group Rept. & J.* 1987, 49–61.
9403 KNOX, G. Antonio Pellegrini and Marco Ricci at Burlington House and Narford Hall. *Burlington Mag.* 130, 1988, 846–53.

NEEDHAM

9404 FRERE, S. S. A food vessel from Needham. *Antiq. J.* 20, 1940, 272–4.
9405 MATHER, C. Some notes on Needham. Illustr. by H. Peters. [Harleston, 1975].
9406 BUSH, A. Needham notes; or, the memoirs of a miller's son. Privately publ., 1988.

NEWTON FLOTMAN

9407 WALKER, R. Newton Flotman: history of a Norfolk village. Newton Flotman, 1973.

NEWTON, WEST

9408 DURST, D. *and others.* Norfolk flax. *J. Norfolk Industrial Archaeol. Soc.* 2 (5), 1980, 37–44.
H.M. Norfolk Flax Establishment at West Newton, important during 2nd World War.

NORTHREPPS

See no. 8727.

NORTHWOLD

See no. 8458.

NORWICH

GUIDEBOOKS

9409 DOUGHTY, G. B. Quaint old Norwich. Stratford, 1895. P.
Small guide produced for Church Congress.
9410 The guide to the Church Congress and ecclesiastical art exhibition to be held at Norwich... including a guide to Norwich by the Rev. [A.] Jessopp. 1895.
9411 VARKE, H. A ramble through Norwich. Norwich, 1898. UEA.
9412 ODDFELLOWS A[NNUAL] M[OVABLE] C[OMMITTEE]. Guide to Norwich... with portraits and numerous illustrations. Norwich, 1901.
9413 LEEDS, H. In the city of gardens. Some impressionist sketches of local life and scenes. Norwich, 1907.
9414 NORWICH CHAMBER OF COMMERCE. Mancroft pocket guide to Norwich. Norwich, [1907].
9415 PURCHAS, A. Norwich: a souvenir of the historic city with notes and illustrations. Norwich, 1911. P.
9416 HOLMES, K. Norwich in pictures. 1954.
See also his *Colourful Norwich* (1958).
9417 THURLOW, A. G. G. The city of Norwich, capital of East Anglia. 1970. P.
9418 MOSELEY, M. J., *ed.* A geographical guide to Norwich. Norwich, 1974.
9419 SIMPSON, R. Literary walks in Norwich. Norwich, 1983.
See also nos. 7591–2, 7595, 7598, 9758–77, 10161.

HISTORY AND ARCHAEOLOGY

HISTORICAL AIDS

9420 BENSLY, W. T., *ed*. Early maps of the city of Norwich. Norwich, 1890.

9421 CAMPBELL, J. Norwich. *In* LOBEL, M. D., *ed*. Atlas of historic towns (1975), vol. 2. [Maps & plans by W. H. Johns].

GENERAL WORKS

9422 WOODWARD, S. Nordovicus antiqua. Illustrations of the early history of Norwich. [Unpubl. ms.], 1826. RCF.

9423 JONES, W. H. Pockthorpe: its mayor and fair. *In* ANDREWS, W., *ed*. Bygone Norfolk (1898), pp. 182–95.
On festival of 'mock Mayor'.

9424 CLAXTON, W. H. Record of local events of Norwich from 575 to 1900. Norwich, [1900]. P. 2nd enlarged ed. 1904.
Continued for 1906 and 1907 in *Claxton's model calendar...* (Norwich, 1909). P.

9425 Citizens of no mean city. Norwich, the East Anglian capital. Norwich, 1910.

9426 SAMUEL, A. M. The Mancroft essays. 1923. Another ed. 1937.
Random musings: a number touch on Norwich subjects.

9427 HILL, G. F. Norwich reminiscences. 1947.

9428 MOTTRAM, R. H. Norwich. *In* MOLONY, E., *ed*. Portraits of towns [1952], pp. 119–24.

9429 DAY, J. W. Norwich through the ages. Ipswich, 1976.

9430 CORFIELD, P. J. Towns, trade, religion and radicalism: the Norwich perspective on English history. Norwich, 1980.
Memorial lecture.

9431 SOLOMONS, G. Stories behind the plaques of Norwich. Norwich, 1981.

ARCHAEOLOGY

9432 DAWKINS, *Sir* W. B. A hoard of articles of the Bronze Age found at Eaton, near Norwich. *Proc. Soc. Antiq.* 2nd ser. 11, 1885, 42–51.

9433 WELLS, C. Dental pathology from a Norwich burial ground. *J. Hist. Medicine and Allied Sciences* 23, 1968, 372–9.

9434 WAINWRIGHT, G. J. The excavation of prehistoric and Romano-British settlements at Eaton Heath, Norwich. *Archaeol. J.* 130, 1973, 1–43.

9435 CARTER, A. *and others*. Excavations in Norwich, 1973–78. The Norwich Survey: 3rd–7th interim reports. *N.A.* 36, 1974/77, 39–71; 99–110; 191–201; 287–304; 37, 1978, 19–55.

9436 SELKIRK, A. Norwich. *Current Archaeol.* 48, 1975, 8–15.

9437 CARTER, A. Sampling in a medieval town: the study of Norwich. *In* CHERRY, J. F. *and others, eds*. Sampling in contemporary British archaeology (Brit. Archaeol. Repts. 50, 1978), pp. 263–77.

9438 ATKIN, M. *and* SMITH, R. Norwich. *Current Archaeol.* 68, 1979, 280–4.

9439 NORWICH SURVEY. The Norwich survey, 1970–1980. Norwich, 1980. P.

9440 CARTER, A. Norwich. *In* MILNE, G. *and* HOBLEY, B., *eds*. Waterfront archaeology in Britain and Northern Europe (CBA research rept. 41, 1981), pp. 139–41.

9441 JENNINGS, S. *and others.* Eighteen centuries of pottery from Norwich. *E.A.A.R.* 13 (1981).

9442 Excavations in Norwich, 1971–1978. *E.A.A.R.* 15 (1982); 26 (1985).

9443 AYERS, B. *and* MURPHY, P. A waterfront excavation at Whitefriars Street car park, Norwich, 1979. *E.A.A.R.* 17, 1983, 1–60, + microfiche.

9444 AYERS, B. Palace Plain, Norwich. *NARG News* 25, 1981, 1–4; 28, 1982, 14–20.

9445 AYERS, B. *and* LAWSON, A. J. Digging under the doorstep: recent excavations in Norwich. Norwich, 1983. P,

9446 ATKIN, M. *and others.* Thetford-type ware production in Norwich. *E.A.A.R.* 17, 1983, 61–97.
Report on 4 kilns dating from 10th to 12th centuries.

9447 ATKIN, M. The chalk tunnels of Norwich. *N.A.* 38, 1983, 313–20.
Sources of building lime and flints over many centuries.

9448 ATKIN, M. *and* MARGESON, S. A 14th-century pewter chalice and paten from Carrow Priory, Norwich. *N.A.* 38, 1983, 374–80.

9449 ATKIN, M. W. *and* EVANS, D. H. Population, profit and plague: the archaeological interpretation of buildings and land use in Norwich. *Scottish Archaeol. Rev.* 3, 1984, 92–8.

9450 LAWSON, A. J. The Mile Cross hoard: 2 early bronze age axes from Norwich. *N.A.* 39, 1984, 82–7.

9451 AYERS, B. *and others.* Excavations within the north-east bailey of Norwich Castle, 1979. *E.A.A.R.* 28, 1985.

9452 AYERS, B. *and others.* Excavations at St. Martin-at-Palace Plain, Norwich, 1981. *E.A.A.R.* 37, 1987.
See also Ayers' 'The growth of a Saxon port' in A. E. Herteig, ed. *Conference on waterfront archaeology in N. European towns,* 2 (Bergen, 1985), pp.46–54.

9453 AYERS, B. St. Margaret in Combusto, Magdalen Street. *NARG News* 48, 1987, 1–6.
Excavation of medieval graveyard.

9454 AYERS, B. Castle Mall: trial work, 1988. Norwich, 1988. P.
See also nos. 9460A, 9796, 9814, 9818, 9829, 9834, 9869

MEDIEVAL

9455 DAVIS, M. D. Hebrew deeds of English Jews before 1290. (Publ. Anglo-Jewish Hist. Exhibition, 2). 1888. Norwich deeds, pp.1–218.

9456 LIPMAN, V. D. The Roth 'Haje' manuscript. *In* SHAFTESLEY, J. M., *ed.* Remember the days (Jewish Hist. Soc. of England, 1966), pp. 49–71.
List of Norwich debtors, 1280s.

9457 STOREY, R. The Norwich riots. *In his* The end of the House of Lancaster (1966), pp.217–25.

9458 CARTER, A. The Anglo-Saxon origins of Norwich: the problems and approaches. *Anglo-Saxon England* 7, 1978, 175–204.

9459 CATHCART, M. F. An introduction to the economic and social structure and settlement patterns of Norwich, prior to the Norman conquest. M.A. thesis, Univ.

of Nebraska, 1983.

9460 PRIESTLEY, U., *ed*. Men of property: an analysis of the Norwich enrolled deeds, 1285–1311. Norwich, 1983.
Papers on acquisition of Blackfriars church site (M. Tillyard); economic topography and structure (S. Kelly); and property transfer and enrollment system (E. Rutledge).

9460A ATKIN, M. *and* MARGESON, S. Life on a medieval street: excavations on Alms Lane, Norwich, 1976. Norwich, 1985. P.

9461 VIRGOE, R. A Norwich taxation list of 1451. *N.A*. 40, 1988, 145–54.

See also nos. 7496, 9437, 9519, 9521, 9645, 9686–92, 9772.

TUDOR AND STUART

9462 EVANS, J. T. The decline of oligarchy in 17th century Norwich. *J. Brit. Stud*. 14, 1974, 46–76.

9463 HINSON, M. D. Apprenticeship and occupation in Norwich, 1580–1625. B.A. thesis, Univ. of Queensland, 1978.

9464 RHODES, D. E. A party at Norwich in 1562. *N.A*. 37, 1978, 116–20.
Given by Guild of St. George for Duke of Norfolk and his guests.

9465 EVANS, J. T. Seventeenth century Norwich: politics, religion and government, 1620–1690. Oxford, 1979.

9466 POUND, J. F. The validity of the freemen's lists: some Norwich evidence. *Econ. Hist. Rev*. 34, 1981, 48–59.
Evidence for occupational patterns in Tudor and Stuart periods.

9467 PRIESTLEY, U. *and* CORFIELD, P. J. Rooms and room use in Norwich housing, 1580–1730. *Post Medieval Archaeol*. 16, 1982, 93–123.

9468 POUND, J. F. Tudor and Stuart Norwich. Chichester, 1988.
See also his 'Government and society in Tudor and Stuart Norwich, 1525–1675'. Ph.D. thesis, Leicester Univ., 1975.

See also nos. 7793, 7797, 7952, 8512, 8888, 9684, 9693–4, 9772–3, 9810.

THE 'STRANGER COMMUNITY'

9469 MINET, W. Notes on the communion cups of the Dutch Church at Norwich. *Proc. Huguenot Soc. of London* 5, 1894/96, 445 ff.

9470 COPPOCK, C. The Walloon community in Norwich: the first hundred years. M.A. thesis, Univ. of E. Anglia, 1967.

9471 FORSTER, L. Literary life of Dutch exiled communities in England, 1567–1603: 1, Norwich. *In* Janus Gruter's English years: studies in the continuity of Dutch literature in exile in Elizabethan England (1967), pp. 25–46.

9472 HADDON, T. The Mayor's courtbooks and the Strangers in Norwich. M.A. thesis, Univ. of E. Anglia, 1967.

9473 DENIS, P. Pour une histoire économique et sociale des refugiés wallons et flamands à Norwich au 16e siècle: travaux récents et sources inexplorées. *Archives et Bibliothèques de Belgique* 46, 1975, 472–88.

9474 FELL, G. The spatial impact of the immigration of the Strangers in Norwich in the late 16th and early 17th centuries. B.A. dissertation, Cambridge, 1975.

9475 BRIGGS, E. R. Reflexions upon the first century of Huguenot churches in England. *Proc. Huguenot Soc*. 23, 1978, 99–119.

9476 RICKWOOD, D. L. The Norwich strangers, 1565–1643. *Proc. Huguenot Soc*.

24, 1984, 119–28.

9477 VANE, C. M. The Walloon community in Norwich: the first hundred years. *Ibid.* 129–40.

CIVIL WAR

9478 The true answer of the Parliament to the petition of the Lord Mayor and Common Councell... Likewise a letter from Norwich of the... blowing up of the magazine there. 1648. BL. P.

18TH CENTURY

9479 The chronicle of the preacher. Norwich, 1753. P.
Mock biblical skit on disturbances of 1752.

9480 Considerations on the causes of the late commotions. By a citizen. Norwich, 1766. P.

9481 JEWSON, C. B. The Jacobin city: a portrait of Norwich in its reaction to the French Revolution, 1788–1802. Glasgow, 1975.

9482 CORFIELD, P. J. The social and economic history of Norwich, 1650–1850: a study in urban growth. Ph.D. thesis, Univ. of London, 1976.

9483 GOODWIN, A. The friends of liberty: the English democratic movement in the age of the French Revolution. 1979.
Much information on Norwich radicalism: see esp. pp. 147–58.

9484 BRETT, P. T. The 'provision' riots in Norwich. 1740, 1766 and 1796. [Unpubl. typescript, 1979].

9485 FAWCETT, T. C. Measuring the provincial enlightenment: the case of Norwich. *18th Century Life* 8, 1982, 13–27,

9486 CAMERON, J. The political economy of decline in the transition to capitalism: Norwich, 1750–1850. (UEA School of Development Studies, Discussion Paper 197). Norwich, 1986.

9487 KILMARTIN, J. Popular holidays and feast days in urban England, 1680–1830: a comparison of Coventry and Norwich. Ph.D. thesis, Univ. of Warwick, 1987.

9487A ROGERS, N. Popular Jacobitism in provincial context: eighteenth-century Bristol and Norwich. *In* CRUICKSHANKS, E. *and* BLACK, J., *eds*. The Jacobite challenge (Edinburgh, 1988), pp. 142–60.

See also nos. 8337, 9515–16, 9520, 9522–4, 9683–4, 9706.

19TH CENTURY

9488 NORFOLK AND NORWICH GENEALOGICAL SOCIETY. Census of Norwich, 1851. [Ed. R. A. F. Page and others]. Norwich, 1975–.
St. Martin-at-Palace and St. Martin-at-Oak covered in *Norfolk Geneal.* 7 (1975); St. Helen, SS. Simon and Jude, St. Michael-at-Plea, St. Ethelred, St. Peter Hungate, St. Edmund, St. James in *ibid* 9, (1977). Continued by pamphlet series: St. George Colegate (1983); St. Michael-at-Thorn (1983); St. Swithin (1984); St. Lawrence (1985); St. John de Sepulchre (1985); St. Margaret (1987).

9489 FAWCETT, T. C. Thorpe Water Frolic. *N.A.* 36, 1977, 393–8.
On Stannard's picture of the 1825 Frolic, and its social setting.

9490 BARRINGER, C., *ed*. Norwich in the 19th century. Norwich, 1984.

9491 CHANEY, G. Some aspects of Norwich radicalism, 1850–1880. [Unpubl., c. 1984].

9492 HARRISON, M. Crowds and history: mass phenomena in English towns, 1790–1835. Cambridge, 1988.
Compares Bristol, Liverpool, Norwich, and Manchester.

See also nos.8305, 8543, 8731, 9482, 9486–7, 9517–18, 9525, 9528–9, 9622.

20TH CENTURY

9493 Visit of H.M. King Edward VII to Norwich, Oct. 25, 1909. [Programmes and souvenir. 3 items]. Norwich, 1909. P.
Presentation of colours to units of Territorials, and laying foundation stone of N. and N. Hospital extension.

9494 NORWICH CORPORATION. Coronation of King George V and Queen Mary: official programme of the celebrations in Norwich. Norwich, 1911.

9495 Visit of His Majesty King George V to Norwich... Official programme. Norwich, 1911. P.

9496 Norwich War Hospital Supply Depot, 29 Surrey Street... 1915–1919. [Norwich, n.d.] P.

9497 NORWICH CITY COUNCIL. Official programme of the visit of H.R.H. Princess Mary. Norwich, 1929.
To open new depts. at Jenny Lind Hospital and Woodrow Pilling Recreation Park.

9498 NORWICH CITY COUNCIL. Souvenir programme and timetable of events for the Silver Jubilee celebrations of H.M. King George V, May 6, 1935. Norwich, 1935.

9499 NORWICH CITY COUNCIL. The coronation celebrations, May 12th, 1937: the official souvenir programme and timetable of events. Ed. H. Leeds. Norwich, 1937.

9500 Norwich Warship Week. Jan. 31 – Feb. 7, 1942. Norwich, 1942. P.

9501 SWAIN, G. Norwich under fire. A camera record. Norwich, [1945]. Another ed. 1982. P.

9502 Norwich roll of honour: Second World War. [Typescript, n.d.]

9503 BANGER, J. R. Norwich at war. Norwich, 1974.

9504 Visit of H.R.H. The Duke of Edinburgh to mark [Norwich's] contribution... to European Architectural Heritage Year. Norwich, 1975. P.

9505 NORWICH CITY COUNCIL. Programme of events in Norwich to celebrate H.M. the Queen's Silver Jubilee. Norwich, 1977.

9506 SILVER JUBILEE PROJECTS GROUP. Jubilee water centre. Norwich, 1978. P.

9507 WALTERS, R. A plaque in Heigham Street. *E.A.M.* July 1979, 504–6.
Records 'plane crash in Nov. 1944.

9508 TEMPLE, C. R. Clifford Temple remembers Norwich. Lowestoft, 1983.

9509 TRAVERS, P. The changing pattern of prestige residence in Norwich, 1871 to 1971: a case study in the geography of segregation. Ph.D. thesis, Univ. of E. Anglia, 1984.

9510 KENT, P. Norwich: 1914–18. *In* GLIDDON, G., *ed*. Norfolk and Suffolk in the Great War (Norwich, 1988), pp.61–73.

MUNICIPAL GOVERNMENT

CIVIC INSTITUTIONS AND POLITICS

GENERAL WORKS

9511 LANE, R. Snap, the Norwich dragon. Norwich, 1976. P.
Central figure in civic pageantry.

9512 EMMERSON, R. The Norwich regalia and civic plate. Norwich, 1984. P.

9513 SLATTER, M. The Norwich Court of Requests – a tradition continued. *J. Legal Hist.* 5, 1984, 96–107.
See also similar article in *N.A.* 39, 1986, 278–85.

9514 GRIFFITHS, E. *and* SMITH, H. 'Buxom to the Mayor': a history of the Norwich freemen and the Town Close Estate. Norwich, 1987.

TO 1835

9515 A letter to John Day Esq., Mayor of Norwich, containing a letter of instruction to Harbord Harbord... and to Edward Bacon..., representatives in Parliament for... Norwich. Norwich, 1768.

9516 A letter to the Society which met at the Angel to celebrate the birthday of C. J. Fox. By one of the people. Norwich, 1799. P.

9517 Corporate retribution; or, the unearthing of the foxes. Norwich, n.d. P.
Early 19th-century satire on Corporation.

9518 The historical memoir of the new farce alias the comical opera, lately performed at the Tory Arms in N...W.. By a reporter. Norwich, 1832. UEA.

9519 GREEN, *Mrs.* J. R. The Common Council of Norwich. *In* Town life in the 15th century (1894), vol.2, pp. 360–401.

9520 O'SULLIVAN, D. S. Politics in Norwich, 1701–1835. M. Phil, thesis, Univ. of E. Anglia, 1975.

9521 JANSSEN, C. A. The waytes of Norwich in medieval and renaissance civic pageantry. Ph.D. thesis, Univ. of New Brunswick, 1977.

9522 PHILLIPS, J. A. Electoral behavior in unreformed England. Princeton, 1982.
Norwich is one of 4 boroughs intensively examined (period 1761–1802).

9523 GUTH, G. J. A. Croakers, tackers, and other citizens: Norwich voters in the early 18th century. Ph.D. thesis, Stanford Univ., 1985.

9524 WEINZIERL, M. The Norwich elections of 1794, 1796, and 1802: conflict and consensus. *Parliaments, Estates & Representation* 7, 1987, 61–9.

See also nos. 8929–31, 9483.

AFTER 1835

9525 BROWNE, W. J. U. A few observations respecting municipal reform suggested by passing events. Norwich [c. 1837]. P.

9526 RYE, W. The recent Norwich election and its lessons. Norwich [1906]. P.

9527 BAXTER, A. Orange and purple. The story of the Conservative Party in Norwich. Norwich, 1952.

9528 SMITH, R. A. H. The passing of the Municipal Corporations Act, 1830–1835, and its political and administrative significance, 1835–1871. M.Phil. thesis, Univ. of E. Anglia, 1974.
Case studies of Norwich, Ipswich, Preston and Hull.

9529 EDWARDS, J. K. Developments in local government organizations and services in Norwich, 1800–1890. [Unpubl. typescript]. Norwich, 1978.

9530 PALGRAVE-MOORE, P. The Mayors and Lord Mayors of Norwich, 1836–1974. Norwich, 1978.

9531 WALD, K. D. Class and the vote before the First World War. *Brit. J. Political Science* 8, 1978, 441–57.

Data from local government elections in Brighton, Bradford, Norwich, Reading and Wolverhampton. Fuller details in author's Ph.D. thesis, 'Patterns of English voter alignment since 1885', (Washington Univ., 1976).

9532 BERNSTEIN, G. L. Liberalism and the progressive alliance in the constituencies, 1900–1914: 3 case studies: Norwich, Leeds and Leicester. *Hist. J.* 26, 1983, 617–40.

9533 Norwich City Council Act, 1984. (L. and P. Acts, xxiii).

9534 CHERRY, S. The Norwich labour movement in the early years. Norwich, 1986. P.

See also nos. 7904A, 8907, 9491.

PLANNING

9535 NORWICH CITY COUNCIL. Norwich town planning scheme: preliminary statement. Norwich, [1925]. P.

9536 NORWICH CITY COUNCIL. Town and Country Planning Act, 1947. Development plan. Written statement. *Followed by* Report and analysis of the survey. Norwich, [1952/55].

9537 NORWICH CITY COUNCIL. The centre of Norwich: a basic plan. By H. W. Rowley, City Engineer. Norwich, 1963.

9538 KINCH, M. B. Departmental reorganization in a local authority: the setting up of the Norwich City Planning Dept. *Public Administration* 52, 1974, 95–109.

9539 NORWICH CITY COUNCIL. Norwich conservation: St. Benedict, Pottergate, Cow Hill. Norwich, [c. 1971].

9540 DAVIS, K. A. The politics of city planning: the Norwich experience. M.Phil. thesis, Univ. of E. Anglia, 1977.

9541 FORD, L. R. Continuity and change in historic cities: Bath, Chester, and Norwich. *Geog. Rev.* 68, 1978, 253–73.

On conservation policy.

9542 NORFOLK COUNTY COUNCIL. Norwich central area local plan. Norwich, 1978.

Preceded by *Draft local plan* (1977).

9543 NORWICH CITY COUNCIL. Norman and Crome Centres: future development. Norwich, 1978. P.

9544 NORWICH CITY COUNCIL. The closure of Elm Hill. Norwich, 1980.

9545 NORWICH CITY COUNCIL. Timberhill – Cattle Market. Planning guidelines. Norwich, 1980.

See also *Draft planning guidelines: a discussion document* (1979); *Alternative schemes* (1983); *Revised planning guidelines* (1984); and *Planning brief: further guidance* (1988).

9546 NORWICH CITY COUNCIL. A leisure pool for Norwich: feasibility study. Norwich, 1980.

9547 NORFOLK COUNTY COUNCIL. Norwich office policy review. Norwich, 1981. P.

9548 NORWICH CITY COUNCIL. Planning brief. St. Mary's Mills, Oak Street. Norwich, 1981. P.

9549 NORWICH CITY COUNCIL. 1981 census: city of Norwich: preliminary analysis. Norwich, 1982.

9550 NORWICH CITY COUNCIL. Newmarket Road plus. Norwich, 1982. P.

9551 NORWICH CITY COUNCIL. Planning guidelines – Norvic and Starte-Rite sites, Colegate/Duke Street. Norwich, 1982. P.

9552 NORWICH CITY COUNCIL. Anglia Square area planning guidelines, May 1982. Norwich, [1982].
See also draft guidelines, Nov. 1981.

9553 NORWICH CITY COUNCIL. Planning guidelines: Sweet Briar Road. Norwich, [1982]. P.

9554 NORWICH CITY COUNCIL. Trees in churchyards. Report. Norwich, 1982. P.

9555 ESTATES AND GENERAL INVESTMENTS PLC. Castle Mall, Norwich: proposals. [1983].
Put forward as alternative to Timberhill development.

9556 NORWICH CITY COUNCIL. King Street area draft planning guidelines. Norwich, 1984. P.
See also proposals for *The Old Barge, King St.* (1984); and *Potential development sites in the King St. area* [c.1988].

9557 NORFOLK COUNTY COUNCIL. Norwich area shopping studies, 1984: preliminary appraisal of results. [Norwich, 1984].

9558 ASHWORTH, G. J. *and* DE HAAN, T. Uses and users of the tourist-historic city: an evolutionary model in Norwich. Groningen (Netherlands), 1986.
Research sponsored by Geografisch Instituut of Groningen University. See also authors' *Residents' reactions to tourism in Norwich and Great Yarmouth* (1985); and associated work, *Norwich: policy in a tourist-historic city* (by M. Berkers and others, 1986)

9559 NORWICH CITY COUNCIL. Riverside: a strategic opportunity. Draft planning guidelines. Norwich, [1988]. P.
See also nos. 9598, 9765–6, 9787–90, 9835, 9837, 9852, 9855.

SECURITY

FIRE SERVICE

9560 VERIOD, B. S. A history of the Norwich City Fire Brigade. Norwich, 1986.
See also no. 9833.

SOCIAL WELFARE

POOR LAW AND CHARITIES

9561 WISEMAN, I. To the payers of the poor's rate, by Isaac Wiseman, Colegate, of the new Guardians. Norwich, 1829.

9562 Royal Commission on the poor laws and relief of distress. Appendix, vol. 15: Report... on endowed and voluntary charities... and the administrative relations of charity and the poor law, by A. C. Kay and H. V. Toynbee. H.C. 1909, xlii. Norwich, pp. 82–112. Little Walsingham, pp. 212–15.
Norwich report separately publ. by Norwich Charity Organisation Society (Norwich, 1909).

9563 NORWICH CORPORATION. Proposed amalgamation of charities under the administration of a central body. Norwich, 1909.

9564 WHITELEY, J. Social investigation and the poor law in Norwich, 1906–14. M.A. thesis, Univ. of E. Anglia, 1968.

9565 STACKHOUSE, J. Changes in the administration of poor relief in Norwich, 1871–1908. M.A. thesis, Univ. of E. Anglia, 1971.

9565A SHAW, L. Aspects of poor relief in Norwich, 1825–1875. Ph.D. thesis, Univ. of E. Anglia, 1980.

CONTEMPORARY SOCIAL SERVICES

9566 NORWICH CITY COUNCIL. An evaluation of future social services expenditure. [By] PA International Management Consultants Ltd. 1972.

9567 Mental illness in Norwich: now and the next 10 years. N.p., n.d. [c. 1972].

9568 NORWICH CITY COUNCIL. Social services in Norwich: a new department, 1971–1973. Norwich, 1973.

9569 NORWICH COUNCIL OF CHURCHES. Norwich night shelter: the first two years. Norwich, 1974. P.
Also annual reports, 1974–.

9570 CHILD POVERTY ACTION GROUP. Learning for living: a collection of facts and comments about the city of Norwich and where to go for help and advice. Norwich, 1975. P.

9571 NORFOLK COUNTY COUNCIL. A–Z: a guide to local organisations concerned with social service [in] Norwich. Norwich, n. d. [c.1975]. 2nd ed., 1978.

9572 BUSH, M. Norwich for the disabled. Norwich, 1977.
See also *Norwich: a guide for the less able* (Norwich, 1984), publ. by City Council.

9573 GOOD PRACTICES IN MENTAL HEALTH PROJECT. Good practices in mental health in Norwich. Norwich, 1980. 2nd ed., 1981.

9574 NORFOLK AND NORWICH ASSOCIATION FOR MENTAL HEALTH. Sembal House, Norwich: a halfway hostel for men and women recovering from mental illness. Norwich, 1986. P.

HOUSING

9575 NORWICH LABOUR PARTY. Housing in Norwich. Norwich, n.d. [c. 1970]. UEA.

9576 HOLLIS, P. L. Slum clearance and the consumer. Norwich, 1971. P. UEA.

9577 HARMAN, J. An introduction to council housing in Norwich. M.A. thesis, Univ. of E. Anglia, 1972.

9578 NORWICH CITY COUNCIL. Local authority housing in Norwich: policy and procedures. Norwich, 1974. P. UEA.

9579 PENTON, J. Old people's housing at Norwich. *Architect. J.* 161, 1975, 1181–91.

9580 NORWICH CITY COUNCIL. Housing list survey. Norwich, 1976.

9581 NORFOLK COUNTY COUNCIL. Norwich area housing land: potential growth locations. March, 1981.
Consists of *Consultative technical report* and *Summary report*. See also: *Proposed alterations* (1981); *Report on public consultation* (1981).

9582 Norwich area study tour: June 16, 1981.
Brochure prepared for members of County Council, City Council, Broadland and S. Norfolk District Councils, to examine future housing land in inner Norwich.

9583 FORREST, R. *and* MURIE, A. An unreasonable act? Central-local government conflict and the Housing Act, 1980. (School for Advanced Urban Studies, study no.1). Bristol, 1985
On dispute between Department of the Environment and Norwich City Council over sale of council houses.

9583A HORSEY, M. *and* MUTHESIUS, S. Provincial mixed development; the design and construction of Norwich council housing under David Percival, 1955–73. Norwich, 1986.
See also no.7552.

UNEMPLOYMENT

9584 NORWICH CITY COUNCIL. Statement...as to the problem of unemployment. Norwich, 1921. P.

9585 SMITH, M. Unemployment and local authorities in Norwich in the 1920s. M.A. thesis, Univ. of E. Anglia, 1972.

9586 NORWICH UNEMPLOYED WORKERS ACTION GROUP. Unemployment and the cuts in Norwich – and how to fight them. Norwich, 1976. P.

9587 SEDDON, J. D. Unemployment and short time working in Norwich. (UEA Development Studies discussion paper, 86). Norwich, 1981.

9588 DAVIES, M. What it's like to be unemployed in Norwich. Norwich, 1986. P.
See also *Towards a classification of the unemployed* (Norwich, 1986), from same data.

PUBLIC HYGIENE, DISEASE AND MEDICAL TREATMENT

9589 COOPER, W. A few remarks on the late Norwich consultation. Norwich, 1851.

9590 WILLIAMS, C. The master wardens and assistants of the gild of barber-surgeons of Norwich, 1439–1723. Norwich, 1900. P.

9591 COLEMAN, W. L. B. The chemists and pharmacists of Norwich and district from c. 1800 to 1875. Wroxham, 1976. P.

9592 JONES, *Sir* F. A. The Norwich schools of surgery. *Annals Roy. College Surgeons of England* 58, 1976, 203–21.

9593 PELLING, M. Tradition and diversity: medical practice in Norwich, 1550–1640. *In* ISTITUTO NAZIONALE DI STUDI SUL RINASCIMENTO. Scienze, credenze occulte, livelli di cultura (Florence, 1982), pp. 159–71.

9594 PELLING, M. Healing the sick poor: social policy and disability in Norwich, 1550–1640. *Medical Hist.* 29, 1985, 115–37.

9595 SLACK, P. The impact of plague in Tudor and Stuart England. 1985.
Contains extensive material on Norwich, esp. pp. 126–43.

9596 WOOD, E. C. The history of chemical analysis in Norwich. *J. Norfolk Industrial Archaeol. Soc.* 4 (2), 1987, 42–5.
Mainly concerns Norwich's first public analysts, Francis and Lincolne Sutton.

9597 PELLING, M. Illness among the poor in an early modern English town: the Norwich census of 1570. *Continuity & Change* 3, 1988, 273–90.
See also nos. 7951–2, 8619.

HOSPITALS AND CHARITABLE INSTITUTIONS
9598 NORWICH CITY COUNCIL. The Bethel Hospital: draft planning guidelines. Norwich, 1985.

9599 JEWSON, C. Doughty's Hospital. Norwich., [1980]. P.

9600 GREAT HOSPITAL. A scheme for the future management and regulation of the charity... Norwich, 1868. RCF.

9601 CASTELL, D. Hellesdon Hospital – the first 100 years: some brief historical notes... Norwich, 1980. P.

9602 BAGOT, L. A sermon preached at the cathedral church in Norwich...[by the Bishop of Norwich] on occasion of the anniversary meeting of the governors of the Norfolk and Norwich Hospital. Norwich, 1783. P. UEA.

9603 COPEMAN, A. C. The birth and parentage of the new Norfolk and Norwich Hospital. Norwich, 1883. P.

9604 NORFOLK AND NORWICH HOSPITAL. Souvenir... of the opening ceremony of the Queen Alexandra Memorial Home by... Queen Mary. Norwich, 1932. P.

9605 [MOTTRAM, R. H.] Norwich Institution for the Blind: 150th anniversary souvenir. Norwich, [1955]. P.
See also brief typescript account by R. W. Malster (1956).

See also nos. 9493, 9497.

PUBLIC WORKS AND UTILITIES

MARKETS

9606 SCOTT, E. E. Weights and measures in the city of Norwich: some historical notes. [Unpubl. typescript, 1974]. P.

9607 PRIESTLEY, U. The Great Market: a survey of nine hundred years of Norwich provision market. Norwich, 1987. P.

PARKS AND CEMETERIES

9608 BENTLEY, R. Consecration of cemeteries apostolical and necessary: a letter to the Mayor of Norwich. 1855.
See also nos. 8566, 9497.

POWER SUPPLIES

9609 NORWICH ELECTRICITY CO. LTD. The Norwich electricity undertaking, 1893–1913. Norwich, 1913. P.

9610 BRITISH GAS LIGHT CO. A short history of the company, 1824–1924. 1924. Norwich, pp.13–19.

WATER SUPPLY AND SEWERAGE

9611 BRAMAH, J. Strictures on a plan by Robert Milne for the improvement of the mills and waterworks in...Norwich. 1798.

9612 NORWICH CITY COUNCIL. Souvenir brochure of the official opening of the Wensum Valley (South) main drainage scheme. Norwich, 1936. P.

9613 NORWICH CITY COUNCIL. Report on the long term development of water resources, 1971–2001. Norwich, 1971. P.

EDUCATION AND RESEARCH

9614 Report of the state of the schools of the associated parishes of St. Stephen,

All Saints, St. John Timberhill, and St. Michael at Thorn, from Michaelmas 1842 to Michaelmas 1843. [Norwich, 1843].

9615 NORWICH CITY COUNCIL. Scheme of education for the area [to 1930]. Norwich, 1920.

9616 NORWICH CITY COUNCIL. The handbook of the education week held in Norwich from Sept. 27th to Oct. 3rd. Norwich, 1925.

9617 NORWICH CITY COUNCIL. Education Act, 1944. Development plan. *Followed by* Further education development plan. Norwich, 1947/48.

9618 READ, D. I. The Norwich reading scheme...for teaching reading in the infant and first-year junior school. 1951.

9619 NORWICH CITY COUNCIL. Education, 1955...a picture of education in the city of Norwich. Norwich, [1955].

9620 BARKER, R. J. B. A history of the Norwich School Board, 1870–1902. Diploma thesis, Cambridge Inst. of Education, 1970.

9621 JARVIS, A. M. Local politics and the development of secondary education in Norwich, 1902–47. M.A. thesis, Univ. of E. Anglia, 1974.

9622 SMITH, W. D. Education and society in Norwich, 1800–1870. Ph.D. thesis, Univ. of E. Anglia, 1978.

See also nos. 7993, 8888.

PARTICULAR SCHOOLS, COLLEGES, ETC.

9623 GOREHAM, G. Central to Middle: a history of Firside Middle School, Hellesdon. [Unpubl. typescript, 1982].

9624 HEWETT SCHOOL. Anniversary brochure, 1970–1982. Norwich, [1982].

9625 JOHN INNES INSTITUTE. John Innes Institute, 1910–1985. Norwich, 1985. P.

9626 THICKNESSE, S. G. Lonsdale School, 1823–1963. Diss, 1963.

9627 RYE, W. The Grammar School of Norwich. Archaeological notes with brief description of the new building and lists of distinguished alumni... Norwich, [1908]. P.

9628 NORWICH HIGH SCHOOL FOR GIRLS. Portrait of a school. Norwich, [1975].

9629 ALLTHORPE-GUYTON, M. *and* STEVENS, J. A happy eye: a School of Art in Norwich, 1845–1982. Norwich, 1982.

9629A UNIVERSITY PROMOTION COMMITTEE. Submissions to the University Grants Committee for the establishment of a University of East Anglia, Norwich. Norwich, 1959. P.

9630 UNIVERSITY OF EAST ANGLIA. Charter and statutes. [Norwich, 1964]. Revised ed., 1985.

9631 UNIVERSITY OF EAST ANGLIA. UEA Bulletin. Nos.1–3; n.s.1–6. Norwich, 1965–73.

9632 UNIVERSITY OF EAST ANGLIA. [Student newspapers and magazines]. Decanter (1965–66); Mandate (1966–1970); Chips (1966–70); Square One (1967); Twice (1970–73); Concrete (1973–75); Once (1974–75); Phoenix (1975–87); Breezeblock (1981–86); Broadly Speaking (Oct.–Nov. 1986); Insight (1987–)

9633 CAMPBELL, M. B. Nonspecialist study in the undergraduate curricula of the new universities and colleges of advanced technology in England. Ann Arbor (Michigan), 1966.
Contains much reference to University.

9634 THISTLETHWAITE, F. The University of East Anglia. *In* ROSS, M. G., *ed*. New universities in the modern world (New York, 1966).

9635 BELOFF, M. The plateglass universities. 1968.

9636 INDUSTRIAL ADMINISTRATION LTD. Survey of Senate and its committees. N.p., 1969.

9637 JOBLING, R. G. The location and siting of a new university [U.E.A.]. *Univ. Quart*. 24, 1969/70, 123–36.

9638 UNIVERSITY OF EAST ANGLIA. Newsletter [fortnightly in term]. Norwich, 1971–.

9639 UNIVERSITY OF EAST ANGLIA. Consultative report of the Constitution Committee. *Followed by* Final report...Norwich, 1973/74.

9640 UNIVERSITY OF EAST ANGLIA. Plans to 1990: submission to University Grants Committee. Norwich, 1985.

9641 UEA SOCIETY. Ziggurat [graduates' newsletter]. Norwich, 1985–.

9642 TILSLEY, G. The foundation of the University of East Anglia. The first steps, 1958–61: a personal reminiscence. [Unpubl. typescript, 1988].

On the University see also nos. 9728–32, 9871–2.

TRADE AND INDUSTRY

GENERAL AND MISCELLANEOUS

9643 NORWICH CORPORATION. Byelaws with respect to the employment of children and street trading by persons under the age of sixteen. Norwich, 1906. P.

9644 NORWICH CITY COUNCIL. Industrial register. Norwich, 1983.

9645 ATKIN, M. Medieval industry in Norwich. *NARG News* 37, 1984, 4–9; 40, 1985, 1–5.
Deals with iron-making and brewing.

9646 NORWICH CITY COUNCIL. Taking Norwich into the 1990s: a forward look at job potential in the Norwich area over the next five years. Norwich, 1987.

9647 GURNEY-READ, J. Trades and industries of Norwich. Norwich, 1988.

9647A UNIVERSITY OF EAST ANGLIA. ECONOMICS RESEARCH CENTRE. Norwich area economic study. Main report: Norwich, a time of opportunity (by P. M. Townroe). *With* Working papers 1–10. Norwich, 1988.

See also nos. 8108, 8731, 9486.

PORT OF NORWICH

9648 NORWICH CHAMBER OF COMMERCE. The port of Norwich: a report. Norwich, 1977. P.

9649 GREAT YARMOUTH PORT AND HAVEN COMMISSIONERS. The port of Norwich: a report prepared by... the Inland Shipping Group of the Inland Waterways Association. Great Yarmouth, 1978. P.

9650 NORFOLK COUNTY COUNCIL. Future options for the port of Norwich. Norwich, 1978.

See also nos. 8093, 8177.

PARTICULAR INDUSTRIES AND TRADES

BANKING AND INSURANCE
See nos. 8111–25, 9854.

BUILDING
9651 Round and about. The newsletter of the house of Jewson. [Yarmouth], c. 1955–.

CHEMICALS
9652 FRIENDS OF THE EARTH. A review of the environmental impacts arising from May and Baker Ltd.'s Norwich factory. Report by A. J. Lees. *Followed by* The May and Baker saga. The ioxynil story: a further contribution...Norwich, 1986.
See also no. 8107.

CLOCK-MAKING
9653 ZIPFEL, A. L. Zipfel and Sons, Norwich clock- and watchmakers. [Norwich], 1987. P.

COKING
9654 DAY, M. John Bolton's cinder oven: an 18th-century industrial re-use of a medieval tower. *Industrial Archaeol. Rev.* 6, 1982, 235–40.

ENGINEERING
9655 NORWICH ENGINEERING SOCIETY. Sixty years of engineering in Norwich [exhibition catalogue]. Norwich, 1983. P.
9656 LOVE, C. Conflicts over closure: the Laurence Scott affair. Aldershot, 1988.

FOOD AND DRINK
9657 J. AND J. COLMAN LTD. Souvenir of Carrow Works, Norwich. Norwich, [1886]. P.
9658 MACKINTOSH, E. D. Norwich adventure: an account of events at Chapelfield Works, 1932–42. Norwich, 1947.
9659 GODFREY, H. The archives of Reckitt & Colman Food Division (formerly J. and J. Colman Ltd.). *Business Archives* no. 39, 1973, 50–54.
9660 NORWICH SCHOOL OF ART. Yellow, white and blue: the advertising art of J. and J. Colman Ltd. [Exhib. brochure]. Norwich, 1977.
Also publ. by Colman's Mustard Shop, 1978.
9661 DAY, M. The Norwich vinegar industry. *J. Norfolk Industrial Archaeol. Soc.* 2 (4), 1979, 11–15.
9662 EDGAR, S. H. History of J. and J. Colman. Norwich, [c.1984].
See also nos. 8138, 9645.

GLASS
9663 DAY, M. Letters from a cupboard: correspondence between a glass works and one of its customers in the 1920s. *Industrial Archaeol.* 15, 1980, 229–35.
Concerns the Norwich Glass Co., Wensum Street.

IRON AND STEEL
See nos. 8141, 9645.

LEATHERWORK AND SHOE-MAKING
9664 The jubilee memorial of Messrs. Howlett and White. Norwich, 1896. P.
9665 The history and development of the Norwich shoe trade. *Footwear Organiser* Feb. 1920, 252 ff.
9666 ADAMS, M. G. The Norwich boot and shoe trade, 1870–1914. M.A. thesis, Univ. of E. Anglia, 1971.
9667 SEXTON, H. J. Address to the Norwich Boot and Shoe Managers' and Foremen's Association, 1952. *J. Norfolk Industrial Archaeol. Soc.* 1 (7), 1974, 5–13.
9668 JONES, D. B. A. Martin and Sons: a shoe factory. *Ibid.* 3 (4), 1984, 130–40.
9669 JONES, D. Business, tact, and thoroughness: a history of the Norvic Shoe Company Ltd. *Ibid.* 4 (1), 1986, 18–26.
    See also no. 8107.

PEWTERERS
9670 FENNER, A. Three Norwich pewterers. *J. Post-Medieval Archaeol.* 8, 1974, 113–119.

PIPE-MAKERS
9671 DAVEY, P., *ed.* The archaeology of the clay tobacco pipe. 1: the Midlands and Eastern England. (Brit. Archaeol. Repts., 63). 1979.
Chapter by M. Karshner on Norwich makers (with note on specimens by A. Oswald), pp. 295–359.
9672 DAVEY, P., *ed.* The archaeology of the clay tobacco pipe. IX: more pipes from the Midlands and Southern England. (Brit. Archaeol. Repts., 146). 1985.
Davey and S. Atkin report on pipes found in 17th century pit on St. Stephen's St. (pp. 309–24); D. J. Woodcock on some attrib. to William Hensell (pp. 325–36).

PRINTING
See nos. 9712, 9714–16.

TELEPHONES
9673 CLAYTON, E. G. The rise and fall of the Norwich Mutual Telephone Co. J. *Norfolk Industrial Archaeol. Soc.* 2 (3), 1978, 6–17.
9674 NORWICH TELEPHONE AREA MUSEUM. Norwich telephones: the early days. Norwich, [1979]. P.
9675 CLAYTON, E. G. The first 100 years of telephones, viewed from Norwich. N.p., 1980.

TEXTILES
9676 CLABBURN, P. Norwich shawls. Norwich, 1975. P.
9677 F. W. HARMER AND CO. 150 years. Norwich, 1975. P.
9678 JONES, J. *and* JONES, J. Pearce's whiting works [at Harford Bridges]. *J. Norfolk Industrial Archaeol. Soc.* 2 (3), 1978, 25–8.
9679 MANN, J. de L. Queries concerning Norwich stuffs. *Textile Hist.* 9, 1978, 173–4.

9680 PRIESTLEY, U. 'The fabric of stuffs': the Norwich textile industry, c. 1650–1750. *Ibid.* 16, 1985,183–210.

For fuller account see her M.A. thesis, 'Norwich stuffs and their makers: a study of the Norwich textile industry. c. 1650–1750' (Univ. of E. Anglia, 1984).

9681 FAWCETT, T. Argonauts and commercial travellers: the foreign marketing of Norwich stuffs in the later 18th century. *Ibid.* 16, 1985, 151–82.

RETAIL TRADE

9682 HARTWELL, W. *and* HATCH, K. Curls of Norwich. Norwich, 1956.

9683 CLABBURN, P. A provincial milliner's shop [Rampant Horse St., Norwich] in 1785. *J. Costume Soc.* 11, 1977, 100–112.

9684 PRIESTLEY, U. *and* FENNER, A. Shops and shopkeepers in Norwich, 1660–1730. Norwich, 1985. P.

9684A HARDINGHAM, V. Some of Norwich's family stores: a study. Norwich, 1986.

See also no. 9714.

RELIGION

GENERAL CHURCH HISTORY

9685 COLMAN, H. C. The religious life of Norwich: a glimpse into the past. Norwich, 1929. P.

MEDIEVAL PERIOD

9686 DOUCET, V. Le studium franciscain de Norwich en 1337, d'apres le MS. Chigi B.V. 66 de la Bibliotheque Vaticane. *Archivum Franciscanum Historicum* 46, 1953, 85–98.

9687 ANDREW, L. The medieval libraries of the religious houses in Norwich. M.A. thesis, London Univ., 1975.

9688 TILLYARD, M. The acquisition by the Norwich Blackfriars of the site for the church, c. 1310–25. *In* Men of property: an analysis of the Norwich enrolled deeds (Norwich, 1983).

9689 CATTERMOLE, P. Notes on Bishop Salmon's charity, 1316–1548, now Norwich School Chapel. Norwich, 1983. P.

9690 TANNER, N. P. The church in late medieval Norwich, 1370–1532. Toronto, 1984.

See also his Oxford D.Phil. thesis, 'Popular religion in Norwich with special reference to the evidence of wills, 1370–1532'.

9691 SHINNERS, J. R. The veneration of saints at Norwich Cathedral in the 14th century. *N.A.* 40, 1980, 133–44.

9692 TANNER, N. P. The Reformation and regionalism: further reflections on the church in late medieval Norwich. *In* THOMSON, J. A. F., *ed.* Towns and townspeople in the 15th century (Gloucester, 1988), pp. 129–47.

See also nos. 8778–86, 9786, 9805–8.

TUDOR AND STUART PERIOD

9693 PAUL, L. S. A survey of the ecclesiastical history of Norwich, 1500–1575. M.A. thesis, Chicago, 1958.

9694 SHEPPARD, E. M. The Reformation and the citizens of Norwich. *N.A.* 38, 1981, 44–58.

See also author's B.A. thesis, 'The Reformation in Norwich, as reflected in the wills of its inhabitants, 1530–60' (Univ. of York, 1978).

See also nos. 9809–10

18TH–20TH CENTURIES

9695 The substance of a public discussion between Thomas Scott and Richard Carlile after the lecture on theology...at the Freemasons Arms, Norwich, 1834. 3rd ed. Norwich, 1837. P. UEA.

9696 RUST, C. T. A list of the incumbents in Norwich from the year 1851 to the year 1891. Soham, [1891]. P.

See also for same period his *List of curates officiating in Norwich...*

9697 NORWICH CITY COMMISSION. Report. Chairman, Rt. Hon. Lord Brooke of Cumnor. 1970.

See also nos. 8722, 8787, 8881.

ROMAN CATHOLICISM

9698 HOLT, T. G. Catholic chapels in Norwich before 1900 – secular and Jesuit. *N.A.* 37, 1979, 153–68.

NONCONFORMITY

9699 JEWSON, C. B. William Watts and William Lindoe. *Baptist Quart.* 14, 1952, 371–4.

Deacon's notes concerning St. Mary's Baptist Church in 18th century.

9700 [BALL, F. P.] Centenary year, 1858–1958: Chapel-in-the-Field Congregational Church. Norwich, 1958.

9701 HILTON, J. Princes Street Congregational Church in the 19th century. [Unpubl. thesis, 1981].

9702 NORWICH DISTRICT PRIMITIVE METHODIST CHURCH. Souvenir of a century of blessing...Norwich, 1907.

9703 Calvert Street [Methodist] Sunday School centenary, 1808–1908. Norwich, 1908.

9704 The Methodist church – Rosebery Road, Norwich, 1818–1968. [Norwich, 1968].

9705 BECKETT, J. *and* BECKETT, J. A church for all seasons. The story of St. Peter's (Park Lane) Methodist Church, Norwich, 1939–1975. Norwich, [c. 1979]. P.

9706 BELLAMY, E. J. Norwich Methodism in the 1750s, with special reference to James Wheatley. [Unpubl. thesis, 1986].

See also earlier version, *A history of Methodism in Norwich in the 1750s* (1977).

9707 PHIPPS, J. An address to the youth of Norwich [on Quaker issues]. 1776.

9708 PENNEY, N., *ed*. 'The first publishers of truth': being early records... of the introduction of Quakerism into the counties of England and Wales. 1907. Norwich, pp. 169–93.

9709 RABAN, J. C. P. Religious conversion: the experience of Mormons in Norwich. M.Phil. thesis, Univ. of E. Anglia, 1973.

See also nos. 8586, 8629, 8887, 9870.

CHURCH AND CHAPEL SOCIETIES

9710 NORWICH Y.M.C.A. A century of service, 1856–1956. Norwich, 1956. P.

CULTURE AND RECREATION

BOOKS AND LIBRARIES

9711 KAY. M. A. Library provision in Norwich before 1850. M.A. thesis, London Univ., 1974.

9712 STOKER, D. The establishment of printing in Norwich: causes and effects, 1660–1760. *Trans. Cambridge Bibliog. Soc.* 7, 1977, 94–111.

9713 STOKER, D. Doctor Collinges and the revival of Norwich City Library, 1657–1664. *Library Hist*, 5, 1980, 73–84.

9714 STOKER, D. The Norwich book trades before 1800. *Trans. Cambridge Bibliog. Soc.* 8, 1981, 79–125.

9715 TOOVEY, S. Martin Kinder and the Walpole Press: a study of a private printing press between 1912 and 1967. Thesis, Norwich School of Art, 1985.

9716 SESSIONS, W. K. *and* STOKER, D. The first printers in Norwich from 1567 – Anthony de Solempne, Albert Christiaensz, and Joannes Paetz. York, 1987.
Stoker's contribution reprints article on Solempne in *Library* 6th ser. 3 (i), 1981, 17–32.

See also nos. 8609, 8623, 8924, 9687, 9746.

MUSEUMS AND GALLERIES

9717 NORFOLK AND NORWICH ARCHAEOLOGICAL SOCIETY. A catalogue of the antiquities in the Norfolk and Norwich Museum. Compiled by H. Harrod. 2 pts. Norwich, 1853. BL.

9718 TAYLOR, J. E. Popular guide to the Norfolk and Norwich Museum. [1872]. BL.

9719 CASTLE MUSEUM COMMITTEE. Catalogue of loan collections of Norwich silver plate; and paintings and prints of famous Norfolk horses, cattle, etc., in the Norwich Castle Museum. Norwich, 1911. P.

9720 NORWICH CITY COUNCIL. Abridged guide to the museums ... Norwich. 1933. Other eds. 1943, 1949.

9721 YOUNG, R. M. R. Teaching toys in the Norwich Museums collection. Norwich, 1966. P.

9722 NORWICH CITY COUNCIL. Treasures of the Norwich museums. Norwich, 1974. P.

9723 GODFREY, H. Colman's museums at Norwich. *Museums J.* 74, 1975, 156–8.
See also Godfrey's article 'The Colman collection of silver mustard pots', *E.A.M.* March 1979, 266–9.

9724 SMITH, S. Lowestoft porcelain in Norwich Castle Museum. 2 vols. Norwich, 1975/85.

9725 LAMBLEY, P. *and others*. A new natural history gallery in Norwich Castle Museum. *Museums J*. 76, 1976, 17–18.

9726 OPEN UNIVERSITY. Women's work and leisure: a guide to the Strangers Hall and Bridewell Museums. Milton Keynes, 1983.
Booklet produced for *The Changing Experience of Women* course.

9727 DURBIN, G. The past displayed: a picture history of the Norwich museums. Norwich, 1984.

SAINSBURY CENTRE

9728 UNIVERSITY OF EAST ANGLIA. The Sainsbury collection: catalogue [of the] works of art given to the University by Sir Robert and Lady Sainsbury...6 vols. in 4. [Norwich, 1977]. UEA.

9729 UNIVERSITY OF EAST ANGLIA. A guide for visitors to the Sainsbury Centre. Norwich, 1978. P.

9730 UNIVERSITY OF EAST ANGLIA. [Catalogue of the] Robert and Lisa Sainsbury Collection: exhibition for the opening of the Centre, April 1978. Norwich, 1978.

9731 JOHNSON, P. Art nouveau: the Anderson collection. [Exhibition catalogue]. Norwich, [c.1981].

9732 SEKULES, V., *ed*. The University of East Anglia collection. Norwich, 1984.
    See also no. 9872.

DRAMA AND THEATRES

GENERAL WORKS
9733 NELSON, A. H. The medieval English stage: Corpus Christi pageants and plays. Chicago, 1974. Chap. 7: Norwich.

9734 DUTKA, J. The lost dramatic cycle of Norwich and the Grocers' play of the Fall of Man. *Rev. of Eng. Stud*. 35, 1984, 1–13.

9735 GALLOWAY, D. Records of early English drama: Norwich, 1540–1642. Toronto, 1985.

PARTICULAR THEATRES
9736 HILDY, F. J. Reviewing Shakespeare's stage craft. Nugent Monck and the Maddermarket Theatre. Ph.D. thesis, Northwestern Univ., 1980.

9737 HARCOURT, B. Theatre Royal, Norwich. Chronicles of an old playhouse. Norwich, 1903.

9738 FAWCETT, T. C. The first undoubted *Magic Flute*. *R.M.A. Research Chronicle* 12, 1975, 106–114.
At Norwich Theatre Royal, 1829.

9739 HOWARD, V. The show must go on: the story of the Theatre Royal, Norwich. Norwich, 1977.

9740 KELLETT, L. The Sewell connection: a family, a community, a theatre. Norwich, 1979. P.
Publ. by Sewell Barn Theatre Trust.

CINEMA

9741 ELGOOD, D. City cinemas, 1903–1978. Norwich, 1978. P.

MUSIC

9742 MATTHEWS, B. George Pike England in Norwich. *Organ* 65, 1986, 74–83.
See also nos.8334, 8337, 8585, 8625, 8718, 8804, 9521, 9867.

APPLIED ARTS

9743 BARRETT, G. N. Norwich silver and its marks, 1565–1702; the goldsmiths of Norwich, 1141–1750. Norwich, 1981.

SOCIETIES AND CLUBS

9744 BOYS' BRIGADE, 5TH NORWICH COMPANY. Coming of age: 1903–24 souvenir. [Norwich, 1924].

9745 EATON GOLF CLUB. Eaton Golf Club: its history and development...Norwich, n.d. P.

9745A MILLNS, W. J. Clarence Chapter no. 116 [Freemasons]. Norwich, 1941. P. FPL.

9745B BRETT, J. T. The Chapter of Perseverance no. 213. Norwich, 1968. FPL.

9746 MECHANICS' INSTITUTION. Catalogue of the library, models, and apparatus...[with] a list of the officers, the laws of the Institution, and the regulations of the library. Norwich, 1833. P. Addenda, 1836. Another ed., 1842.

9747 NORWICH AND DISTRICT PEACE COUNCIL. Newsletter. Norwich, 1982–.

9748 NORWICH DISTRICT FOOTPATH SOCIETY. Bulletin. Norwich, 1965–.

9749 NORWICH LADS' CLUB. An illustrated history of the club founded in 1918. Norwich, [c.1934].

9750 DAIN, J. H. Police welfare work among boys. [1938]. P.
See also his earlier account 'The Norwich Lads' Club: welfare work by the police', *Police J*. July 1929.

9751 NORWICH LADS' CLUB. Re-opening of the Norwich Lads' Club, King Street... official programme. Norwich, 1951. P.

9752 The Norwich Preservation Trust. Norwich, [1974]. P.

9753 HEPWORTH, P. *and* OGDEN, J. 60 eventful years: the Diamond Jubilee of the Norwich Society, 1923–1983. Norwich, 1983.

9754 CREASEY, J. Round Table: the first 25 years of the...movement. 1953.
Norwich origins. For early account see J. L. Hanly, *The Round table: what it is, what it does* (Norwich, 1932). P.

9755 WATSON, B. Some kind of club: no. 6 Group, Norwich, Royal Observer Corps. Norwich, 1984.
Volunteer adjunct to RAF.

9756 M., C. The Scots Society of St. Andrew. Norwich, 1901. RCF.

9757 TILLETT, J. H. The reply of the executive of the Norwich Auxiliary of the U.K. Alliance to the statements on local option made by Mr. J. H.Tillett, M.P., at St. Andrew's Hall... Norwich, [1882]. P.
Local temperance organization.

TOPOGRAPHY

GENERAL TOPOGRAPHICAL AND ARCHITECTURAL FEATURES

9758 RYE, W. Taste and want of taste in Norwich. Norwich, 1904.

9759 NORWICH SOCIETY. A journey along the waterways of Norwich. Norwich, 1969.

9760 GOREHAM, G. Yards and courts of old Norwich. Norwich, 1974. P.

9761 SHAW, M., *ed*. Norwich old and new. Wakefield, 1974.
Photographs covering period 1850 onwards.

9762 NORWICH CITY COUNCIL. Heritage over the Wensum. Norwich., 1975.

9763 YOUNG, J. R. The inns and taverns of old Norwich. Norwich, 1975.

9764 BURTON, J. R. The church Over the Water. [Unpubl. typescript, 1976].
Comprehensive history and topography of Coslany, Colegate and Fyebridge, the 'Great Ward Over the Water'.

9765 DIX, G. Norwich: a fine old city. *In* REYNOLDS, J., *ed*. Conservation planning in town and country (Liverpool, 1976), pp. 67–86.
See also similar piece in *Town Planning Rev.* 46, 1975, 417–34.

9766 HUMAN, B. Conservation-over-the-water. *E.A.M.* Jan. 1977, 104–7.
Restoration of Colegate area.

9767 GOREHAM, G. Norwich heritage. 2 vols. Norwich, 1977/81.

9768 ROSE, M. Three house extensions in Norwich [in Riverside Close and College Road]. *Architects J.* 169, 1979, 321–31.

9769 NORWICH CITY COUNCIL. Historic plaques presented to the city by Mr. E. Garfield Williams. Norwich, 1981. P.

9770 DAY, M. Railway cottages, Norwich. *Transport Hist.* 12, 1981, 74–7.
Description of 24 artisan's cottages built by Norfolk Railway (1845) near Thorpe Station.

9771 HEPWORTH, P. Norwich in old picture postcards. Zaltbommel (Netherlands), 1982.

9772 SMITH, R. *and* CARTER. A. Function and site: aspects of Norwich buildings before 1700. *Vernacular Architecture* 14, 1983, 1–14.

9773 PORTER, S. Thatching in early modern Norwich. *N.A.* 39, 1986, 310–12.

9774 HOOTON, C. Pubs and people of Norwich. Norwich, 1987. P.

9775 NORWICH SOCIETY. Norwich pubs survey, 1986. 2 vols. [Unpubl. typescript]. Norwich, 1987.
4-page summary publ. by Society and City Council, 1986.

9776 PLUNKETT, G. A. F. Disappearing Norwich. Lavenham, 1987.

9777 STANDLEY, P. Norwich: a portrait in old picture postcards. Vol.1. Market Drayton, 1988.

See also no. 8475.

ARTISTS' VIEWS

9778 NINHAM, H. Nine original etchings of picturesque antiquities. 1842.

9779 STIMPSON, P. E. Old views of Norwich: sketches from *The highways and byways of old Norwich*. 1887. RCF.
Separate issue of plates from M. Knights' book. (*B.N.H.* 5726).

9780 LARGE, W. M. Sketches of ancient Norwich in line and pencil. N.p., [1920].

9781 TUCK, H. W. Norwich. A book of drawings. Norwich, 1932. P.

9782 SPENCER, N. Norwich drawings: a collection of drawings of old Norwich.

Norwich, 1978. P.

9783 POOLE, D. Norwich sketches. Sprowston, 1981.

INDIVIDUAL DISTRICTS, BUILDINGS, ETC. A–Z

9784 GREENWOOD, J. R. The brasses of All Saints, Norwich. *Trans. Monumental Brass Soc.* 12, 1979, 215–18.

9785 JAMES, Z. The history of 45 All Saints Green, 1788–1973. [Unpubl. typescript, 1973]. P.

9786 SUTERMEISTER, H. The Norwich Blackfriars: an historical guide to the friary and its buildings up to the present day. Norwich, 1977. P.

9787 NORWICH CITY COUNCIL. Bowthorpe master plan. Norwich, 1974.
Cf. also the *Bowthorpe draft plans* (Norwich, 1973, 1974); and *Bowthorpe design guide* (Norwich, 1975).

9788 NORWICH CITY COUNCIL. For Bowthorpe people. Norwich, [1978]. P.

9789 CAMINA, M. M. Bowthorpe, the implementation of a dream: a case-study in the frustration of local government. Norwich, 1980.

9790 NORFOLK COUNTY COUNCIL. Sainsbury's at Bowthorpe: the impact of a new retailing facility... Norwich, 1981.

9791 SIMPSON, R. Bowthorpe: a community's beginnings. Norwich, 1982.

9792 AYERS, B. St. Michael's Church, Bowthorpe. *NARG News* 41, 1985, 5–10.
On Bowthorpe see also no. 7550.

9793 SMITH, A. Bracondale memories. *E.A.M.* April 1979, 342–3.

9794 KELLY, G. I. The manor house, 54 Bracondale: a history. [Unpubl., 1983].

CARROW PRIORY. See no. 9448.

9795 FISKE, R. C. The stables on the old shirehouse site of Norwich Castle Bailey. *NARG News* 36, 1984, 1–5.

9796 AYERS, B. Norwich castle keep. *Ibid.* 45, 1986, 1–3.
See also summary of lecture by P. Drury in *Bull. Norfolk Research Committee* 37, 1987, 7–9; and nos. 9451. 9454.

CATHEDRAL: GENERAL GUIDES AND HISTORIES

9797 KING, R. J. Norwich Cathedral. *In* Murray's handbook to the cathedrals of England: Eastern division (1881), pp. 141–214.

9798 JESSOPP, A. Norwich. *In* BONNEY, T. G., *ed.* Cathedrals, abbeys and churches of England and Wales (1891), pp. 90–100.

9799 BUCKINGHAM, E. Sketches in Norwich Cathedral. Norwich, 1907.

9800 FAIRBAIRNS, W. H. Notes on the cathedrals [series]: Norwich. [c. 1928]. P. BL.

9801 WEBSTER, A. Norwich Cathedral: a short guide. Norwich, 1976. P.

9802 SAMPSON, A. Norwich Close. Wellington (Somerset), 1977.

9803 NEW, A. S. B. A guide to the cathedrals of Britain. 1980. Norwich, pp. 275–86.
Pp. 284–6 describe Catholic cathedral of St. John the Baptist.

9804 PEVSNER, N. *and* METCALF, P. The cathedrals of England: midland, eastern and northern England. 1985. Norwich, pp. 250–70.
Revised version of description in *Buildings of England* series.
See also nos. 8472.

CATHEDRAL: THE MEDIEVAL PRIORY

9805 DODWELL, B., *ed.* The charters of Norwich Cathedral Priory. 2 vols. *Pipe Roll Soc.* n.s. 40, 1974; 46, 1985.

9806 DODWELL, B. William Bauchun and his connection with the Cathedral Priory at Norwich. *N.A.* 36, 1975, 111–18.
9807 DODWELL, B. History and the monks of Norwich Cathedral Priory. *Reading Medieval Stud.* 5, 1979, 33–56.
9808 YAXLEY, D., *ed.* The prior's manor-houses: inventories of 11 of the manor-houses of the Prior of Norwich...1352 A.D. Guist, 1988.

See also no. 8031.

CATHEDRAL: DEAN AND CHAPTER

9809 The statutes of the cathedral church of Norwich. [Norwich], n.d.
Modern reprint of statutes of 1620, with material on their interpretation.

9810 METTERS, G. A., *ed.* The parliamentary survey of Dean and Chapter properties in and around Norwich in 1649. *N.R.S.* 51, 1985 [publ. 1988].

See also no. 8572.

CATHEDRAL: STRUCTURAL HISTORY AND FEATURES

9811 L'ESTRANGE, J. The cloches of Norwich Cathedral, etc. *N.A.M.* 2, 1883, 149–58.
9812 RYE, W. The precincts of Norwich Cathedral. *N.A.M.* 2nd ser. 1, 1906, 48–51.
See also short pamphlet by Rye attacking recent Chapter alterations to Close, *Vandalism at Norwich* (Norwich, 1903).
9813 COLEBY, C. C. Norwich Cathedral cloister. Norwich, n.d. P.
9814 FERNIE, E. C. Excavations at the facade of Norwich Cathedral. *N.A.* 36, 1974, 72–5.
9815 FERNIE, E. C. The ground plan of Norwich Cathedral and the square root of two. *J. Brit. Archaeol. Assoc.* 129, 1976, 77–86.
9816 FERNIE, E. C. The Romanesque piers of Norwich Cathedral. *N.A.* 36, 1977, 383–6.
9817 FERNIE, E. C. Two aspects of Bishop Walter de Suffield's Lady Chapel at Norwich Cathedral. *In* ORMROD, W. M., *ed.* England in the 13th century: proceedings of the 1984 Harlaxton Symposium (Grantham, 1985), pp. 52–5.
9818 FERNIE, E. C. An architectural and archaeological analysis of the sanctuary of Norwich Cathedral. *N.A.* 39, 1986, 296–305.

CATHEDRAL: FURNITURE AND DECORATIVE FEATURES

9819 SHERMAN, H. S. *Ludus Coventriae* and the bosses in the nave of Norwich Cathedral: the Christian history of Man in two disciplines. Ph.D. thesis, Michigan State Univ., 1976.
9820 SHERMAN, H. S. Diverging tendencies in Gothic art: two sculptures of Abraham and Isaac at Norwich Cathedral. *15th Century Stud.* 1, 1978, 275–86.
9821 WHITTINGHAM, A. B. Norwich Saxon throne: ancient Bishop's throne. *Archaeol. J.* 136, 1979, 60–68.
9822 UNIVERSITY OF EAST ANGLIA. Medieval sculpture from Norwich Cathedral. [Sainsbury Centre exhibition catalogue]. Norwich, 1980.
9823 WHITTINGHAM, A. B. Norwich Cathedral bosses and misericords. Norwich, 1981. P.
9824 FRANKLIN, J. A. The Romanesque cloister sculpture at Norwich Cathedral

Priory. *In* THOMPSON, F. H., *ed.* Studies in medieval sculpture (Soc. of Antiquaries, occasional papers n.s.3, 1983), pp.56–70.

9825 WHITTINGHAM, A. B. The Erpingham retable or reredos in Norwich Cathedral. *N.A.* 39, 1985, 202–6.

CATHEDRAL: MUSICAL HISTORY

See nos. 8334, 8585, 8625.

9826 NUTHALL, T. Christ Church, New Catton: biography of a church. [Norwich, 1980].

9827 PLUNKETT, G. A. F. Churchman House, St. Giles's Street, Norwich. *N.A.* 36, 1974, 76–84.

9828 A brief history of Cotman Road, Norwich. Norwich, 1985. P.

9829 SAUNDERS, A. D. The Cow Tower, Norwich: an East Anglian bastille? *Medieval Archaeol.* 29, 1985, 109–19.

9830 CRESCENT HISTORY GROUP. The Crescent, Norwich: listing of occupiers, 1825–1978. Norwich, 1978. P.

EARLHAM. See nos. 8535–6.

9831 EATON, F. R. Notes on the parish church of Eaton. Norwich, 1953. P.

9832 HEPWORTH, P. Eaton parish and its churches. Norwich, 1978. P.
On Eaton see also nos. 9432, 9434.

9833 BERRY, G. A. Norwich city fire station competition. *Builder* 3 Apr. 1931, 610–18.

9834 AYERS, B. Fishergate, Norwich, 1985. *NARG News* 42, 1985, 1–6.
Excavation report.

9835 Dream city: rehabilitation of Friars Quay, Norwich. *Architect. Rev.* 158, 1975, 283–6.

9836 DUNN, I. *and* SUTERMEISTER, H. The Norwich Guildhall: a history and guide. Norwich, [1978]. P.

9837 O'DONOGHUE, R. A Victorian suburb [Heigham]: some aspects of town planning in 19th-century Norwich. *N.A.* 38, 1983, 321–8.

9838 JOBY, R. S. Hellesdon past and present. Part 1. Norwich, 1977.

9839 HIPPER, K. A history of Hellesdon village. [Norwich], 1978.

9840 HELLESDON PARISH COUNCIL. Hellesdon: a community guide. Hellesdon, 1982. 2nd ed. 1985.

9841 FENNER, G. The church of St. Mary at Hellesdon. *NARG News* 41, 1985, 13–22.

9842 'Inverleith', Norwich, designed by Mr. P. Morley Horder and Mr. A. G. Wyand. *In* WEAVER, L., *ed.* Small country houses of today (1911), pp. 67–70.
Built in Lime Tree Road for Mr. Davidson Walker.

9843 KELLY, G. I. The Ironmongers' Arms public house, 1 St. John Maddermarket. [Unpubl.], 1984. P.

9844 BUSTON, W. The Norman house in Norwich and the 'Music house'. *Country Life* Aug. 1942, 360–61.

9845 KELLY, G. I. Read Woodrow Ltd., King Street: the background to the freehold site from 1783 until 1965. [Unpubl.], 1981.

9846 CONDON, E. King Street, a guided walk. Norwich, 1983. P.

9847 PELLEW, G. A sermon preached at the consecration of the church of St. Mark, New Lakenham. Norwich, 1844. P.

9848 FISHER, C. Old Lakenham Water Mill. *J. Norfolk Industrial Archaeol. Soc.* 2 (4), 1979, 6–10.

9849 KELLY, G. I. The Louis Marchesi public house, 17 Tombland. [Unpubl.], 1984. P.

9850 46, Mancroft Street, Norwich. *J. Norfolk Industrial Archaeol. Soc.* 1 (6), 1974, 11–19.
Description of a mid-19th century worker's cottage.

9851 A unified Mousehold. By a group of people interested in retaining and improving Mousehold Heath. [Duplicated]. 1964. P.

9852 NORWICH CITY COUNCIL. The Mousehold Study. 3 parts. Norwich, 1978–81.

9853 NORWICH CITY COUNCIL. Mousehold Heath: a history. Norwich, 1984.

9854 CLEMENTS, B. Island site: a brief history of the [Norwich Union] head office buildings from 1797. Norwich, 1983.

PALACE PLAIN. See nos. 9444, 9452, 9864.

9855 SKIPPER AND ASSOCIATES (ARCHITECTS). Report to the Town Clerk on behalf of the St. Benedict's and District Traders' Association and Broadland Housing Association [re St. Benedict's revitalisation]. Norwich, [1971].

9856 ORTON, C., *ed.* St. Benedict's remembered: a community booklet. Norwich, 1980. P.

9857 COILEY, D. E. M. The church of St. George Tombland. Norwich, 1974. P.

9858 HORTH, J. R. St. George Tombland, Norwich: reconstituted family groupings derived from the first parish register, 1538–1707. Goodmayes, Essex, 1982.

9859 EADE, *Sir* P. St. Giles. a lecture. Norwich, 1870.

9860 McBRIDE, E. The story of the cathedral of St. John the Baptist, Norwich. N.p., [c. 1978]. P.
See also no. 9803.

9861 McLEAN, M. *and* UPJOHN, S. Guide to St. John Timberhill. [Norwich, 1982].

9862 McLEAN. M. St. Julian's Church and Lady Julian's cell. Norwich, 1979. P.

9863 WILLIAMS J. F. The brasses of St. Margaret's Church, Norwich. *Trans. Monumental Brass Soc.* 9, 1954, 118–25.

9864 BEAZLEY, O. St. Martin-at-Palace Church, Norwich. *NARG News* 52, 1988, 17–22.

9865 NEVILL, H. R. Kett's Castle. A lecture [on St. Michael's Chapel]. Norwich, 1857. P.

9866 VICTORIA AND ALBERT MUSEUM. Exhibition of medieval paintings from Norwich [St. Michael-at-Plea]. [Notes by] P. Tudor-Craig. 1956. P.

9867 [Entry deleted]

9868 MILLICAN, P. A threat to Elm Hill. [Appeal re church of SS. Simon and Jude]. Norwich, 1951. P.

ST. STEPHEN'S CHURCH. See no. 8614.

9869 JENNINGS, S. *and* ATKIN, M. A 17th-century well group from St. Stephen's Street, Norwich. *N.A.* 38, 1984, 13–37.
Account of pottery and clay pipes found on site.

9870 VIRGOE, J. The Tabernacle; a lost Norwich building. *NARG News* 46, 1986, 6–11.

9871 Arup at East Anglia. Music Centre, University of East Anglia. *Architect. Rev.* 157, 1975, 130–9.

9872 Sainsbury Centre for the Visual Arts, University of East Anglia. *Architect. Rev.* 164, 1978, 345–62.
See also *Architects' J.* 167, 1978, 622–5; and 180, 1984, 39–44; *RIBA J.* 85, 1978, 318; *Burlington Mag.* 120, 1978, 565; *Museums J*, 78, 1979, 167–9.

9873 WHITTINGHAM, A. B. *and* GREEN, B. The White Swan Inn, St. Peter's Street, Norwich. *N.A.* 39, 1984, 38–50.

ORMESBY PARISHES

See nos. 8641, 8826.

OULTON

9874 PARTRIDGE, E. Oulton Meeting House. *NARG News* 11, 1977, 16–20.

OVERSTRAND

9875 ANDERSON, V. Overstrand Belfry School, 1830–1980. N.p., 1980. P.

OXBOROUGH

9876 BELOE. E. M. Oxborough. Notes for an address to the members of the N.N.A.S. on their visit. King's Lynn, 1890. P.

9877 MILES, P. A French parterre in Norfolk: the garden of Oxburgh Hall. *Country Life* 167, 1980, 1480–2.

9878 PASTON-BEDINGFELD, *Sir* E. Heraldry at Oxburgh. Oxburgh, 1983. P.

9879 ROSE, E. J. *and* JENNINGS, S. The excavation of a brick-lined shaft and its contents at Oxburgh Hall. *Post-Medieval Archaeol.* 19, 1985, 35–47.

9880 FARROW, C. W. The descent of Oxborough. *Norfolk Ancestor* 4, 1986, 34–7.

9881 NICOLSON, N. Oxburgh Hall. *In* FORD, B., *ed.* Cambridge guide to the arts in Britain: vol.2, the Middle Ages (Cambridge, 1988), pp.88–95.

OXNEAD

9882 HARRIS, J. "Oh happy Oxnead". Oxnead and the Yarmouth collection. *Country Life* 179, 1986, 1630–2.

PANXWORTH

See no. 8141.

PASTON

9883 CAPES, J. M. The Paston barn. *E.A.M.* Nov. 1981, 17–19.
See also nos. 8580, 8811.

PENTNEY

See no. 7712.

PICKENHAM

Sale catalogue
9884 Pickenham Hall. Furniture, etc. of Mr. G. Moreton. Christie's, Oct. 1986

PLUMSTEAD

9885 COXFORD, B. *and others*. Little Plumstead brickworks. *J. Norfolk Industrial Archaeol. Soc.* 3 (3), 1983, 107–12.

POSTWICK

9886 CARTER, A. Postwick: the story of a Norfolk village. Postwick, 1987.

POTTER HEIGHAM

9887 BROADS AUTHORITY. Potter Heigham bridge local plan: draft plan for consultation. *Followed by* Final plan. Norwich, 1983/85.
　　See also no. 8051.

PULHAM PARISHES

9888 ROSE, E. J. Pulham St. Mary Magdalen: a constructional mystery. *N.A.* 38, 1982, 193–5.
　　See also nos. 7855, 7895.

QUIDENHAM

Sale catalogue
9889 Quidenham Hall. Library (remaining portion). Hodgson, London, 1949.

RACKHEATH

See no. 8549.

RANWORTH

9890 [ENRAGHT, H. J.] Ranworth. A village and church on the Broads. Norwich, [c.1908]. Numerous later eds. P.
9891 PEARSON, R. O. Ranworth rood screen, Norfolk. Drawn by R. O. Pearson. N.d. RCF.
9892 BROADS AUTHORITY. Ranworth Staithe: design case study. Prepared... by Owers and Lumley, associates, Cambridge. Norwich, 1983.
9892A MUIR, M. Ranworth Old Hall: North Barn. *NARG News* 47, 1986, 1–10.

RAYNHAM PARISHES

See nos. 8043, 8411, 8414, 8675, 8908–11, 10058.

REDENHALL

9893 BROWN, A. The parish of Redenhall with Harleston and Wortwell. Ramsgate, 1974.

REEDHAM

9894 WAILES, R. Berney Arms Mill, Reedham. 1957. P. 2nd ed., 1982.

REEPHAM

9895 BARRINGER, J. C. Reepham: a market town and its neighbours. An exhibition organised by Reepham branch of the W.E.A. Reepham, 1975. P.
9896 BROADLAND DISTRICT COUNCIL. Reepham town centre plan. Norwich, 1979.
9897 BROADLAND DISTRICT COUNCIL. Reepham local plan: draft written statement. Norwich, 1986.
   See also 7536.

REPPS WITH BASTWICK

See no. 8070.

REYMERSTON

See no. 8458.

RIDDLESWORTH

See no. 8458.

RINGLAND

See no. 8822.

RINGSTEAD

See nos. 7710, 8712.

ROCKLAND ALL SAINTS

See no. 8458.

ROCKLAND ST. MARY

9898 CHALCRAFT, C. W. T. Rockland St. Mary. Norwich, 1988.

ROLLESBY

See nos. 8427, 8850.

ROUGHAM

9899 TRETT, R. Rougham brickworks. *J. Norfolk Industrial Archaeol. Soc.* 2 (4), 1979, 70–72.
9900 LONG, P. The Rougham [supernatural] phenomenon. *E.A.M.* Feb. 1982, 189–91.
See also no. 8462.

ROYDON

9901 COTTON, S. The parish church of St. Remigius, Roydon. Roydon, 1984. P.
See also no. 8549.

RUDHAM, EAST

9902 STUART, J. K. Farewell; a sermon preached in St. Mary's parish church, East Rudham...Norwich, 1855. P. UEA.
See also no. 8713.

RUNTON PARISHES

9903 MATTHEWS, F. H. *and* CREASY, J. Runton parish church of the Holy Trinity. A brief history. N.p., 1967. P.
9904 LEAKE, G. F. An undated field book relating to Runton. Cert. in Local Hist., Cambridge Board of Extra-Mural Studies, 1977.
9905 LEAKE, G. F. Further notes on the Reformation in another Norfolk parish. *Bull. Norfolk Research Committee* 38, 1987, 15–18.
9906 LEAKE, G. F. East and West Runton: two villages, one parish. North Walsham, 1988. P.
See also no. 8634.

RUSHFORD

See no. 8458.

RUSTON, EAST

See no. 8051.

RYBURGH, GREAT

9907 MANNING, I. M. Great Ryburgh. *J. Norfolk. Industrial Archaeol. Soc.* 2 (2), 1977, 12–20.

RYSTON

9908 CHERRY, J. A 12th-century mortar from Ryston Hall. *N.A.* 38, 1981, 67–73.
See also no. 8549.

SAHAM TONEY

9909 BROWN, R. A. Coin evidence at the Romano-British site at Woodcock Hall, Saham Toney. *NARG News* 4, 1976, 1–4; 10, 1977, 9–14.
See also comments by J. Smallwood on Icenian coins, *ibid.* 20, 1980, 10–13.
9910 BROWN, R. A. The Iron Age and Romano-British settlement at Woodcock Hall, Saham Toney. *Britannia* 17, 1986, 1–58.
9911 REID, A. Saham Toney and the English Civil War. *Bull. Norfolk Research Committee* 35, 1986, 11–14.
Constable's accounts of 1644 and 1650 involving recruitment expenses.
9912 BROWN, R. A. A group of gold-plated Roman coins from Woodcock Hall. *N.A.* 40, 1988, 171–9.

SALHOUSE

9913 FARROW, C. W. A calendar of Salhouse poor law documents. *Norfolk Ancestor* 4, 1986, 38–42.

SALLE

9914 LINNELL, C. L. S. Salle [Church]. N.p., 1955. P.
9915 R., D. Salle, a Norfolk parish church. 2nd ed. [Salle], 1984. P.

SALTHOUSE

9916 VINES, A. Romano-British site at Salthouse. *Bull. Norfolk Research Committee* 26, 1981, 9–13.
9917 BROOKS, P. Salthouse: village of character and history. North Walsham, 1984. P.

SANDRINGHAM

9918 A catalogue of the valuable, curious, and rare library of books, the property of the late H. H. Henley, Esq., at Sandringham Hall...which will be sold by auction...2 July. [King's Lynn, 1834].
9919 W., G. Sandringham: a complete description of the royal residence and estate... King's Lynn, 1874. BL.
9920 BUXTON, A. The King in his country. 1955.
Recounts George VI's visits to Sandringham.
9921 ASHTON, P. T. Sandringham Church (St. Mary Magdalene) and the gardens of Sandringham House. 1958. P. Several later eds.
9922 MESSENT, C. J. W. The architecture on the royal estate of Sandringham: an architectural history with reproductions of pencil sketches. Blofield, 1974.

9923 WINTON, M. J. Sandringham House: a royal home for Edward and Alexandra. King's Lynn, 1975. P.

9924 HEPWORTH, P. Royal Sandringham. Norwich, 1978.

9925 Sandringham. [Official guide]. Sandringham, 1978. P.

9926 WHITLOCK, R. Royal farmers. 1980. Chap. 5: Sandringham estate.

9927 [Entry deleted].

See also nos. 7589, 7591, 7595, 7628, 8334.

SANTON

See no. 8549

SAXLINGHAM

9928 ROSE, E. J. Saxlingham Place or Heydon Hall, Saxlingham [with later addendum]. *N.A.* 38, 1983, 336–43; 40, 1987, 93–100.

SAXLINGHAM NETHERGATE

9929 'Belcoombe', Saxlingham, designed by Mr. F. W. Troup. *In* WEAVER, L., *ed.* Small country houses of today (1911), pp. 160–64.

9930 MUIR, M. A small, unofficial dig in Saxlingham. *NARG News* 14, 1978, 8–17.
Moated site.

9931 MUIR, M. From slate to computer. A history of education in Saxlingham Nethergate. Norwich, 1987.

See also no. 7560.

SAXTHORPE

See no. 8040.

SCOLE

9932 GALE, C. H. Roman remains in Scole. *Proc. Suffolk Inst. Archaeol.* 22, 1936, 263–86; 23, 1937, 24–30.

9933 HALLOWS, J. Scole from past to present. Ipswich, [1963]. RCF.

9934 ROGERSON, A. Excavations at Scole, 1973. *E.A.A.R.* 5, 1977, 97–224.

9935 LEVERETT, J. Bygone memories of Scole over the past 70 years. Felixstowe, [1978].

SCOTTOW

See no. 8458.

SCOULTON

9936 KELLY, M. A traditional Norfolk earth-walled building [The Old Rectory, Scoulton]. [Unpubl. typescript, 1976].

SCULTHORPE

9937 BALDWIN, J., *ed.* 40 years of R.A.F. Sculthorpe, 1943–83. Fakenham, 1986.

SEA PALLING

9938 PESTELL, R. E. Palling: a history shaped by the sea. North Walsham, 1986.

SEDGEFORD

9939 HAMMOND, J. Sedgeford. Stoke Ferry, [c. 1977]. P.
9940 HAMMOND, J. Gnatingdon, deserted medieval village or mislaid manor? *NARG News* 37, 1984, 10–16.
  See also nos. 8030, 8040.

SEETHING

See no. 7847.

SENNOWE

9941 ASLET, C. Sennowe Park. *Country Life.* 170, 1981, 2242–5, 2298–301.

SHADWELL PARK

9942 GIROUARD, M. Shadwell Park. *In his* The Victorian country house (Oxford, 1971), pp. 95–8.
9943 LE ROUGETEL, H. Tall oaks from little acorns. 18th century landscaping at Shadwell Park. *Country Life* 164, 1978, 1974–5.

SHARRINGTON

9944 BLATCHLY, J. M. The brasses of Sharrington, Norfolk. *Trans. Monumental Brass Soc.* 12, 1978, 159–68.

SHELFANGER

9945 SHELFANGER WOMEN'S INSTITUTE. Shelfanger: a Norfolk village, past and present. Tivetshall, [1985]. P.
9946 All Saints. Shelfanger, 1975. P.
See also nos. 7775, 8546, 8549.

SHERINGHAM

9947 JONES, P. T. The story of the churches of Sheringham illustrated. Gloucester, [c. 1935]. Another ed. [1950]. P. BL.

9948 LINNELL, C. L. S. All Saints, Upper Sheringham. N.p., 1960. P.

9949 ERROLL, A. C. Life and death in Norfolk villages [Sheringham and Sidestrand]. 3 pts. Privately publ., 1974–76.

9950 BURKI, D. *and others*. Sheringham past and present. [Duplicated]. 1975. P.

9951 BROOKS, P. Sheringham: the story of a town. Cromer, 1980. P.

9952 MALSTER, R. W. The Sheringham lifeboats, 1838–1981. Cromer, 1981.

9953 SHERINGHAM CHAMBER OF TRADE. Sheringham residents directory. Wisbech, [c. 1981].

9954 BROOKS, P. A Sheringham album. North Walsham, 1985.

9955 CRASKE, S. *and* CRASKE, R. Sheringham: a century of change. North Walsham, 1985.

9956 YAXLEY, S., *ed*. Sherringhamia: the journal of Abbot Upcher, 1813–16. Stibbard, 1986.

9957 CECIL, M. *and* MORTIMER, J. Sheringham Hall. *World of Interiors* March 1987, 102–15.

9958 WATERSON, M. Repton recognised. *Landscape* 7, 1988, 62–7.
On National Trust's acquisition of Sheringham Hall.

Sale catalogue
9959 Sheringham Hall. Furniture, pictures, etc. Oct. 1986 (Christie's).
See also nos. 7591, 8411, 8870.

SHIPDHAM

9960 SPENCE, K. J. A Shipdham centenary [the Congregational Church]. N.p., 1981. P.

9961 WOODS, M. Shipdham past and present. Shipdham, 1987.
See also his *A view of Shipdham, 1: 1890–1940* (1985); and other pamphlets.
See also no. 7526.

SHOTESHAM

9962 WADE, K. The excavation of a brick clamp at Shotesham St. Mary. *Post-Medieval Archaeol*. 14, 1980, 187–9.

Sale catalogue
9963 Shotesham Park. Library. 24 Sept. 1979.
See also no. 7560.

SHOULDHAM

9964 WELLS, C. An urned cremation from a late Bronze Age cemetery at Shouldham. *Archaeol. J*. 133, 1976, 38–42.

9965 SMALLWOOD, J. A medieval tile-kiln at Abbey Farm, Shouldham. *E.A.A.R*. 8, 1978, 45–54.

9966 DURST, D. *and others.* The Shouldham survey. *J. Norfolk Industrial Archaeol. Soc.* 2 (4), 1979, 16–25.

SLOLEY

9967 BOWDITCH, P. *and* OGILVIE, P. Our heritage: Sloley Voluntary Controlled Primary School. [Sloley], 1974.
9968 NEVILLE, *Sir* R. A secondhand monument? *Norfolk Standard* 3 (5), 1983, 68–72.
Concerns armorial window and monument in Sloley Church, and connection with Cubitt family.

SMALLBURGH
9969 ROSE, E. Wayford Bridge, Smallburgh. *E.A.A.R.* 8, 1978, 23–8.
Possible site of Roman ford.

SNETTISHAM

9970 MAITLAND, R. W. The Snettisham ghost. 1956. P.
9971 GIROUARD, M. Ken Hill. *In his* The Victorian country house (Oxford, 1971), pp. 161–4.
9972 HARDING, R. W. A tour of Snettisham. N.p., [1982].
9973 BINGHAM, J. A famous victory: an account of the early years of Snettisham Parish Council. Snettisham, 1983. P.
Controversy over access to Ken Hill.
9974 JAMES, E. M. Old Hall, Snettisham, and the Styleman family. *N.A.* 38, 1983, 343–57.
9975 SNETTISHAM PARISH COUNCIL. Snettisham's common rights. [By John Bingham]. Snettisham, [c. 1984]. P.
9976 POTTER, T. A Roman jeweller's hoard from Snettisham. *Antiquity* 60, 1986, 137–9.

SOMERTON
9977 MORTIMER, R. The prior of Butley and the lepers of West Somerton. *Bull. Inst. Hist. Research* 53, 1980, 99–103.

SOUTHACRE
9978 STEPHENSON, M. A note on the brass of Thomas Lemon, priest, 1534, at Southacre. *Trans. Monumental Brass Soc.* 5, 1906, 157–8.

SOUTHERY
9979 FYSH, J. P. G. *and* FYSH, A. V. G. A. Six of one... the curate and the churchwarden in combat. *Norfolk Ancestor* 3 (4), 1984, 52–7.
Dispute at Southery 1838–40.

SPARHAM

9980 LINNELL, C. L. S. St. Mary's, Sparham. N.p., 1959. P. 2nd ed. 1976, by M. J. Sayer.

SPIXWORTH

See no. 8294.

SPORLE

9981 DAVISON, A. Petygards and the medieval hamlet of Cotes. *E.A.A.R.* 14, 1982, 102–107.
Deserted village in Sporle parish.

SPROWSTON

9982 TRICKER, R. W. Parish of Sprowston. Church of SS. Mary and Margaret and St. Cuthbert: a short guide. Sprowston, 1976.
See also no. 8061.

STALHAM

9983 HENDERSON, S. J. N. Handbook of information on the caring and educational resources for Stalham area. (Norwich Archdeaconry Committee for Social Responsibility). Stalham, [1979].
9984 FARMAN, D. *and others.* Stalham and district in times past. Chorley (Lancs.), 1982.
9985 FARMAN, D. 150 years of service: Stalham Fire Brigade, 1833–1983. Wymondham, 1983.

STANFIELD

See no. 7687.

STANFORD

See no. 8549.

STANHOE

9986 BECKETT, G. Family reconstitution [parish of Stanhoe]. *NARG News* 11, 1977, 2–10.

STARSTON

9987 RICHES, R. Oddments: an account of happenings in the Waveney Valley area. Harleston, [c. 1976].
Concentrates on Starston.
See also no. 7560.

STIBBARD

9988 HOWELL, K. M. The parish of Stibbard: census index, 1841–81. Harrogate, 1987.

STIFFKEY

9989 STERN, E. Account of labourers' wages and other charges kept for Sir Nathaniel Bacon of Stiffkey Hall, 1588–1598. Cert. in Local Hist., Cambridge Board of Extra-Mural Studies, 1977.
9990 SMITH, A. H. A squire and his community: the Stiffkey project. *Bull. of Local Hist., East Midland Region* 16, 1981, 13–19.
9991 CAMPBELL, L. The women of Stiffkey [in the late 16th century]. M.A. thesis, Univ. of E. Anglia, 1985.
See also no. 8414.

STOCKTON

9992 PRONK, S. E. Stockton's stone charters: a survey of the epitaphs in the churchyard of St. Michael's Church. [Stockton, 1976]. P.

STOKE FERRY

9993 COATES, D. Stoke Ferry: the story of a Norfolk village. Henley-on-Thames, 1980.
See also no. 7366.

STOKE HOLY CROSS

9994 SMITH, A. C. Tapestry of Stoke. Stoke Holy Cross, 1977.
See also nos. 7560, 8647.

STOKESBY

See no. 8563.

STOW BARDOLPH

9995 [DASHWOOD, G. H.] Sigilla antiqua. Engravings from ancient seals... in the muniment room of Sir Thomas Hare, Bt., of Stowe-Bardolph. 2 vols. 1847/62.
See also no. 7775.

STOW BEDON

See no. 8458.

STRATTON PARISHES

9996 St. Mary's Church, Long Stratton. Long Stratton, 1975.
9997 LONG STRATTON CONGREGATIONAL CHURCH. 150th church anniversary year, 1826–1976: a short history of the church and programme of special events. [Long Stratton, 1976]. P.
9998 COOKE, R. Long Stratton: history of the village. [Long Stratton, 1978]. P.
9999 AMERY, C. and WINNINGTON, T. South Norfolk District offices. *Architects J.* 170, 1979, 923–38.
10000 SOUTH NORFOLK DISTRICT COUNCIL. Long Stratton local plan. Long Stratton, 1988.
Preceded by *Consultation draft* and *Summary of main issues/comments* (both 1987).
10001 ADDINGTON, S. The Wood Greens and Crow Green. *NARG News* 40, 1985, 5–9.
See also nos. 7509, 9170.

STRUMPSHAW

10002 BUCKTON, B. F. The village and church of Strumpshaw, 1257–1957. [Strumpshaw, 1957].
10003 PEART, S. Strumpshaw: a village at that time of day. Strumpshaw, 1981.
See also author's article in *E.A.M.* June 1982, 354–6.

SWAFFHAM

10004 SMITH, *Rev.* G. V. V. Long ago in Swaffham. Swaffham, [1904]. P. BL
10005 The Swaffham almanac, 1933. Swaffham, 1933. RCF.
10006 HILLS, C. and WADE-MARTINS, P. The Anglo-Saxon cemetery at the Paddocks, Swaffham. *E.A.A.R.* 2, 1976. 1–44.
10007 McCRIRICK, J. The early days of Swaffham coursing club. Swaffham, 1976. P.
10008 WINCOTE, K. W. H. Plowright and Sons, engineers and ironfounders. *J. Norfolk Industrial Archaeol. Soc.* 1 (9), 1975, 11–16.
10009 BRECKLAND DISTRICT COUNCIL. Swaffham local plan. Dereham, [c. 1982]. P.
10010 KENDLE, L. C. Kendle's old Swaffham. Norwich, 1982. Another ed. 1985.
Old photographs.
10010A RIPPER, B. Some 18th-century tithe maps of Swaffham. *Bull. Norfolk Research Committee* 32, 1984, 16–18.
10011 GRETTON, J. R. A history of Hamond's High School, Swaffham, 1736–1986. Swaffham, 1986.
10012 LYONS, M. C. Swaffham parish library: a catalogue of printed books and manuscripts. Dublin/Norwich, 1987.
See also nos. 7552, 7570.

SWAFIELD

See no. 8563.

SWANNINGTON

10013 WORTLEY, J. D. The story of Swannington Parish Church from prehistoric times. Norwich, 1936. P. BL.

SWANTON ABBOT

10014 Swanton Abbot School, 1876–1976: 100 years of learning and teaching. Swanton Abbot, [1976]. P.
See also no. 8458.

TACOLNESTON

10015 Tacolneston School centenary anniversary. [Tacolneston], 1977.
See also no. 7560.

TASBURGH

10016 LAWSON, A. J. A beaker from Tasburgh. *N.A.* 36, 1975, 183–4.
10017 ADDINGTON, S. The hedgerows of Tasburgh. *N.A.* 37, 1978, 70–83.
10018 ADDINGTON, S. The Reformation in a Norfolk village, 1500–1635. *Bull. Norfolk Research Committee* 36, 1986, 13–16.
See also no. 7509

TAVERHAM

10019 KING, D. J. An antiphon to St. Edmund in Taverham Church. *N.A.* 36, 1977, 387–91.
10020 Taverham: a fine village. Taverham, 1983.
See also 8549.

TERRINGTON PARISHES

10021 FRANKLIN, F. S. Terrington St. Clement through the ages. [Unpubl. typescript, 1974]. P.
10022 GREER, A. Education in Terrington St. John: an historical interpretation. Wisbech, 1984.
10023 GREER, S. *and others, eds.* Terrington Scti Johns ... register book. Vol.1, 1538–1600; vol.2, 1601–50. Wisbech, 1985/87.
See also no. 7800.

THETFORD

GENERAL HISTORIES AND GUIDES

10024 KNOCKER, G. M. Theodford: the story of Anglo-Saxon Thetford. Thetford, n.d. P.

10025 CLARKE, W. G. A short historical guide to the ancient borough of Thetford. Thetford, 1908. Another ed., variant title, 1909.

10026 THETFORD AND DISTRICT CHAMBER OF COMMERCE. A short historical and descriptive guide to the ancient borough of Thetford. Thetford, 1948.
See also Chamber's later *Thetford official guide. By John Kitson* (1983).

10027 OSBORNE, D. A view of Thetford past. 3 parts. Thetford, 1984–87.
Views from picture postcards etc.

10028 CROSBY, A. A history of Thetford. Chichester, 1986.

10029 Thetford: antiq burg. Thetford, 1985.

See also nos. 8331, 8758, 9105.

ARCHAEOLOGY

10030 DUNMORE, S. *and* CARR, R. The late Saxon town of Thetford. *E.A.A.R.* 4, 1976.

10031 NORWICH CASTLE MUSEUM. The Thetford Roman treasure. [Exhibition catalogue]. Norwich, 1982.

10032 ROGERSON, A. *and others.* Excavations in Thetford, 1948–59 and 1973–80. *E.A.A.* 22, 1984.

10033 JOHNS, C. Faunus and Thetford: an early Latian deity in late Roman Britain. *In* HENIG, M. *and* KING, A., *eds.* Pagan gods and shrines of the Roman Empire (Oxford Univ. Committee for Archaeology, monograph 8, 1986), pp. 93–103.

See also no. 7732.

PLANNING

10034 THETFORD URBAN DISTRICT COUNCIL. Statement with documents relating to the proposed sewerage scheme. Thetford, 1909.
See also associated report by consultant E. Bailey-Denton.

10035 THETFORD ROTARY CLUB. Thetford town expansion: report on social survey. Thetford, 1964. P.

10036 BRECKLAND DISTRICT COUNCIL. Thetford town centre plan review. 2 parts. E. Dereham, 1979.

See also no. 7552.

TRADE AND INDUSTRY

10037 LANE, M. R. Burrell Showman's road locomotives: the story of Showman type road locomotives manufactured by Charles Burrell & Sons Ltd. Hemel Hempstead, 1971.

10038 MADDOCK, A. Burrell's of Thetford. Norwich, 1979. P.

10039 Survey of Fisons' Vitriol and Manure Works, Two Mile Bottom, Thetford. *J. Norfolk Industrial Archaeol. Soc.* 2 (1), 1976.

10040 THETFORD MOULDED PRODUCTS LTD. A century of moulding in Thetford. Thetford, 1979. P.

10041 GOODWIN, C. Thetford pulp ware. *J. Norfolk Industrial Archaeol. Soc.* 3, 1985, 164–8.
Process used by company now known as Thetford Moulded Products prior to introduction of plastics, i.e. 1870s to 1950s.

10042 COOKE, R. *and* COOKE, S. Thetford waterworks. *J. Norfolk Industrial Archaeol. Soc.* 2 (4), 1979, 26–61.

CLUBS AND SOCIETIES

10042A SHORT, W. J. 50 years Thet Lodge [Freemasons]. Thetford, 1958. FPL.

THE PRIORIES

10043 WASSON, J. Visiting entertainers at the Cluniac Priory, Thetford, 1497–1540. *Albion* 9, 1977, 128–34.

10044 HARE, J. N. The priory of the Holy Sepulchre, Thetford. *N.A.* 37, 1979, 190–200.

10045 WILCOX, R. Thetford Cluniac Priory excavations, 1971–4. *N.A.* 40, 1987, 1–18.

THOMPSON

See no. 8458.

THORNHAM

10046 LINNELL, C. L. S. All Saints Church, Thornham. N.p., 1962. P.
See also no. 7691.

THORPE MARKET

See no. 8458.

THORPE ST. ANDREW

10047 HODGETTS, M. Brough Hall, Catterick, and Thorpe Hall, Norwich: a comment. *Recusant Hist.* 13, 1976, 157–8.

10048 GREGORY, A. Early Romano-British pottery production at Thorpe St. Andrew. *N.A.* 37, 1979, 202–7.

10049 BROADLAND DISTRICT COUNCIL. Thorpe St. Andrew (Pound Lane) local plan. Norwich, 1984.
See also *Public participation statement* (1984); and further *Written statement* (1986).

10050 ROSE, E. J. *and* DAVISON, A. J. 'St. Catherine's, Thorpe' – the birth and death of a myth. *N.A.* 40, 1988, 179–81.
Questions attribution of church foundations uncovered in 1951.

10051 ROSSI, A. P. Contrasts and parallels. Two conservation case studies: Greenhill [Wirksworth] and Thorpe Hall. *Trans. Ancient Monuments Soc.* n.s. 32, 1988, 73–100.

THREXTON

See no. 8549.

THURNE

10052 MACDERMOTT, G. M. Thurne. Norwich, 1923. P.

THURSFORD

10053 CUSHING, G. *and* STARSMORE, I. Steam at Thursford. Newton Abbot, 1982.
On authors' steam engine collection.

See also no. 8458.

THWAITE

See no. 8256A.

TIBENHAM

10054 ROSE, E. J. The Aslacton painting of Channonz Hall, Tibenham, and an early cartographic illustration. *N.A.* 40, 1987, 109–11.
Painting on panelling at Limestone House, Aslacton.

TILNEY PARISHES

10055 JUKES, H. A. L. The Tilney papers: a note-worthy parochial collection of historical manuscripts and printed books. *N.A.* 36, 1976, 233–40.

10056 BRISTOW, C. Tilney families. Tonbridge, 1988.

TITTLESHALL

See no. 7686.

TIVETSHALL

10057 Tivetshall: reminiscences of the past, based on ... study by Tivetshall School. Tivetshall, 1977. P.

TOFT MONKS

See no. 8938.

TOFTREES

10058 WADE-MARTINS, S. Cannister Hall Farm [Toftrees]. *J. Norfolk Industrial Archaeol. Soc.* 2 (3), 1978, 22–4.
Disused farm on Raynham Estate.

TOFTS, WEST

See no. 8549.

TOTTINGTON

See no. 8058.

TRIMINGHAM

See no. 8849.

TROWSE

10059 HEALY, F. A round barrow at Trowse: early Bronze Age burials and medieval occupation. *E.A.A.R.* 14, 1982, 1–34.
10060 British Railways (Trowse Bridge) Act, 1985. (Local Acts, xxx).
    See also no. 7560.

TRUNCH

10061 FISKE, R. C. A history of Trunch. [Duplicated]. 1964–65.
10062 CHESHIRE, J. G. St. Botolph's Church, Trunch. Norwich, [c.1920].
10063 GOODRICH, P. The church of St. Botolph's, Trunch: a guidebook. Rewritten, with historical additions. Norwich, 1935. P. BL.
10064 WINKLEY, G. W. D. Church of St. Botolph, Trunch. Cley, [1976]. P.
10065 AMIS, A. Trunch Methodist Church: the first 50 years, 1937–1987. [Trunch, 1987].

TUDDENHAM, NORTH

10066 NELSON, R. E. North Tuddenham. *NARG News* 48, 1987, 6–14.
Sketch of its archaeological history.

TUNSTEAD

See nos. 8462, 8519.

UPWELL

10067 JEANS, R. Upwell: history of a Fenland village. Shaftesbury, 1987.

WACTON

10068 BARRINGER, J. C. *and others*. The Wacton project, 1977. *Bull. Norfolk Research Committee* 18, 1977, 11–13.
10069 [History of Wacton]. *Ibid.* 24, 1980, 10–16.
Short articles on hedges (S. Addington), the Common (L. McMurdo), and 16th century yeoman families (B. Cornford).
See also no. 7560.

WALPOLE PARISHES

10070 WALPOLE, R. C. The Walpole villages and their people. 1979.
See also no. 8458.

WALSHAM, NORTH

10071 North Walsham official guide. [North Walsham, 1927]. Many later eds.
10072 COLLINS, S., *ed.* An historical outline of Bradfield and North Walsham Congregational Church. [Typescript]. 1957.
10072A EATON, F. R. Bi-centenary of Lodge of Unanimity no. 102 [Freemasons]. Norwich, 1958. P. FPL.
Note also earlier anon. history, *Unanimity Lodge no. 102* (1908).
10073 HOWARD, A. The changing economic and social geography of North Walsham since 1960. [Unpubl. dissertation, 1973].
10074 Beyond the fringe: North Walsham County Primary School, 1874–1974. North Walsham, [1974].
10075 EMERSON, S. *and others*. North Walsham past and present. Part 1. Norwich, 1975.
10076 NORFOLK COUNTY COUNCIL. The North Walsham area: a case study in alternative patterns of village development. Norwich, 1976.
10077 100 years: North Walsham High School, 1877–1977. [North Walsham], 1977. P.
10078 FORDER, C. A history of the Paston School: supplementary notes to the 2nd edition of 1975. N.p., 1980.
Refers to 2nd ed. of *B.N.H.* 6702.
10079 MARSHALL, K. N. Inscriptions on tombstones, lodger-stones and wall monuments in St. Nicholas' Parish Church, North Walsham. [Unpubl. typescript, 1981].
10080 North Walsham Girls' High School: [history and reminiscences]. North Walsham, 1982.
10081 BARRINGER, C., *ed.* North Walsham in the eighteenth century: from research by the History Group of the North Walsham branch of the WEA. N. Walsham, 1983.

10082 McMANUS, M. *and others.* North Walsham in old picture postcards. Zaltbommel (Netherlands), 1984.
See also nos. 7536, 7589, 8687–8.

WALSHAM, SOUTH

10083 AMOS, G. S. A history and description of South Walsham. S. Walsham, 1981.
10084 WARREN, P. South Walsham: the agrarian economy in the late 16th century. *Bull. Norfolk Research Committee* 30, 1983, 11–15.

WALSINGHAM

10085 B., T. A. An English churchman's guide to Walsingham. Walsingham, 1912. P.
10086 [PATTEN, A. H.] The pilgrim's manual to the shrine of Our Lady of Walsingham. Walsingham, 1928. 6th ed., 1957.
See also his *Pilgrimage of Our Lady of Walsingham* (1922); *Walsingham. Everybody's guide book* (Walsingham, [1939]); and *Mary's shrine of the Holy House, Walsingham* (Walsingham, 1954).
10087 MORTIMER, C. G. Our Lady of Walsingham. [1934]. P.
10088 DICKINSON, J. C. The shrine of Our Lady of Walsingham. Cambridge, 1956.
10089 BOND, H. A. The Walsingham story through 900 years, 1061–1961. Walsingham, [1960].
10090 STEPHENSON, F. Walsingham. A story of faith through time. Holt, 1969.
10091 FISHER, C. Walsingham lives on. 1979.
10092 ROLLINGS, P. Walsingham in times past. Chorley, 1981.
10093 Three Victorian pamphlets on Walsingham. Bedford, 1982
Facsimiles of J. Lee Warner's notes on Little Walsingham Church and the Priory; and R. Hart's *Shrines and pilgrimages of Norfolk.*
10094 FISHER, C. Walsingham: a place of pilgrimage for all people. Walsingham 1983.
10095 SMITH, C. A pocket guide to Walsingham. 1988.
10096 [PATTEN, A. H.] A short guide to St. Mary's Church, Little Walsingham. Sutton, [1934]. P. BL.
10097 BARNES, J. St. Mary's Church, Walsingham. [Walsingham], 1982. P.
See also nos. 8462, 9562.

WALTON, WEST

10098 SILVESTER, R. J. West Walton: the development of a siltland parish. *N.A.* 39, 1985, 101–17.
See also no. 7800.

WARHAM

See no. 7691.

WATTON

10099 [GRIGSON, E. R.] Congregational Church, Watton: a historical sketch...[1872]. P.

10100 CALEY, W. B. R. An old East Anglian town [Watton]. *In* ANDREWS, W., *ed.* Bygone Norfolk (1898), pp. 130–47.

10101 Watton in an earlier age, 1700–1900 [W.E.A. compilation]. Watton, 1975.

10102 HENIG, M. *and* BROWN, R. A. Silver and gold Roman finger ring from Watton. *N.A.* 37, 1979, 201–2.

10103 WATTON AND DISTRICT CHAMBER OF TRADE. Information, trade, and services directory. Watton, 1982.

10104 BRECKLAND DISTRICT COUNCIL. Watton local plan. Dereham 1983.
Preceded by *Discussion document* (1983).

10105 CHAPMAN, C. F. Grandad's Watton. 2 parts. Watton, 1985. P.

10106 JESSUP, G. Watton through the ages. Watton, 1985.

See also no. 8546.

WEASENHAM

See no. 7686.

WEETING

10107 GREGORY, T. A hoard of late Roman metal work from Weeting. *N.A.* 36, 1976, 265–72.

10108 GREGORY, T. Excavations at Weeting, 1979. *NARG News* 21, 1980, 7–10.

WELLINGHAM

See no. 7686.

WELLS

10109 HODSKINSON, J. *and others*. The reports of Messrs. Hodskinson, Grundy, Hogard and Nickalls on the state and causes of the decay of Wells Harbour. 2 pts. N.p., 1782. BL.
See article on Hodskinson's report by G. Tonkin, *E.A.M.*, June 1981, 380–81.

10110 NICHOLSON, N. Aspects of life in Wells-next-the-Sea. [Wells], 1981.

See also no. 7628.

WELNEY

See no. 8768.

WENDLING

10111 JOLLY, C. Wendling County Primary School centenary, 1876–1976: notes on the village. Wendling, 1976. P.

See also no. 7845.

WEREHAM

10112 MILSOM, M. E. Short history of Wereham School, 1876–1976. Wereham, 1980.

WEST ACRE

10113 POWELL, R. A portrait from Norfolk's past: two Westacre gentlemen. *E.A.M.* Dec. 1981, 92–3.
On farm-workers at High House Farm.

10114 JAMES, E. *and* JONES, R. Lime kiln at West Acre. *J. Norfolk Industrial Archaeol. Soc.* 3 (3), 1983, 113–16.

WESTON LONGVILLE

10115 [WINSTANLEY, R. L.] Five Weston poor law documents. *Quart. J. Parson Woodforde Soc.* 17 (3), 1984, 17–25.
See also earlier article 'The poor law at Weston', *ibid.* 16 (2), 1983.

See also nos. 8589, 8677, 8934.

WESTWICK

See nos. 8458, 8687–8.

WEYBOURNE

10116 SANDRED, K. I. Weybourne: a parish- and river-name in Norfolk. *In* BENSKIN, M. *and* SAMUELS, M. L., *eds.* So meny people, longages and tonges: philological essays... presented to Angus McIntosh (Edinburgh, 1981), pp. 161–6.

10117 ARNGART, O. The place-names Weybourne and Wooburn. *J. Eng. Place-name Soc.* 18, 1982/83, 5–8.

10118 BROOKS, P. Weybourne: peaceful mirror of a turbulent past. North Walsham, 1984. P.

10119 FUNNELL, B. Weybourne watermill. *J. Norfolk Industrial Archaeol. Soc.* 3 (4), 1984, 123–9.

See also no. 8472.

WHITLINGHAM

See no. 8197.

WHITWELL

10120 MANNING, I. M. Whitwell Hall tannery. *J. Norfolk Industrial Archaeol. Soc.* 1 (8), 1975, 14–16; 3 (3), 1983, 102–6.

WICKHAMPTON

10121 JAMES, M. R. The wall paintings in Wickhampton Church. *In* INGLEBY, C., *ed.* Supplement to Blomefield's Norfolk (1929), pp. 125–42.
　　See also no. 8256A.

WICKLEWOOD

10122 WADE, D. Wicklewood Mill: recollections of Denis Wade, miller. *J. Norfolk Industrial Archaeol. Soc.* 1 (5), 1973, 5–13.
10123 NORFOLK WINDMILLS TRUST. Wicklewood windmill. Norwich, 1981. P.
　　See also nos. 8624, 8923.

WICKMERE

10124 FASSNIDGE, C. W. The tomb of the last Earl of Orford at Wickmere. *Norfolk Standard* 2 (2), 1979, 21–5.

WIGGENHALL PARISHES

See nos. 8458, 8912.

WIGHTON

10125 LAWSON, A. Excavations at Whey Curd Farm, Wighton. *E.A.A.R.* 2, 1976, 65–100.
Roman (?) enclosure.
　　See also no. 7691.

WILBY

See no. 8458.

WIMBOTSHAM

See no. 7775.

WINCH, EAST

10126 ALVIS, E. J. Short historical notes upon the parish of East Winch. [c. 1908]. P. RCF.

WINFARTHING

See no. 7775.

WINTERTON

10127 WINTERTON SEAMAN'S FRIENDLY SOCIETY. Articles...for the purpose of providing against sickness and infirmity. Yarmouth, [1828]. P.

WITCHINGHAM, GREAT

10128 JAMES, G. C. A guide to St. Mary's Parish Church, Great Witchingham. [1976]. P.
See also no. 8675.

WITTON (nr. North Walsham)

10129 REEVE, J. E. St. Margaret's churchyard, Witton, North Walsham. B.A. thesis, Nottingham Univ., 1979.
10130 LAWSON, A. J. *and others*. The archaeology of Witton. *E.A.A.R.* 18, 1983.

WIVETON

10131 GIDNEY, L. Some neolithic axes and a surface collection from Church Farm, Wiveton. B.A. thesis, London Univ., 1977.
10132 FAWCETT, R. St. Mary at Wiveton in Norfolk and a group of churches attributed to its mason. *Antiq. J.* 62, 1982, 35–56.

WOLFERTON

10133 CROWN, J. Rendezvous of royals [Wolferton railway station]. *E.A.M.* Apr. 1981, 284–6.

WOLTERTON HALL

10134 Catalogue of pictures, statues, [etc.]...at Wolterton. [Unpubl. typescript, n.d.]. RCF.
See also no.8916.

WOODBASTWICK

See no. 7536.

WOOD DALLING

See no. 8458.

WOODTON

10135 BALDWIN, L. M. History of Woodton. (Friends of the Round Tower Churches Society). Lowestoft, 1980.

WORSTEAD

10136 Worstead Baptist Church. A souvenir of the 225th anniversary, 1717–1942. [Worstead, 1942]. P. RCF.
10137 [WATTS, S.] A walk-round guide. Worstead Church. N. Walsham, 1973. P.
See also no. 8519.

WORTHING

10138 WOOLMER, B. Worthing Tannery. *J. Norfolk Industrial Archaeol. Soc.* 2 (5), 1980, 45–8.

WRENINGHAM

See no. 7953

WRETHAM

10139 MEGAW, E. *and* HENIG, M. A Roman intaglio from East Wretham Heath. *In* MARKOTIC, V., *ed*. Ancient Europe and the Mediterranean (Warminster, 1977), pp. 111–14.
See also nos. 8060, 8458.

WROXHAM

10140 SINCLAIR, M. Why did Wroxham supersede Coltishall as a regional centre? Cert. in Local Hist., Cambridge Board of Extra-Mural Studies, 1977.
10141 NORFOLK COUNTY COUNCIL. Wroxham and Hoveton local plan: draft interim guidelines. Norwich, 1988.

WYMONDHAM

10141A [DOVE, L.] Centenary of Doric Lodge no. 1193, 1867–1967. Wymondham, 1967. FPL.
On this masonic lodge see also no. 8378B.
10142 BARRINGER, J. C. Dial Farm, Wymondham. *Bull. Norfolk Research Committee* 14, 1974, 9–12.
10143 WILLIAMS N. H. The history of Wymondham Grammar School, 1559–1903. [Unpubl. typescript, 1978].
10144 WILSON, J. H. The Wymondham market cross. Wymondham, 1979. P.
10145 YAXLEY, P. G. Wymondham's old inns. Wymondham, 1982. P.
10146 WILSON, J. H., *ed*. Wymondham inventories. Norwich, 1983.

10147 WYMONDHAM AND DISTRICT CHAMBER OF TRADE AND COMMERCE. Wymondham information and trade directory. Wymondham, 1983.

10148 HAWKINS, J. The Quakers of Wymondham. Wymondham, 1984. P.

10149 MARCH, G. O. Local government in Wymondham, 1894–1974. [Unpubl.], 1984.

10150 MANNING, I. M. The CWS Brushworks, Wymondham. *J. Norfolk Industrial Archaeol. Soc.* 3, 1985, 169–73.

10151 YAXLEY, P. Memories of old Wymondham. Dereham, 1985.

10152 SOUTH NORFOLK DISTRICT COUNCIL. Wymondham local plan. Long Stratton, 1986.

See also *Consultation draft* (1985); and *Consideration...of Inspector's report [on public enquiry]* (1987).

10153 Restoration of the historical and well-known abbey church of Wymondham in Norfolk. 1905. P. RCF.

10154 BETTS, M. Jewel or ornament. The illustrated story of the historic organ in the [Wymondham] Abbey Church. [Wymondham], n.d. P. RCF.

10155 JARVIS, F. Wymondham Abbey. 1933. Enlarged eds. 1948, 1954.

10156 YAXLEY, S. Wymondham Abbey before the dissolution: the episcopal visitations of 1492–1532. Stibbard, 1986.

See also nos. 8334, 8472, 8812.

YARMOUTH, GREAT

ALMANACS AND ANNUALS

10157 The Yarmouth almanack, 1864–66. Great Yarmouth, [1863–65]. BL.

10158 The Yarmouth Mercury almanac and yearbook... for 1881. Great Yarmouth, [1880]. BL.

GUIDE-BOOKS

10159 NALL, G. Nall's [penny, threepenny, etc.] Yarmouth guide. Various eds. Gt. Yarmouth, 1866–73. BL.

10160 Yarmouth illustrated: historical and descriptive; art. commerce and trade. Brighton, 1892. UEA.

10161 Guide to the Church Congress and ecclesiatical art exhibition held in Great Yarmouth; including some notes...on Yarmouth [by K. M. Guthrie] and on Norwich [A. Jessopp]. 1907.

10162 HEDGES, A. A. C. What to see in Great Yarmouth and district. Gunton, 1978. P.

HISTORY AND ARCHAEOLOGY

GENERAL WORKS

10163 Yarmouth past and present. By one familiar with both. 2nd ed. Norwich, 1889.

10164 NATIONAL REGISTER OF ARCHIVES. Handlist of the archives of date before 1835 preserved in the Town Clerk's department. 1965.

10165 ECCLESTONE, A. W., *ed.* A Yarmouth miscellany. Gt. Yarmouth, 1974.

10166 LEWIS, C. Great Yarmouth: history, herrings and holidays. Cromer, 1980. P.

10167 ECCLESTONE, A. W. Yarmouth haven. Gorleston, 1981.

ARCHAEOLOGY

10168 ROGERSON, A. Excavations on Fuller's Hill, Great Yarmouth. *E.A.A.R.* 2, 1976, 131–246.

10169 MCEWEN, A. Priory Plain, Great Yarmouth [excavation report]. *Yarmouth Archaeol.* 1 (4), 1982, [unpaginated].

MEDIEVAL PERIOD

10170 SAUL, A. R. Great Yarmouth in the 14th century: a study of trade, politics and society. D.Phil. thesis, Oxford Univ., 1975.

10171 RUTLEDGE, E. *and* RUTLEDGE, P. King's Lynn and Great Yarmouth: 2 thirteenth century surveys. *N.A.* 37, 1978, 92–114.
Yarmouth survey (1286), pp. 110–12.

10172 SAUL, A. Great Yarmouth and the Hundred Years War in the 14th century. *Bull. Inst. Hist. Research* 52, 1979, 105–15.

10173 SAUL, A. English towns in the late middle ages: the case of Great Yarmouth. *J. Medieval Hist.* 8, 1982, 75–88.

10174 RUTLEDGE, P. Two Little Yarmouth deeds. *Yarmouth Archaeol.* 2 (i), 1984, 17–19.

10175 SAUL, A. Local politics and the Good Parliament. *In* POLLARD, A. J., *ed.* Property and politics: essays in later medieval history (Gloucester, 1984), pp. 156–71.
Disputes between Yarmouth and Lowestoft in Parliament of 1376.

10176 RUTLEDGE, P. The earliest Yarmouth bailiffs. *N.A.* 40, 1988, 181–5.
See also no. 10220.

TUDOR AND STUART PERIODS

10177 FULLER, N. The argument of Master Nicholas Fuller in the case of Thomas Lad and Richard Maunsell... 1607. BL.
Lad was a Yarmouth merchant accused of taking part in a conventicle.

10178 ROBERTS. J. Great Yarmouths exercise. In a very compleat and martiall manner performed by their artillery men... [in] May last. 1638. BL.

10179 DAVIES, R. Journal of the Very Rev. Rowland Davies, Dean of Ross, from March 8 1688/89 to Sept. 29 1690. Ed. R. Caulfield. *Camden Soc.* 1st ser. 68, 1857.
Davies held lectureship at Yarmouth from July 1689 to Feb. 1690, while a refugee from Ireland.

10180 RUTLEDGE, P. Calendar of Great Yarmouth enrolled apprenticeship indentures, 1563–1665. *Norfolk Geneal.* 11, 1979.

10181 RUTLEDGE, P. The goods of William Smyth. *Yarmouth Archaeol.* 2 (2), 1985, 51–5.
Probate inventory of Yarmouth town clerk, 1580.

10182 GRUENFELDER, J. K. Jeffrey Neve, Charles I, and Great Yarmouth. *N.A.* 40, 1988, 155–63.

See also nos. 8087, 10216–17.

18TH–20TH CENTURIES

10183 An answer to the reply of the Revd. G. Hallatt to the Socialists' address. By a Yarmouth socialist. Yarmouth, 1839. P. BL.

10184 HALLATT, G. A refutation of the... charges... published in the Socialists' Newspaper... in reference to Mr. Brindley's late visit to Yarmouth. Yarmouth, 1840. P. BL.

10185 ECCLESTONE, A. W. Great Yarmouth, 1886–1936. Gorleston, 1977.

10186 RYE, G. *and* TOOKE, C. Great Yarmouth: the fortifications [1750–1914]. *Yarmouth Archaeol.* 2, 1984/87, 9–12, 26–32, 89–98, 133–45.

10187 TEMPLE, C. Clifford Temple remembers Great Yarmouth and Gorleston. Lowestoft, 1984.

See also nos. 8810, 10219.

MUNICIPAL GOVERNMENT

THE CORPORATION

10188 GREAT YARMOUTH LABOUR PARTY. Great Yarmouth and Gorleston Municipal Elector. Nov. 1936; Nov. 1937. BL.
Municipal elections newspaper.

10189 Great Yarmouth Borough Council Act, 1981. (L. and P. Acts, xxx).

PLANNING

10190 GREAT YARMOUTH BOROUGH COUNCIL. A report on the planning and reconstruction... Yarmouth, 1943.

10191 GREAT YARMOUTH BOROUGH COUNCIL. Town and Country Planning Act, 1947. Development plan, 1952–72. Written analysis of the survey. 2 pts. [Gt. Yarmouth, 1952/54.] BL.

10192 GREAT YARMOUTH BOROUGH COUNCIL. Great Yarmouth seafront district plan. Yarmouth, 1980.
Preceded by *Great Yarmouth seafront: report of survey* (1978).

10193 GREAT YARMOUTH BOROUGH COUNCIL. Great Yarmouth town centre district plan: report of survey and policy document. 2 parts. Yarmouth, 1980.
See also *Policies for advertisement control: town centre conservation areas.* (1981).

10194 GREAT YARMOUTH BOROUGH COUNCIL. Market Gates general improvement area. Yarmouth, 1981.

10195 GREAT YARMOUTH BOROUGH COUNCIL. The port and South Denes district plan: issues and possibilities. Yarmouth, 1981.
See also *Statement of proposals* (n.d.)

10196 GREAT YARMOUTH BOROUGH COUNCIL. Innovations in leisure: a sea-front redevelopment [the Marina]. Yarmouth, [1982].

10197 ASHWORTH, G. J. *and others.* The structure of tourist supply in a seaside resort: the example of Great Yarmouth. Groningen (Netherlands), 1984.
See also Ashworth and T. Z. De Haan, *Modelling the seaside resort: Great Yarmouth* (Groningen, 1985); and their *Residents' reactions to tourism in Norwich and Great Yarmouth* (Groningen, 1985. P.)
   See also nos. 7516, 7552.

ELECTIONS

10198 Yarmouth election petition, 1906: J. Martin White, petitioner, v. Arthur Fell, respondent. 1906.

SOCIAL WELFARE

10199 Peggotty's annual: official magazine of the Great Yarmouth and Gorleston hospitals. No.1. Yarmouth, 1939.

10200 STAFFORD, E. For those in peril. Ed. A. A. C. Hedges. Great Yarmouth, n.d. P.
History of Sailors' Home, now Maritime Museum.

10201 NORFOLK AREA HEALTH AUTHORITY. Consultative document on the rationalisation of health services in Great Yarmouth and Waveney as a result of the...new district hospital...at Gorleston. Norwich, 1980. P.

10202 DAVIES, M. Unemployment in Great Yarmouth: an interim research report (UEA School of Economic and Social Studies). Norwich, 1986.

PUBLIC WORKS AND UTILITIES

HARBOUR
10203 NICKALLS, J. A report to the Commissioners for repairing, improving, and maintaining the harbour of Great Yarmouth. 1784. P.

10204 RENNIE, J. Report to the Commissioners...on the state of the bar and haven, and the measures advisable...for improving the same. Yarmouth, 1819. P.

10205 GREAT YARMOUTH PORT AND HAVEN COMMISSIONERS. Great Yarmouth port and industry handbook. [Annual]. Yarmouth, 1980–.

10206 Great Yarmouth Outer Harbour Act, 1986. (L. and P. Acts, xxii).
   See also nos. 8093, 8178.

TRANSPORT
10207 BARKER, T. Transport in Great Yarmouth. 3 vols. Chipping Sodbury, 1980/83.
Vol.1 covers trams, 1902–18; Vol.2 trams and buses, 1919–33.

10208 FISHER, C. The quayside tramways of Great Yarmouth. *J. Norfolk Industrial Archaeol. Soc.* 3, 1985, 153–63.

DRAINAGE
10209 GREAT YARMOUTH CORPORATION. Proceeding respecting drainage of the Denes. Yarmouth, 1849. P.

EDUCATION

10210 BLUE-COAT CHARITY SCHOOL. Rules, 1845. Annual reports, 1844, 1849–58, 1868, 1871–89. Great Yarmouth, [1845–90]. UEA.

10211 BLUE-COAT CHARITY SCHOOL. Copy orders of Charity Commissioners, 1896 and 1899. Great Yarmouth, 1902. P. UEA.

TRADE AND INDUSTRY

10212 READER, W. J. Birds Eye, the early years. 1963.

10213 McEWEN, A. The salt industry at Cobholm, Great Yarmouth. *J. Norfolk Industr. Archaeol. Soc.* 1 (5), 1973, 3–4.

10214 LEWIS, C. The Maritime Museum for East Anglia [Great Yarmouth]. *Ibid.* 1 (6), 1974, 21–3.

10215 TOOKE, C. S. Glass stopper blowing at Gt. Yarmouth. *Ibid.* 2 (1), 1976 [no pagination].

10216 TITTLER, R. The English fishing industry in the 16th century: the case of Great Yarmouth. *Albion* 9, 1977, 40–60.

10217 MICHELL, A. R. The port and town of Great Yarmouth and its economic and social relationships with its neighbours on both side of the seas, 1550–1714: an essay in the history of the North Sea's economy. Ph.D. thesis, Cambridge Univ., 1978.

10218 ECCLESTONE, A. W. The Victoria Building Company. *Yarmouth Archaeol.* 1 (i), 1979, 17–22.

10219 MURPHY. J. D. The town and trade of Great Yarmouth, 1740–1850. Ph.D. thesis, Univ. of E. Anglia, 1979.

10220 SAUL, A. The herring industry at Great Yarmouth, c. 1280 – c. 1400. *N.A.* 38, 1981, 33–43.

10221 HAWKINS, L. W. The Ocean fleet of Yarmouth. Sprowston, 1983.

10222 TOOKE, C. S. The ballast trade in the port of Great Yarmouth. *Yarmouth Archaeol.* 2 (1), 1984, 13–16.

10223 FEWSTER, M. I. The Yarmouth herring industry, 1880–1960. M.Phil. thesis, Univ. of E. Anglia, 1985.
See also her articles, 'Traditional herring curing in Great Yarmouth', *J. Norfolk Industrial Archaeol. Soc.* 4 (1), 1986, 7–17; and 'Bloomfield's Ocean House, Great Yarmouth', *ibid.* (2), 1987, 53–8.

10224 BERRY, R. G. 'Bauleah', an East Anglian-Indian enterprise. *Yarmouth Archaeol.* 2 (3), 1986, 67–73.
Concerns silk manufacture of Grout and Co., and its Yarmouth manager John Brown.

10225 MCEWEN, A. Yarmouth iron foundries. *Ibid.* 2 (4), 1987, 111–15.
On fishing industry see also nos. 8083, 8087.

RELIGION

10226 Spiritual wants in the parish of Great Yarmouth. [Gt. Yarmouth], 1849. P. RCF.

10227 [VINCENT, S.] The vicar [Rev. G. Venables] and Mr. Vincent on the tendency of the principles of dissent: an attack and a defence...for the perusal of fair-minded men in Great Yarmouth. Yarmouth, [1878]. P.

CULTURE AND RECREATION

10227A A short history of Friendship Lodge no. 100 [Freemasons]. Yarmouth, 1909. P. FPL.

10228 GALLOWAY, D. The 'Game Place' and 'House' at Great Yarmouth, 1493–1595. *Theatre Notebook* 31, no.2, 1976, 6–9.

10229 YOUNG, R. Treasures of the Yarmouth museums. Norwich, 1976. P.

10230 GOATE, E. W. Great Yarmouth and the cinematograph, 1897–1915. *Yarmouth Archaeol.* 1 (2), 1980, 1–10.

10231 GREAT YARMOUTH REFERENCE LIBRARY. Great Yarmouth associations, societies, organisations, 1979–80. Yarmouth, 1979.

See also no. 8375.

TOPOGRAPHY

GENERAL TOPOGRAPHICAL AND ARCHITECTURAL FEATURES

10232 YALLOP, A. W. In and about ancient Yarmouth. A portfolio of reproductions of old and unique pictures of byegone Yarmouth. Great Yarmouth, 1905.

10233 GREAT YARMOUTH AND DISTRICT ARCHAEOLOGICAL SOCIETY. Historic Yarmouth. Yarmouth, 1980. P.

10234 TOOKE, C. S. The rows of Great Yarmouth. North Walsham, 1987.

INDIVIDUAL DISTRICTS, BUILDINGS, ETC.

10235 RYE, C. G. Great Yarmouth: Blackfriars Church [excavations]. *N.A.* 35, 1973, 498–502; 37, 1979, 208.

10236 FARMER, R. L. The Nelson Monument. *E.A.M.* July 1977, 376–7.

10237 DUNMORE, S. 221–222 Northgate Street, Great Yarmouth. *E.A.A.R.* 8, 1978, 73–86.

10238 GOSLING, G. St. George's, Great Yarmouth: a short history. Yarmouth, [1980]. P.

10239 WILLINK, J. W. St. Nicholas' Church: its chequered and fascinating history. Yarmouth, 1906.

10240 HAWKINS, F. Parish church of St. Nicholas, Great Yarmouth. A brief history and photographic record. N.p., [c. 1943]. P.

10241 HEDGES, A. A. C. Great Yarmouth priory and parish church. Yarmouth, [1979]. P.

10242 Pier and Harbour (Great Yarmouth Wellington Pier) Confirmation Act, 1980. (L. and P. Acts, xxxiii).

INDEX OF AUTHORS, INSTITUTIONS, ETC.

Abigail, R., 9179
Acle Society, 8939
Acomb, H. W., 9134
Adams, M. G., 9666
Adams, N., 8984, 9221
Adderson, R. S., 8391
Addington, S., 7509, 10001, 10017–18, 10069
Adkin, L., 7993
Agnew and Sons Ltd., 9254
Agricultural Development and Advisory Service, 7680, 8064
Aickman, D. J., 9342
Airs, M., 8414
Albright, M., 7473
Alcock, L., 9037
Alderton, D. L., 8099
Alexander, J., 7997
Alexander, M., 8689
Alexander, W., 7941
All Hallows, Community of, 9128–9
Allchin, A. M., 8781
Allen, D. G., 9241
Allen, G. F., 8201
Allen, H. C., 9241
Allen, I. C., 8203
Allerston, P. A., 7570
Allerton, E. C., 9049
Alley, R., 8635
Allmand, C. T., 8697
Allthorpe-Guyton, M., 8656, 8905, 9629
Alnand, S., 8689
Alsford, S., 7901
Alsop, J. D., 7917
Alvis, E. J., 10126
Amery, C., 9999
Ames, C. L., 8715
Amis, A., 10065
Amison, P., 8008
Amos, G. A., 10083
Amussen, S. D., 7775, 9067
Anckorn, G., 7628
Anderson, A. C., 9033
Anderson, M., 8631A
Anderson, O. S., 7483
Anderson, V., 8727, 9875
Andrew, L., 9687
Andrews, W., 8287
Anglia Television, 7658, 8145
Anglian Water Authority, 7568, 7572, 8357
Annan, R., 7423
Annan, T., 7423
Apfel, W. H., 7825
Apling, H., 8440

Archer, B. H., 8152
Archer, J. E., 7822
Archer, R. E., 8827
Archibald, M. M., 9211, 9213
Armes, W., 9311A
Armstrong, C. A. J., 8697
Armstrong, P., 7354
Arnell, B., 9236
Arnell, L., 9236
Arngart, O., 7485, 10117
Arthur, P., 9038
Ashbee, P., 7703
Ashby, R., 8281
Ashcroft, M. Y., 8657
Ashley, S. J., 8972, 9389
Ashton, P. T., 9921
Ashton, R., 9333
Ashworth, G. J., 8156, 9558, 10197
Aslet, C., 9941
Atherton, H. M., 8908
Atkin, M., 7745, 9438, 9446–9, 9645, 9869
Atkin, S., 9672
Atkin, S. J., 8591
Atkinson, C. W., 8791
Attleborough Chamber of Trade, 8953
Auker, R. H., 9348
Austin, *Mrs.* S., 8728
Automobile Association, 7633
Ayers, B., 9443–5, 9451–4, 9460A, 9792, 9796, 9834
Aylsham Local History Society, 8966
Ayton, J., 7518

B., J., 8989
B., T. A., 10085
Back, D. H. L., 9162
Backhouse, J., 8888
Badham, S., 8614
Bagot, L., 9602
Bagshaw, R., 8580
Bagshawe, R., 7728
Bailey, M., 8044
Baker, B. G., 7600
Baker, D., 8789
Baker, G. M., 8578
Baldwin, J., 9157, 9937
Baldwin, L. M., 10135
Ball, F. P., 9700
Bamford, H. M., 7702
Banger, J. R., 9503
Banks, S., 7824A, 7910
Barber, J., 8644
Barber, M., 7906
Barber, R., 8859

Bardswell, F. A., 8529
Barker, R., 8690
Barker, R. J. B., 9620
Barker, T., 10207
Barlow, J., 8523
Barnard, G. V., 8501
Barnes, J., 10097
Barnes, J. S., 9063
Barnes, P., 8378
Barnes, P. B., 8072A
Barnett, P. W., 8418
Barr, D., 8583
Barran, F., 7635
Barrett, C. R. B., 7584
Barrett, G. N., 9743
Barrett, J., 7699
Barrett, K. D. L., 9095
Barrett, W. H., 8296, 8299
Barrett-Lennard, T., 9267
Barringer, J. C., 7355, 7703, 7898, 8427, 8949, 9384, 9490, 9895, 10068, 10081, 10142
Barritt, R. A., 8584
Barry, T. H., 7606
Barthorp. M., 7927
Bartlett, K., 8305
Barton, C., 9353
Barwood, N. E., 9025
Bassett, P., 8390
Bastin, J., 7928
Batcock, N., 8476
Bately, J., 9369
Bates, F., 8585
Bates, M., 7665
Battley, S. L. M., 7779. 9317
Batty Shaw, A., 7969, 7974, 8619, 8848
Baty, E., 8473
Bax, A., 7625
Baxter, A., 9527
Baxter, J. C., 7810
Bayne, A. D., 7661
Beadle, H. R. L., 8330–1
Beagrie, N., 7693
Bearman, P. S., 7774
Beaumont, C., 8940
Beauroy, J., 9306
Beazley, O., 9864
Beckett, C., 8191
Beckett, G., 7510, 9986
Beckett, J., 9705
Beckett, M. D., 8202
Beckham, E., 8279
Beckley, R., 7683
Bedell, A. J., 7751
Beech, G., 9225
Beer, B. L., 7784, 7788
Bell, S., 8551

Bell, T., 8361–2
Bellamy, E. J., 9706
Bellinger, R., 8547
Beloe, E. M., 7595, 7648, 8489, 9876
Beloff, M., 9635
Benham, H., 7863, 7883
Bennett, F. J., 7376
Bennett, H. S., 7757
Bennett, J., 8316–17
Benskin, M., 10116
Bensly, W. T., 9420
Bentham, C. G., 7966, 7971
Bentley, R., 9608
Benton, E. O., 8589
Bergsma, J. R., 8156
Berkers, M., 9558
Bernstein, G. L., 9532
Berry, G., 8882
Berry, G. A., 9833
Berry, R. G., 10224
Berry, V., 8880
Betts, M., 10154
Bevis, T. A., 7464, 8497
Billett, M., 8421
Bilyard, J., 9217
Bingham, J., 9973, 9975
Binney, M., 9198–9
Binski, P., 9149
Bird, M. C. H., 8055
Birks, H. G. B., 7353
Bishop, B., 8592
Bishop, J. S., 8148
Bishop, S. M., 8804
Blackburn, S., 8593
Blackman, D. J., 9332
Blair, J., 8476
Blake, J. H., 7379–80
Blakeney Preservation Society, 8993
Blatchly. J. M., 8494, 8968, 9944
Bloemendal, F. A. H., 7635
Blofeld, G., 8594
Blomefield, M., 8598
Bloom, A., 7463, 8599
Bloom, U., 8600–1
Blue Coat Charity School (Yarmouth), 10210–11
Blyth, M. M., 8602
Boening, J., 8904
Bolingbroke, L. G., 7595
Bond, H. A., 10089
Bond, R., 9074
Bonfield, L., 9306
Booker, J., 8099
Booth. S., 8834
Bootman, R., 8335
Booty, H., 8604
Borsa, J., 8505

Bosanquet, N., 7975
Bourne, U., 8443
Bouwens, D., 8432
Bowden-Smith, R., 9272
Bowditch, P., 9967
Bowen, H. C., 8032
Bowman, M. W., 7844
Bowyer, B., 8702
Bowyer, M. J. F., 7837, 7841
Boyd-Bayley, E., 8896
Boyes, J., 8180
Boys' Brigade, 9744
Bradfer-Lawrence, H. L., 9060, 9312
Bradford, E., 8841
Bradley, E., 8225
Bradley, Richard, 7699
Bradley, Ritamary, 8782
Bradshaw, R. H. W., 7366
Braithwaite, D., 9337
Bramah, J., 9611
Bramerton Group Council, 9005
Brandon, J. A., 8445
Brandon, R., 8445
Branford, C. W., 8174
Brathwaite, C. A., 7477
Bray, D., 7875
Breckland District Council, 7554A–7, 8101,
    8956, 8977, 9110, 9113, 9397, 10009,
    10036, 10104
Brereton, C. D., 7934
Bressingham Parish Council, 9012
Brett, J. T., 9745B
Brett, P. T., 9484
Brewster, D. E., 8219
Brewster, K. A., 8450
Bridges, A., 9380
Brigden, R., 8134
Briggs, E. R., 9475
Brigham, R., 8374
Brindley, H. H., 8482
Brisley and Elmham Rural Deanery, 8451
Bristow, C., 10056
British Association, 7595
British Association of Social Workers, 7978
British Gas Light Co., 9610
British Road Federation, 8169
Britnell, R. H., 8862
Brittain, H., 7418, 7424
Broadland District Council, 7457, 8101,
    9018, 9896–7, 10049
Broads Authority, 7448, 9887, 9892
Brooks, P., 8994, 9070, 9264, 9917, 9951,
    9954, 10118
Broom, A. S., 8616
Brown, A., 9893
Brown, A. S., 8381
Brown, P., 7749

Brown, R., 7622
Brown, R. A., 8241, 9061, 9909–10, 9912,
    10102
Brown, R. D., 7839
Brown, R. J., 8435
Browne, W. J. U., 9525
Bruce, R., 8054
Brumwell, P. M., 7925
Buckingham, E., 9799
Buckton, B. F., 10002
Bujak, P. E., 8957–8
Bulkeley, L., 8897
Bull, J., 8007
Bullock, D. A., 9188
Bunting, G., 8889
Burgess, B., 8071
Burgess, C., 7718, 9039
Burgess, M. W., 7696
Burki, D., 9950
Burleigh, R., 7719
Burn, M. P., 8626
Burney, C., 8627
Burnham, B., 8229
Burt, R. M., 9136, 9378
Burton, J., 7721
Burton, J. R., 8629, 9268, 9764
Burton, W. P., 9048
Bush, A., 9406
Bush, M., 9572
Bussey, A., 7961
Buston, W., 9844
Butcher, D. R., 7617, 9078
Butlin, R. A., 7772
Butterfield, R. I., 7801
Buxton, Anthony, 8630
Buxton, Aubrey, 9920
Buxton, E. E., 8631
Buxton, Sir T. F., 8632

Caley, W. B. R., 10100
Calthrop, M. M. C., 8270
Calvert, D. K., 9043
Cambridge University Library, 8799
Cameron, H. K., 9359
Cameron, J., 9486
Camina, M. M., 9789
Camm, B., 8483
Campaign Against Norwich Airport Expan-
    sion, 7886
Campaign For Real Ale, 8382
Campbell, B. M. S., 7497, 8029, 8034–5,
    8037–8, 8045, 9073, 9232, 9381
Campbell, C., 8634
Campbell, J., 9421
Campbell, L., 9991
Campbell, M. B., 9633
Capes, J. M., 9883

Carlile, R., 9695
Carnell, P., 7747
Carnie, T. W., 7590
Caro, A. J., 7965
Carr, R., 10030
Carrington, A. C., 9192
Carson, T. E., 8230, 8242
Carter, Alan, 8424, 8429, 9299, 9435, 9437, 9440, 9458, 9772
Carter, Anne, 7790. 9886
Carter, J., 8717
Carter. M. J., 7821
Cartwright, A. R., 7352
Castell, D., 9601
Castle Museum, Norwich. *See* Norwich Castle Museum
Cathcart. M. F., 9459
Catling, M., 8995
Cattermole, P., 8467, 9689
Cattermole, R. H., 8910A
Caulfield, R., 10179
Cecil, M., 9957
Central Office of Information, 7619, 8092
Centre of East Anglian Studies, 7643, 7645, 7652, 7657, 8160
Chalcraft, C. W. T., 9898
Champness, M. V. D., 8162
Chaney, G., 9491
Chapman, C. F., 9084, 10105
Chapman, H. W., 8759
Chapman, K. R., 8138
Charlesworth, A., 7822. 7826
Cherry, B., 8457
Cherry, J., 9908
Cherry, J. F., 9437
Cherry, S., 9534
Cheshire, J. G., 10062
Chesney, R. W. L., 8638
Cheyne, N., 9127
Child Poverty Action Group, 9570
Christie, P., 9226
Church, R., 7940
Civil Aviation Authority, 7888
Clabburn, P., 7814, 9676, 9683
Clark, A. M., 8933
Clark, C. L., 8673
Clark, E. G., 7759
Clark, P., 7493–4
Clark, P.[F.], 8218
Clark, R., 8084
Clark, R. H., 8196, 9335
Clark, W. B., 9375
Clarke, H., 7675, 9299, 9301, 9303–4, 9332
Clarke, R. R., 9037
Clarke, S. K., 9093
Clarke, W. G., 7345, 10025
Clarkson, A. T., 8376

Clayton, E. G., 9673, 9675
Clayton, K. M., 7389
Claxton, W. H., 9424
Cleaver, J., 7851
Clements, B., 9854
Cleveland, D., 7413, 7659
Clewes, D., 8309
Clifton, P., 9237
Clough, T. H. M., 8108, 9107, 9183
Clout, H. D., 8158
Clover, R. D., 9105
Clutton-Brock, J., 7723
Coad, J. G., 9058–9
Coates, D. E., 9004, 9993
Coe, A. E., 7398
Coiley, D. E. M., 9857
Coke, H. J., 8642
Coldham, P. W., 8544
Coleby, C. C., 9813
Coleman, J., 9287
Coleman, S. J., 8295
Coleman, W. L. B., 9591
Coles, J. M., 7468, 7471
Colledge, E., 8779
Collie, M., 8610
Collings, J., 7798
Collins, P., 8354
Collins, R. N., 8216
Collins, R. P., 8639
Collins, S., 10072
Collis, L., 8788
Colman, (J. and J.) Ltd., 9657
Colman, H. C., 9685
Colman, J. J., 7913, 8345
Colman Foods, 8526
Condon, E., 9846
Conservative Party, 7513
Cook, B., 9163
Cook, M., 9114
Cook, O., 7415
Cooke, R., 10042
Cooke, Rod, 9998
Cooke, S., 10042
Coombs, D., 9039
Cooper, A. H., 8520
Cooper, A. P., 7608
Cooper, B., 8353
Cooper, C. G., 7609
Cooper, R. R., 8065
Cooper, S. M., 9311
Cooper, W., 9589
Copeman, A. C., 9603
Coppock, C., 9470
Corfield, P. J., 9430, 9467, 9482
Cornford, B., 7412, 7450, 7764A, 7765, 8184, 8254, 8427, 8641, 9226A, 10069
Cornforth, J., 8411, 9002, 9233, 9256, 9259,

9273
Cornwall, J., 7785, 7787
Cory, R. H., 7466
Cotton, B. D., 8430
Cotton, S., 8234, 8243, 8246, 8458–9, 8463, 8465, 8467–8, 8470–1, 8474, 8486, 9901
Council for Small Industries, 8131
Country Life (publ.), 7612, 8411
Countryside Commission, 7441, 7454, 7571
Cowley, I., 8212
Cowley, J. K., 7607
Cowlin, D., 8718
Cowper, W., 8662
Cox, B. H., 7484
Coxford, B., 9885
Cozens-Hardy, H. T., 8664
Craig-Smith, S. J., 7409
Craske, R., 9955
Craske, S., 9955
Crawford, H., 7720
Creasey, J., 9754
Creasy, J., 9903
Creighton, E. R. C., 8631
Crescent History Group, 9830
Cresswell, I., 8384
Cressy, D. A., 7771, 8002
Cringleford Historical Society, 9086
Crisp, F. A., 8564
Crombac, G., 8637
Cromer and North Norfolk Festival, 9092
Cromer Protection Commissioners, 9088
Crook, C. E., 7448
Crosby, A., 10028
Crotch, W. W., 7992
Crowe, G., 8305
Crowley, J., 7948
Crown, J. I., 8802, 8986, 10133
Crowther, C., 7926
Cubitt, M., 9220
Cudworth, C. L., 8397
Cullum, F., 8675
Cuming, H. S., 7736
Cunliffe, R., 9343
Cushing, G., 10053
Cushion, B., 7508
Custance, T., 8676

Dain, J. H., 9750
Daley, P. V., 7433
Dalton, W. H., 7378
Darby, H. C., 7469, 7748
Darby, J., 8015
Darby, J. (fl. 1875), 8052
Darley, G., 8246
Darling, M. J., 9035
Darsley, R., 8209
Darwin, B., 8365–6

Dashwood, G. H., 9995
Daubeney, A. R. V., 9166, 9168
Davage, M., 8364
Davey, P., 9671–2
Davies, C., 7872
Davies, G. C., 7417
Davies, M., 9588, 10202
Davies, R., 10179
Davis, K. A., 9540
Davis, M. D., 9455
Davis, N., 8319, 8856, 8864–5
Davison, A. J., 7416, 7510–11, 9210, 9212, 9981, 10050
Davy, T., 8525, 9114–15
Dawes, C., 9260
Dawkins, *Sir* W. B., 9432
Day, J. W., 7435–6, 8060, 8917–18, 9296, 9429
Day, M., 9654, 9661, 9663, 9770
Day, P., 9020
Daynes, G. W., 8379
Deacon, R., 8311
Dean, M. A., 8460
Dearden, S., 8605
Debenham, F., 7348
De Brisay, K. W., 8135
De Chair, S., 8682
De Haan, T. Z., 9558, 10197
Dejohn, V. A., 7794
De La Mare, A. C., 9258
Dence, C. S., 9062
Denis, P., 9473
Dent, D. L., 7448, 7573
Department of Education and Science, 8010
Department of Employment, 9338
Department of the Environment, 7519, 7569
Department of Trade, 7887, 7889–90
Department of Transport, 7894
Dickinson, J. C., 10088
Dickinson, R. E., 8091
Dickman, S., 8240, 8781
Digby, A., 7945, 7947
Dimmick, R., 8005
Disney, H. B., 8177
Dittbrenner, C. H., 7943
Dix, G., 9765
Dixon, E. S., 8774
Dixon, G. M., 7832, 8300, 8310
Dixon, R., 8517
Dixon-Scott, J., 7603
Doarks, C., 7448
Dodd, A. B., 7427
Dodd, J. P., 8067
Dodds, M., 9141
Dodwell, B., 9805–7
Dodwell, R., 7588
Doggett, M., 8220

Dollin B. W., 7692, 9288
Dorman, B. E., 7616
Doucet, V., 9686
Douet, A., 8075
Doughty, G. B., 9409
Doughty, H. M., 7421
Dove, L., 10141A
Drackett, P., 7627
Drake, M., 8479
Draper, W. H., 8322
Drayton Association, 9133
Driscoll, R. J., 7455
Drudy, P. J., 7495, 7514, 7518, 8065A
Drudy, S. M., 7495
Drury, P., 9796
Duff, D., 8667. 8849
Duleep Singh, *Prince* F. V., 8555
Dunbabin, J. P. D., 7817
Dunmore, S., 10030, 10237
Dunn, I., 9836
Dunn, R. M., 7291
Durbin, G., 9727
Durst, D. W., 8999, 9408, 9966
Dutka, J., 9734
Dutt, W. A., 7694, 8321
Dyke, G. W., 9308
Dymond, D., 7371

Eade, *Sir* P., 7955, 9859
Earle, A., 9024
East Anglia Consultative Committee, 7532–5
East Anglia Economic Planning Council, 7499, 7874, 8013–14
East Anglia Regional Strategy Team, 7517
East Anglia Tourist Board, 8153
East Anglian Regional Health Authority, 7964, 7968, 7975, 7980
East Anglian Regional Studies Group, 7512
East of England Art Union, 8498
East Suffolk and Norfolk River Authority, 7567
Eastern Council for Sport, 8342
Eastern Counties Railway Co., 8186–7
Eastern Gas, 9153
Eastwood, J., 8364
Eaton, F. R., 8380, 9831, 10072A
Eaton, R., 9102
Eaton Golf Club, 9745
Ebbage, S., 8026
Eccles, M., 8315
Ecclestone, A. W., 9186, 10165, 10167, 10185, 10218
Eden, P., 8047
Edgar, S. H., 9662
Edrich, R. G., 7498
Edwards, D. A., 7374, 7679, 8032, 9009
Edwards, E. H., 8911

Edwards, J. K., 9529
Edwards, W. C., 8567
Edwards, W. F., 9265, 9372
Elgood, D., 9741
Elliott, C. R., 7840, 9377
Ellis, P. B., 8733
Ellis, R., 8404
Elton, D. H., 9137
Elwes, H., 8291
Elwin, W., 8692
Elworthy, A., 8787
Elworthy, G., 8787
Emerson, P. H., 7419, 7422, 7426, 7815–16
Emerson, S., 10075
Emmerson, R., 9512
Emmison, F. G., 9253
English Heritage, 8531
Enraght, H. J., 9890
Erroll, A. C., 9949
Estates and General Investments Plc, 9555
Evans, D. H., 9449
Evans, G. E., 7830
Evans, J. G., 7364
Evans, J. T., 9462, 9465
Evans, K. A., 8135
Evans, M. C., 8767
Evans, N., 7655, 8149
Everett, C. G. G., 8217
Everitt, A. T., 7646
Everitt, G., 9028
Everitt, N., 8369
Everitt, W. S., 8022
Evison, V. I., 7741

Faden, W., 7355
Fairbairns, W. H., 9800
Fairfax-Blakeborough, J. F., 8375
Fairfield, S., 7625
Fairhead, A. E., 9126
Fairweather, F. H., 8446
Fakenham Association Against Horse Stealers, 9151
Fakenham Festival, 9154
Fakenham Local History Society, 9156
Farley, V., 9057
Farman, D., 9984–5
Farmer, D. H., 8239
Farmer, R. L., 10236
Farnell, W. K., 7994
Farrar, J. M., 9175
Farrer, E., 8568
Farrow, C. W., 8714, 8974, 9124, 9880, 9913
Farson, D., 8926
Fassnidge, C. W., 10124
Fawcett, R., 8452–3, 8462, 8465, 10132
Fawcett, T. C., 8337, 8508, 8671, 9485, 9489, 9681, 9738

Fearn, R. M. G., 7972
Feeney, B. J., 7758, 7906
Felce, E., 7606, 8116
Fell, G., 9474
Fenn, I., 8700
Fennell, G., 7984
Fenner, A., 9085, 9670, 9684
Fenner, G., 9085, 9841
Fenwick, G., 8611
Ferguson, J. P., 8640
Fernie, E. C., 9814–18
Festing, S., 8085, 8665
Fewster, M. I., 8141, 10223
Feyerharm, W. R., 8001
Field, J., 8280
Finch, J. S., 8623
Finch, R., 7883
Fines, J. D., 8227
Firth, C. B., 8224
Fisher, B., 9394
Fisher, Christopher, 8197, 9379, 9848, 10208
Fisher, Claude, 10091, 10094
Fisher, E. C., 8351
Fisher, F. D., 8703
Fisher, J. R., 8873A
Fisher, *Lady* R., 8704
Fiske, R. C., 8559, 8721, 8843, 9795. 10061
Fitzgerald, B. S. V., 8606
Flack, S., 9011
Fleming, M., 9135
Flenley, R., 9307
Fletcher, A., 7775
Fletcher, A. J., 7764
Fletcher, R., 7668
Flint, B., 8433
Flower, C. T., 7899
Foley, T., 8836
Fone, J. F., 8170, 8543, 8719
Ford, Boris, 9881
Ford, Brinsley, 8706, 9161
Ford, L. R., 9541
Forder, C., 10078
Forman, J., 8298
Forestry Commission, 7346, 7369
Forrest, A. J., 7613
Forrest, R., 9583
Forster, L., 9471
Foster, I. L., 9037
Fountaine, M., 8707
Fowler, E., 7823, 8648
Fowler, P. J., 7506, 8032
Fox, *Sir* C., 7708
Fox, H. S. A., 7772
Frankel, M. S., 7908
Franklin, F. S., 10021
Franklin, J, A., 9824
Fraser, A., 8610

Freeman, E. A., 8444
Freeman, R. A., 7842
French, C., 7459
Frere, S. S., 9404
Friends of Brinton, 9013
Friends of the Earth, 9652
Friends of the Round Tower Churches Society, 10135
Fritz, P. S., 7809
Frostick, C., 8562
Frostick, R., 7375
Fry, K., 8711
Fryer, F. A., 8582, 8846
Fuller, N., 10177
Fuller, T., 8532
Funnell, B., 10119
Fussell, G. E., 8059, 9383
Fysh, A. V. G. A., 8712, 9979
Fysh, J. P. G., 8712, 9979

Gaddis, E. R., 8931
Gale, C. H., 8981, 9932
Galloway, D., 8332, 9735, 10228
Gardiner, T., 8312
Garrod, R. P., 8299
Garrod, R. R., 9082
Gedge, D., 8625
Geological Survey, 7376–82, 7387
George, M., 7439
Gibbins, R. W., 7991
Gibbs, A. W., 7885, 8373
Gibbs, E. H., 8644
Gidney, L., 10131
Gifford, A., 8306, 8913
Gilbert, H., 9165
Gilchrist, O., 8649
Giles, M., 7373
Gillespie, I., 8355
Gillett, H. E. H., 8288–9
Girouard, M., 9942, 9971
Glasscoe, M., 8240, 8781
Glenn, A., 7396
Glendenning, S. E., 9003
Gliddon, G., 7835
Glover, J., 8717
Goate, E. W., 9187, 10230
Godfrey, H., 9659, 9723
Godwin, H., 7347, 7467
Goffin, M., 8854
Goldberg, N. L., 8668, 8670
Gooch, B., 7917
Gooch, R., 8720
Good Practices in Mental Health Project, 9573
Goodall, J. A., 9176
Goode, W. J., 8466
Goodey, C., 7443

Goodman, A. E., 8789
Goodman, J., 8835, 8893
Goodrich, P., 10063
Goodwin, A., 9483
Goodwin, C., 10041
Goodwins, B. M., 8722
Goodwyn, E. A., 7810, 8325, 8817, 9097, 9395
Gore. L. L., 9278
Goreham, G., 9190, 9623, 9760, 9767
Gosling, G., 10238
Gottfried, R. S., 7950
Gould, A., 8102
Gourvish, T., 8139
Gransden, A., 9370
Graves, C. L., 8996
Gray, M. G., 8282
Grayston, C., 9120
Great Eastern Railway Society, 8190
Great Hospital, 9600
Great Yarmouth and District Archaeological Society, 7641, 10233
Great Yarmouth Borough Council, 9044, 9182, 9224, 10190–6
Great Yarmouth Corporation, 10209
Great Yarmouth Labour Party, 10188
Great Yarmouth Port and Haven Commissioners, 9649, 10205
Great Yarmouth Reference Library, 10231
Greaves, R., 8371
Green, B., 7670, 7717, 7741, 8980, 9390, 9873
Green, C., 9183
Green, C. J. S., 9006. 9009
Green, G. C., 8724
Green, J., 7858
Green, Mrs. J. R., 9316, 9519
Green, R., 8894
Greenwell, W., 7713–14
Greenwood, J. R., 8885, 8959, 9170, 9784
Greenwood, R., 8493
Greer, A., 10022
Greer, S., 10023
Greeves, J., 8725
Gregory, A., 7689, 7691, 7731, 7735, 8943, 9011, 9021, 10048, 10107–8
Gregory, R., 8967
Gregory, T. See Gregory, A.
Gretton, J. R., 8794–5, 10011
Grice, E., 8329
Griffiths, E., 8042, 9514
Grigg, A. J., 7902
Grigson, E. R., 10099
Grigson, G. E. H., 7610
Grimmer, H. S., 9200
Grimsley, G. E., 8419
Grint, B. S., 7456

Griston, J., 8183
Grose. J., 9100
Grove, R., 7476
Gruenfelder, J. K., 10182
Grundy, C. R., 8908
Guiver, J., 8018
Gunn, S. J., 8613
Gurney, D., 7691, 7693, 7734
Gurney-Read, J., 9647
Guth, G. J., 9523
Guthrie, K. M., 10161

Haddon, T., 9472
Hadfield, J., 7614
Hagan, G., 9130
Haggard, Sir H. R., 8734
Haggard, L. R., 8736
Haines, C. W., 8173
Haines, H., 8488
Hales, J., 7618, 7666, 7671, 7959, 8737
Hall, D., 7468, 7471
Hallam, H. E., 7395, 8036A
Hallatt, G., 7857, 10184
Hallows, J., 9933
Hamburger, L., 8574
Hamlin, P. E., 8548, 8566
Hammond, J., 9939–40
Hammond, Mrs. P., 8852
Hanawalt, B. A., 7930–1
Hanly, J. L., 9754
Hannaford, C. A., 7434
Harbord, E., 7933
Harbord, R. P., 8742
Harbour, H., 7585
Harcourt, B., 9737
Harding, R. W., 9972
Hardingham, V., 9684A
Hardwicke, Earl. See Yorke, P.
Hare, J. N., 10044
Harland, E. M., 8745
Harland, H. J., 7404
Harland, M. G., 7404
Harley, B., 8770
Harley, L. S., 8402
Harman, J., 9577
Harmer (F.W.) and Co., 9677
Harper-Bill, C., 8232, 8241
Harris, A. P., 9174
Harris, B. J., 8762
Harris, C. (pseud.), 7829
Harris, J., 9882
Harris, J. R., 7768
Harris, M., 8436
Harris, N., 8840
Harris, S., 8027
Harrison, M., 9492
Hart, C., 7742

Hart, R., 10093
Hartcup, A., 9255
Hartley, C., 8515
Hartwell, W., 9682
Harvey, C., 8133
Harvey, P. D. A., 8030
Haskell, A. S., 8857
Haslam, H. M., 7559, 7565
Haslam, R., 8979, 9204
Haslam, S. M., 8024
Hassall, W. O., 8646, 9253
Hastings, M., 7838
Hatch, K., 9682
Hawcroft, F. W., 8892
Hawes, T. L. M., 8596. 9085
Hawkes., C. F. C., 9037
Hawkins, F., 10240
Hawkins, J., 10148
Hawkins, L. W., 10221
Hayes, D. R., 7882
Haymon, S., 8747
Haynes, R. M., 7966, 7971
Hayton, D., 7916
Hayward, W. G. R., 8992
Healey, M. J., 8102
Healy, F. M. A., 7698, 7711, 7724, 9008, 10059
Hearn S., 8860
Hedges, A. A. C., 7868, 8442, 10162, 10200, 10241
Heeley, J., 8154
Hellesdon Parish Council, 9840
Hellyer, A., 9172
Hemingway, A., 8510. 8660
Hemnell, P. R., 8202
Henderson, F., 7862
Henderson, H., 8661
Henderson, H. J. R., 8065
Henderson, S. J. N., 9983
Henderson, T. S., 8914
Hendrey, H. D., 8536
Henfrey, H. W., 8481
Henig, M., 8527, 10033, 10102, 10139
Henney, J., 7657
Hepworth, P., 7620. 9753, 9771, 9832, 9924
Herteig, A. E., 9452
Hesford, B., 9358
Heslop, T. A., 8527
Hethersett Society, 9228
Hewett School, 9624
Hey. R. D., 7448, 7573
Heywood, S., 8477, 9147
Heyworth, P. L., 8319
Higgins, D., 7884
Higgins, D. S., 8734
Highfield, J. R. L., 7763
Hildy, F. J., 9736

Hill, C. M., 7525
Hill, G. F., 9427
Hill, L. A., 8318
Hill, O., 8411
Hills, C. M., 7743, 9138, 9142–5. 10006
Hilton, J., 9701
Hinchliffe, J., 9010
Hinde, P., 8143
Hines, J., 7744
Hingham Festival, 9239
Hingham Society, 9240
Hinson, M. D., 9463
Hipper. K., 9839
Historical Association, 7642
Historical Manuscripts Commission, 7754, 8932
Hoare, A., 7789, 9389A
Hoare, H., 8752
Hoare, L., 8751
Hoare, W. P., 9089
Hobley, B., 9303
Hodgetts, M., 10047
Hodgson, D., 8518
Hodskinson, J., 10109
Holcomb, A. M., 8657
Holden, C. C., 9094
Holderness, B. A., 8039
Holleyman, G. A., 8936
Hollingsworth, A., 7635
Hollis, D. W., 9111
Hollis, P. L., 7904A, 9576
Holman, R., 9341
Holme, C., 8530, 8650
Holmes, C., 7799
Holmes, D., 9374
Holmes, K., 9416
Holt, T. G., 8696, 9698
Home G. C., 7601
Home, M. (pseud.), 8753
Homeland Association, 7589
Honer, D. E., 9363A–4
Hood, C. M., 7756, 7783
Hooke, D., 7746
Hooper. B., 8746
Hooper. J., 8287, 9087
Hooton, C., 9774
Hope, N., 8688
Hope. W. H. St.J., 7896
Hopkinson, B., 7634
Horder, M., 7636
Horsey, M., 9583A
Horth, J. R., 8754, 9858
Hoseason, J., 7847
Hoskins, W. G., 7358
Hoste, Sir W., 8755
Houlbrooke, R. A., 7780, 8250–1
Houston, W., 9076

Howard, A., 10073
Howard, J., 7932
Howard, V., 9739
Howell, K. M., 9988
Howkins, A. J., 8078–9, 8081
Howlett and White, 9664
Howlett, R., 8223
Howman, P. J. L., 8764
Howman, R., 8763
Howsell, H., 7393
Hudson, K., 7670
Hughes, A., 8336
Hughes, G., 9229
Hughes, H. T., 8278
Hughes, T. M., 7383
Hulme, A-M., 9237
Human, B., 9766
Humphreys, A. E., 9152
Humphreys, A. L., 7649
Hunstanton and District Festival, 9274
Hunt, A., 9260
Huntley, F. L., 8739
Hurst, J. G., 7737
Hussey, C., 8411
Hutchinson, Sir J., 8069

Ilbery, B. W., 8102
Industrial Administration Ltd., 9636
Ingleby, C., 8446, 9108
Innes, H., 7631
Insley, J., 7740
Institute of Geological Sciences, 7387–8
Institution of Civil Engineers, 7401
International Hospital Federation, 7983
Ive, J. G. A., 7803
Ives, E. W., 7776
Ives, R., 9248

Jackman, B., 8478
Jackson, J. C. K., 8723
Jacob, D. E., 8635A
Jacob, W. M., 8261
Jacobi, R. M., 9080
Jacobs, M., 8511
Jaggar, G., 7800
Jakes, B., 9207
James, A., 8768
James, D. E. H., 7903
James, E. M., 9340, 9362, 9974, 10114
James, G. C., 10128
James, H. V., 7820
James, M. H., 8286
James, M. R., 9015. 10121
James, Z., 9785
Jamieson, Mackay and Partners, 7516
Janson, H., 7399
Janssen, C. A., 9521

Jantzen, G. M., 8786
Jarvis, A. M., 9621
Jarvis, F., 10155
Jarvis, S. M., 7938
Jay, D., 8766
Jeans, R., 10067
Jeffery, J., 8769
Jeffs, R., 7763
Jenkins, S. C., 8213
Jennings, P., 8524
Jennings, S., 9441, 9869, 9879
Jenyon, A. R., 7367
Jerrold, W., 7598
Jervoise, E., 8175
Jessopp. A., 7999, 9410, 9798, 10161
Jessup, G., 10106
Jewitt, L., 7896
Jewson and Sons Ltd., 9651
Jewson, C. B., 8615, 8775, 8819, 8924, 9481, 9599, 9699
Jobling, R. G., 9637
Joby, R. S. F., 7356, 8151, 8181, 8192, 8194, 8204, 8214, 9838
John Innes Institute, 9625
Johns, C., 7732, 9246, 10033
Johns, W. H., 9421
Johnson, C. T., 9173
Johnson, D. E., 7834, 7836, 8341, 8372
Johnson, M. B., 8603, 9385
Johnson, P., 9731
Johnson, W. E., 7368
Johnston, D. E., 9009
Johnston, L., 7581
Joice, R., 8873, 8899
Jolly, C., 7876, 8276, 8683, 9194, 9244, 10111
Jolly, W. T. F., 9077
Jones, A., 8570
Jones, B. A., 8776
Jones, D., 9668–9
Jones, D. (b.1941), 7818
Jones, Sir F. A., 9592
Jones, G. R., 8283
Jones, H., 8367
Jones, Mrs. H., 8534, 8708
Jones, Jane, 9678
Jones, John, 9678
Jones, Sir L. E., 8777
Jones, M. G., 8126
Jones, P. T., 9947
Jones, R., 10114
Jones, S., 8769
Jones, S. R., 7611
Jones, W. H., 8826, 9423
Jordan, C., 8940
Jordan, J. A., 7603
Jordan, R., 8273

Jordan, W. K., 7948A
Joyce, B. R., 7559
Jukes, H. A. L., 8249, 10055
Jukes-Brown, A. J., 7382

Karshner, M., 9671
Kay, M. A., 9711
Kaye, B., 8991
Keeble, D., 8102
Keeley, H. C. M., 7690
Keith, E. C., 8351
Keith, J., 8062
Kelbrick, N., 8326
Kellett, L., 9740
Kelly, G. I., 9355A, 9794, 9843, 9845, 9849
Kelly, M., 9936
Kelly, S., 9460
Kendle, L. C., 10010
Kennett, D. H., 7629, 7669, 8168, 8406, 9016
Kenny, R. W., 8578
Kent, C., 7414
Kent, P., 7921A, 9352, 9510
Kenworthy-Browne, J., 8416
Kerrison, A. E., 9152A
Kestner, F. J. T., 7408
Kett, H., 8748
Kett, J., 9066
Ketton-Cremer, R. W., 7808, 7936, 8666, 8744, 8818, 8908
Key, R., 8276
Key, J., 8576A
Keymer, T., 8920
Killingsworth, V., 7755
Kilmartin, J., 9487
Kilvington, R. P., 7557
Kinch, M. B., 9538
King, A., 10033
King, D. J., 8480, 9104, 10019
King, D. J. C., 8405
King, James, 8662–3
King, John, 8796
King, R. J., 9797
King's Lynn and West Norfolk Council, 7558, 8017, 8172, 9132, 9216, 9276, 9279, 9319–21
King's Lynn Borough Council, 9334
King's Lynn Civic Society, 9330
King's Lynn Museum, 8581, 9346
King's Lynn Preservation Trust, 9349
King's Lynn Rotary Club, 9294
King's Lynn Society of Arts and Sciences, 9293
Kinnes, I., 7710
Kinsey, B. K., 7891, 7895
Kinsman, R. S., 8898
Kirk, T., 8942
Kitson, J., 10026
Kivell, M. S., 8104

Knecht, R. J., 7776
Knights, M., 7662, 8285, 9087
Knocker, G. M., 10024
Knowles, A. K., 9007
Knox, G., 9403
Kudo, N., 7621

Labour Party, 7520, 7919, 8005, 9575, 10188
Lacassagne, C., 8741
Lade, R., 8028
Lagorio, V. M., 8782
Lamb, C., 7615
Lambert, D., 8800
Lambley, P., 9725
Lamont-Brown, R., 8565
Lancaster-Rennie, J., 7843
Land, S. K., 7786
Lane, M. R., 10037
Lane, R., 9511
Lane, R. M., 7935
Langham, G. H., 8533
Large, W. M., 9780
La Rochefoucauld, F. de, 7579
Lathe, A., 9219
Latter Day Saints, 8552
Law, J. R., 9848
Lawson, A. J., 7471, 7697, 7699, 7700, 7705, 7712, 8969, 8978, 9039, 9083, 9214, 9277, 9445, 9450, 10016, 10125, 10130
Lawson, A. K., 8947
Lawson, N. G., 9201
Leake, G. F., 9904–6
Leather, J., 8083
Leeds, H., 7431, 9413
Lees, A. J., 9652
Lee Warner, J., 10093
Legge, R. H., 8346
Le Grice, J., 8803
Lemon, A., 7505, 8095
Lenny, J. G., 7481
Le Rougetel, H., 9943
Lester, G. A., 8863
L'Estrange, J., 9811
Le Strange, Sir N., 7794
Le Strange, R., 8491
Leverett, J., 9935
Levine, G. J., 8561, 9017
Lewin, J., 9327
Lewis, A., 9222
Lewis, C., 7670, 7878, 8087, 10166, 10214
Lewis, P., 9222
Liebermann, F., 7752
Limbrey, S., 7364
Lindley, K., 7802
Lindley, P., 7593
Lindley, P. G., 8475
Lindsay, D., 8577, 8705

Ling, W. E., 8805
Linnell, C. L. S., 8490, 8990, 9392, 9914, 9948, 9980. 10046
Lipman, V. D., 9456
Lippincott, H. F., 7794
Liscombe, R. W., 8925, 9031
Littlewood, J., 8806
Livet, G., 8741
Livingstone, S., 7819
Llewellyn, R., 8785
Lloyd-Prichard, M. F., 8111
Loads and Sons, 9090
Lobel, M. D., 9421
Local Government Operational Research Unit, 7904
Lochrie, K., 8792
Lockhart, B. L., 8579
Lockwood, J., 9026
Loddon Rural District Council, 9366
Lodey, M. J., 8963
Loftus, C., 8808
Loftus, G. W. F., 8378B
London Society of East Anglians, 8533
Long, N., 7881
Long, P., 9900
Long, U., 8809
Long Stratton Congregational Church, 9997
Longe, A., 8294
Longsdon, E. H., 8970
Longworth, I., 7723
Lonsdale, M. E., 9242
Lord, J. F., 9013
Love, C., 9656
Lowe, P., 8074
Luckett, H., 8581
Lummis, T., 8086, 8088, 8090
Lupson, E. J., 8810
Lynn, R., 8094
Lynn Advertiser, 9322
Lynn Dispensary, 9324
Lynn News and Advertiser, 9295
Lyons, M. C., 10012
Lyons, S. M., 8255

M.,C., 9756
McBride, E., 9860
McCabe, R. A., 8740
McCann, J., 8431
McClure, P., 7496
MacCulloch, D., 7787, 7792
McCririck, J., 10007
McCutcheon, E. M. J., 7507, 7946, 9203
Macdermott, G. M., 10052
Mace, H., 9088A
McEwen, A., 9040, 9185. 10169, 10213, 10225
McGrail, S., 9301

McIlwain, J. T., 8784
Mack, A. H., 9109A
Mack, M., 8811
McKean, C., 8370, 8400
Mackenzie, M. L., 8797
Mackeown, M., 9263
McKinley, R., 8553
Mackintosh, E. D., 9658
McKitterick, D. J., 8799
McLean, M., 9861–2
McManus, M., 10082
McMurdo, L., 8427, 10069
McWilliam, N., 8695
Madden, D. C., 9271
Maddern, P. C., 7766
Maddison, J., 9002
Maddock, A., 10038
Maddock, S., 8309
Mahl, M. R., 8575
Maisonneuve, R., 8781
Maitland, R. W., 9970
Major, J. K., 9197
Major, K., 8686
Malcolmson, R., 8571
Maling, J. J., 8624, 9121
Mallalieu, H., 8506
Malster, R. W., 7866, 7869, 8136, 9096, 9605, 9952
Manby, G. W., 8178, 8813–14
Mann, J. D., 8193
Mann, J. de L., 9679
Manning, I. M., 7375A, 9064, 9907, 10120, 10150
Manning, K., 9249
Manning, S. A., 7449
Mansfield, H. O., 8456
March, G. O., 10149
Margeson, S., 9448
Margoliouth, M., 8284
Marks, R., 8758
Marlowe, C., 7462, 8292
Marr, L., 8461
Marriott, W., 8191
Marsden, W., 8537
Marshall, K. N., 10079
Marshall, M. A. N., 7864
Marsters, T., 7853
Martin, K., 9198
Martin, R. G., 9275
Martingell, H. E., 9080
Martins, S. W. See Wade-Martins, S.
Marzac-Holland, N., 8238
Mason, J., 7879
Mather, C., 9405
Matthews, B., 9742
Matthews, F. H., 9903
Maw, P. G., 8449

Mayhew, P., 8820
Megaw, E., 10139
Melling, C. T., 8132
Mellor, D., 9030
Mellor, I., 8906
Mercer, R. J., 7718, 7722
Meredith. H., 7602
Meredith, R., 8696
Meriton, H., 7852
Messent, C. J. W., 8450A, 9922
Metcalf, P., 9804
Meteorological Office, 7393
Metters, G. A., 9309, 9810
Michell, A. R., 10217
Middleton, C. S., 7444
Middleton J., 7975
Midgley, P. W., 9297
Midland and Great Northern Circle, 8199
Miket, R., 7718
Mileham, J., 8618
Miles, D., 7731
Miles, P., 9877
Millatt, T. B., 8822
Miller, A. C., 8572, 8807, 9310
Miller, C., 8815
Miller, C. D., 7871
Miller, P., 8441
Miller, R. G., 8590
Miller, S. H., 7392, 7460–61
Millican, P., 9868
Milligan, W. F., 7741
Millman, J., 8772
Millns, W. J., 8745A
Mills, D., 7910
Mills, J. F. C., 7865
Milne, G., 9303
Milne, K., 7805
Milner, J., 7761
Milsom, M. E., 10112
Minet, W., 9469
Ministry of Health, 7958
Ministry of Housing, 7384
Mitchels, E., 7634
Mitchels, M., 7634
Moated Sites Research Group, 7687
Moffat, H., 8215
Moir, J. R., 8801
Molinari, P., 8778
Molony, E., 9428
Monopolies Commission, 9112
Moore, A. W., 7812, 8513, 8516, 8658
Moore, N. J., 8401
Moran, J., 9155
Morgan, V., 7773
Morimoto, N., 8031
Morley, F. V., 7599
Morris, S. E., 9055

Morriss, A. H., 8350
Mortimer, C. G., 10087
Mortimer, J., 9957
Mortimer, R., 9977
Mortlock, D. P., 8464
Mosby, J. E. G., 9245
Moscrop, W. J., 8053
Moseley, M. J., 7500. 7504, 7521, 7528, 7939, 8015, 8097, 8160, 9418
Moss, B., 7442, 7445–6, 7448, 7451–2, 7459
Mott, R. F., 8729
Mottram, R. H., 8824–5, 9428, 9605
Moye, L. E., 8828
Moynes, J. C., 7793
Mueller, J. M., 8793
Muir, D. E., 8829
Muir, M., 9892A, 9930–1
Muir, P., 8991
Muir, R., 7370
Mumby, J., 9150
Muncaster, M. J., 7963
Munnings, Sir A., 8832
Munnings, T. C., 8046
Murby, T., 7344
Murie, A., 9583
Murphy, J. D., 10219
Murphy, P., 7459, 7688, 7690, 9443
Murray, G. C., 8072
Muscroft, S., 7309
Muskett, P., 7811, 7827
Muthesius, S., 9583A

Naish, G. P. B., 8837
Nall, G., 10159
Napier, P., 8868
National Agricultural Advisory Service, 8064
National Agricultural Labourers' and Rural Workers' Union, 8077
National Catholic Congress, 8269
National Extension College Trust, 8008
National Front, 7920
National Maritime Museum, 8838
National Register of Archives, 10164
National Trust, 8997, 9001
National Union of Teachers, 8004, 8006
Nature Conservancy Council, 7440
Naughton, G., 9254
Nelson, A. H., 9733
Nelson, R. E., 10066
Neve, E., 8207
Nevill, C., 9369A
Nevill, Lady D., 8844
Nevill, G., 8844
Nevill, H. R., 7998, 9865
Nevill, R. H., 8844
Neville, Sir R., 9968
Neville-Rolfe, C. W., 9215

New, A. S. B., 9803
Newby, D., 8503
Newby, H., 7522, 8080
Newhall, N., 8694
Newman, J., 9000
Newman, L. F., 8310A
Nichols, A. E., 8244
Nichols, J. A., 8228
Nicholson, N., 9223, 10110
Nickalls, J., 10203
Nickless, E. F. P., 7387
Nicolson, N., 9881
Ninham, H., 9778
Norfolk Agricultural Association, 8052
Norfolk Agricultural Station, 8061
Norfolk and Norwich Archaeological Society, 7651, 8383–4, 9717
Norfolk and Norwich Art Circle, 8514
Norfolk and Norwich Association for Mental Health, 9574
Norfolk and Norwich Genealogical Society, 8539, 8542, 8546, 8549–51, 9488
Norfolk and Norwich Horticultural Society, 8385
Norfolk and Norwich Hospital, 9604
Norfolk and Norwich Naturalists' Society, 8386
Morfolk and Norwich Savings Bank, 8114
Norfolk and Suffolk Association of Baptist Churches, 8274
Norfolk and Suffolk Aviation Museum, 7892
Norfolk Archaeological Rescue Group, 7638
Norfolk Archaeological Unit, 7676
Norfolk Architects' Association, 8387
Norfolk Area Health Authority, 7501, 7962, 7979. 7981, 10201
Norfolk Area Joint Liaison Committee, 7960
Norfolk Arts Forum, 8320
Norfolk Canoeing Association, 8377
Norfolk Churches Trust, 8265, 8458
Norfolk Club, 8388
Norfolk Conservation Corps, 8389
Norfolk County Chess Association, 8344
Norfolk County Council, 7362, 7391, 7411, 7457, 7536–54, 7831, 7956, 7979, 7985–6, 7989–90, 8000, 8003, 8011, 8100, 8103, 8157, 8159, 8161, 8409–10, 9158, 9318, 9542, 9547, 9557, 9571, 9581, 9650, 9790, 10076, 10141
Norfolk County Cricket Club, 8347
Norfolk County Library, 7650, 8607
Norfolk Drama Committee, 8327
Norfolk Education Industry and Commerce Group, 8012
Norfolk Heraldry Society, 8556, 8558
Norfolk Heritage, 7644
Norfolk Naturalists' Trust, 8390

Norfolk News Co., 7828
Norfolk Railway Society, 8391
Norfolk Record Office, 7656, 8309, 8538
Norfolk Rural Music School, 8333
Norfolk Society, 7357, 8393
Norfolk Windmills Trust, 8438, 8982, 9109, 10123
Norgate, T. S., 8140
Norman, J. C., 8806
Norris, M., 8493
Norris, R., 9243
North Norfolk District Council, 8101
North Yorkshire Record Office, 8657
Norton, T. W., 8403
Norton, W. E., 8845
Norwak, M., 8308
Norwich, J. J., 8408
Norwich Airport Joint Committee, 7893
Norwich and District Peace Council, 9747
Norwich and Norfolk Chamber of Commerce, 8105
Norwich Archdeaconry Committee for Social Responsibility, 9983
Norwich Castle Museum, 7664, 7674, 7709, 7782, 8500, 8569, 8732, 8831, 9550, 9719, 10031
Norwich Chamber of Commerce, 9414, 9648
Norwich Charity Organisation Society, 9562
Norwich City Council, 7804, 9494, 9497–9, 9505, 9535–7, 9539, 9543–6, 9548–54, 9556, 9559, 9563, 9566, 9568, 9572, 9578, 9580, 9584, 9598, 9612–17, 9619, 9643–4, 9646, 9720, 9722, 9762, 9769, 9787–8, 9852–3
Norwich City Commission, 9697
Norwich Community Workshop, 7660
Norwich Complete Suffrage Union, 7859
Norwich Corporation. See Norwich City Council
Norwich Council of Christian Congregations, 7976
Norwich Council of Churches, 9569
Norwich Diocesan Synod, 8018
Norwich District Footpath Society, 9748
Norwich District Primitive Methodist Church, 9702
Norwich Electricity Co. Ltd., 9609
Norwich Engineering Society, 9655
Norwich Health Authority, 7967, 7970, 7973, 7987–8
Norwich High School for Girls, 9628
Norwich Industrial Mission, 7977, 8098
Norwich Labour Party, 9575
Norwich Lads' Club, 9749, 9751
Norwich Mechanics' Institution, 9746
Norwich Preservation Trust, 9752
Norwich Public Library, 8595, 8847

Norwich School of Art, 9660
Norwich Society, 9759, 9775
Norwich Telephone Area Museum, 9674
Norwich Trades Council, 8096
Norwich Unemployed Workers Action Group, 9586
Norwich Union, 8117–20
Norwich Y.M.C.A., 9710
Nunn, H. L., 8066
Nuthall, T., 9826
Oddfellows' Conference, 9412
Oddy, J. A., 8875A
O'Donnell, R., 8684
O'Donoghue, R., 9837
Office of Works, 8396
Ogden, J., 9753
Ogilvie, P., 9967
Oliver, J., 7394
Open University, 7653, 9726
Oppé, A. P., 8651
O'Riordan, A. M., 7440
O'Riordan, T., 7445, 7447, 7529–30, 7574–5
Ormrod, W. M., 9817
Orna, B., 8407
Orna, E., 8407
Orr, J., 8056
Orton, C., 9382, 9856
Orwin, C. S., 8056
Osborne, D., 10027
Oscar and Peter Johnson Ltd., 8506A, 8669, 8901
O'Sullivan, D. S., 8921, 9520
Oswald, A., 9671
Oswell, G. R., 9345
Overton, M., 8033, 8036, 8041
Owen, A. E. B., 8135
Owen, D. M., 9302, 9305
Owen, J., 7856
Owens, G. L., 8798
Owens, L., 8359
Owens, S. E., 7527
Owers, A. C., 8068–9

Packman, J., 7531, 8100
Pagan, H. E., 8109
Page, G. G., 8447
Page, R. A. F., 9488
Paget, G., 8334
Palgrave, D. A., 8850, 8971
Palgrave-Moore, P. T. R., 8275, 8540, 8545, 8560, 8951, 9530
Parish, E. J., 8851
Parissien, S., 9402
Park, D., 9284
Parker, A., 7465
Parker, R. A. C., 8645
Parry, A., 8853

Parry, P. H., 7791
Parsons-Norman, G., 7406, 7428
Partridge, B., 7565
Partridge, E. G., 8950, 8954–5, 9159, 9874
Paston, E., 8678
Paston-Bedingfield, Sir E., 9878
Patrides, C. A., 8620
Patten, A. H., 10086, 10096
Patten, J., 7492–3, 7769, 7772
Patterson, A. H., 7407, 7432, 7807
Paul, L., 8867
Paul, L. S., 9693
Pawley, M., 9280
Payne, S. J., 7448
Peacock, A. C., 9328
Peacock, A. J., 7817
Pearson, R., 7365
Pearson, R. O., 9891
Peart, S., 8415, 9019, 10003
Peaton, A., 7594
Pedrick, M., 8523
Peet, D. J., 8252
Pegg, R. E. F., 8163
Pellew, G., 9847
Pelling, M., 7951–2, 9593–4, 9597
Pelphrey, B., 8783
Penney, N., 9708
Penny, J. S., 8348
Penoyre, Jane, 8422
Penoyre, John, 8422
Penton, J., 9579
Perceval, C. S., 7646
Perkins, J., 8550
Perry, G., 8198
Pestell, R. E., 9036, 9205, 9938
Peters, H., 9405
Pevsner, N., 9804
Phillips, B., 8964
Phillips, F. A., 9181
Phillips. J. A., 9522
Phipps, J., 9707
Pickard, I., 7486
Pidley, M. R., 8653
Pierssene, A., 8182
Pigott, B. A. F., 8687, 8870
Piper, C., 9122
Pirie, J., 9178
Plouviez, J., 7727
Plunkett, G. A. F., 8485, 9776, 9827
Pocock, T., 8756
Pollard, A. J., 8699
Pollard, M., 7402
Poole, D., 8521–2, 9783
Pooley, G., 9068, 9081
Popplewell, L., 8211
Porter, E., 8296
Porter, S., 9773

Post, J. B., 7767
Potter, C., 8073
Potter, H. E., 8343
Potter, T., 7732, 9976
Poulson, J., 8307
Pound, J. F., 8253, 9466, 9468
Pound, R., 8833
Powell, R., 7475, 9027, 10113
Pratt, S. J., 7580
Prest, W., 8576
Priest, E. W., 7604, 8395
Priestley, U., 9460, 9467, 9607, 9680, 9684
Prince, H. C., 7350
Pringle, P., 8709
Pritchard, G., 7681
Proctor, F., 8441
Proctor, J. M., 8423
Pronk, S. E., 9992
Pryor, F. P., 8752
Public Record Office, 7753, 7900
Puddy, E. I., 8221, 9189
Pugh, P. M., 8633
Purchas, A., 9415
Putnam, G., 9145
Pye, D., 7465

R., D., 9915
Raban, J. C. P., 9709
Rabuzzi, D. A., 8302
Raby, J. W., 9313
Rahtz, P., 9145
Railway Development Society, 8205
Rajnai, M., 8507, 8509, 8516, 8654, 8659
Randell, A. R., 8872–3
Ranson, R., 8895
Ravensdale, J., 7370
Ray, A. L., 7523
Read, D. I., 9618
Read, J., 9187
Reader, W. J., 10212
Reading, E., 9396
Record Commission, 7750, 8248
Reeve, J. E., 10129
Reeve, L. M., 8058
Reid, A. W., 7948, 8945–6, 8947A, 9101, 9218, 9911
Rennert, J., 8672
Rennie, J., 10204
Reynolds, J., 9765
Rhodes, D. E., 9464
Rhodes, J., 8206
Ribbans, F. B., 8935
Ribeiro, A. F. V., 8627
Richards, A. B., 8150
Richards, J. D., 9148
Richardson, J., 7942
Richardson, R. C., 8876

Riches, R., 9207, 9987
Richmond, C., 8823, 8861
Richmond, H., 9354, 9356
Rickwood, D. L., 9034, 9476
Ridler, A. M., 8609
Ridyard, S. J., 8247
Ring, G., 9180
Ritchie, J. E., 8878
Rix, L., 9297
Rix Family Alliance, 8879
Roast, T. R., 8454
Roberts, C. V., 8464
Roberts, J., 10178
Roberts, Sir P., 9072
Robertson, B., 8635
Robins, P. A., 9386
Robinson, A. H. W., 7351
Robinson, B., 7632. 7701, 7735, 8171
Robinson, E. K., 7596
Robinson, J. M., 8757, 9247
Roe, D. A., 7695
Roe, P. J., 8048
Rogers, D., 9252
Rogers, D., (b. 1939), 8166
Rogers, J. V., 7845
Rogers, N., 9487A
Rogerson, A. J. G., 7689, 8972, 8980, 8984, 9195, 9221, 9389, 9934, 10032, 10168
Rollings, P., 10092
Rolt, M. S., 8628
Roper, C., 7586
Rose, E. J., 8171, 9068, 9104, 9266, 9879, 9888, 9928, 9969, 10050, 10054
Rose, J., 8710
Rose, M., 9768
Rosenheim, J. M., 7806, 7915, 8685
Ross, A., 8761
Rossi, A. P., 10051
Rothery, C., 8210
Roulston, M., 8179
Rowlands, S., 8961
Royal Archaeological Institute, 8399
Royal College of Physicians, 8621
Royal Institute Gallery, 8504
Ruddy, I. M., 8930
Russell, A., 8264
Russell, R., 8180
Rust, C. T., 9696
Rutledge, E., 9300, 9460, 10171
Rutledge, P., 7651, 8428, 9300, 10171, 10174, 10176, 10180–1
Ryan, P., 8271
Ryan, R. J., 8121–3
Ryder, R., 8636
Rye, C. G., 8434, 10186, 10235
Rye, W., 7420, 7647, 8563, 8883, 9526, 9627, 9758, 9812

Ryskamp, C., 8662

S., W., 7850
Sadgrove, M., 8884
Sainsbury Centre for Visual Arts, 8875, 9728–30, 9822
Saint Faith's Society, 9269A
Salmon, N., 7578
Sampson, A., 8987, 9802
Sampson, C., 8293
Samuel, A. M., 9426
Samuels, M. L., 10116
Sanderson, E. W., 8951
Sandred. K. I., 7487–91, 10116
Sanecki, K. N., 8874
Sant, M. E. C., 8097
Sapsford, D., 8019. 8104
Sapwell, J., 8960
Saul, A. R., 10170, 10172–3, 10175, 10220
Saunders, A. D., 9829
Saunders, D., 9051
Saunders, S., 9051
Save Britain's Heritage, 8469
Savory, A., 8352
Sawyer, M. E., 8780
Sayer, F. D., 8023
Sayer, M. J., 7760, 8076, 8416, 8540–1, 9980
Sayers, G. R., 8993
Scarfe, N., 7579
Scarff, E. P., 8231
Scarisbrick, J. J., 7776
Schazmann, P-E., 8588
Schmidt, L., 8643, 9256–7
Scot, T., 7848–9
Scotland, N. A., 8260, 8277, 8915
Scott, C. W., 7405
Scott, E. E., 9606
Scott, M., 8436
Scott, T., 9695
Scott, W., 9285
Scout Association, 8394
Seago, E., 8890
Seal-Coon, F. W., 8236
Seaman, P. J., 7907–8, 7911
Seddon, J. D., 9587
Sekules, V., 8695, 9732
Selkirk, A., 9436
Selten, B., 8554
Senior, C., 9350
Serpell, M. F., 8701, 9289, 9368
Sessions, W. A., 8760
Sessions, W. K., 9716
Sewell, B., 8677
Sexton, H. J., 9667
Shaw, A. B. See Batty Shaw, A.
Shaw, J. M., 7529
Shaw, L., 9565A

Shaw, M., 7833, 9761
Shaw, M. N., 8812
Shelfanger Women's Institute, 9945
Shelton, S. S., 8164
Sheppard, E. M., 9694
Sheringham Chamber of Trade, 9953
Sherlock, D., 9269
Sherman, H. S., 9819–20
Shinners, J. R., 8237, 9691
Shipp, H., 8891
Short, W. J., 10042A
Shotton, F. E., 8063
Siegmund-Schultze, D., 8790
Sieveking, G. de G., 7720
Silvester, R. J., 7472, 10098
Simms, N., 7637
Simper, R., 8301
Simpson, J. H., 8765
Simpson, Ray, 9791
Simpson, Roger, 9419
Simpson, R. J., 8519, 9054, 9087A, 9160
Simpson, W., 8897
Sims, R. E., 7353, 7364
Sinclair, M., 10140
Sinclair, O., 9075
Skeat, T. C., 9251
Skelton, P. N., 9171
Skertchly, S. B. J., 7460
Slack, P., 7787, 9595
Slatter, M., 7939, 9513
Smallwood, J., 7730, 9909, 9965
Smedley, N., 8129
Smith, A., 9793
Smith, A. C., 8437, 8439, 9994
Smith, A. H., 8290
Smith, A. Hassell, 7778, 7792, 8578, 9514, 9990
Smith, A. J., 8052
Smith, A. R., 8698–9
Smith, B., 7905
Smith, C., 10095
Smith, D. M., 8222
Smith, E. G., 9286
Smith, G. V. V., 10004
Smith, J., 8324
Smith, Sir J. E., 8339
Smith, M., 9585
Smith, R., 9438, 9772
Smith, R. A., 7716
Smith, R. A. H., 9528
Smith, R. M., 7944
Smith, Sheenah, 9724
Smith, Simon, 7524
Smith, Stan, 7905
Smith, T. P., 9361
Smith, W. D., 8726, 9622
Smith, W. R., 9205A

Smithdon and Brothercross Friendly Society, 7949
Smythies, W., 7850
Snelling, J. M., 9371
Snettisham Parish Council, 9975
Society of Genealogists, 8545
Soil Survey, 7385
Solomon, J. D., 9391
Solomons, G., 9431
Sotherton, N., 7784
Souden, D., 7493
South, D., 7410
South Norfolk District Council, 7360, 7559–65, 8016, 8106, 9123, 9206, 9209, 9230–1, 10000, 10152
Southwell, T., 7595
Sparkes, W., 9336
Spence, K. J., 9960
Spencer, B., 7762
Spencer, N., 8496, 9782
Spinks, W., 8494
Sports Council, 8340
Sprunger, K. L., 8937
Spurdens, D., 8363
Stackhouse, J., 9565
Stafford, E., 10200
Stancsyszyn, R., 7387
Standley, P., 9777
Standley, V. H., 7453, 8051
Stanley, E., 8257, 9202
Stanley, E. H., Baron, 8900
Stanley-Millson, C., 9000
Stannard, J., 8130
Starr, F., 9069
Starsmore, I., 10053
Steers, J. A., 7400
Steffens, R. J., 9196
Steggall, P., 7626
Stenton, D. M., 7929
Stephen, G. A., 8499, 8535, 9087
Stephens, R., 9253
Stephenson, F., 7438, 10090
Stephenson, M., 9978
Stern, E., 7777, 9989
Stevens, J., 9629
Stevens, M., 8507
Stevenson, J., 7775
Stibbons, B., 9099
Stibbons, F., 7605, 8902
Stibbons, P. J. R., 7413, 8089, 9096, 9099
Stibbons, T., 9281
Stimpson, P. E., 9779
Stoker, D., 8144, 8323, 8597, 9712–14, 9716
Stone, E., 8691
Stone, L., 7773
Stone, M. C., 9079
Stone, R. K., 8314A

Storey, R., 9457
Stranger's Hall Museum, 7804
Stratton, D. G., 8093
Straw, A., 7389
Streeten, A. D. F., 9058
Stride, K. B., 8043
Strugnell, K. W., 7867
Stuart, F. C., 8632
Stuart, J. K., 9902
Sturge, W. A., 7707, 7715
Suffling, E. R., 7425, 7429
Summers, D., 7403, 7474
Summers, P., 8557
Surman, C. E., 9106
Surtees, S. F., 7725
Sussex, V. J., 8164–5, 9117
Sutermeister, H., 9786, 9836
Sutherland, Mrs. S., 8903
Swain, G., 9501
Swan, V. G., 9033
Swift, D. E., 8731
Swinger, P. W., 8208
Symes, E. S., 7663

Talbot, H. J., 8484
Tanner, N. P., 8233, 9690, 9692
Taylor, A., 7726
Taylor, G. H., 8189
Taylor, J. E., 9718
Taylor, R., 9354
Temple, C. R., 7870, 9508, 10187
Thacker, C., 8531
Thackeray, D. W. R., 7739
Thetford Chamber of Commerce, 10026
Thetford Moulded Products Ltd., 10040
Thetford Museum, 7654
Thetford Rotary Club, 10035
Thetford Urban District Council, 10034
Thicknesse, S. G., 9626
Thirsk, J., 8039
Thistlethwaite, F., 9634
Thistlethwaite, J., 8679
Thomas, C., 9208
Thomas, D., 8830
Thomas, D. H., 8009
Thompson, F. H., 9824
Thompson, P., 8088
Thompson, R., 9241
Thompson, T. W., 8313
Thompson, W. A., 9272
Thomson, D. G., 7957
Thomson, J. A. F., 9692
Thorold, H., 8472
Thurlow, A. G. G., 9417
Tillett, J. H., 7861, 8647, 9757
Tilly, C., 7770
Tillyard, M., 9460, 9688

Tillyard, R., 7361
Tillyard, V., 8512
Tilsley, G., 9642
Tisdall, E. E. P., 8573
Tittler, R., 7779, 10216
Tolhurst, P. D., 8425
Tomlinson, H., 8487
Tonkin, G., 7877
Tooke, C. S., 8070. 8200. 9041–2, 9045–7, 10186, 10215, 10222, 10234
Tookey, J., 8524
Tooley, B., 8866
Toovey, S., 9715
Toulson, S., 8167
Townroe, P. M., 9647A
Townshend, G. E. G. E., *Marchioness*, 8909
Travers, P., 9509
Trett, P., 8882
Trett, R., 7733, 8713, 9339, 9376, 9899
Trewin, I., 8912
Tricker, R. W., 8458, 9982
Tuck, D. W., 9339
Tuck, H. W., 9781
Tudor-Craig, P., 9866
Tullett, G. A., 7437
Turner, C., 7854
Turner, D. E., 9400
Turner, J., 7349
Turner, M., 7910
Turner, P., 8693
Turner, R. K., 7448, 7576
Twiddy, J., 7853A
Tyack, N. C. P., 7796
Tyler, M., 8263
Tymms, S., 7582

University of Birmingham Library, 8773
University of East Anglia, 7409, 8020–1, 8104, 8107, 8998, 9282, 9629–41, 10202. *See also* Centre of East Anglian Studies, Sainsbury Centre
Unwin, P., 8674
Upjohn, S., 9861

Valdar, S., 8771
Vallance, A., 8112
Van Damme, E., 9364
Vane, C. M., 9477
Vansittart, J., 8711
Varke, H., 9411
Veal, C. N., 9293
Veriod, B. S., 9560
Versey, G. R., 7748
Vickers, R. E., 7845
Victoria and Albert Museum, 9866
Vincent, J., 8900
Vincent, J. E., 7597

Vincent, S., 10227
Vines, A., 9916
Virgoe, J., 9870
Virgoe, N., 8413, 9141
Virgoe, R., 7763, 7776, 7914, 8877, 9461
Vogler, B., 8741
Vyse, J. W. M., 8941, 8962

W., C., 7855
W., G., 9919
Wacher, J., 9032
Waddington, D., 8187
Wade, D., 10122
Wade, K., 9363, 9962
Wade-Martins, P., 7374, 7506, 7677, 7729, 7738, 8946, 9014, 9139–41, 9146, 9177, 9355, 10006
Wade-Martins, S., 7672, 8049–50, 8429, 9139–40, 10058
Wailes, R., 9894
Wainwright, G. J., 9434
Wake, T., 8392
Wakeling, C., 8412
Wald, K. D., 9531
Wales, T., 7944
Walford, E., 9023
Walker, R., 9407
Walker, S. E, 8155
Walker, W. H. T., 7781
Walklett, H., 8586
Wallace, D., 8240
Wallace, D. B., 7514
Wallwork, K. L., 7351
Walmsley, M., 7526, 9399
Walpole, *Lady* N., 8916
Walpole, R. C., 10070
Walsh, J., 8779
Walters, R., 9507
Walthew, K., 8816
Walton, J. A., 9013
Walton, P. C., 8082
Ward, Lock and Co.[publ.], 7591–2
Warner, *Sir* F., 8147
Warner, M., 8511
Warner, P., 8245
Warren, P., 10084
Washbourn, R., 7359
Wasson, J., 8332, 10043
Water Resources Board, 7566
Waterson, M., 9164, 9958
Watkins, M., 7623, 7630, 7667, 7673
Watling, H., 8481
Watson, B., 9755
Watson, F. W., 8346
Watson, J., 8137
Watson, J. F., 8975
Watson, J. N. P., 9290

Watton Chamber of Trade, 10103
Watts, S., 10137
Weaver, L., 9842
Webb, D. H., 9345A
Webster, A., 9801
Webster, C., 7951
Webster, S., 9050
Weedon, G., 8528
Weikel, A., 8587
Weinzierl, M., 9524
Welch, C., 9285
Wells, C., 9433, 9964
Wells, W., 9291
Wesby, Mrs. E., 7954
West, H. M., 8303
West, R. G., 7353, 7390
West, S. E., 7741
West Norfolk and Lynn Hospital, 9325–6
West Norfolk District Council. See King's Lynn and West Norfolk District Council
West Norfolk Local History Society, 7640
Westall, O. M., 8122
Westman, B. H., 7930–1
Westwood, J., 8304
Whall, W. B., 8919
Whatmore, D. E., 8735
Wheeler, B. D., 7448
Wher, C., 7855
Whitaker, W., 7378, 7381–2
White, S. R., 9337
White, W., 7583
White, W. J. W., 7814
Whitefoote, J., 8738
Whitehead, G., 8279
Whiteley, J., 9564
Whitelock, D., 8226
Whites, Renard and Co., 8113
Whitfield, C., 9254
Whitfield, P. W., 8259
Whiting, A., 8922
Whitlock, R., 9926
Whittaker, A. C., 8199
Whittet, T. D., 8110
Whittingham, A. B., 8871, 9821, 9823, 9825, 9873
Whytehead, R. L., 9116
Wigby, F. C., 8923
Wilcox, C. J., 7387
Wilcox, R., 9056, 10045
Wilks, J. C., 8448
Williams, C., 9590
Williams, D., 9038
Williams, I. A., 8502
Williams, J. F., 9022, 9863
Williams, N. H., 10143
Williams, P., 9195
Williamson, H., 8736

Williamson, J. G., 8030
Williamson, T, (b. 1894), 7926
Williamson, T, (b. 1955), 7372, 7706, 7746
Willink, J. W., 10239
Wills, N. T., 8025
Wilson, A. M., 8927
Wilson, D. R., 7684
Wilson, J., 9076
Wilson, John, 8356, 8358
Wilson, J. H., 10144, 10146
Wilson, R., 9298, 9315, 9344, 9351
Wilton, J. W., 7685, 8235
Wincote, K. W., 10008
Windeatt, B. A., 8781
Windham, W., 8929
Winfrey, Sir R., 8931A
Winkley, G. W. D., 8417, 10064
Winnington, T., 9999
Winstanley, R. L., 7909, 8716, 8934, 10115
Winstedt, E. O., 8314
Winter, L., 8839, 8842
Winterton Seaman's Friendly Society, 10127
Winton, M. J., 9347, 9923
Wiseman, I., 9561
Wodehouse, C. N., 9360
Wood, A. C., 7900
Wood, E. A., 8886
Wood, E. C., 9596
Wood, F. A., 8628
Wood, R., 8693
Wood, S., 9323
Woodcock, D. J., 9672
Woodforde, J., 8934
Woods, M., 9961
Woodward, H. B., 7377
Woodward, S., 9422
Woolmer, B., 10138
Workers Educational Association, 8983, 9895, 10101
Worstead Baptist Church, 10136
Wortley, J. D., 10013
Wren, W. J., 7873
Wright, A. C., 8195
Wright, D., 7365
Wright, L., 8320
Wright, R. R., 8328
Wright, S., 8887
Wyer, S., 9238
Wymer, J. J., 7704, 8976, 9283
Wymondham Chamber of Trade, 10147
Wyndham, K. S. H., 8858

Xenos, S., 8125

Yallop, A. W., 10232
Yarham, E. R., 7880
Yates, E. M., 9387–8

Yaxley, D., 7624, 8413, 8985, 9146, 9271A, 9398, 9808
Yaxley, P. G., 10145, 10151
Yaxley, S., 9956, 10156
Yonekawa, S. I., 7363
Yorke, P., *3rd Earl Hardwicke*, 7480
Youell, G., 8938

Young, *Sir* C. G., 8928
Young, J. R., 9763
Young, R. M. R., 9721, 10229
Youngs, F. A., 7897

Zamoyska, B., 9029
Zipfel, A. L., 9653